The 2 X 2 Game

THE 2 X 2 GAME

by
Anatol Rapoport
Melvin J. Guyer
and
David G. Gordon

Ann Arbor   THE UNIVERSITY OF MICHIGAN PRESS

ISBN 0–472–08742–8

Library of Congress Catalog Card No. 74–25947

Published in the United States of America by
The University of Michigan Press and simultaneously
in Rexdale, Canada, by John Wiley & Sons Canada, Limited

Manufactured in the United States of America

To our children:

ANYA, SASHA, and TONY

MATTHEW

MEGGIE and KATIE

Preface

This book is an attempt to summarize and interpret what has been learned in some fifteen years of experimentation with a comparatively new research tool, the simplest possible format of a game of strategy. The format appears attractive because, on the one hand, experiments with it yield unambiguously observable and easily quantifiable behavior patterns (frequencies of choices between two alternatives); on the other hand, the approach necessitates the introduction of concepts of considerable psychological or social-psychological interest; for example, competition and cooperation, dominance and submission, considerations of expediency and of equity, etc. In this way, it seems to the authors that the method of experimental games has provided opportunities for extending the methods of "hard" experimental psychology to areas beyond its traditional domain, which had been largely confined to conditioning experiments, rote learning, short-term memory spans, reaction times, and the like.

From the point of view of "hard" experimental psychology, however, the book has a serious methodological shortcoming. In many cases, especially those involving experiments performed by the authors, the statistical significance of the results is omitted. The reason is that we were primarily interested not in "establishing" hypotheses but rather in generating them. The point is that a great many hypotheses serving as "explanations" of observed behavior patterns are all but devoid of interest if to begin with they are strongly suggested by common sense. A typical example is what we have called the "monotonicity hypothesis" (cf. chapter 4), according to which the higher a player's payoff in a particular cell of the game matrix, the more frequently will the corresponding strategy be chosen either by the individual player in an iterated game or in a population of players. The hypothesis is corroborated in an overwhelming majority of the cases, but the results only confirm a simple-minded expectation, and it seems a waste of effort to evaluate the statistical significance of the confirmation in each case. In contrast, the equally simple-minded "repetition hypothesis" (cf. chapter 4), to the effect that the frequency of repeating a strategy choice following each outcome is monotonically related to the corresponding payoffs, is often violated. Many of the violations could turn out to be statistically *not* significant, thus not constituting grounds for rejecting the hypothesis. But it is precisely the violations that are interesting, for they suggest conjectures about psychological pressures that override an elementary reinforcement model. To support such conjectures, the significance of the discrepancies should be established. However, to do this in each particular case would completely deflect our efforts from the chosen direction: to chart an area of psychologically interesting hypotheses or conjectures. The test of such hypotheses, chosen especially for their psychological or social-psychological interest, should be undertaken as a separate task, for which new experiments should be specifically designed.

The preparation of this book involved considerable technical difficulties and much tedious work, and we are greatly obligated to those who gave us invaluable help. Our heartfelt thanks go to Professor John Fox of the University of Alberta, Edmonton, Canada, for the production of the several hundred game matrices by programing computer graphics; to Adele Henry for the painstaking composition of the tabulated data; to Claire Adler, Research Associate at the Mental Health Research Institute, University of Michigan, for the editing and preparation of the entire manuscript which went through several drafts and also for the book's makeup, and to Barbara Perkel for typing assistance.

The help of the Mental Health Research Institute in providing assisting personnel and services, and of the Canada Council in providing support for research done in Toronto, is gratefully acknowledged.

We cherish the memory of coauthor David Gordon, whose untimely death in November, 1972, was a severe personal loss to us.

ANATOL RAPOPORT
MELVIN GUYER

Contents

Part I

Introduction to Part I

It stands to reason that the "essentials" of the studied situation should be preserved in its theoretical description and that the "inessentials" should be pared away. But this common sense principle only defers the question to a decision of what are the "essentials."

This book will be concerned with decisions in situations that, in general, involve conflicts of interests. One theory that deals with these decisions, called the theory of games, is a normative, not a descriptive theory. That is, it does not purport to describe how actual people make decisions in situations involving conflicts of interests; rather it purports to discover how certain idealized actors, called *rational players*, can be expected to make decisions in such situations.

In a way, therefore, the theory of games can be defined as a theory of "rational decisions in conflict situations." The definition sounds informative, but, as we shall see, the definition of "rationality" in many typical conflict situations is beset with ambiguities. Game theory strives to single out the "essentials" of situations involving a conflict of interests. To the extent that these singled out features capture what is deemed to be actually essential in such situations, game theory can serve as a *basis* of a behavioral science of decisions in conflict situations.

Here, singling out the "essentials" of a conflict situation, we shall follow game-theoretic paradigms. We shall not, however, confine our attention to the normative aspects. We shall also be interested in descriptive and predictive aspects of behavioral theories related to conflict. We shall be investigating, among others, just that question: to what extent can game theoretic models get at the "essentials" and be made a basis for an experimental approach to a behavioral (i.e., descriptive) science of conflict?

In its strict game-theoretic sense, a *game* has the following features.

3

1. There is a set of decision makers, called *players*. The set comprises of at least two.

2. At specified instances, one or more players must make decisions by choosing among a specified set of alternatives. These decisions determine the resulting *situations* of the game. Thus, a *play* of a game is a sequence of situations.

3. Each situation in turn determines which of the players is to make the next decision (whose "move" it is) and the range of choices open to him.

4. Certain specified situations define the end of the particular play of the game.

5. A situation in which a particular play of a game ends is called an *outcome* of the game. Associated with each outcome is a set of *payoffs*, positive or negative numbers, one awarded to each of the players. The payoffs represent gains or losses.

6. A *rational player* is one who, having taken into account all the information available to him by the rules of the game, makes his choices in such a way as to maximize the actual or the statistically expected payoff to accrue to him (and to him only) in the outcome of the game.

Some decision situations involving only one player are also sometimes called games, specifically *games against nature*. What distinguishes games against nature from games proper is the circumstance that, in the former, only the single player gets payoffs. We may, nevertheless, view Nature as another decision maker who, although she gets no payoffs, "decides" to effect certain combinations of events, called the *states of the world*, which, together with the player's decisions, determine the situations that obtain. Thus the outcome of the game depends not only on what the player does but also on what Nature does. In contrast to a genuine player, however, Nature is indifferent toward the outcomes. That is to say, since she gets no payoffs, she is not expected to make her choices in accordance with calculations of what the single bona fide player may do.

In decisions called *decisions under risk*, it is assumed that Nature chooses among the possible states of the world in accordance with certain probabilities. A real player, as we shall see, may also make his decisions probabilistically (letting a random device choose for him). But a player facing another bona fide player with interests of his own must take into account what the latter may do in pursuit of *his* interests. Since Nature has no "interests," no such considerations need be made in a game against nature.

In sum, the difference between a decision under risk and a genuine game can be formulated thus: in the former, it is possible, in principle, to get some information concerning the probabilities with which Nature will choose among the states of the world, *without* reference to the specific structure of the game played and the payoffs associated with the outcomes. In a genuine game, if the opposing player (or players) choose probabilistically, the probabilities with which the moves are chosen must be assumed to be governed by the strategic considerations peculiar to the specific game and the specific situation.

A drastic simplication of the conceptual framework just described was introduced by J. von Neumann (1928) through the concept of *strategy.* If the number of choices open to each player is finite, and if there is a termination rule which guarantees that the game ends in a finite number of moves, then the total number of situations that can occur in a play of a game is also finite, although it may be very large.

A strategy is defined as a set of specifications that a player can make concerning his choice in every situation that may conceivably occur. Then the totality of these *sets of specifications*—even though super-astronomically large—is also finite. The course of the play of a game is determined if each player chooses *one* of his available strategies. These choices are thought of as being made simultaneously (or independently) by all players, necessarily so, since at the start of the game no player knows the future moves of the others. This reformulation leads to the following conception of a game.

1. Each of the players has a set of available strategies. We denote the j-th strategy of the i-th player by $s_j^{(i)}$. The number of strategies available to different players are not necessarily equal. Thus i ranges from 1 to n (the number of players), and the i-th player's strategies range from 1 to n_i.

2. Each player chooses a particular strategy from his available set.

3. Suppose player 1 chose his j-th strategy; player 2, his k-th strategy, etc. . . , and player n, his z-th strategy. Then the n-tuple $[s_j^{(1)}, s_k^{(2)}, \ldots, s_z^{(n)}]$ specifies the corresponding outcome of the game and the associated payoffs are represented by the n-tuple $[x^{(1)}, x^{(2)}, \ldots, x^{(n)}]$, where $x^{(i)}$ is the payoff to player i.

A game so conceptualized is called a game in *normal form.* It can be represented by an n-dimensional array, where each dimension represents a player; the coordinates of a dimension, his strategy choices; the entries in the array, the payoff n-tuples.

The simplest example of this paradigm is obtained by reducing to a minimum the number of players and the number of strategies available to each. Since, by definition, the smallest number of players in a game proper (as distinct from games against nature) is two, and since each player must have a choice between at least two alternatives, it follows that the "smallest" possible games are those that involve exactly two players, each having two strategies available.

Such games, with which we shall be exclusively concerned in this book, are called *2 × 2 games*. The two players are represented by the two factors of the product. Each "2" represents the number of strategies available to each player. According to this notation, we would designate by "2 × 3" a game in which one of the two players had two strategies while the other had three; by "2 × 2 × 2," a three-person game in which each of three players had two strategies available, and so on.

The structure of a 2 × 2 game in normal form is represented by a matrix with two rows, two columns, and, consequently, four entries, each entry being a pair of numbers. The two horizontal rows of the matrix represent the two strategies available to one of the players. We shall call this player Row. The vertical columns represent the two strategies available to the other player, whom we shall call Column. Row's two strategies will be labeled by capital letters with subscript 1; Column's by capital letters with subscript 2.

The four cells of the matrix represent the four possible outcomes of the game. The four outcomes will be denoted by ordered pairs of subscripted letters, Row's choice always being first; e.g., A_1A_2, S_1T_2, D_1C_2, etc. The entries in the matrices will denote the payoffs to the two players. The payoff in the lower left corner of each cell is to Row; that in the upper right corner, to Column. Matrix 1.1 is a general 2 × 2 game matrix.

1

Strategic Structure

A theory is supposed to reduce a potentially infinite complexity to a perceivable structure. It does so by incorporating into its descriptive statements (explicitly or implicitly) a *typology* in which classes of objects or events rather than individual instances are distinguished. In this way "differences that make no difference" in a given context are ignored.

In its predictive statements, a theory (again, explicitly or implicitly) postulates the recurrence of "identical" conditions under which presumably "identical" events will be observed.

Taxonomies and assumptions of identity distort "reality" but make it accessible to systematic investigation.

It is, of course, impossible to give a general answer to the question of how much simplification or idealization can be imposed on a given context without severing the links between a theory and what it deals with. The "trade-off" between tractability and verisimilitude of theoretical models is something to be evaluated in each specific case.

1.1

The structure of a 2×2 game in normal form is completely contained in the information provided by its payoff matrix. In making his choices, the rational player is guided only by the prospects of his own payoff associated with the possible outcome. The crucial feature of a game is, of course, the circumstance that neither player controls the outcome himself: the two *jointly* determine the outcome. Therefore, in considering which strategies to choose, each player must also take into account which strategy the other may choose. Of this he has no direct knowledge, but he may be able to infer something by putting himself into the other's shoes, as it were. This inclusion of the other player's position in making one's own decision is the essence of "rational choice" in the context of game theory.

The theory of "rational choice" in a 2 × 2 game becomes rather simple if the game is of a special type called a *constant-sum game*. In a constant-sum game, the sums of the payoffs to the two players are the same in all four entries. It follows that in a constant-sum game the interests of the players are diametrically opposed. This is so, because the larger the payoff to one, the smaller it must be to the other. In particular, if the sum of the payoffs is always zero, the game is called a *zerosum game*.

It is easily seen that any constant-sum game is *strategically equivalent* to a zerosum game. To verify, compare the two games represented by 1.2a and 1.2b.

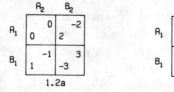

In 1.2a, the sum of the payoffs is zero in all four outcomes. In 1.2b, the sum is constant (−2) in all four outcomes.

Matrix 1.2b is obtained from matrix 1.2a by adding 5 to each of Row's four payoffs and by subtracting 7 from each of Column's four payoffs. Equivalently, we can assume that Row has been paid 5 units of payoff just for playing the game represented by 1.2a, while Column has been charged 7 units for playing that game. Since the magnitudes of the fees paid or charged are independent of how the players choose, it follows that these additional payments, whether positive or negative, ought not to make a difference in how the players choose. If a choice is rational in 1.2a, it is also rational in 1.2b. It is in this sense that the two games are strategically equivalent. Therefore, we shall refer to such games indiscriminately as either constant-sum or zerosum games.

As shown above, if the sum of the payoffs in every outcome is constant, the interests of the players are diametrically opposed. But the converse need not be true. In 1.3, the sums of the payoffs are different in all four cells; yet the interests of the two players are still diametrically opposed, since the outcome that gives Row the largest payoff, A_1B_2, gives Column the smallest, and indeed the orders of magnitude of the payoffs in the four outcomes are exactly reversed for the two players. We shall call these games *games of complete opposition*. Clearly, constant-sum games are a subset of this class.

1.3   1.4

Games that are not games of complete opposition will be called *games of partial conflict*, or *mixed-motive games*. In them, the interests of the players partially coincide in that both may prefer one outcome to another. An example is shown in 1.4.

Note that both players prefer outcomes A_1A_2 and B_1B_2 to outcomes A_1B_2 and B_1A_2. With respect to these preferences, therefore, the interests of the players coincide. However, Row prefers B_1B_2 to A_1A_2 while Column prefers A_1A_2 to B_1B_2. So, with respect to these preferences, the interests of the players are in conflict.

A fundamental question raised in game theory is the following: How should a rational player, confronted with a game in matrix form, choose his strategy? Let us examine this question in the context of a zerosum 2×2 game. In some such games, the answer is obvious. Consider the game represented by 1.5.

1.5

Observe that in this game, Row's larger payoff is associated with the choice of A_1, regardless of how Column chooses. We then say that strategy A_1 *dominates* B_1. Similarly, for Column, strategy A_2 dominates strategy B_2. Therefore, if Row is rational, he must choose A_1; if Column is rational, he must choose A_2. The outcome of this game is thereby determined, namely A_1A_2. Neither player can do better by choosing the other strategy.

Matrix 1.6 represents a slightly more complicated situation.

	A_2	B_2
A_1	-1 / 1	-10 / 10
B_1	0 / 0	5 / -5

1.6

Here Column, looking at his payoffs alone, cannot decide which strategy he should choose. For, if Row chooses A_1, then A_2 is Column's better strategy, but if Row chooses B_1, then B_2 is Column's better strategy. However, if Column takes Row's payoffs into account, he sees that, for Row, strategy A_1 dominates B_1. Column can expect, therefore, that Row, being rational, will certainly choose A_1. Then there is no question what Column should choose, namely A_2. Thus the outcome of this game is also determined: A_1A_2.

In the game represented by 1.7, the reasoning followed above does not apply, since neither player has a dominating strategy.

	A_2	B_2
A_1	0 / 0	-8 / 8
B_1	-3 / 3	1 / -1

1.7

When the unambiguously "better" strategy is unavailable, a rational player might consider choosing the strategy that portends the "lesser of two evils." Consider the game from Row's point of view. If he chooses A_1, the worst that can happen to him is outcome A_1A_2, which awards him a payoff of 0. If he chooses B_1, the worst that can happen is outcome B_1B_2, in which he gets -1. Clearly, A_1A_2 is the better of the two "worse" outcomes; so A_1 is indicated. Column, pursuing the same line of reasoning, might come to the conclusion that A_2 is the better choice for him. Can we then expect that both players will be satisfied that the best they could do in this game is to get the payoff associated with A_1A_2? Hardly. For, if Row were sure that Column, guided by the principle of the "lesser evil," will choose A_2, he, Row, would doubtless choose B_1, for his payoff is larger in B_1A_2 than in A_1A_2. But Column, being as farsighted as Row, might have anticipated *that* conclusion and chosen B_2, thus effecting B_1B_2, where Row gets the *smallest* payoff. This sort of reasoning ("he thinks that I think that he thinks . . .") leads to endless regression and to no satisfactory conclusion. Game theory provides a way out of this impasse, provided we include consideration of *statistically expected payoffs*. The game-theoretic solution of constant-sum games without dominating strategies will be discussed in chapter 3.

Analysis of *non*constant-sum games presents new problems. Consider again the game represented by 1.4.

1.4

Row, of course, would like the outcome to be B_1B_2, where he gets 10. Column would like it to be A_1A_2, where he gets 7. If each player chooses the strategy that contains his most preferred outcomes, the result is B_1A_2 in which both get less than they would have got in either A_1A_2 or B_1B_2. If Row could be sure that Column, trying for his largest payoff, will choose A_2, then Row could safely choose A_1 and get 2. However, Row cannot be sure of Column's choice, since Column may be going through the same reasoning, that is, expecting Row to go for *his* largest payoff (to choose B_1). Column might then choose B_2, in which case, Row, thinking that A_1 is "safe," will lose a unit. Column, who also thought that he was playing safe with B_2, will lose 10 units.

Now, if the players could communicate, they could conceivably come to an agreement to avoid the two outcomes bad for both, A_1B_2 and B_1A_2. Then they would face the problem of choosing between A_1A_2 and B_1B_2, for which their preferences are opposite. The theory of so-called cooperative nonconstant-sum games (where communication and bargaining are permitted) will be discussed in chapter 3. In that chapter we shall also examine solutions of the sort proposed in game theory for noncooperative nonconstant-sum games where opportunities for communication or for making binding agreements do not exist. As we shall see, these solutions are often unsatisfactory even in the normative sense, let alone as models of a descriptive theory.

Nevertheless, people do make decisions in real situations that are analogous to noncooperative nonconstant-sum games. How do they do it? To answer this question we must make observations. However, merely recording observations is not sufficient. We must make some sort of sense of what we observe, comparing decisions of different people in different situations in the hope of discovering some regularities from which we can draw some tentative conclusions, or, at least, hypotheses to be further tested by further observations. These conclusions or hypotheses should relate the regularities (if any) observed about the way people make decisions in conflict situations to the features of the situation and, perhaps, to the characteristics of the people involved.

Real life situations being notoriously complex, and freely acting people notoriously erratic, it is extremely difficult to pursue such a program "in situ," as it were. It seems desirable to design situations "in vitro," where the structure of "conflicts" can be precisely described and where people's attention can be directed to the specific, controlled features of the conflicts. Gaming experiments offer this opportunity and, if we are simplifying the conflict situation to make it tractable, we may as well reduce it to the simplest possible. The 2 × 2 game is such a situation.

The question is repeatedly asked: what can we infer from whatever we discover about people's decisions in simple, formal games that is relevant to real life conflicts? The frank answer is that we do not know. Sometimes it seems that even a 2 × 2 game can capture enough of the essentials of a conflict so that we *ought* to be able to make inferences of the sort expected on utilitarian grounds. However, *every* inference drawn from empirical evidence is, in the last analysis, only a hypothesis to be tested in analogous situations. Only in the physical sciences, where conditions can be reproduced with great accuracy, are we safe in assuming that our expectations will be corroborated with near certainty. In situations involving human behavior, no such expectations are warranted, because we can never know whether we can reproduce the conditions under which we had made previous observations. In other words, experiments involving human *behavior* (as distinguished from simple reactions to physical stimuli) are extremely difficult to perform under controls sufficient to get reliable, reproducible results. Consequently, if there is any hope of eventually constructing scientific theories of human behavior, we must first learn to perform controlled experiments with a view of drawing inferences from them that at least have *apparent* relevance to human motivations, learning, decisions—above all, to interactions. Gaming experiments include all these features, and experiments on 2 × 2 games are the simplest and most tractable that include the most important of them. The value of such experiments is that they can teach us not necessarily how people behave in real life but how we can study certain aspects of characteristically human behavior systematically, from the ground up, as it were.

2

Taxonomies of 2 X 2 Games

Our first task is to classify all 2×2 games according to some scheme that reveals similarities and differences among them.

The structure of a game represented by a payoff matrix is entirely determined by the distributions of the payoffs in the cells of the matrix. In game theory, it is usual to view the payoffs as reflections of the players' utilities for the different outcomes. The question of *how* these utilities are actually determined is a question to be investigated separately. The designation of the payoffs by numbers implies that the utilities have already been determined. Clearly, the magnitudes of these numbers have a bearing on the considerations that determine a choice of strategy. For the time being, however, we shall consider only the rank order of each player's four payoffs: the largest, the second largest, the next to smallest, and the smallest. We shall also assume, for the time being, that all four payoffs of each player are different, so that each player has a strict preference for the outcomes in accordance with the order of magnitude of the associated payoffs. Therefore, in this context, it will suffice to label the four payoffs of each player 1, 2, 3, and 4, 4 being the most preferred payoff. Then the payoff matrix of every 2×2 game will be determined by a particular configuration of eight numbers (1 through 4 twice) in the four cells. Payoffs so represented will be called *ordinal* payoffs.

Now, the numbers 1, 2, 3, and 4 can be placed in the four cells in $4! = 24$ different ways to represent all the possible preference orders of, say, Row, for the four outcomes. Similarly, these numbers can be

14

placed independently in 24 different ways to represent Column's preference order. There are, therefore, $24 \times 24 = 576$ distinct matrices to represent all possible 2×2 games under our assumption that a game is determined only by the (strict) orders of preference of the players for the outcomes.

Obviously, the 576 distinct matrices do not represent that many strategically distinct games. For, if we interchange, say, the rows of a matrix, a different matrix will result but not a strategically different game, because the second matrix was obtained from the first simply by relabeling Row's two strategies. Therefore, the two matrices should be considered as representing the same game. An example is shown in 2.1a and 2.1b.

2.1a   2.1b

The same reasoning applies to the interchange of columns and to the interchange of both rows and columns. Likewise, relabeling the players should not result in a different game even though the matrix may be transformed as a result. An example is shown in 2.2a and 2.2b.

2.2a   2.2b

In some games, the interchange of *players* results in exactly the same matrix. Such games will be called *symmetric*. A game that is symmetric when defined in terms of ordinal payoffs will be called *ordinally symmetric*. Every symmetric game is ordinally symmetric, but an ordinally symmetric game is not necessarily symmetric. When we wish to emphasize that a game is symmetric (not just ordinally symmetric), we shall say that it is *numerically symmetric*. If a game is not even ordinally symmetric, it will be called *ordinally asymmetric*. When the context is clearly that of ordinally defined games, "symmetric" ("asymmetric") will mean ordinally symmetric (ordinally asymmetric). Symmetric games "look alike" to both players. The game represented by 2.2a and 2.2b is not ordinally symmetric; the game represented by 2.3a and 2.3b is: although the players have been relabeled, the matrices look alike.

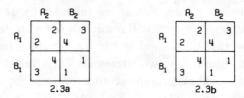

It turns out that an ordinally symmetric game can be represented by four different matrices, as shown by 2.4a–2.4d.

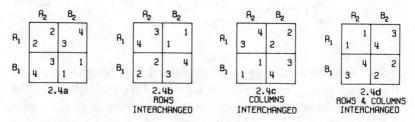

It turns out that an asymmetric game can be represented by eight different matrices, as shown by 2.5a–2.5h.

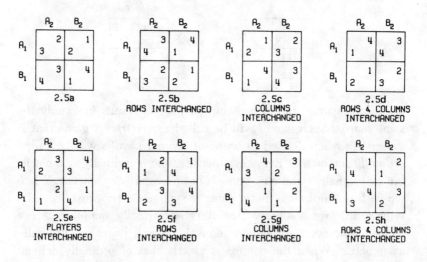

Next, it is easy to verify that there are exactly 12 strategically non-equivalent symmetric games. Consequently, there must be 66 strategically nonequivalent asymmetric games, since $576 = 4 \times 12 + 66 \times 8$. This makes $12 + 66 = 78$ 2×2 games in all, a set small enough to be completely enumerated.

We now seek some method of classifying these seventy-eight games. To begin with, three categories suggest themselves: games of complete opposition, games of partial opposition (mixed-motive games), and games of no opposition (no-conflict games). Games of complete opposition and mixed-motive games have been discussed and illustrated (cf. 1.2 and 1.4). In a no-conflict game, the same cell of the payoff matrix contains the largest payoffs of both players, as shown by 2.6.

$$
\begin{array}{c|c|c|}
 & S_2 & T_2 \\
\hline
S_1 & \begin{array}{cc} & 4 \\ 4 & \end{array} & \begin{array}{cc} & 3 \\ 3 & \end{array} \\
\hline
T_1 & \begin{array}{cc} & 1 \\ 2 & \end{array} & \begin{array}{cc} & 2 \\ 1 & \end{array} \\
\hline
\end{array}
$$

2.6

In this game, we should certainly expect $S_1 S_2$ to be the outcome if both players are rational. (Recall that a rational player is concerned only with his own payoff.) Row can safely choose S_1 *because* Column can safely choose S_2, and Column can safely choose S_2 *because* Row can safely choose S_1.

Before making further partitions in the set of seventy-eight games, we introduce the notions of a *natural outcome, equilibrium,* and of *Pareto-optimality.*

On intuitive grounds, a *natural outcome* of a 2×2 game is one which is characterized by a certain stability; that is, one expected to occur with the greatest frequency in a game played by rational players as we have defined them. In no-conflict games, the outcome that accords the largest payoff to both players should certainly be designated as the natural outcome. Similarly, in a game where both players have a dominating strategy (cf. p. 10), the outcome resulting from the choice of these strategies by both players will also be designated as the natural outcome. Next, if only one player has a dominating strategy, it will be assumed that he will choose it and that the other player will choose the strategy which is the "better response" to the other's dominating strategy. This pair of choices will be the natural outcome.

An *equilibrium outcome* is one from which neither player can shift without impairing his payoff, assuming that the other player does not shift. For instance, outcome B_1A_2 in matrix 2.4a is an equilibrium outcome. Now, if a 2×2 game with distinct payoffs has at least one dominating strategy, it is easy to see that the natural outcome is the only equilibrium outcome of the game. However, if a 2×2 game has no dominating strategy, then it may have two or no equilibrium outcomes. Further, if a game has two equilibria, the natural outcome (to be presently defined for these games) may be one of them, or it may not. Therefore, a further classification of games without dominating strategies can be made according to whether they have two or no equilibria, and according to whether the natural outcome is an equilibrium.

It remains to define the natural outcome for games that have no dominating strategies. The "solution" of constant-sum games of this type is given in terms of so-called mixed strategies, to be discussed in chapter 3. Since the solution in terms of mixed strategies involves the concept of a statistically expected payoff, it follows that such solutions can be discussed only if the statistical expectation of a payoff can be defined. In classical game theory, payoffs are supposed to be given on an *interval scale* which permits the definition of a statistical expectation. In the present classification of games, however, we assume only an ordinal scale for the payoffs. Statistical expectation, hence a solution in terms of mixed strategies, has no meaning in this context, and the natural outcome of a game without dominating strategies cannot be defined in terms of mixed strategies.

We therefore resort to the following definition. The natural outcome of a 2×2 game without dominating strategies is the intersection of *maximin* strategies—a maximin strategy being one that contains the larger of the two smaller payoffs associated with each strategy. For instance, in 2.4a, Row's smaller payoff associated with B_1 is 1, while the smaller payoff associated with A_1 is 2. Therefore, A_1 is Row's maximin strategy in that game. Similarly, A_2 is Column's maximin strategy. Consequently, A_1A_2 is the natural outcome of that game. Observe that in this game the natural outcome is not an equilibrium. The two equilibria are B_1A_2 and A_1B_2.

An outcome of a game is called *Pareto-optimal* if there is no other outcome in which *both* players get a larger payoff. A 2 × 2 game may have one, two, three, or four Pareto-optimal payoffs. For instance, the natural outcome of a no-conflict game (cf. 2.6) is clearly the only Pareto-optimal outcome of that game. Conversely, if the game has only one Pareto-optimal outcome, it must be a no-conflict game. In 2.4 there are two Pareto-optimal outcomes; in 2.31 (cf. p. 25), there are three. If a game is of complete opposition, all outcomes are Pareto-optimal, and conversely. A natural outcome, as we have defined it, may or may not be Pareto-optimal. Also an equilibrium may or may not be Pareto-optimal. An outcome that is not Pareto-optimal will be called *Pareto-deficient*.

Our discussion so far suggests that all 2 × 2 games with distinct payoffs on an ordinal scale can be classified as follows:

1. according to whether they are no-conflict games, or games of complete opposition, or games of partial opposition;
2. according to whether or not their natural outcomes are equilibria, Pareto-optimal, both, or neither;
3. according to whether they have two, one, or no dominating strategies.

In what follows, we shall introduce several other criteria of classification. The resulting taxonomy (Rapoport and Guyer, 1966) was motivated by an attempt to arrange the seventy-eight games according to the "stability" of the natural outcome. Empirically, this stability might be manifested by the frequency with which the outcome is chosen among a population of subjects playing the game just once, or by the frequencies with which it is chosen in a sequence of iterated plays. As we shall see, these criteria often give different results.

On the basis of a classification, we can construct a "taxonomic tree," where each branching represents a criterion of classification. The structure of this tree will, of course, depend on the order in which the criteria are examined. It would be desirable to construct the tree in such a way that the branchings are determined by criteria in decreasing order of importance. Ideally, each criterion would divide the games into sets in a monotone order of stability, so that all the games of a more stable set will turn out empirically to be more stable than any game in a less stable set. In other words, we would obtain a *lexicographic* order of games ranked according to stability, as words are ranked alphabetically in a dictionary: first, according to the precedence established by the first letter; second, within this class, according to the precedence established by the second letter, and so on. However, we have no assurance that the order so established among games will be empirically corroborated. Thus the taxonomy has only the status of a hypothesis to be put to an empirical test. Any systematic discrepancies between the observed relative frequencies of occurrence of the natural outcome and the relative frequencies established by the lexicographic hypothesis will be points of departure for alternative approaches.

The three largest categories will be called *phyla*. Borrowing further from the terminology of biological taxonomy, we shall call the subdivisions of these phyla *classes, orders, genera,* and *species.* Each of the seventy-eight games will be a separate "species." Games with different numerical payoffs assigned to a game of a given species will be called *variants* of a given species or game.

Among our suggested criteria of stability, the first is whether the natural outcome is or is not an equilibrium. Thus we shall distinguish two classes: E (natural outcome is an equilibrium) and e (natural outcome is not an equilibrium). Next, class E will be subdivided into two subclasses: P (the natural outcome is a Pareto-optimal equilibrium) and p (the equilibrium is Pareto-deficient). It will turn out that the subclass p contains only four games, one of which is the well-known Prisoner's Dilemma.

Our three orders will be D_2, D_1, and D_0, according to whether the game has two, one, or no dominating strategies.

The genera will be defined in accordance with the pressures acting on the players, assuming that the outcome of a play was the natural outcome. That is to say, we shall consider the motivation which may induce a player to shift away from the natural outcome if he assumes that the other does not switch. The following pressures will be taken into account:

Competitive pressure. A player may be more attracted to an outcome in which he gets a relatively larger payoff than the co-player gets, even though his own payoff in that outcome is absolutely smaller than in the natural outcome. Accordingly, if at least one player is motivated to shift (unilaterally) in order to get a relatively larger payoff, we shall say that competitive pressure is acting.

It should be kept in mind that when we speak of one player's payoff being larger than the other's in the context of ordinally defined payoffs, we mean *ordinally* larger; for instance, when the first player gets his second largest payoff, while the other gets his next-to-smallest. When the payoffs are defined numerically, Row's payoff may be numerically smaller than Column's while being ordinally larger. For this reason, competitive pressure may be present in a game with numerical payoffs and absent in the same game if the payoffs are defined ordinally, and vice versa.

Threat and force pressures. The next two types of pressure relate to the player's estimate of his chances to effect his most preferred outcome in *repeated* plays. If a game is not a no-conflict game, at least one player fails to obtain his largest payoff in the natural outcome. In our notation, the natural outcome will always be S_1S_2. This is possible, since we are free to label the rows and columns of the game matrix. The player who gets the smaller payoff in the natural outcome will be called the *disgruntled* player. Assume that he is Row. If S_1S_2 is an equilibrium, two cases are distinguished: (*i*) Row's largest payoff is in S_1T_2 and (*ii*) Row's largest payoff is in T_1T_2. Consider now Row's chances of getting the largest payoff (in iterated play) if this payoff is in S_1T_2. This can happen only if Column shifts away from the natural outcome while Row sticks to S_1. Now, if by shifting unilaterally, Row effects an outcome where Column gets a smaller payoff than if Column were to shift unilaterally (thereby giving the largest payoff to Row), we shall say that the natural outcome is *threat-vulnerable.*

Suppose now that Row's payoff in T_1T_2 is larger than in S_1S_2, and consider his chances of getting it. This can happen if, after Row's unilateral shift to T_1S_2, Column is induced to shift to T_1T_2, and this will be the case if Column gets a larger payoff in T_1T_2 than in T_1S_2. Natural outcomes in games of this sort will be called *force-vulnerable.* Some natural outcomes will be called force-vulnerable even if Row's (the disgruntled player's) largest payoff is in S_1T_2, provided both Row and Column get more in T_1T_2 than in T_1S_2. By switching from S_1S_2 to T_1S_2, Row "forces" Column to switch to T_1T_2, gaining thereby (relative to his payoff in T_1S_2) and also getting the opportunity to switch to S_1T_2 to get the largest payoff.

Matrices 2.7, 2.8, and 2.9 are examples of games with natural outcomes that are, respectively, threat-vulnerable, force-vulnerable, and both threat- and force-vulnerable.

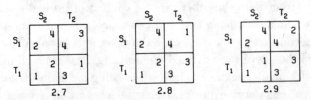

The pressures described can act in combination. Accordingly, we list our genera in accordance with the singly acting or combined pressures acting on a player who gets less than his largest payoff in the natural outcome:

Genus o: no pressures

Genus c: competitive pressure only

Genus t: natural outcome only threat-vulnerable

Genus f: natural outcome only force-vulnerable

Genus ct: threat-vulnerable with competitive pressure

Genus cf: force-vulnerable with competitive pressure

Genus tf: both threat- and force-vulnerable

Genus ctf: both threat- and force-vulnerable with competitive pressure.

One would hope that the genera could be arranged in a monotone order of stability, but such an order does not easily suggest itself since we have no a priori idea about the relevant importance of the pressures. Besides, the relevant importance may be quite different in games played once and in iterated games. For instance, threat-vulnerability and force-vulnerability may be more important than competitive pressure in iterated games, but clearly they are all but irrelevant in games played once. We can, perhaps, assume that natural outcomes subjected to combined pressures are less stable than those subjected to pressures of one kind. Therefore, assuming iterated plays where all pressures are relevant, we shall designate natural outcomes of no-conflict games subjected to no pressures as *strongly stable;* those of other games without pressures, *stable;* those subjected to single pressures, *weakly stable;* those subjected to combinations of two or three pressures and those that are not equilibria, *unstable.* Note that these designations do not quite correspond to those used in the earlier taxonomy (Rapoport and Guyer, 1966).

No-conflict Games (Phylum N)

In the games of this phylum, the natural outcome is obviously an equilibrium. Therefore, all no-conflict games belong to class E. Furthermore, since the natural outcome in these games is obviously Pareto-optimal, the subclass p of this class is empty. The class contains all three orders, D_2, D_1, and D_0. And since the natural outcome can be neither threat-vulnerable nor force-vulnerable, the only genera are o and c. The taxonomic tree of phylum N is shown in figure. 2.1 .

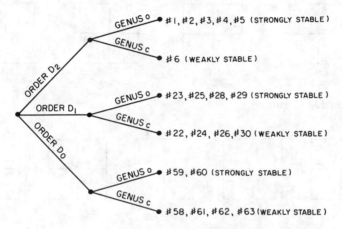

Fig. 2.1. Taxonomic tree for phylum N.

The numbers at the end points of the tree refer to the games as they are listed in the earlier ordinal taxonomy (Rapoport and Guyer, 1966). To avoid confusion, we have not renumbered them here. The complete list of games in numerical order is given in Appendix I.

The taxonomic enumeration of the twenty-one games in phylum N follows.

Order D_2. Genus o:

	4		3
4		3	
	2		1
2		1	

2.10
GAME #1

	4		3
4		3	
	2		1
1		2	

2.11
GAME #2

	4		2
4		3	
	3		1
2		1	

2.12
GAME #3

	4		2
4		3	
	3		1
1		2	

2.13
GAME #4

	4		1
4		3	
	3		2
1		2	

2.14
GAME #5

Order D_2. Genus c:

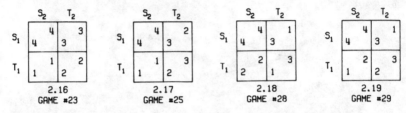

2.15
GAME #6

Order D_1. Genus o:

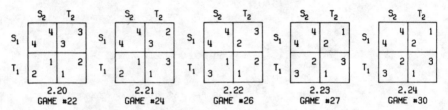

2.16   2.17   2.18   2.19
GAME #23   GAME #25   GAME #28   GAME #29

Order D_1. Genus c:

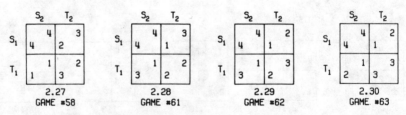

2.20   2.21   2.22   2.23   2.24
GAME #22   GAME #24   GAME #26   GAME #27   GAME #30

Order D_0. Genus o:

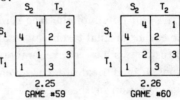

2.25   2.26
GAME #59   GAME #60

Order D_0. Genus c:

2.27   2.28   2.29   2.30
GAME #58   GAME #61   GAME #62   GAME #63

Mixed-motive Games (Phylum M)

This phylum includes all games that are not no-conflict games and
that have at least one Pareto-deficient outcome. The taxonomic trees

(figures 2.2, 2.3, and 2.4) show the nonempty genera of this phylum.

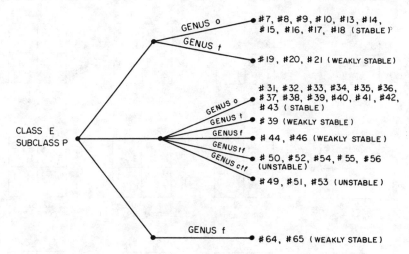

Fig. 2.2. Taxonomic tree for phylum M, class E, subclass P.

Order D₂. Genus o:

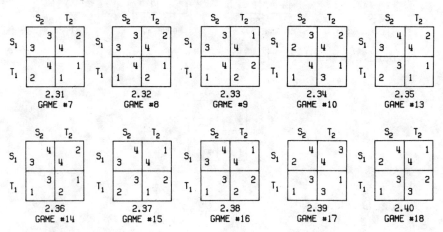

Order D₂. Genus o:

Order D₁. Genus o:

2.44 — GAME #31

	S₂	T₂
S₁	3 , 4	2 , 2
T₁	1 , 3	4 , 1

2.45 — GAME #32

	S₂	T₂
S₁	3 , 4	2 , 1
T₁	1 , 3	4 , 2

2.46 — GAME #33

	S₂	T₂
S₁	3 , 4	1 , 2
T₁	2 , 3	4 , 1

2.47 — GAME #34

	S₂	T₂
S₁	3 , 4	1 , 1
T₁	2 , 3	4 , 2

2.48 — GAME #35

	S₂	T₂
S₁	2 , 4	3 , 2
T₁	1 , 3	4 , 1

2.49 — GAME #36

	S₂	T₂
S₁	2 , 4	3 , 1
T₁	1 , 3	4 , 2

2.50 — GAME #37

	S₂	T₂
S₁	3 , 4	2 , 3
T₁	1 , 2	4 , 1

2.51 — GAME #38

	S₂	T₂
S₁	3 , 4	1 , 3
T₁	2 , 2	4 , 1

2.52 — GAME #40

	S₂	T₂
S₁	3 , 4	4 , 1
T₁	2 , 2	1 , 3

2.53 — GAME #41

	S₂	T₂
S₁	3 , 4	4 , 1
T₁	1 , 2	2 , 3

2.54 — GAME #42

	S₂	T₂
S₁	3 , 3	4 , 1
T₁	2 , 2	1 , 4

2.55 — GAME #43

	S₂	T₂
S₁	3 , 3	4 , 1
T₁	1 , 2	2 , 4

Order D₁. Genus t¹:

2.56 — GAME #39

	S₂	T₂
S₁	2 , 4	3 , 3
T₁	1 , 2	4 , 1

Order D₁. Genus f:

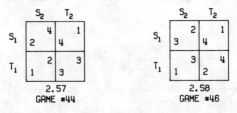

2.57 — GAME #44

	S₂	T₂
S₁	2 , 4	4 , 1
T₁	1 , 2	3 , 3

2.58 — GAME #46

	S₂	T₂
S₁	3 , 2	4 , 1
T₁	1 , 3	2 , 4

---

[1] We classify the natural outcome of this game "threat-vulnerable" even though Row's largest payoff is not in S₁T₂. The point is that Row gets more in S₁T₂ than in S₁S₂ and has an effective threat in T₁S₂.

Order D_1. Genus tf:

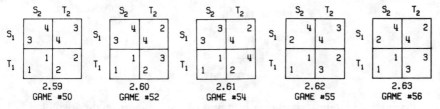

	2.59	2.60	2.61	2.62	2.63
	GAME #50	GAME #52	GAME #54	GAME #55	GAME #56

Order D_1. Genus ctf:

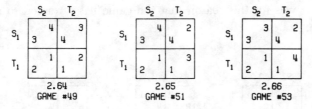

	2.64	2.65	2.66
	GAME #49	GAME #51	GAME #53

Order D_0. Genus f:

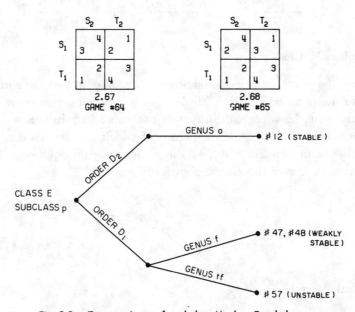

2.67
GAME #64

2.68
GAME #65

GENUS o #12 (STABLE)

ORDER D_2

CLASS E
SUBCLASS p

ORDER D_1

GENUS f #47, #48 (WEAKLY STABLE)

GENUS tf #57 (UNSTABLE)

Fig. 2.3. Taxonomic tree for phylum M, class E, subclass p.

Class E. Subclass p

This subclass contains four games. One, belonging to order D_2, is Prisoner's Dilemma.

Order D₂:

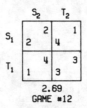

2.69
GAME #12

Prisoner's Dilemma is the only game of the seventy-eight in which the natural outcome is a stable but Pareto-deficient equilibrium. Perhaps it was for this reason that the game has attracted so much attention.

Order D₁:

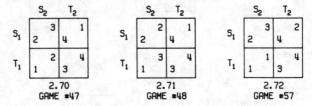

2.70   2.71   2.72
GAME #47   GAME #48   GAME #57

Phylum M. Class e

Since the existence of a dominating strategy implies that the natural outcome is an equilibrium, all of these games belong to order D_0. It is useful, however, to distinguish two suborders. In one, e_2, the games contain two equilibria, neither of which, however, is the natural outcome. In the other, e_0, the games have no equilibria. The taxonomic tree of this class is shown in figure 2.4.

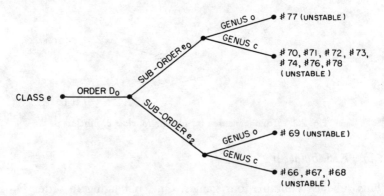

Fig. 2.4.   Taxonomic tree for phylum M, class e.

Order D_0, Suborder e_0. Genus o:

2.73
GAME #77

Order D_0, Suborder e_0. Genus c:

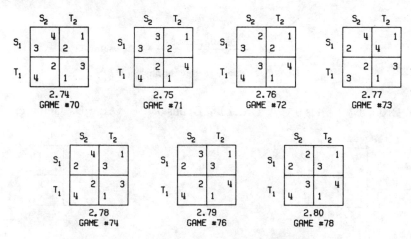

Order D_0, Suborder e_2. Genus o:

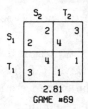

2.81
GAME #69

Order D_0, Suborder e_2. Genus c:

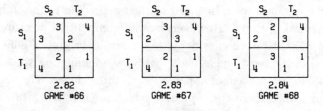

Games of Complete Opposition (Phylum Z)

This phylum contains only three games, shown in figure 2.5.

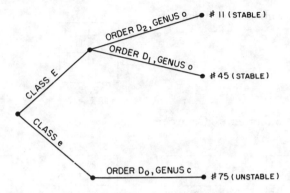

Fig. 2.5. Taxonomic tree for phylum Z.

Order D_2. Genus o: Order D_1. Genus o: Order D_0. Genus c:

<table>
<tr><td></td><td>S_2</td><td>T_2</td></tr>
<tr><td>S_1</td><td>3
2</td><td>1
4</td></tr>
<tr><td>T_1</td><td>4
1</td><td>2
3</td></tr>
</table>

2.85
GAME #11

<table>
<tr><td></td><td>S_2</td><td>T_2</td></tr>
<tr><td>S_1</td><td>2
3</td><td>1
4</td></tr>
<tr><td>T_1</td><td>3
2</td><td>4
1</td></tr>
</table>

2.86
GAME #45

<table>
<tr><td></td><td>S_2</td><td>T_2</td></tr>
<tr><td>S_1</td><td>3
2</td><td>1
4</td></tr>
<tr><td>T_1</td><td>2
3</td><td>4
1</td></tr>
</table>

2.87
GAME #75

These three are the prototypes of the three constant-sum games discussed in chapter 1.

The relation of the present taxonomy to the earlier one proposed by Rapoport and Guyer (1966) is apparent. There the first criterion of stability was the existence and number of dominating strategies (the "classes"), corresponding to the "orders" in the present taxonomy. In games with at least one dominating strategy, the natural outcome, as was shown (p. 10), is the only equilibrium. Consequently, the games were further classified according to the stability of the natural outcome. However, neither competitive pressure nor Pareto-optimality were considered. As a result, Prisoner's Dilemma appeared in the most stable class (with two dominating strategies) while the no-conflict games appeared in all three classes. The present taxonomy avoids these consequences which seem rather artificial.

Borderline and "Degenerate" Games

If we abandon the requirement of strict preference ranking of the outcomes, i.e., allow ordinal equality, hence also numerical equality of payoffs of the same player, we get a considerably larger set of strategically distinct 2×2 games. This set contains 732 games (Guyer and Hamburger, 1968). We shall refer to it as the complete set. No systematic classification of this set has been attempted. However, some games with numerically equal payoffs to the same player are useful in certain experimental situations. We shall order these games serially beginning with #79.

Equalizing certain payoffs allows us to construct "borderline games." Consider Prisoner's Dilemma (game #12) in which the payoffs associated with S_1S_2 keep decreasing. As long as these payoffs are larger than the payoffs associated with unilateral departure from the natural outcome, the game is still Prisoner's Dilemma. But as soon as the decreasing payoffs become smaller than those associated with unilateral cooperation, the game turns into game #66 (Chicken). So, when the equality is reached, we obtain a "borderline" game on the juncture of Prisoner's Dilemma and Chicken. Other such borderline games can be obtained similarly. The principal use of equalizing payoffs is to eliminate a particular pressure so as to study the effects of another pressure.

Of special interest are so-called degenerate games, in which one or both players are indifferent between the two choices. An example is shown in 2.88.

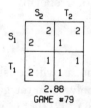

2.88
GAME #79

In this game, neither player can affect his own payoff by choosing between the two strategies, but each can affect the other's payoff. In fact, the outcome bad for both, T_1T_2, will result if each yields to competitive pressure and tries to impair the other's payoff (at no cost to himself, if he switches unilaterally from S_1S_2). This game offers an opportunity to study the effect of competitive pressure when it is neither magnified nor diminished by other pressures. We shall have occasion to examine some experimental results on games of this sort in chapter 18.

Other Classifications

In discussing the strategic and psychological features of 2×2 games we shall be relating them to the *ordinal taxonomy* presented here. Other taxonomies based on numerical instead of merely ordinal payoffs have been proposed and will be mentioned in relation to matters to which they seem to us to be most relevant. For example, Harris's classification (Harris, 1972) is made essentially with respect to certain numerical indices characterizing each game with payoffs given on an interval scale. This classification will be described in connection with a discussion of game indices (chapter 4).

Some authors have singled out certain special classes of 2×2 games as worthy of attention. H. Hamburger's *separable games* (1969) constitute one such class. Its importance seems to be in the circumstance that these games can be presented to experimental subjects in a form that brings out particular psychological aspects. This class of games will be discussed in chapter 5 ("Method").

R. B. Braithwaite (1955), in his book *Game Theory as a Tool for the Moral Philosopher*, has developed an approach to the 2×2 game that can be applied only to some games which we shall call Braithwaite games. These games will be discussed in chapter 3 ("Game-Theoretic Concepts"). That same chapter is the proper place for discussing other classifications of nonconstant-sum noncooperative games singled out by game theoreticians.

A Note on Notation

The rows of a 2×2 game matrix will be labeled S_1 and T_1, the columns, S_2 and T_2, when and only when the game is represented in the standard format described on p. 17; that is, with the natural outcome in the upper left corner. An exception will be made in game #66 (Chicken). In this game, the choices will be labeled C_i ($i = 1, 2$), corresponding to S_i, and D_i, corresponding to T_i, even though the game will be presented in standard format. Prisoner's Dilemma will at times be represented with the natural outcome in the lower right corner instead of upper left, and the corresponding choices will be labeled D_i, while the other choices will be labeled C_i. Thus it should be kept in mind that, while the outcome C_1C_2 will always be in the upper left corner in both these games, it is the natural outcome in

Chicken but the diagonally opposite one in Prisoner's Dilemma. These departures from what we hope to establish as standard notation for 2 × 2 games are made in the interest of consistency with a widely accepted notation in game-experimental literature.

Whenever any other game is not in standard format (as when we reproduce the notation of other authors), we shall use A_i and B_i to label the rows and columns.

In the text, choices will be denoted the same way, that is, by roman capitals with subscripts 1 or 2 referring to Row and Column respectively. Whenever there is no danger of ambivalence, subscripts may be omitted.

Outcomes will be denoted by pairs of subscripted capitals, with Row's choice always first, e.g., S_1T_2, D_1C_2, etc.

Choices in parentheses, e.g., (S_2), will refer to relative frequencies of choices in iterated games. The frequencies will always be given as percentages, e.g., $(S_2) = 76$. Choices in brackets will refer to the fractions of *subjects* making the choices indicated. These fractions will also be given as percentages. For instance, $[S_2] = 60$ means that 60 percent of the subjects chose S_2 as Column in a game experiment consisting of single plays, one by each subject. If the game is symmetric, the subscript will usually be omitted. For instance, $[C] = 40$ may mean that 40 percent of the subjects (either as Row or as Column) chose C in a single play Prisoner's Dilemma (or Chicken). The same notation will be used for outcomes with brackets referring to fractions of pairs.

Probabilities of choices and outcomes will be denoted by Pr( ) or Pr(|), where the vertical bar, as usual, indicates conditional probability. The conditioning event will always be the preceding outcome. Thus $Pr(S_1 \mid S_1T_2)$ means the conditional probability that Row chooses S_1, given that the preceding outcome (in an iterated game) was S_1T_2.

Conditional frequencies, being also estimates of conditional probabilities, will be denoted by Greek letters corresponding to the roman letters denoting the payoffs in the associated outcomes, as given in the general 2 × 2 game matrix 1.1. Thus β_1 is an estimate of the probability $Pr(T_1 \mid T_1S_2)$. Note that Row's payoff in T_1S_2 is denoted by b_1. Similarly α_i refers to a_i, γ_i to c_i, δ_i to d_i, each being an estimate of the probability that a player *repeats* his previous choice after the outcome associated with the indicated payoff. Complements of the repetition probabilities will be denoted by tildes. Thus, $\tilde{\gamma}_2 = 1 - \gamma_2 = \hat{P}r(T_2 \mid T_1S_2)$.

Again, exceptions will be made in Prisoner's Dilemma and in Chicken in the interest of preserving a convention. In these games, the conditional frequencies will be designated by x_i, y_i, z_i, and w_i, which always denote conditional frequencies of C choices instead of conditional frequencies of repeated choices.

Designations of payoffs are shown in matrix 1.1. Payoffs in Prisoner's Dilemma and Chicken *only* will sometimes be designated as shown in 2.89.

$$
\begin{array}{c c}
 & \begin{array}{cc} C_2 & D_2 \end{array} \\
\begin{array}{c} C_1 \\[2em] D_1 \end{array} &
\begin{array}{|c|c|}
\hline
R_2 \quad\; & T_2 \quad\; \\
R_1 & S_1 \\
\hline
S_2 \quad\; & P_2 \quad\; \\
T_1 & P_1 \\
\hline
\end{array}
\end{array}
$$

2.89

Confusion of S_i and T_i as designations of payoffs with the similar designations of choices is minimal here because the choices are labeled differently.

Game matrices and equations will be numbered serially within each chapter. References to equations, mathematical expressions, or inequalities will always be numbers in parentheses; to game matrices, simply numbers. Thus (3.2.) means equation or expression or inequality 2 of chapter 3; 3.2. means game matrix 2 in chapter 3. Occasionally a reference will be made to a matrix in the mathematical rather than the game-theoretic sense; for instance, a matrix of transition probabilities of a Markov chain (chapter 24) is treated as a mathematical expression.

Whenever a game is designated by number sign, #, it will always mean the game so numbered in the earlier ordinal taxonomy (Rapoport and Guyer, 1966) and so listed in the Game Index, or to the games from the complete set from #79 on.

Variants of games will be designated by roman numerals, sometimes not consecutively, again to adhere to their designations in earlier literature.

Mass frequency distributions will be denoted as vectors. For instance, (45, 10, 08, 37) may mean that outcomes S_1S_2, S_1T_2, T_1S_2

and T_1T_2, or C_1C_2, C_1D_2, D_1C_2, and D_1D_2 (always in those orders) were observed with frequencies indicated.

Strategy mixtures (cf. chapter 3) will also be designated by vectors, except that the components will be fractions or decimals. Thus (.25, .75) may mean that a player uses a mixed strategy in the proportions indicated, S or C always being given first.

Game-Theoretic Concepts

Constant-Sum Games

The mathematical theory of games was first formulated in the context of the two-person zerosum (or constant-sum) game. A two-person zerosum game with a finite number of strategies available to each player is represented by the payoff matrix. Since the payoffs in each cell are negatives of each other, the general zerosum 2×2 game will be represented by 3.1.

3.1

Two cases are distinguished: games with a *saddle point* and those without. A saddle point is an entry in the payoff matrix in which the payoff to Row is at the same time minimal in its row and maximal in its column, while the payoff to Column is at the same time minimal in its column and maximal in its row. If the game is constant-sum, it is clear that if one of these two conditions is satisfied, so is the other.

Consider the set of all of Row's payoffs that are minimal in their respective rows. Assume that Row chooses the strategy, i.e., row, where this minimum is maximal. Likewise, consider the set of all of Column's payoffs that are minimal in their respective columns and assume that Column chooses the column that contains the maximal of these minimal payoffs.

If a constant-sum game has a saddle point, the result of this pair of choices is a saddle point. Furthermore, it can be shown that

1. if there are several saddle points, then the payoffs in them to Row and to Column, respectively, are all equal;
2. if Row and Column choose *any* strategy containing a saddle point, then the joint choice determines a saddle point.

We shall now show that if a 2×2 zerosum, i.e., constant-sum, game has a saddle point, then either all of each player's payoffs are equal, or at least one of the players must have a dominating strategy. In the first case, the game is trivial. We suppose that it is not. Note that, if the game is zerosum, then $a_2 = -a_1$; $b_2 = -c_1$; $c_2 = -b_1$; $d_2 = -d_1$. Let the outcome A_1A_2 be a saddle point. Then, by definition of saddle point, $b_1 \leq a_1 \leq c_1$. It now follows that either $c_1 \geq d_1$, or $b_1 \leq d_1$, or both. For, supposing the contrary, $c_1 \leq d_1$ and $b_1 \geq d_1$, then $c_1 \leq d_1 \leq b_1$. But we have supposed that $b_1 \leq a_1 \leq c_1$. Combining these inequalities, we have $b_1 = a_1 = c_1 = d_1$, contrary to our assumption that the game is not trivial. Now if $c_1 \geq d_1$, then since also $a_1 \geq b_1$, Row's A_1 strategy dominates B_1. If, on the other hand, $b_1 \leq d_1$, then, since $a_1 \leq c_1$, it follows that $-a_1 \geq -c_1$ and $-b_1 \geq -d_1$, so that Column's A_2 strategy dominates B_2. This completes the proof.

In a sense, therefore, the 2×2 zerosum game with a saddle point is "solved" by prescribing to the player with a dominating strategy that strategy, and to the other player, the best counter strategy. The justification of the prescription is the circumstance that neither player can do better if faced with a rational opponent.[1] It is also clear that the two maximin strategies intersecting in a saddle point are in equilibrium.

The justification can be extended to games of complete opposition without saddle points, provided we extend the range of choices to include so-called *mixed strategies*. Suppose a player uses some random device to decide which choice he shall make. Since there are two choices, the random device should yield one of two outcomes.

---

[1] We shall reserve the term "opponent" for the other player in a game of complete opposition. In all other cases, the other player will be called a *co-player*.

By fixing the probabilities of these outcomes, the player in effect chooses a mixed strategy. For instance, if the device is a fair coin, the choices have been made equiprobable. If the device is a fair die, which prescribes A if a "six" is rolled and B otherwise, the player has fixed the probabilities of choosing A or B at 1/6 and 5/6 respectively. In general, a mixed strategy in a 2×2 game will be denoted by a probability vector $(x, 1-x)$ for Row or $(y, 1-y)$ for Column $(0 < x, y < 1)$; or simply by x or y, as the probability of choosing a specified strategy.

Suppose now that Row chooses A_1 with probability x and Column chooses A_2 with probability y. Since the actual choices of particular strategies are made independently on each play, the four outcomes will occur with the following probabilities:

$$Pr(A_1A_2) = xy; Pr(A_1B_2) = x(1-y); Pr(B_1A_2) = (1-x)y;$$
$$Pr(B_1B_2) = (1-x)(1-y). \tag{3.1}$$

Consequently, the expected payoff to Row will be (cf. 3.1)

$$xya + (1-x)yb + x(1-y)c + (1-x)(1-y)d. \tag{3.2}$$

Since the game is zerosum, the expected payoff to Column will be the same quantity with the opposite sign.

We shall now show that Row can choose his mixed strategy $(x, 1-x)$ in such a way that he will be *guaranteed* a certain minimal expected payoff. Similarly, Column can choose $(y, 1-y)$ so as to guarantee himself a minimal expected payoff. Because in a zerosum game one player's minimal payoff is the other's maximal, it follows that neither player can do better if the opponent chooses the above mentioned mixed strategy. These strategies are therefore *optimal* for both players. They are called *maximin* (getting the maximum of the minima) or *minimax* (keeping the opponent's payoff to the minimum of the maxima). Minimax and maximin strategies are identical in a zerosum game, but not necessarily in a nonzero-sum game, as we shall see.

First we establish the following property of 2×2 zerosum games. If the game has no saddle point, then each of two diagonally placed payoffs of each player is larger than each of the other two payoffs. That is, we must have either Min $(a, d) >$ Max (b, c) or Min $(b, c) >$ Max (a, d). Since we are free to interchange rows and columns, let us suppose that a is the largest of Row's payoffs. (If there is no largest, all the payoffs are equal, and the game, being trivial, presents no interest.) Then, if the above mentioned condition is violated, we have

$$\text{Either } a \geqslant b \geqslant d \geqslant c, \text{ i.e., } -c \geqslant -d \geqslant -b \geqslant -a \qquad (3.3)$$

$$\text{or} \quad a \geqslant c \geqslant d \geqslant b, \text{ i.e., } -b \geqslant -d \geqslant -c \geqslant -a \qquad (3.4)$$

$$\text{or} \quad a \geqslant b \geqslant c \geqslant d, \text{ i.e., } -d \geqslant -c \geqslant -b \geqslant -a \qquad (3.5)$$

$$\text{or} \quad a \geqslant c \geqslant b \geqslant d, \text{ i.e., } -d \geqslant -b \geqslant -c \geqslant -a. \qquad (3.6)$$

If (3.3) or (3.5) holds, Column has a dominating strategy; if (3.4) or (3.6) holds, Row has a dominating strategy. In each case, therefore, the game has a saddle point contradicting our assumption.

Assuming a game without a saddle point, we can without loss of generality suppose that $a \geqslant d \geqslant b \geqslant c$ with at least one strict inequality to avoid trivial games, hence $(a + d) > (b + c)$.

We shall now compute the maximin mixed strategies of a zerosum 2×2 game and thereby demonstrate their existence.

Suppose there exists a number v, denoting Row's minimum guaranteed expected payoff. We seek Row's mixed strategy $(x, 1 - x)$ that will guarantee at least v to Row. If Column chooses A_2, Row's expected payoff will be $ax + b(1 - x)$; if Column chooses B_2, it will be $cx + d(1 - x)$. By definition of v, we must have

$$ax + b(1 - x) \geqslant v \qquad (3.7)$$

$$cx + d(1 - x) \geqslant v. \qquad (3.8)$$

Since the game is zerosum, Column's expected payoff will be the negative of Row's. Therefore, if Column's mixed strategy $(y, 1 - y)$ guarantees Column *his* minimal expected payoff, it will also keep Row's down to, at most, v. Accordingly, assuming in turn that Row will choose A_1 or B_1, we must have

$$ay + c(1 - y) \leqslant v \qquad (3.9)$$

$$by + d(1 - y) \leqslant v. \qquad (3.10)$$

If the number v in fact exists, we should find x and y to satisfy all four inequalities. In particular, if we can find x and y to satisfy the inequalities as *equalities*, the inequalities will be automatically satisfied because the imposed relations are all "less than or equal to." The question then hinges on whether the equations are consistent. To see whether they are, we solve the first two for x and v, then the last two for y and v. Consistent solutions must yield the same value of v.

Indeed, solving (3.7) and (3.8) as equations, we obtain

$$x = \frac{d-b}{a+d-b-c} ; \tag{3.11}$$

$$v = \frac{ad-bc}{a+d-b-c} . \tag{3.12}$$

Solving (3.9) and (3.10), we obtain

$$y = \frac{d-c}{a+d-b-c} ; \tag{3.13}$$

$$v = \frac{ad-bc}{a+d-b-c} . \tag{3.14}$$

Because of the inequalities we have imposed on the payoffs, x and y are between 0 and 1 and so represent probabilities. The parameter v is called the *value* of the game (Row's expected payoff).

There is another way of looking at the problem of computing the equilibrium mixed strategies in the 2 × 2 game. Rearranging the terms of (3.2), we obtain

$$\begin{aligned}
& xya + yb - xyb + xc - xyc + d - xd - yd + xyd \\
&= y(xa + b - xb - xc - d + xd) + xc + d - xd \\
&= y[x(a - b - c + d) + b - d] + xc + d - xd. \tag{3.15}
\end{aligned}$$

Now Row can choose x so as to make the coefficient of y in (3.15) vanish; namely,

$$x = \frac{d-b}{a-b-c+d} , \tag{3.16}$$

which is precisely Row's maximin strategy. It follows that, if Row chooses his maximin strategy, his expected payoff will be the same regardless of the strategy, pure or mixed, chosen by Column. Mutatis mutandis, Column also can make his payoff independent of Row's choice by choosing the maximin strategy.

Next, consider what happens if Row shifts from his maximin strategy in either direction. If he does, the coefficient of y in (3.15) will become either positive or negative, since it is a linear function of x with either a positive or negative derivative. If this coefficient becomes positive, Column can minimize Row's payoff, thus maximizing his own by choosing $y = 0$; if it is negative, he can do the same by choosing $y = 1$. Thus any departure from the maximin strategy can be taken advantage of by the opponent, who can forthwith choose the appropriate *pure* strategy. Consequently, the pair of maximin strategies is the only equilibrium unless $a + d = b + c$. But, since we have assumed $\text{Min}(a, d) > \text{Max}(b, c)$, this implies also that $a = b = c = d$, in which case the game is trivial.

We now have a normative solution for all 2×2 zerosum games, namely the (pure or mixed) maximin strategy prescribed to each player, which, except in trivial games, is unique. The method can be extended to all games of complete opposition even if they are not strictly constant-sum.

Nonconstant-sum Noncooperative Games

If we try to extend the method of solving 2×2 games of complete opposition to games of partial opposition, we immediately meet with difficulties. Consider the concept of saddle point. In a game of complete opposition, if Row's payoff in a given outcome is minimal in its row and maximal in its column, then Column's corresponding payoff is minimal in its column and maximal in its row. Hence, what is a saddle point for Row is also a saddle point for Column. In a game of partial opposition, this is not necessarily the case, as can be seen in game #47.

	S_2	T_2
S_1	3 2	1 4
T_1	2 1	4 3

3.2
GAME #47

Row's payoff in S_1S_2 is minimal in its row and maximal in its column; so this outcome is a saddle point from Row's point of view. Column's payoff in S_1S_2, however, is maximal in both its column and its row; so the outcome is not a saddle point from Column's point of view. In fact, Column's payoff matrix has no saddle point.

In developing a theory of the (noncooperative) nonconstant-sum game, game theoreticians have concentrated on the concept of the equilibrium outcome. Although S_1S_2 in game #47 is not a saddle point for both players, it is an equilibrium in the sense that neither player can improve his payoff by unilaterally shifting from that outcome. It happens to be the only equilibrium in this game and so is a natural candidate for a "solution" of the game. Note, however, that S_1S_2 is not Pareto-optimal; so that treating it as a normative solution, i.e., prescribing it to "rational" players, raises questions about the meaning of "rationality" in this context. For the moment we postpone the discussion of this question since there are other difficulties to contend with.

Some games (belonging to order D_0 in our taxonomy) have two equilibria, which are always placed diagonally opposite. As an example, consider game #68 in which T_1S_2 and S_1T_2 are both equilibria.

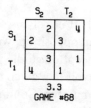

3.3
GAME #68

If an equilibrium is to be the prescribed solution, how is one to prescribe it: that is, what choice is one to prescribe to each player *individually* (which is what must be done if they make their choices independently)? Suppose we prescribe the strategy that contains the equilibrium outcome where the payoff to the player advised is the larger of the two. Then Row will choose T_1, Column will choose T_2. The result will be T_1T_2, which is not an equilibrium. If we prescribe the strategy containing the equilibrium with the smaller payoff, the outcome will be S_1S_2, again not an equilibrium. If we prescribe choices that will result in a specific equilibrium, say, T_1 to Row and S_2 to Column, the outcome will favor Row, whereas there is no reason for either player to have an advantage in game #68, since it is a symmetric game.

Such difficulties do not always characterize a nonconstant-sum game. We have already seen that in game #47, S_1S_2 is the only equilibrium. Hence there is no difficulty in prescribing it as the solution of the game *if* the equilibrium criterion is to be decisive. However, the other difficulty—namely that the prescribed solution would not be Pareto-optimal—remains.

In coming to grips with these problems, game theoreticians introduced a number of additional concepts. We shall present them in the context of 2×2 games, where they are much simpler than in the general case.

Let x and y stand for Row's and Column's respective strategy choices, pure or mixed. Let $M_1(x, y)$ and $M_2(x, y)$ be the corresponding (actual or expected) payoffs to Row and Column respectively. Suppose x and y result in an equilibrium outcome. We shall then call them an *equilibrium pair*.[2] Let x' and y' be another equilibrium pair. The two equilibrium pairs are called *equivalent* if $M_1(x, y) = M_1(x', y')$ and $M_2(x, y) = M_2(x', y')$. The two equilibrium pairs are called *interchangeable* if (x, y') and (x', y) are also equilibrium pairs. Games in which all pairs of equilibrium pairs are both equivalent and interchangeable are called Nash-solvable. All two-person constant-sum games are Nash-solvable.

An equilibrium pair of a nonconstant-sum 2×2 game can be found by the method illustrated on page 40, except that here, the strategies will not in general be maximin strategies. Consider the general 2×2 game as given by matrix 1.1. Assume that Row chooses the mixed strategy $(x, 1 - x)$, and Column chooses $(y, 1 - y)$, where x and y can now range from 0 to 1 inclusive, so that pure strategies are also included. The expected payoff to Row will be

$$M_1(x, y) = a_1xy + c_1x(1 - y) + b_1(1 - x)y + d_1(1 - x)(1 - y)$$
$$= x[y(a_1 + d_1 - b_1 - c_1) + c_1 - d_1] + y(b_1 - d_1) + d_1.$$
$$(3.17)$$

Now Row's payoff can be made independent of his strategy if

$$y = \frac{d_1 - c_1}{a_1 + d_1 - b_1 - c_1}. \qquad (3.18)$$

[2] The existence of at least one such pair in every game in matrix form was proved by J. Nash (1950).

However, y is a strategy, pure or mixed, only if $0 \leqslant y \leqslant 1$, and this inequality will be satisfied only if either

$$0 \leqslant d_1 - c_1 \leqslant a_1 + d_1 - b_1 - c_1$$
$$\text{or} \quad 0 \geqslant d_1 - c_1 \geqslant a_1 + d_1 - b_1 - c_1. \tag{3.19}$$

The first inequalities imply $a_1 \geqslant b_1$, $d_1 \geqslant c_1$; the second imply $a_1 \leqslant b_1$, $d_1 \leqslant c_1$. If $c_1 = d_1$ and $a_1 = b_1$, Row is indifferent between his strategies and from his point of view the game is trivial. Otherwise, we see that Row cannot have a dominating strategy.

A similar argument shows that if Row can make Column's payoffs independent of his choice of strategy, then, except in a game trivial from Column's point of view, Column cannot have a dominating strategy.

It follows that none of the games of the strict ordinal taxonomy belonging to orders D_2 or D_1 can have a mixed strategy equilibrium pair. But all of them have exactly one pure strategy equilibrium pair, which is obviously equivalent and interchangeable with itself. Therefore, all games of these two orders are Nash-solvable.

Next, we conclude that games #70 to #78 are all Nash-solvable. Because neither player has a dominating strategy in these games, each has a mixed strategy equilibrium pair which can easily be shown to be unique.

On the other hand, none of the games with two equilibria, not even the no-conflict games, are Nash-solvable, because their equilibrium pairs, being diagonally placed, are not interchangeable. Game #68 was shown to be an example.

Let us now return to the question raised earlier, namely whether the equilibrium criterion is always suitable to define a normative solution of a game of partial conflict. Observe that the equilibrium solution of game #78 (assuming the payoffs now to be numerical instead of only ordinal) is achieved by the strategy pair $(.5, .5)$, $(.5, .5)$ and yields an expected payoff of 2.5 to each player. On the other hand, T_1S_2 of that game yields 4 to Row and 3 to Column; that is, more to *each* player than the equilibrium pair. There are even some games with a unique pure strategy equilibrium, where both players get less than in another outcome, namely the games of subclass p– #12, #47, #48, and #57. The Pareto-optimal outcomes of these games cannot be considered solutions in Nash's sense because they are not equilibria. But then, do not these examples cast aspersion on the equilibrium as a criterion of a solution?

Luce and Raiffa (1957) have proposed another concept of solution, namely the solution in the *strict* sense. To define this solution, we need the concept of *joint dominance* of one strategy pair by another. In the context of the 2×2 game, strategy pair $[x, y]$ jointly dominates another $[x', y']$ if $M_i(x, y) > M_i(x', y')$, $i = 1, 2$. A strategy pair jointly dominated by another is called *jointly inadmissible;* one not jointly dominated by another is called *jointly admissible.* A game is said to be solvable in the strict sense (i) if there exists an equilibrium pair among the jointly admissible strategy pairs and (ii) if all jointly admissible equilibrium pairs are both interchangeable and equivalent.

The definition implies that the solution must be both an equilibrium and Pareto-optimal. According to this definition of solvability, some of the games in the ordinal taxonomy that are not Nash-solvable are solvable in the strict sense; for instance, game #63.

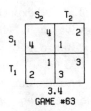

GAME #63

Since the two equilibria are not interchangeable, the game is not Nash-solvable. But since only admissible pairs are now considered and there is only one such pair, namely S_1S_2, which is trivially equivalent to and interchangeable with itself and is moreover an equilibrium, game #63 is solvable in the strict sense.

On the other hand, game #12 (cf. 2.69) which is Nash-solvable, is not solvable in the strict sense, because none of its admissible strategy pairs, T_1T_2, S_1T_2, and T_1S_2 is an equilibrium.

Clearly, if we are willing to call a game solvable if it is so either in the strict sense or in Nash's, we subsume more games under the solvable category. There still remain games, however, that are not solvable in either Nash's or in the strict sense, namely, the games of partial conflict with two equilibria.

J. Harsanyi (1962) has proposed a concept of solution for a non-cooperative game that makes all such games solvable. However, he has "paid" for this extension by redefining a "noncooperative" game. The usual definition of a noncooperative game is one where the players cannot communicate, hence cannot coordinate their strategy choices. Harsanyi defines a noncooperative game as one in which the players are not able to make *enforceable* agreements to choose some particular strategy pair. They are, however, allowed to communicate. The possibility of communication greatly facilitates the establishment of a unique solution. In fact, as we shall see, when both communication and enforceable agreements are made possible, the solutions are not limited to equilibria, hence can, in fact must, be Pareto-optimal. This is not so in Harsanyi's solution because, in his view, the absence of enforceable agreements excludes nonequilibrium strategy pairs from consideration as solutions.

Consider, then, all the equilibrium pairs. The problem is to eliminate pairs until only equivalent and interchangeable ones remain. If the game is Nash-solvable to begin with, all of its equilibrium pairs are equivalent and interchangeable and thus determine a unique solution in the sense of a fixed expected payoff to each player. A game may not be Nash-solvable by virtue of having noninterchangeable equilibrium pairs. But some of these may be jointly dominated by others, as in game #63 (cf. p. 45). If so, then in Harsanyi's procedure, the dominated equilibrium pairs are eliminated. If thereby only interchangeable equivalent pairs remain, a solution in the above sense is again determined. Note that the elimination of dominated pairs is somewhat but not quite analogous to the procedure employed in determining a solution in the strict sense. In the latter, an equilibrium pair jointly dominated by *any* strategy pair is eliminated from consideration. Therefore, a solution in the strict sense must be Pareto-optimal. In Harsanyi's procedure, only equilibrium pairs jointly dominated by other equilibrium pairs are eliminated. Hence, Harsanyi's solution need not be Pareto-optimal.

Further reduction is effected either by "coordination" or by invoking the principle of "risk dominance." We shall confine ourselves to illustrating each of these principles by an example. The first is a game from the complete set (cf. p. 31), shown in 3.5.

This is a no-conflict game, since both players are indifferent between A_1A_2 and B_1B_2. The game is not Nash-solvable because the two equilibrium pairs are not interchangeable. It is not solvable in the strict sense because neither pair can be eliminated as inadmissible. Harsanyi's procedure, however, allows communication for the purpose of *coordination*. Since both players are indifferent between A_1A_2 and B_1B_2, they can "agree" on either one of these outcomes and choose accordingly. Note that an *enforcement* of this agreement is unnecessary, because neither player gains anything (on the contrary, loses) by breaking it.

3.5
GAME #85

The other example is game #66.

3.6
GAME #66

T_1S_2 and S_1T_2 are uninterchangeable equilibrium pairs; so the game is not Nash-solvable. Both pairs being jointly admissible, neither can be eliminated as jointly dominated by the other; so the game is not solvable in the strict sense. Roughly, the principle of risk dominance says that Row, by insisting on T_1S_2 (where he gets more), faces a larger risk than Column, should agreement be impossible. Similarly, Column faces a larger risk than Row if he insists on S_1T_2. There is, however, another equilibrium pair in this game, namely the mixed strategy pair (.5, .5), (.5, .5), which gives each player 2.5. Here the risk is equalized. This strategy pair constitutes Harsanyi's solution of this game. Note that it is not Pareto-optimal. The Pareto-optimal pair S_1S_2 cannot be attained, for without an enforceable agreement each player would be tempted to shift away from S_1S_2. In Harsanyi's estimation, the non-Pareto optimality of the solution of many non-cooperative games is simply the unfortunate consequence of the absence of *enforceable* agreements.

Like other game-theoretic concepts, the concept of equilibrium was developed in a purely theoretical, not empirical, context. To what extent the theory of equilibria can be geared to empirical content is part of a larger question pertaining to game theory as a tool of behavioral science. For the moment we shall by-pass this question in order to examine some further implications of the equilibrium concept.

Mathematically, an equilibrium strategy pair of a game is analogous to a mechanical equilibrium in the sense of representing a certain balance of forces. Pursuing the analogy further, we can examine the stability of equilibrium strategy pairs. Roughly, a mechanical equilibrium is stable if the departure of a system from it instigates forces in the direction opposite to the departure, thus tending to restore the equilibrium state. If, on the other hand, departure instigates forces in the same direction so as to drive the system even further from the equilibrium state, the equilibrium is called unstable.

Both stable and unstable equilibria can be observed in 2×2 games. Consider game #78.

3.7
GAME #78

If Row chooses mixed strategy x and Column chooses y, the expected payoffs to Row and Column respectively will be

$$M_1(x, y) = 2xy + 3x(1 - y) + 4(1 - x)y + (1 - x)(1 - y)$$
$$= x(-4y + 2) + 3y + 1. \tag{3.20}$$

$$M_2(x, y) = 2xy + x(1 - y) + 3(1 - x)y + 4(1 - x)(1 - y)$$
$$= y(2x - 1) - 3x + 4. \tag{3.21}$$

Thus $x = y = 1/2$ is an equilibrium strategy pair. Let us now see what happens if for some reason y slightly increases. As long as Row sticks to $x = 1/2$, Column's payoff is not affected thereby, since the coefficient of y in (3.21) remains zero. However, *Row's* expected payoff decreases, since the coefficient of x in (3.20) becomes negative. Row can counteract this loss by decreasing x. Thereupon, the coefficient of y in (3.21) becomes negative, and Column, in order to counteract the decrease in his payoff, will decrease y. In summary, an initial increase of y instigates "forces" that lead to an eventual decrease. An analogous counteracting tendency can be shown when y initially decreases or, indeed, when either variable departs from its equilibrium value in either direction. Thus the equilibrium in game #78 has the mathematical property of stability.

Consider now game #66.

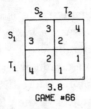

3.8
GAME #66

Again, we compute the expected payoffs associated with an arbitrary pair of strategies x and y.

$$M_1(x, y) = 3xy + 2x(1 - y) + 4(1 - x)y + (1 - x)(1 - y)$$
$$= x(-2y + 1) + 3y + 1. \tag{3.22}$$

$$M_2(x, y) = 3xy + 4x(1 - y) + 2(1 - x)y + (1 - x)(1 - y)$$
$$= y(-2x + 1) + 3x + 1. \tag{3.23}$$

In this game, if y increases from its equilibrium value of $1/2$, M_1 decreases, and Row is motivated to decrease x, which, in turn, makes the coefficient of y in (3.23) positive. This motivates Column to increase y, which, in turn, puts additional pressure on Row to decrease x further. Here an initial departure from the equilibrium tends to be magnified, so that the equilibrium is unstable. Note that continued decrease of x accompanied by an increase of y will "drive the system" toward the outcome T_1S_2, while an increase of x accompanied by a decrease of y will drive it towards S_1T_2. These two outcomes are the "mechanically" stable equilibria of this game. If players were mechanisms, responding only to forces acting "here and now," we would expect T_1S_2 or S_1T_2 to be the only outcomes of game #66. That this is empirically far from being the case reminds us of the obvious fact that people are governed by other considerations besides immediate motivational "forces."

Cooperative Games

As we have seen, a most serious shortcoming of the equilibrium concept as the basis for a solution of a nonconstant-sum game is that equilibria of such games are frequently Pareto-deficient. Harsanyi argues that only equilibria can be considered solutions of noncooperative games in consequence of the impossibility of effecting an enforceable agreement. If we accept this argument, then the only way to arrive at solutions that are always Pareto-optimal is by introducing enforceable agreements (as well as communication and bargaining) into the theory of games. This is what is done in the theory of the *cooperative* game. In such a game, although the interests of the players can be and generally are (partially) in conflict, it still makes sense for them to cooperate in order to ensure Pareto-optimality of the outcome. If a game has more than one such outcome, it is among them that the preferences of the players are in conflict. Thus the theory of the "cooperative" game is as much concerned with the conflict aspect as with the cooperative aspect of a mixed-motive game.

Before considering the 2×2 game proper, we shall examine an even more elementary case of a partial conflict of interests, namely simple bargaining. Take a seller and a buyer. The seller is willing to sell an object at any price above a certain minimum price; the buyer is willing to buy it at any price below a certain maximum price. If the maximum price the buyer is willing to pay is less than the minimum price the seller is willing to accept, obviously no agreement is possible. So, assume that the buyer's maximum exceeds the seller's minimum. The range of prices spanned by these two amounts constitutes the *negotiation* set. In the negotiation set, the object may go for any price. But, naturally, the seller wants to get as much as possible and the buyer wants to pay as little as possible.

So far, we have been talking about prices as amounts of money. It is, however, necessary to consider the possibility that the "worth" of a particular increment of money is not necessarily proportional to the *size* of the increment; that is, the utility of money is not necessarily a linear function of the amount of money. How the utility of money varies with the amount of money probably differs among individuals. We can assume, however, that the function representing this variation is monotone nondecreasing. That is to say, more money is worth at least as much as less money if only because the amount of money representing "negative utility" can be given away or even thrown away. Aside from assuming that the utility of money is a nondecreasing function of the amount of money, we shall assume nothing about the "shape" of that function.

Now we plot in a space of two dimensions the utilities of the possible sales prices for which the object will be sold. The horizontal coordinate will represent the seller's utilities for the sales price; the vertical coordinate, the buyer's. The negotiation set will be, accordingly, represented by a "curve" (which may also be a straight line or a broken line). The slope of the curve must, in general, be negative, because the larger the utility of the selling price is for the seller, the smaller it is for the buyer.

In addition to the negotiation set, there is another point on our graph that represents the utilities accruing to the seller and the buyer in the event that they cannot agree on the price. This point, called *status quo* (or, in the business world, "no sale") is, of course, associated with smaller utilities for both parties than any of the points on the negotiating set. The entire picture is shown in figure 3.1.

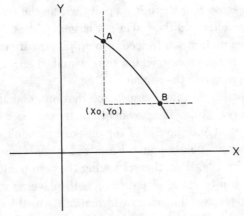

Fig. 3.1. Diagrammatic representation of the simple bargaining problem. Horizontal coordinate: seller's utility; vertical coordinate: buyer's utility. Curve segment AB: negotiation set. Pont (x_0, y_0): utilities associated with "no sale."

The region enclosed by a vertical and a horizontal line drawn through the "no sale" point, and the portion of the curve intercepted, is called the *feasible region*. The buyer and the seller can, by an appropriate arrangement (possibly including "throwing money away"), attain any point (representing their respective utilities) within or on the boundary of the region.

The problem is now to single out a point in this region that can be defended as being in some sense the "most reasonable" solution of the bargaining problem, i.e., a point that will represent the utilities of a "fair" selling price.

One way of attacking this problem is to specify exactly in mathematical terms what one might mean by a "reasonable" solution. To begin with, since the solution must be general, i.e., applicable to all possible sellers and buyers who may find themselves in similar situations, one might demand that the solution should not depend on the labeling of the players. In other words, if the roles of the seller and the buyer were interchanged, the selling price should still represent the same pair of utilities. Accordingly, we write explicitly:

Axiom 1. (Symmetry) The solution is invariant with respect to the labeling of the players.

Axiom 2. (Pareto-optimality) The solution lies on the negotiation set.

(Note that the curve representing the negotiation set is Pareto-optimal in the sense that there is no point within the feasible region where *both* the seller and the buyer get larger utilities than on some point on the negotiation set. Indeed, if both players are rational, they will not throw money away, which they would in effect be doing if the solution were inside the region.)

Axiom 3 depends on the circumstance that, in general, the utility scale is an interval scale. This means that there is no way to determine the zero point and the size of the unit of a person's utility scale. Therefore, the zero points and the units may be chosen independently and arbitrarily. If so, then changing the zero point or the unit or both of the utility scales of either or both players independently by performing positive linear transformations, should in the same way transform the utilities they get at the solution. Therefore,

Axiom 3. The solution is invariant under positive linear transformations.

Now imagine the bargaining problem to be changed to a different one by deleting some portion of the feasible region while the status quo point remains the same. If the solution has not thereby been eliminated, then the solution of the new problem should be the same as that of the old. Mutatis mutandis, adding a new region should either transfer the solution to the new region or, if it does not, should not change the solution. Therefore,

Axiom 4. The solution should be invariant with respect to irrelevant alternatives.

To see the meaning of this axiom in a simpler decision situation, imagine that a man in choosing between alternatives $A_1 \ldots , A_n$ prefers A_i to all others. Suppose, further, that a new alternative A_{n+1} has been added. It could happen that now A_{n+1} is preferred to all the rest. In that case, the new alternative is not "irrelevant." But if the man's preference does *not* shift to the new alternative, then A_i should still be his most preferred alternative.

Nash (1953) has shown that one and only one point of the payoff space satisfies all four axioms. We know by axiom 2 that the point should be on the negotiation set. It can be found there as follows. Consider all possible rectangles such that one of the corners is the status quo point ("no sale") (x_0, y_0) and one is on the curve segment AB of figure 3.1. Among these rectangles, one will have the largest area. The corresponding point on the curve AB is the solution of the simple bargaining problem.

Analytically, the solution is found as follows. Let the equation of the curve AB be $y = f(x)$. Set the derivative with respect to x of the expression $(x - x_0)[f(x) - y_0]$ equal to zero and solve for x. Let the solution be x^*. Then the solution of the bargaining problem is the point $[x^*, f(x^*)]$ on the curve AB.

This method of solving the simple bargaining problem will now be extended to solve the cooperative 2×2 game.

Plot the pairs of payoffs associated with the four possible outcomes of the game. Figure 3.2 represents the game with 3.9 as the payoff matrix.

	A_2		B_2	
A_1		4		0
	0		2	
B_1		-2		-2
	-1		-3	

3.9

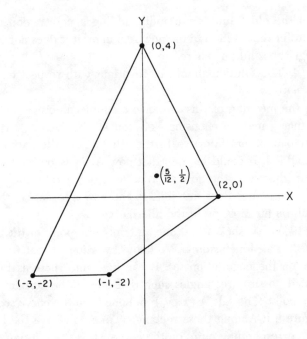

Fig. 3.2. Diagrammatic representation of a 2 × 2 game.

The *convex hull* of these four points will determine the region of feasible payoffs. If the points determine a convex quadrilateral, then the quadrilateral is the convex hull. If the quadrilateral is concave, then the convex hull will be a triangle with one of the points inside. If all four points lie in a straight line, they represent either a no-conflict game (if the slope is positive) or a game of complete opposition (if the slope is negative). These last two cases are of no interest in the theory of cooperative games since, in the former case, the solution is trivial and, in the latter case, "cooperation" is meaningless. As can be seen from figure 3.2, the convex hull of 3.9 is a quadrilateral.

By choosing an appropriate pair of strategies, pure or mixed, the two players can arrive at any point inside or on the boundary of the quadrilateral as their statistically expected payoffs. For instance, let Row choose A_1 with probability 3/4 and Column choose A_2 with probability 1/3. Then Row's expected payoff will be

$$3/4 \times 1/3 \times 0 + 3/4 \times 2/3 \times 2 + 1/4 \times 1/3 \times (-1)$$
$$+ 1/4 \times 2/3 \times (-3) = 5/12.$$

Column's expected payoff will be

$$3/4 \times 1/3 \times 4 + 3/4 \times 2/3 \times 0 + 1/4 \times 1/3 \times (-2)$$
$$+ 1/4 \times 2/3 \times (-2) = 1/2.$$

The pair of payoffs represented by the point $(5/12, 1/2)$ is inside the quadrilateral (cf. figure 3.2).

Note that the line segment joining the points $(0, 4)$ and $(2, 0)$ is the set of Pareto-optimal outcomes in this game. According to axiom 2, the solution should be on this line segment. Any point on it can be effected by an appropriate pair of coordinated strategies: the end points, by the pure strategies available in the game; the points in between, by mixtures of the two pairs. One of these points must be the solution.

Now, if there were some point in the feasible region representing a possible pair of payoffs that could be taken as a status quo point, the solution of the two-person game would reduce to that of the simple bargaining problem in which the status quo point is given. In the 2×2 game, however, the status quo point is not given a priori; it must be deduced. The deduction of the status quo point for a general two-person game is one of J. Nash's contributions to game theory (Nash, 1953). This is how it works.

Suppose each player selects a strategy among those available to him (including all the mixtures of his two pure strategies) and announces that, if the two players cannot agree on a Pareto-optimal solution, he will choose that strategy. Call such a strategy a "threat strategy." A pair of threat strategies determine a point inside or on the boundary of the payoff quadrilateral. It can serve as the status quo point, thus reducing the game to a simple bargaining problem.

Let us see how the optimal threat strategy can be found for each of the players. Here "optimal" refers to the individual interests of the players: Row wants the solution to be as far as possible to the right on the Pareto-optimal line, while Column wants it to be as far up as possible. These desires are in conflict because the slope of the optimal line is negative. On the other hand, the two players also have a common interest, namely that the solution should be *on* the Pareto-optimal line. Thus the concept of the threat point combined with Pareto-optimality captures the character of the game of partial conflict.

To find the threat point, let us suppose that the threat strategies have already been chosen and that they determine the point (X_0, Y_0)

within the quadrilateral. The position of the solution (x^*, y^*) of the resulting bargaining problem will depend on X_o and Y_o.

Let us examine the nature of this dependence in 3.9, as represented by figure 3.2. The equation of the line joining points $(0, 4)$ and $(2, 0)$ is $y = -2x + 4$. If the threat point is (X_o, Y_o), we get the solution of the bargaining problem by setting

$$\frac{d}{dx}[(x - X_o)(-2x + 4 - Y_o)] = -4x + 2X_o - Y_o + 4 = 0.$$
(3.24)

The solution is

$$x^* = X_o/2 - Y_o/4 + 1;$$
(3.25)

$$y^* = -2x^* + 4 = -X_o + Y_o/2 + 2.$$
(3.26)

It follows that x^* will be the larger, the larger is X_o and the smaller is Y_o; and the opposite is true of y^*. In effect, therefore, in choosing their strategies to determine (X_o, Y_o) the two players are playing a game of complete opposition, because their interests with regard to the position of X_o and Y_o are diametrically opposed.

Now, according to axiom 3 above, the solution of the game must be invariant with respect to positive linear transformations. Therefore, we can change the scale of either player's payoffs without changing the strategic structure of the game. Accordingly, if we multiply Column's payoffs by $1/2$, we obtain the following solution of the transformed game as a function of the threat point coordinates X_o and Y_o:

$$x^* = X_o/2 - Y_o/4 + 1;$$
(3.27)

$$y^* = -X_o/2 + Y_o/4 + 1;$$
(3.28)

$$x^* + y^* = 2.$$
(3.29)

Equation (3.29) shows that, with appropriate choice of payoff units, the game of complete opposition representing the opposite attempts of the players regarding the position of (X_o, Y_o) can be represented as a constant-sum game. This game is obtained from the original game by "normalizing" it, so that the equation of the Pareto-optimal line becomes $x + y = 2$, and by replacing the payoffs of the normalized game by their algebraic differences. The normalized game is shown in 3.10 and the "difference" (zerosum) game is shown in 3.11.

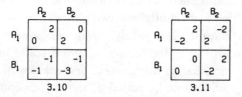

| | 3.10 | | 3.11 |

The players can now determine the threat point (X_o, Y_o) by solving the zerosum game represented by 3.11. That game has no saddle point; hence its solution is a mixed strategy pair, namely (1/3, 2/3) for Row and (2/3, 1/3) for Column. These, then, are the strategies that determine the threat point (X_o, Y_o) in the original game. (They are the same strategies that determine the threat point in the normalized game, being invariant with respect to linear transformations.)

Applying the threat strategies to 3.9, we obtain

$$X_o = 0 \times 1/3 \times 2/3 + 2 \times 1/3 \times 1/3 + (-1) \times 2/3 \times 2/3$$
$$+ (-3) \times 2/3 \times 2/3 = -14/9; \tag{3.30}$$

$$Y_o = 4 \times 2/3 \times 1/3 + (-2) \times 2/3 \times 2/3 + (-2) \times 2/3 \times 1/3$$
$$= -4/9. \tag{3.31}$$

Using the threat strategies as the status quo point of a bargaining problem and noting that the equation of the Pareto-optimal line is $y = 4 - 2x$, we obtain the solution

$$\frac{d}{dx}[(4 + 4/9 - 2x)(x + 14/9)] = -2x + 40/9 - 2x - 28/9 = 0 \tag{3.32}$$

$$x^* = 1/3; y^* = 10/3. \tag{3.33}$$

Observe that 3.9 has a single equilibrium at A_1A_2, which is, therefore, the solution of the *noncooperative* game in the sense of Nash, in the strict sense, and in the sense of Harsanyi. It is Pareto-optimal, so that objection to Pareto-deficient equilibrium solutions cannot be brought against it. The fact that, in the setting of the cooperative game, Row gets a concession from Column (that is, gets 1/3 rather than 0) stems from the opportunity available to Row to make threats, which, coupled with Column's threat, leads to the compromise solution. This game is an example of a game in which it is to one player's advantage but not to the other's to come to the bargaining table.

One might think that "jointly" the two players can get 4 (in A_1A_2), which is more than they get "jointly" in the compromise. This, however, is only an artifact of the particular payoff scales used. A "joint payoff" has no meaning in this context because payoffs given only on an interval scale cannot be added. If the payoffs could be added and redistributed, it would obviously be to the advantage of both players to effect the outcome that gives them the largest combined payoff and then use some "criterion of equity" to divide this sum. This is, in fact, the principle used in solving cooperative games with more than two players. However, the theory of the N-person game is not discussed in this book.

The compromise can be realized as follows. Note that Row's payoff is "one-sixth of the way" between his least preferred payoff (0) and his most preferred payoff (2) on the Pareto-optimal line. Accordingly, the players can decide between these two outcomes by a random device that effects A_1A_2 with probability 5/6 and A_1B_2 with probability 1/6. Or else, if the game can be played many times, the players can agree to jointly choose A_1A_2 five-sixths of the time and A_1B_2 one-sixth of the time. That is to say, Column, being in a more advantageous position in this game, has his way five-sixths of the time. This result is independent of the particular scales used to represent the payoffs.

Two other solutions of the cooperative game have been proposed. Like Nash's solution, they depend on the solution of a zerosum game in which the payoffs are payoff differences of the original game. They differ in the sort of "normalization" used to obtain the zerosum game, and in the way the final solution is obtained from the solution of that game.

In normalizing the original game, H. Raiffa (1953) assigns zero to each player's smallest payoff and one to the largest. The other payoffs are determined by preserving the original ratios of payoff differences (that is, the payoffs are transformed linearly so that the zero point and the unit are fixed as indicated). From this normalized game a zerosum game is obtained by replacing the payoffs with their algebraic differences. The zerosum game is then solved.

The solution of the original game is obtained by joining the outcome of the zerosum game and the Pareto-optimal line by a line inclined 45° to the X-axis. The solution of the zerosum game determines the "relative advantage" of one player over the other. Along the 45° line, this relative advantage is maintained, since the difference between x and y is a constant on that line. Thus, maintaining the relative advantage determined by the "conflict" aspect of the game, the players "cooperate" by increasing both their payoffs to the maximum attainable values on the Pareto-optimal line.

To illustrate Raiffa's method, let us apply it to solve the game represented by 3.9. The normalized game is shown in 3.12 and the difference game in 3.13.

		A_2	B_2			A_2	B_2
A_1		1	1/3	A_1		2/5	-2/3
		3/5	1			-2/5	2/3
B_1		0	0	B_1		-2/5	0
		2/5	0			2/5	0
		3.12				3.13	

The solution awards 2/11 to Row and −2/11 to Column. Hence x − y = 4/11 (Row has the advantage). The equation of the Pareto-optimal line of 3.12 is $y = -(5/3)x + 2$, and the intersection of this line with $y = x - 4/11$ gives Row 39/44 and Column 23/44. To translate these payoffs into payoffs associated with 3.9., we perform the inverse transformation that carries the normalized payoffs back into the original ones. These transformations are $y' = 6y - 2$ for Column and $x' = 5x - 3$ for Row. Accordingly, the solution of the original game is $x^* = 63/44$; $y^* = 50/44$.

Observe that Raiffa's solution favors Row while Nash's favors Column. In Nash's solution, the relative bargaining positions of the two players, as reflected in available threats, is the principal determinant of the outcome. Evidently in this game, Column has a greater threat leverage than Row. Raiffa's solution is more like an arbitration scheme. It puts the utilities of both players on the same unit interval, i.e., invokes an "equity principle" which in this particular game works in Row's favor.

R. B. Braithwaite (1955) has proposed a solution essentially similar to Raiffa's, except that the game is normalized in a different manner. Each player has at his disposal a maximin strategy which, if used, guarantees to the player a certain minimal payoff regardless of the other's strategy, and a minimax strategy, which, if used, keeps the payoff of the other to at most his guaranteed minimum. Assume that in a 2×2 game neither player's payoff matrix (considered as a matrix of a zerosum game) has a saddle point. Then the maximin and the minimax strategies of both players are mixed. If the maximin strategies are mixed (which Braithwaite assumes), then, if both players choose them, each will actually get his guaranteed minimum as the statistically expected payoff.

Let now one player use his maximin strategy while the other uses his minimax. The first player will then get his "security level payoff," but the other may get more than his security level. Record the difference. Now reverse the roles and record the excess over the security level obtained by the other player as he shifts from his maximin to the minimax. According to Braithwaite's arbitration scheme, the game should be normalized in such a way that each player gains as much as the other when shifting from maximin to minimax while the other sticks to his maximin.

The difficulty with this scheme is that it can be applied only to games in which both excesses are positive or at least have the same sign. To illustrate his method, Braithwaite used a variant of game #64 where this condition is met. It is violated in other types of 2×2 games (for instance in game #72) where the excesses can be of opposite sign. The difficulty can be formally by-passed if we allow negative linear transformations of the payoffs, but such transformations would be difficult to justify.

In some games Braithwaite's method is inapplicable even if negative linear transformations are allowed. Consider once more 3.9 where both players have dominating strategies. Row's maximin strategy is A_1; Column's is A_2.[3] The outcome gives Row 0 and Column 4. (Note that while Row gets his "security level," Column gets more. This could not happen if neither player had a dominating strategy.) Now Row's minimax strategy is B_1 and Column's is A_1 (the same as

---

[3] Strictly speaking, both A_2 and B_2 are maximin strategies for Column, but A_2 weakly dominates B_2 and so should be preferred.

his maximin strategy). Consequently, Column's excess in "shifting" to the minimax while Row stays with the maximin is 0, whereas Row's excess in shifting to the minimax while Column stays with the maximin is -1. A linear transformation that will equalize the two excesses does not exist, and Braithwaite's solution cannot be applied.

M. Kilgour (1974) derived criteria for deciding whether Braithwaite's arbitration scheme can be applied to any 2×2 game. He defines the following categories of games, or, in our terminology, game *variants,* since his criteria depend on payoffs given on an interval (not an ordinal) scale.

A *Braithwaite game* is one in which the gains of each player, as he shifts from his maximin to his minimax strategy while the co-player stays with the maximin, are both positive.

An *anti-Braithwaite game* is one where both these excesses are negative.

An *improper Braithwaite game* is one in which both of the excesses are zero.

A *non-Braithwaite game* is one in which only one of the excesses is positive or zero.

Since we have defined game species in terms of ordinal payoffs, the question of interest to us is whether a variant of a game that is a Braithwaite game remains a Braithwaite game when the payoffs of the players are changed by a positive *monotone* transformation. Braithwaite's arbitration scheme can be said to be applicable to these game species. We might also assume the scheme to be applicable to game species that are either Braithwaite games or anti-Braithwaite games in all of their variants except, possibly, when a monotone transformation carries them from one of these categories to the other, so that they pass through the "improper" category in a "borderline" variant.

Kilgour examined all of the seventy-eight games of the Rapoport and Guyer taxonomy and found the following twenty-five games to be either Braithwaite games or anti-Braithwaite games in all of their variants, except possibly in their borderline "improper" variants: Games (#1, #2, #3, #4, #5, #6), (#24, #25, #27, #28, #29, #30), #31, #32, #33, #34, #37, #38, (#59, #60, #63), #64, #66, #68, #69.[4]

----

[4] The games in parentheses are no-conflict games. Clearly arbitration is irrelevant in the context of these games.

We were somewhat surprised to find that among these games, which can be arbitrated by Braithwaite's scheme, the only one that remains a Braithwaite game (with both excesses positive) in all of its variants is Chicken (game #66). Braithwaite's own game, "The Two Musicians" (see Braithwaite, 1955) which in the ordinal taxonomy appears as game #64, is a so-called generalized Braithwaite game: in some of its variants the two excesses are both positive, in some they are both negative.

Meta-game Theory

The theory of the noncooperative game, as we have seen, revolves around singling out the equilibria of a game. If a game has a pure strategy single equilibrium, the corresponding outcome can in one sense be considered the "solution" of the game. If a 2×2 game has two equilibria or no equilibrium, an equilibrium can be defined in terms of mixed strategies. The crucial feature of such games is that, if one player uses the appropriate mixed strategy, the other player's payoff is the same regardless of what strategy, pure or mixed, he uses. The pair of such mixed strategies can then be considered as the solution of the game. We have seen further that such solutions are generally Pareto-deficient and, therefore, leave something to be desired.

Another way of finding new equilibria in a game is by extending the concept of "strategy" in another direction by defining so-called meta-strategies.

The relation of a meta-strategy to a strategy proper is analogous to the relation of a strategy to a move. Suppose that a 2×2 game is presented in matrix form and that one of the players, say, Row, is to choose first, his choice becoming known to Column before Column is to choose. This rule violates the definition of a game in normal form because, when a game has been given in normal form, it is assumed that the players must choose independently, i.e., simultaneously. However, if the players choose sequentially, the game can be considered to have been given in *extensive* form, which specifies the order of the moves. This new game in extensive form can be reduced to a game in normal form, but the resulting game will no longer be a 2×2 game; it will be a 2×4 game in which Row has two strategies and Column has four.

The two strategies available to Row are still the same, namely A_1 and B_1. But now, *before the play starts*, Column can choose from four different strategies, each being a specification of what he will do in each of the two situations resulting from Row's choices. These four strategies are the following:

M_1: I shall choose A_2 regardless of how Row chooses.
M_2: If Row chooses A_1, I shall choose A_2; otherwise, B_2.
M_3: If Row chooses A_1, I shall choose B_2; otherwise, A_2.
M_4: I shall choose B_2 regardless of how Row chooses.

Note that in the original 2×2 game, since Column has no knowledge of Row's choice, the "conditional strategies," M_2 and M_3, were not available to Column, only the "unconditional" strategies, M_1 and M_4, were available. Suppose now that, before the game starts, Column writes one of these four strategies (M_1, M_2, M_3, or M_4) on a piece of paper; Row writes down one of his two strategies, A_1 or A_2; each gives his piece of paper indicating his strategy choice to a referee. The referee can now determine the outcome of the game.

Suppose, for example, Column chose his strategy M_2, which states that his choice is the same as Row's. Column cannot literally make this choice, since he does not know how Row has chosen. But the referee, who also has Row's choice, can make it for him. Say Row has chosen A_1. The referee announces that Row chose A_1 and that Column chose "as Row did," and that, consequently, the outcome of the game is A_1A_2. A game so constructed from another game by introducing meta-strategies is called a meta-game of the first order.

Let us now construct a meta-game from a 2×2 game and examine it for equilibria. Take the game represented by 3.9. The corresponding meta-game, now a 2×4 game where Column chooses among meta-strategies, is shown as 3.14.

	M_1	M_2	M_3	M_4
A_1	4 / 0	4 / 0	0 / 2	0 / 2
B_1	-2 / -1	-2 / -3	-2 / -1	-2 / -3

3.14

This game has two equilibria, at (A_1M_1) and at (A_1M_2). The payoffs in these outcomes are the same as the payoff in the equilibrium (natural) outcome of the original game. So this 2×4 meta-game can be expected to result in the same payoffs to Row and to Column as the original game.

On the other hand, the meta-game in which Row's choices are meta-strategies (of a 4×2 game shown in matrix 3.15) has, besides the two original equilibria, an additional one at M_3B_2, which is Row's most preferred outcome.

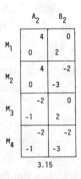

3.15

In this game, therefore, the outcome preferred by Row (who is the disgruntled player in this game) can at least be taken into consideration as a possible outcome of the noncooperative game. It is easy to see why this comes about. In making meta-strategies available to the disgruntled player, we give him the opportunity to choose a strategy to which the privileged player's best answer is "to give in." Still, since the outcome favoring Row does not appear as an equilibrium in *both* meta-games of the first order, it cannot yet be considered as a "meta-equilibrium" of the game.

Let us now go a step further. We might try to construct a 4×4 game in which each player will have the same four meta-strategies (M_1, M_2, M_3, M_4). However, it turns out that the resulting 4×4 matrix does not represent a well-defined game. For, suppose each player chooses M_2. The referee reads Row's strategy: "I shall choose A_1 if Column chooses A_2; otherwise, B_1." He turns to Column's paper and reads: "I shall choose A_2 if Row chooses A_1; otherwise, B_2." Collating the two decisions still does not tell the referee how the two players *actually* chose.

In order to construct a well-defined game, we must still take another step in the same direction. Let Column now have available the first four meta-strategies, and let Row have at his disposal sixteen meta-meta-strategies. The resulting game is a meta-game of the second order (a "meta-meta game").

For instance, one of Row's meta-meta-strategies may read: "If Column chooses M_1, I shall choose A_1; if M_2, I shall choose B_1; if M_3, also B_1; if M_4, A_1." Suppose Column chose M_2. The referee reads Column's message: "I shall choose A_2 if Row chooses A_1; otherwise, B_2." He reads Row's message as given above. Since Column *in fact* chose M_2, this means that Row chose B_1. But Column's choice contingent on Row's B_1 is B_2 (see the statement of M_2). Therefore, the outcome is B_1B_2.

We see that Row's sixteen meta-meta-strategies come from the fact that, corresponding to each of Column's four choices, he can indicate either A_1 or B_1 ($2 \times 2 \times 2 \times 2 = 16$). This 16×4 game is represented by 3.16 (p. 66).

Similarly, we construct a 4×16 game in which Row has four meta-strategies while Column has sixteen meta-meta-strategies. This game is shown as 3.17 (p. 67).

Examining these two matrices for equilibrium points, we find that there are several. Most of them give to the two players the same payoffs as the natural outcome in the original game. However, among them we also find the outcome A_1B_2: in the 16×4 game at $M_{12}^{(2)}M_4$; in the 4×16 game at $M_3M_3^{(2)}$.

Let us now see whether the 16×4 game has any dominating strategies. Recall that a dominating strategy is one which is "best" against all other strategies in the sense that a player choosing it does no worse and possibly better than by choosing any other strategy, regardless of the strategy chosen by the other player. We see that $M_1^{(2)}$ is a dominating strategy for Row. Therefore, by the principle of individual rationality, he must choose it. Assuming that Row does choose his dominating strategy, Column maximizes his payoff by choosing either M_1 or M_2, and the outcome is the same as in the original game. However, we see that in the 16×4 game Column has a dominating strategy, namely, $M_3^{(2)}$ or $M_6^{(2)}$. In that game, Column must choose one of these. Row maximizes by choosing M_3, getting the largest payoff.

This game is conceptualized as a pair of meta-meta games as described; in one of them Row gets the largest payoff. Column's dominant position, which he enjoyed in the original game, has been shaken.

	M_1	M_2	M_3	M_4
$M_1^{(2)}$: AAAA	4 / 0	4 / 0	0 / 2	0 / 2
$M_2^{(2)}$: AAAB	4 / 0	4 / 0	0 / 2	-2 / -3
$M_3^{(2)}$: AABA	4 / 0	4 / 0	-2 / -1	0 / 2
$M_4^{(2)}$: ABAA	4 / 0	-2 / -3	0 / 2	0 / 2
$M_5^{(2)}$: BAAA	-2 / -1	4 / 0	0 / 2	0 / 2
$M_6^{(2)}$: AABB	4 / 0	4 / 0	-2 / -1	-2 / -3
$M_7^{(2)}$: ABAB	4 / 0	-2 / -3	0 / 2	-2 / -3
$M_8^{(2)}$: BAAB	-2 / -1	4 / 0	0 / 2	-2 / -3
$M_9^{(2)}$: ABBA	4 / 0	-2 / -3	-2 / -1	0 / 2
$M_{10}^{(2)}$: BABA	-2 / -1	4 / 0	-2 / -1	0 / 2
$M_{11}^{(2)}$: BBAA	-2 / -1	-2 / -3	0 / 2	0 / 2
$M_{12}^{(2)}$: BBBA	-2 / -1	-2 / -3	-2 / -1	0 / 2
$M_{13}^{(2)}$: BBAB	-2 / -1	-2 / -3	0 / 2	-2 / -3
$M_{14}^{(2)}$: BABB	-2 / -1	4 / 0	-2 / -1	-2 / -3
$M_{15}^{(2)}$: ABBB	4 / 0	-2 / -3	-2 / -1	-2 / -3
$M_{16}^{(2)}$: BBBB	-2 / -1	-2 / -3	-2 / -1	-2 / -3

3.16

	$M_1^{(2)}$ A A A	$M_2^{(2)}$ A A B	$M_3^{(2)}$ A B A	$M_4^{(2)}$ A B A	$M_5^{(2)}$ B A A	$M_6^{(2)}$ A B B	$M_7^{(2)}$ A B A B	$M_8^{(2)}$ B A A B	$M_9^{(2)}$ A B B A	$M_{10}^{(2)}$ B B B A	$M_{11}^{(2)}$ B B A A	$M_{12}^{(2)}$ B B B A	$M_{13}^{(2)}$ B B A B	$M_{14}^{(2)}$ B A B B	$M_{15}^{(2)}$ A B B	$M_{16}^{(2)}$ B B B
M_1	4 / 0	4 / 0	4 / 0	4 / 0	0 / 2	4 / 0	4 / 0	0 / 2	4 / 0	0 / 2	0 / 2	0 / 2	0 / 2	0 / 2	4 / 0	0 / 2
M_2	4 / 0	4 / 0	4 / 0	-2 / -3	4 / 0	4 / 0	-2 / -3	4 / 0	-2 / -3	4 / 0	-2 / -3	-2 / -3	-2 / -3	4 / 0	-2 / -3	-2 / -3
M_3	-2 / -1	-2 / -1	0 / 2	-2 / -1	-2 / -1	0 / 2	-2 / -1	-2 / -1	0 / 2	0 / 2	-2 / -1	0 / 2	-2 / -1	0 / 2	0 / 2	0 / 2
M_4	-2 / -1	-2 / -3	-2 / -1	-2 / -1	-2 / -1	-2 / -3	-2 / -3	-2 / -3	-2 / -1	-2 / -1	-2 / -1	-2 / -1	-2 / -3	-2 / -3	-2 / -3	-2 / -3

3.17

At this point, the question naturally arises as to what would happen if we extended the strategy space still further to meta-games of third and higher orders. A theorem proved by Nigel Howard (1966) states that further extensions reveal no new equilibria, so that the process is "closed" after just two steps.

The meta-game model removes the objection to the theory of non-cooperative games where only equilibria are considered as "rational" outcomes. Recall that the objection stemmed from the circumstance that in some important instances equilibria are Pareto-deficient, and in some instances intuitively acceptable outcomes are not equilibria. The meta-game of the second order exhibits more outcomes as equilibria, and among these, outcomes discarded in the equilibrium-based theory make their appearance. With several equilibria on hand, if the game is not Nash-solvable, Harsanyi's theory can be applied. Particularly, in the game under discussion, Harsanyi's theory leads to precisely the same solution as Nash's theory of the *cooperative* game, provided the threat point determined by the latter is the point of reference in invoking the principle of risk dominance (cf. p. 46).

The transformation effected by the meta-game version is even more striking in the case of game #12 (Prisoner's Dilemma). The 16×4 meta-meta-game is shown in 3.18. In that game, Row's meta-meta-strategy, $M_4{}^{(2)}$, dominates all others. He, therefore, must choose it, and Column maximizes by choosing M_2. Mutatis mutandis, because this game is symmetric, $M_4{}^{(2)}$ is Column's dominating strategy in the 4×16 meta-game. Thus, in the meta-strategy space of the second order, Prisoner's Dilemma appears resolved because the cooperative outcome T_1T_2 results from *individually* rational choices.

The extension of the "repertoire of strategies" to meta-strategies is no less reasonable than the extension to mixed strategies. We have seen that the latter extension "solves" zerosum games that have no equilibria by exhibiting equilibria in mixed-strategy space. Similarly, the extension to meta-strategies "solves" some games in which individual "rationality" indicates one choice and collective "rationality" another.

It may appear that formulating a noncooperative game as a meta-game is tantamount to bringing in communication by the back door, as it were. It is not surprising, therefore, that "cooperative solutions" and outcomes favoring the less advantaged player, which had not

	M_1	M_2	M_3	M_4
$M_1^{(2)}$: SSSS	2 / 2	2 / 2	1 / 4	1 / 4
$M_2^{(2)}$: SSST	2 / 2	2 / 2	1 / 4	3 / 3
$M_3^{(2)}$: SSTS	2 / 2	2 / 2	4 / 1	1 / 4
$M_4^{(2)}$: STSS	2 / 2	3 / 3	1 / 4	1 / 4
$M_5^{(2)}$: TSSS	4 / 1	2 / 2	1 / 4	1 / 4
$M_6^{(2)}$: SSTT	2 / 2	2 / 2	4 / 1	3 / 3
$M_7^{(2)}$: STST	2 / 2	3 / 3	1 / 4	3 / 3
$M_8^{(2)}$: TSST	4 / 1	2 / 2	1 / 4	3 / 3
$M_9^{(2)}$: STTS	2 / 2	3 / 3	4 / 1	1 / 4
$M_{10}^{(2)}$: TSTS	4 / 1	2 / 2	4 / 1	1 / 4
$M_{11}^{(2)}$: TTSS	4 / 1	3 / 3	1 / 4	1 / 4
$M_{12}^{(2)}$: TTTS	4 / 1	3 / 3	4 / 1	1 / 4
$M_{13}^{(2)}$: TTST	4 / 1	3 / 3	1 / 4	3 / 3
$M_{14}^{(2)}$: TSTT	4 / 1	2 / 2	4 / 1	3 / 3
$M_{15}^{(2)}$: STTT	2 / 2	3 / 3	4 / 1	3 / 3
$M_{16}^{(2)}$: TTTT	4 / 1	3 / 3	4 / 1	3 / 3

3.18

been equilibria in the original game, now present themselves as equilibria. In other words, a sort of "broadening of horizons" occurs, as it does in negotiations. This is probably a correct interpretation. However, as long as game theory purports to be a theory of *rational* decision in conflict situations, there is no reason why situations of partial conflict should not be pictured by rational players *as if* communication between them were always possible, even if it is not in a particular instance. Further, there is no reason why rational players should not guide their decisions by principles that would be adopted if communication were possible. If we can choose a definition of "rationality" (which, after all, has never been unambiguously and rigorously prescribed), there is no reason why such a definition cannot incorporate the ability to take advantage of mutually advantageous decisions made possible by "tacit" or "imagined" communication.

4

Approaches to a
Behavioral Theory

The difficulties in the way of linking game theory to an experimentally testable theory are several. To begin with, game-theoretic analysis can be applied only if the payoffs entered in the game matrix actually represent utilities given on an interval scale. In principle, these utilities could be determined by specially designed experiments. In experimental games, however, such determination is not usually carried out, first, because it might be of questionable reliability, second, because it would detract from the usual purpose of the experiments, which is not so much to test the "rationality" of the players as to relate the subjects' decisions to given experimental situations, including the payoffs actually displayed in the game matrix.

Next, there are difficulties in interpreting the normative results of game theory. We have seen that the "solutions" of many games are pairs of mixed strategies. Strictly speaking, a mixed strategy is realized by the use of a random device, as explained in chapter 3, p. 38. Therefore, if the purpose of an experiment is to see whether subjects, in fact, make their choices as prescribed by game-theoretic solutions, they should be provided with such a device. However, providing a device amounts to instructing the subjects to use it. Thus the primary question, whether the subjects indeed determine their choices by chance, is automatically answered in the affirmative by structuring the situation rather than on the basis of empirical evidence.

To be sure, this difficulty can be overcome by interpreting the *frequencies* of the subjects' choices as probabilities associated with them. This interpretation, however, cannot be applied to experiments in which a game is played only once. In single play experiments, an analogue of choice frequency is the fraction of subjects choosing this or that strategy. To interpret this fraction as the probability of choice by a single subject is tantamount to assuming that each subject in the population uses the same random device to determine his choice. Although in some instances we shall make this assumption, it is admittedly a very strong one as well as somewhat far-fetched.

Finally, as we shall see, most of the game-theoretic prescriptions cannot be taken as serious contenders in a behavioral theory because, as a rule, they are disconfirmed except in most trivial situations (always assuming, to be sure, that the payoffs are the actual utilities). Nevertheless, game theory is a convenient point of departure of a behavioral theory, for its very failure can suggest more realistic behavioral models, provided the discrepancies between observed behavior and the prescriptions of the model can somehow be interpreted.

In this chapter, we abandon the prescriptive models of "rational" behavior in conflict situations and begin from the other end, as it were. Instead of assuming that the players are "rational" in the game-theoretic sense, we shall begin by assuming the contrary, that the players are guided only by the simplest, most naive considerations or are reacting to "immediate stimuli." Starting with this assumption as a base line, we can add complications, that is, more "far-sighted" considerations, as we go along. In this way, a behavioral theory might be built up gradually by adding and/or discarding hypotheses to be experimentally tested at each step. In particular, the question of whether the payoffs actually represent utilities will no longer be relevant since our hypotheses will relate directly to the payoffs actually entered in the game matrix; so that, if we find on occasions that the players do *not* make choices apparently calculated to maximize *payoffs,* these observations will simply be taken into account in our subsequent hypotheses. Recall that we have already suggested deviations from payoff-maximizing choices by introducing "competitive pressure" as a factor affecting the "stability" of the natural outcome. In fact, the concept of the natural outcome itself was derived from the hypothesis that the players will tend to avoid the strategy that contains the smallest payoff. This decision rule does not necessarily maximize expected payoff.

Our simple hypotheses concerning subjects' choices in 2×2 games will all relate to probabilities of choices to be estimated by observing relative frequencies either of choices in iterated games or as fractions of subjects making a particular choice. Such probabilistic hypotheses are dictated by the universal observation that, in almost all situations, human behavior appears to be "erratic," that is, hardly ever (except in most trivial situations) predictable with certainty.

Some of our hypotheses will relate choice frequencies to the structure of the game, that is, to the game species. Characteristically, these hypotheses will rest on an assumption that subjects can differentiate the rank order of the payoffs (as this is done in the ordinal taxonomy) but not necessarily the numerical magnitudes of the payoffs. Other hypotheses will relate choice frequencies to the numerical magnitudes of the payoffs. These usually will be applied to comparing different variants of the same game. Some hypotheses or models will relate to the time courses of choice frequencies. These will be called *dynamic;* those that do not relate to the time courses will be called *static.*

Static Hypotheses

1. *The stability of the natural outcome.* The empirical measure of the "stability" of the natural outcome will be the relative frequency of its occurrence either in iterations of a game or in a population of subjects. Stability will be assumed to depend on the category to which the game in question belongs. Some such assumptions seem intuitively reasonable. For instance, we would guess that the natural outcomes of class E games, where they are equilibria, would be more stable than those in class e, where they are not equilibria. Also, we would assume that games of order D_2 have the most stable natural outcomes; those of order D_1 the next most stable, and those of order D_0 the least stable. It is more difficult to imagine the effects of the different sorts of "pressures" that we have used to define our genera. Therefore, no explicit hypotheses will be made concerning the relative stability of natural outcomes in games within an order. Any pronounced differences, however, will be noted and used to generate

hypotheses concerning these effects, to be further tested empirically.

2. *The Repetition Hypothesis.* This hypothesis, which will be denoted by H_r, relates the frequency with which a choice is repeated to the rank of the associated payoff. Consider the conditional probability that a player will repeat his choice, given the specific outcome that occurred on the previous play of an iterated game. According to H_r, these frequencies will be monotonically related to the payoff ranks. That is, the repetition of a choice of strategy will be the most frequent following the outcome that awarded the player his largest payoff, etc. The hypothesis derives from a simple-minded assumption regarding the effects of reinforcement.

3. *The Shift Hypothesis* (H_s). The repetition hypothesis, H_r, could also be rationalized as follows: Column (Row) supposes that Row (Column) will repeat his choice. Therefore, a repetition on Column's (Row's) part will produce the same outcome, whereas a shift will produce the other outcome in the same row (column). The relative attractiveness of the outcome determines the relative frequencies of repetitions. The Shift Hypothesis (H_s) states that the larger the *difference* between these two payoffs (in the direction of the shift), the more tempting it is to shift.

Whereas H_r applies to games with ordinally defined payoffs, a stronger scale is required if the Shift Hypothesis is to be meaningful. At least the rank order of payoff *differences* must be defined. The interval scale is sufficient but not necessary to establish this rank order.

4. *The Monotonicity Hypothesis.* The next hypothesis relates to the numerical values of the payoffs rather than to their rank orders, as does H_r, or to the rank order of the payoff differences, as does H_s. It is, therefore, primarily relevant to comparing behavior in different variants of the same game, where payoff magnitudes can be varied without changing the game species. This hypothesis will be called the Hypothesis of Monotonicity and denoted by H_m.

Consider the general game represented by 1.1, reproduced here as 4.1 for convenience.

	A_2	B_2
A_1	a_2 / a_1	b_2 / c_1
B_1	c_2 / b_1	d_2 / d_1

4.1

For Row, the "attractiveness" of A_1 is reflected in the magnitudes of a_1 and c_1. Therefore, if we change Row's payoffs by increasing a_1 or c_1 while all the other payoffs remain the same, we may suppose that the frequency of A_1 choices by Row will increase. Similarly, since the attractiveness of A_2 to Column is reflected in the magnitudes of a_2 and c_2, we may suppose that increasing a_2 or c_2 will result in larger frequencies of A_2 choices. The effects of increasing other payoffs are analogous.

In summary, the Hypothesis of Monotonicity states that the frequency of choices of a strategy is a monotone increasing function of the payoffs associated with either of the outcomes contained in that strategy. This hypothesis is a sort of generalization of a "game against nature" model of the 2×2 game (cf. p. 4). If the game were so conceived, a rational player would choose the strategy that maximizes the expected payoff. H_m states, in effect, that the probability of choosing a strategy is a monotone increasing function of the associated expected payoff. Note that considerations associated with the co-player's probable choice are left out.

The Game Index

The Hypothesis of Monotonicity can be viewed as a simplified version of a more general hypothesis that relates frequencies of choices to the entire payoff matrix. Since the general 2×2 game matrix has eight payoffs, the most general hypothesis of this sort would specify the choice frequencies as functions of eight variables. In a 2×2 game, as long as we fix our attention on the unconditional frequencies of choices, each game can be characterized by two functions of the eight payoffs, each function representing the frequency of one of the two strategies chosen by each player. Let us call these functions $\Sigma_1(a_1, a_2, b_1, c_2, c_1, b_2, d_1, d_2)$ and $\Sigma_2(a_1, a_2, b_1, c_2, c_1, b_2, d_1, d_2)$, being respectively frequencies of S_1 and S_2 when the game is in standard format. The index of a game will be defined as this pair of functions.

The proposed functions indicate how an index is to be calculated from the payoffs. If the calculation involves arithmetic operations on the payoffs, the question arises as to which operations are "permissible" or meaningful. The answer depends on the kind of scale on which the payoffs are indicated. The scale, in turn, is defined by the kinds of transformations that can be performed on the payoffs without affecting the strategic structure of the game. For instance, in constructing the ordinal taxonomy, we assumed that the payoffs are given only on an ordinal scale. This means that if we change the payoffs of a player in any way, so long as the order of magnitudes of his four payoffs remains undisturbed, the resulting matrix still represents the same game, hence must have the same index, if its index is to be compared with indices of other games. There is ample evidence that an index in the sense just defined, characterizing a given *species* of a 2 × 2 game, does not exist, because systematic changes in S_1 and S_2 frequencies have been observed when payoffs are varied numerically in variants of the same species.

Recall that in game theory it is assumed that the payoffs are given on an interval scale. This means that, if the payoffs of a player are transformed by a positive linear transformation, the resulting matrix represents the same game. If indices of all games are to be invariant with respect to positive linear transformations, severe restrictions must be put on the sort of functions that determine the index of the game.

For simplicity, consider a symmetric game so that

$$\Sigma_1(a_1, \ldots d_2) = \Sigma_2(a_1, \ldots d_2) = \Sigma(a, b, c, d).$$

Then, if the payoffs are given on an interval scale, the following equation must be satisfied:

$$\Sigma(a, b, c, d) = \Sigma(ma + n, mb + n, mc + n, md + n), \quad (4.1)$$

where m is a positive constant and n an arbitrary constant.

To fix ideas, we shall examine the simplest functions of this type, namely, the quotients of linear polynomials in the differences of the payoffs.

For further simplification, we shall confine ourselves to a particular game, namely, a numerically symmetric variant of #12, Prisoner's Dilemma. Following the usual notation in the literature, we shall designate the two strategies of both players by C and D and place the natural outcome in the lower right corner instead of the upper left. We shall also use the notation for the payoffs adopted by many authors, as shown in 4.2.

Prisoner's Dilemma is defined by the inequality $T > R > P > S$. Our index, denoted by Δ, will now represent the frequency of D

$$\begin{array}{cc} C_2 & D_2 \end{array}$$

	R	T
C_1	R	S
D_1	S	P
	T	P

4.2

choices, since these intersect in the natural outcome. We single out all bilinear functions (quotients of linear polynomials) in the payoff differences. It can be easily shown that all such homogeneous bilinear functions can be written in the form

$$\Delta(T, R, S, P) = \frac{g_1(T - S) + g_2(R - S) + g_3(P - S)}{g_1'(T - S) + g_2'(R - S) + g_3'(P - S)}. \quad (4.2)$$

There are, of course, many possible representations of the same expression. We might, for example, write

$$\Delta(T, R, P, S) = \frac{h_1(R - P) + h_2(T - R) + h_3(P - S)}{h_1'(R - P) + h_2'(T - R) + h_3'(P - S)}, \quad (4.3)$$

where $h_2 = g_1$; $h_1 - h_2 = g_2$; $h_3 - h_1 = g_3$, etc.

Equation (4.3) contains all the "pressures" characteristic of Prisoner's Dilemma. The difference $(T - R)$ represents the pressure to choose D in pursuit of the largest payoff, assuming that the co-player chooses C. The difference $(R - P)$ represents the pressure to choose C in an attempt to avoid the Pareto-deficient natural outcome D_1D_2; $(P - S)$ represents the pressure to choose D in case the other has chosen likewise. However, since these differences appear in both the numerator and in the denominator, and since the signs of the coefficients have not yet been determined, we still do not know how the index depends on the payoffs.

Let us see whether Δ can be restricted still further. Consider a "degenerate" Prisoner's Dilemma game (cf. p. 30), in which $R = P$. In this game, the pressure to choose C has been completely eliminated; so we can assume that Δ attains its largest value. Let us arbitrarily fix this largest value at 1. Setting $\Delta(T, R, R, S)$ in (4.3) = 1, we deduce

$$h_2(T - R) + h_3(R - S) = h_2'(T - R) + h_3'(R - S), \quad (4.4)$$

which is a restriction on the coefficients h_2, h_3, h_2', h_3'.

Next, if we set $T = R$, $P = S$, disregarding competitive pressure, the pressure toward D vanishes; so we assume that Δ attains its smallest value, which we choose to be 0. Setting $\Delta(R, R, P, P) = 0$, we obtain $h_1 = 0$.

Our index has now been reduced to

$$\Delta(T, R, P, S) = \frac{h_2(T - R) + h_3(P - S)}{h_1'(R - P) + h_2(T - R) + h_3(P - S)}. \quad (4.5)$$

Dividing the numerator and the denominator by h_1', we obtain

$$\Delta(T, R, P, S) = \frac{m(T - R) + n(P - S)}{(R - P) + m(T - R) + n(P - S)} \quad (4.6)$$

$$= 1 - \frac{R - P}{(R - P) + m(T - R) + n(P - S)},$$

where $m = h_2/h_1'$; $n = h_3/h_1'$.

Thus our index for a numerically symmetric Prisoner's Dilemma game depends on the difference of payoffs and on two parameters, m and n.

We shall now show that the index satisfies the hypothesis of monotonicity. In the process, we shall obtain also an interpretation of the parameters m and n.

According to the hypothesis of monotonicity, Δ, being a measure of the tendency to choose D, should increase as T or P increases and should decrease as R or S increases. The dependence of Δ on T, R, P, and S can be observed by taking partial derivatives with respect to these variables. Denoting $[(R - P) + m(T - R) + n(P - S)]$ by K, we have

$$\frac{\partial \Delta}{\partial R} = \frac{-m(T - P) - n(P - S)}{K^2}; \quad (4.7)$$

$$\frac{\partial \Delta}{\partial T} = \frac{m(R - P)}{K^2}; \quad (4.8)$$

$$\frac{\partial \Delta}{\partial S} = \frac{-n(R - P)}{K^2}; \quad (4.9)$$

$$\frac{\partial \Delta}{\partial P} = \frac{m(T - R) + n(R - S)}{K^2}. \quad (4.10)$$

To satisfy H_m, we must have $\frac{\partial \Delta}{\partial T} > 0$, hence $m > 0$, and $\frac{\partial \Delta}{\partial S} < 0$, hence $n > 0$. If m and n are both positive, inequalities $\frac{\partial \Delta}{\partial R} < 0$ and $\frac{\partial \Delta}{\partial P} > 0$ are also satisfied, and all the partial derivatives have signs in accord with H_m.

Equations (4.8) and (4.9) reveal also the significance of the parameters m and n. Their relative magnitudes reflect the relative importance of T and S, that is, the payoffs associated with the unilateral outcomes D_1C_2 and C_1D_2 in generating the pressure toward D. This relation is of some psychological interest and will be discussed more fully in chapter 23.

If we ascribe special values to m and n, the index is simplified still further. For instance, if $m = 1$, $n = 0$, Δ reduces to $(T - R)/(T - P)$; if $m = 0$, $n = 1$, Δ reduces to $(P - S)/(R - S)$; if $m = n = 1$, Δ reduces to $1 - (R - P)/(T - S)$. As we shall see in chapter 23, all of these indices were used by different authors in attempts to account for behavior in Prisoner's Dilemma and in other more or less related 2×2 games.

It should be noted that the particular restriction of Δ to the form of (4.6) is a consequence of the inequalities that characterize Prisoner's Dilemma. In another game, Chicken (#66), often treated in experimental game literature as a variant of Prisoner's Dilemma, the method of fixing parameters by considering degenerate variants leads to a different reduction.

The numerically symmetric game of Chicken is defined by the inequalities $T > R > S > P$. We again define Δ as a measure of the tendency to choose D. In order to eliminate completely the pressure to choose C, we must set $R = P$. However, in Chicken, since $R > S > P$, setting $R = P$ would then make $R = S = P$. Substituting into (4.3) and setting $\Delta = 1$, we obtain

$$\Delta(T, R, R, R) = \frac{h_2(T - R)}{h_2'(T - R)} = 1; \quad h_2 = h_2'. \tag{4.11}$$

Next, in order to eliminate the pressure to choose D (again neglecting competitive pressure), we must set $R = T$. Substituting into (4.3), we obtain

$$\Delta(R, R, S, P) = h_1(R - P) + h_3(P - S) = 0. \tag{4.12}$$

Substituting into (4.3) reduces the latter to

$$\Delta = \frac{h_2(T-R)}{h_1'(R-P) + h_2(T-R) + h_3'(P-S)} \qquad (4.13)$$

$$= \frac{(T-R)}{p(R-P) + (T-R) + q(S-P)},$$

where $p = h_1'/h_2$; $q = -h_3'/h_2$. (For convenience in further calculations, we have made all payoff differences positive.)

We now test our index for concordance with the hypothesis of monotonicity. Setting $p(R-P) + (T-R) + q(S-P) = L$, we obtain

$$\frac{\partial\Delta}{\partial T} = \frac{p(R-P) + q(S-P)}{L^2} > 0; \qquad (4.14)$$

$$\frac{\partial\Delta}{\partial R} = \frac{-p(T-P) - q(S-P)}{L^2} < 0; \qquad (4.15)$$

$$\frac{\partial\Delta}{\partial S} = \frac{-q(T-R)}{L^2} < 0; \qquad (4.16)$$

$$\frac{\partial\Delta}{\partial P} = \frac{(p+q)(T-R)}{L^2} > 0. \qquad (4.17)$$

If $p > 0$, $q > 0$, all the inequalities are in accord with H_m, and Δ ranges from 0 to 1 as required.

As noted, we have left competitive pressure out of consideration. If we include it, fewer of the original six parameters (of which five are independent) can be eliminated. For instance, let us assume that in Prisoner's Dilemma Δ becomes zero only when competitive pressure is eliminated by setting $T = S$. But this implies $T = R = P = S$, and the game becomes trivial. Consequently, only one parameter can be eliminated, leaving four independent parameters. In Chicken, competitive pressure can be eliminated by setting $R = T = S$, which implies $h_3 = h_1$. Consequently, in this game, two parameters can be eliminated, leaving three independent ones. We shall not examine these more general models further.

An index can be built up in another way. Consider all possible difference ratios of the payoffs of the form $(x-y)/(z-w)$, where x, y, z, and w are some permutation of a_i, b_i, c_i, and d_i ($i = 1, 2$). Associated with each player's payoffs there are $4! = 24$ such ratios. Not all of them, however, are functionally independent. For instance,

$$\frac{d_1 - a_1}{c_1 - b_1} = \frac{a_1 - d_1}{b_1 - c_1} = \left[\frac{b_1 - c_1}{a_1 - d_1}\right]^{-1}, \text{etc.} \qquad (4.18)$$

It can be shown that every one of the twenty-four difference ratios can be obtained as a function of just two functionally independent ratios. For example, let

$$r_1 = \frac{a - d}{b - c} \text{ and } r_2 = \frac{a - c}{b - c}$$

be the two fundamental ratios. Then

$$\frac{c - d}{b - c} = r_1 - r_2, \quad \frac{b - c}{b - a} = (1 - r_2)^{-1}, \text{etc.} \qquad (4.19)$$

In short, r_1 and r_2 can be taken as "building blocks" in constructing an index to serve as a measure of the frequency of S responses of any numerically symmetric 2×2 game invariant under linear transformations of the payoffs. If the game is not symmetric, four such ratios are required, two for each player.

R. J. Harris used this method in constructing his index for any 2×2 game. Harris labels each player's largest payoff t_i ($i = 1, 2$). He places this payoff into an arbitrarily chosen cell of the payoff matrix. The payoff to the same player in the diagonally opposite cell is labeled s_i. Row's payoff in the same column with t_1 is labeled r_1, and that in the same row with t_1 is labeled p_1. Column's payoff in the same row with t_2 is labeled r_2; that in the same column with t_2 is labeled p_2.[1] Thus game #70, for example, would be represented in Harris's notation by 4.3.

4.3

Next, the following two ratios are calculated:

$$r_a^{(i)} = \frac{p_i - s_i}{t_i - s_i}; \qquad r_b^{(i)} = \frac{t_i - r_i}{t_i - s_i} \qquad (i = 1, 2).$$

[1] This notation is suggested by that of Prisoner's Dilemma (cf. 4.2).

The pair of ratios defines a point in a two-dimensional region, to be defined presently. Because the ratios are invariant with respect to linear transformations, the payoffs can all be assumed to be positive without loss of generality. Next, because t is the largest payoff, r_b is restricted to non-negative values. The value of r_a, on the other hand, is restricted to $r_a < 1$. Taking the horizontal axis of a cartesian plane to represent r_a and the vertical r_b, we see that the point (r_a, r_b) is free to range over the quadrant bounded by the horizontal axis below and the vertical line $r_a = 1$ on the right. This quadrant is divided into six regions, as shown in figure 4.1. The region in which the point lies will be completely determined by the rank order of r, p, and s, as shown in table 4.1.

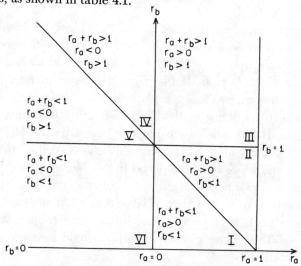

Fig. 4.1.   The six regions of Harris's taxonomy.

TABLE 4.1

Ordinal magnitudes of r, p, and s			Restrictions on r_a, r_b			Region
r > p;	r > s;	p > s	$r_a + r_b < 1$;	$r_a > 0$;	$r_b < 1$	I
r < p;	r > s;	p > s	$r_a + r_b > 1$;	$r_a > 0$;	$r_b < 1$	II
r < p;	r < s;	p > s	$r_a + r_b > 1$;	$r_a > 0$;	$r_b > 1$	III
r < p;	r < s;	p < s	$r_a + r_b > 1$;	$r_a < 0$;	$r_b > 1$	IV
r > p;	r < s;	p > s	$r_a + r_b < 1$;	$r_a > 0$;	$r_b > 1$	V
r > p;	r > s;	p < s	$r_a + r_b < 1$;	$r_a < 0$;	$r_b < 1$	VI

An asymmetric game is determined by two such points, each representing a player's ratio pair $(r_a^{(i)}, r_b^{(i)})$ $(i = 1, 2)$. A numerically symmetric game will be represented by a single point, since the ratio pairs of the two players will be equal. An ordinally symmetric game will be represented by two points in the same region (they will coincide if the game is numerically symmetric).

It follows that Harris's index separates the seventy-eight games of the ordinal taxonomy into twenty-one categories: fifteen categories of games characterized by pairs of points in distinct regions ($1/2 \times 6 \times 5 = 15$) and six categories of games with pairs of points in the same region. As pointed out, all the ordinally symmetric games fall into the latter six categories. Since there are twelve such games, one might surmise that there are two in each region. It turns out, however, that each of the fifteen two-region categories contains four games, and the six single-region categories contain eighteen games, not twelve. Thus, besides the twelve ordinally symmetric games, six others are included in those categories.

To see why this is so, consider game #14 shown in standard notation, 4.4, and in Harris's 4.5.

	4		2
3		4	
	3		1
1		2	

4.4

	t_2		r_2
p_1		t_1	
	p_2		s_2
s_1		r_1	

4.5

In this game $r_1 < p_1$; $r_1 > s_1$; $p_1 > s_1$; $r_2 < p_2$; $r_2 > s_2$; $p_2 > s_2$.

Therefore, according to table 4.1, both ratio pairs are in region II. Game #14 appears to be "symmetric" in Harris's scheme because his point of anchorage is not the natural outcome, as in the ordinal taxonomy, but each player's largest payoff. Assume that a player fixes his attention on the outcome containing his largest payoff and considers his order of preference for the following three events: (1) he shifts unilaterally from that outcome; (2) the co-player shifts unilaterally; (3) they both shift. The six possible orders of preference determine the region in which his ratio pair (r_a, r_b) lies. It is not surprising, therefore, that games that fall into each of Harris's categories are sometimes quite dissimilar from the point of view of the ordinal taxonomy. For instance, region I contains game #12 (Prisoner's Dilemma), game #6 (a no-conflict game), game #9, a symmetric game with a stable equilibrium, and game #21, an asymmetric game with a threat-vulnerable equilibrium.

Whether the categorization introduced by Harris's index is reflected in behavior is, of course, an empirical question. In particular, comparing observed behavior with the implications of the two taxonomic schemes, we would be asking the following question: which outcome is more salient for a player, the natural outcome (with reference to which the categories of the ordinal taxonomy are deduced) or the outcome containing his largest payoff, in terms of which Harris's index taxonomy is derived? In particular, Harris's taxonomy suggests the following hypothesis: in games #21, #14, #15, #72, #73, and #76, with identical quadruples of payoffs, as well as in the twelve numerically symmetric games, the behavior of the "average Row" ought to be identical with that of the "average Column" (since all these games appear to be symmetric in Harris's scheme). The ordinal taxonomy predicts this result for only the twelve ordinally symmetric games with identical payoff quadruples. Results obtained for game #21 (Guyer and Rapoport, 1969) indicate that, in this game at least, the behavior of Row and Column are widely different. Unfortunately, the numerical payoffs of the two players were not identical in that game; hence a disconfirmation of the above hypothesis cannot be concluded.[2]

The Iterated Game as a Stochastic Process

The search for an index by which to characterize all 2×2 games is the concern of a static theory, in which processes are not taken into account. When a theory incorporates the time dimension (examines processes, that is, sequences of events) it is said to be *dynamic*. The mathematical model that suggests itself as a description of an iterated game is a *stochastic process*. Such a process can be thought of as the behavior of a system that at any particular time finds itself in one of a number of specified states. At specified moments of time, the system either repeats the state in which it has just been or shifts to

---

[2] *Added in proof.* In one of Frenkel's experiments with single plays and numerically standardized payoffs (cf. chapter 7), substantial discrepancies were observed between $[S_1]$ and $[S_2]$ in games #21 (77 vs. 87) and #73 (55 vs. 94). No discrepancies of comparable magnitude were observed in any of the twelve ordinally symmetric games.

another state. These passages from state to state are governed by probabilities, called *transition probabilities,* which may themselves depend on the "history" of the process, that is, on the sequence of states in which the system has been. They may also depend on time explicitly.

Formally, a stochastic process is described as a family of random variables, each variable being characterized by a value of a parameter. To define the process fully, one must specify, not only the probability distributions of each random variable in the family, but also all the joint probability distributions of arbitrary sets of these variables. Stochastic processes singled out for theoretical investigations or used as models of phenomena are those which can be fully described sufficiently simply. In the simplest case, the system "chooses" the next state to be in by means of some random device with fixed probabilities, independent of either the time explicitly or of the previous states "visited" by the system.

Of special interest are stochastic processes known as *stationary Markov chains,* just one step of complexity removed from the foregoing. Assume that the system can be in any of n distinct states, indexed by 1, 2, . . . , n. At each moment of time when a transition is made, the next state is chosen with a probability that depends *only* on the state in which the system finds itself at the moment of transition. Thus, the whole process is completely specified by an initial probability vector $\vec{p}(0) = (p_1(0), p_2(0), \ldots, p_n(0))$ and the n^2 transition probabilities from any of the n states to any other, including the same state.

The transition probabilities are conveniently represented by a matrix:

$$P = \begin{bmatrix} p_{11} & p_{12} & \cdots & p_{1n} \\ p_{21} & p_{22} & \cdots & p_{2n} \\ & \cdots\cdots\cdots & & \\ p_{n1} & p_{n2} & \cdots & p_{nn} \end{bmatrix} \qquad (4.20)$$

Clearly, the p_{ij} must satisfy the condition $\sum_{j=1}^{n} p_{ij} = 1$.

Once the initial vector and the matrix P are given, we can calculate the probability that the system will be in any of the n states at any time, that is, after any number of transitions. For example, the probability that at time $t = 1$ the system will be in any of the n states is given by the following set of equations:

$$p_j(1) = \sum_{i=1}^{n} p_i(0)\, p_{ij}, \quad j = 1, 2, \ldots, n. \tag{4.21}$$

And in general, having calculated the probability vector for any time t, we can calculate it for time $t + 1$; for

$$p_j(t+1) = \sum_{i=1}^{n} p_i(t)\, p_{ij}, \quad j = 1, 2, \ldots, n. \tag{4.22}$$

These equations can be written in terms of products of a horizontal vector by the matrix P, thus:

$$\vec{p}(0)P = \vec{p}(1), \tag{4.23}$$

$$[\vec{p}(1)P]P = \vec{p}(0)P^2 = \vec{p}(2), \tag{4.24}$$

and in general,

$$\vec{p}(t) = \vec{p}(0)P^t. \tag{4.25}$$

From (4.25), it appears that the "future" probability vector at time t depends on the initial probability vector $\vec{p}(0)$. There is, however, an important class of Markov chains, called ergodic chains, in which the probability vector becomes "progressively more independent" of the initial vector. That is, the vector $\vec{p}(t)$ tends to a limit as t increases without bound, and this limit is independent of the initial probability vector.

If the Markov chain is ergodic, the limiting probability vector can be calculated by solving the system of (4.22) after $\vec{p}(t+1)$ has been replaced by $\vec{p}(t)$ and $1 - p_1 - p_2 - \ldots p_{n-1}$ has been substituted for p_n.

We shall now consider a Markov chain as a mathematical model of an iterated 2×2 game. The four states of the "system" are now the four outcomes S_1S_2, S_1T_2, T_1S_2, and T_1T_2. After each play, the system can either remain in the same state or shift to another, depending on the choices of the players on that play. It is easy to see that the transition probabilities of this Markov chain will be determined by the conditional choice probabilities of the players. Of these there are eight: α_i, β_i, γ_i, δ_i $(i = 1, 2)$, defined on p. 33. The transition probabilities p_{ij} $(i, j = 1, \ldots, 4)$ can be calculated in terms of these. For instance, let us calculate p_{23}, i.e., the probability that following state 2 (S_1T_2), state 3 (T_1S_2) occurs. This happens if Row chooses T_1 following S_1T_2 while Column chooses S_2 following S_1T_2. The two events being independent, their joint probabilities are the product of their respective probabilities. Therefore, $p_{23} = \tilde{\beta_1}\tilde{\gamma_2}$.

The Markov chain model is dynamic in the sense that it predicts the time course of the probability distribution of the four outcomes, given the initial distribution and the transition probabilities. Systematic changes of behavior patterns accompanying repeated experiences are usually ascribed to "learning." Can we then say that, if a protocol (or a pool of protocols) of an iterated game is adequately described by a Markov chain, the players are "learning something" in the course of repeated plays? According to the above mentioned conception of learning, we can. However, let us examine in greater detail the "psychological rationale" for this Markov chain model. This model is usually deduced from the so-called single element model (Atkinson and Estes, 1963) of a conditioning process. This single element (an abstractly conceived neural pathway) is assumed to be conditioned either to the one choice or to the other. When an outcome occurs, the element either remains conditioned to the choice just made or becomes conditioned to the other choice. The probability of either event depends on the outcome. These probabilities are reflected in the conditional probabilities of choice. So "learning" in this narrow sense is a sequence of decisions based on the outcome of the last decision, e.g., "The last outcome was satisfactory; now I shall repeat my choice," or "The last outcome was unsatisfactory; now I shall change my choice." These decisions are themselves probabilistic with biases determined by the payoffs associated with the occurring outcomes. But the *biases* are fixed. So, although probabilities of *choice* change, the probabilities of repetitions or shifts do not.

A more general stochastic model of learning, called the linear model, postulates a large number of elements, from which a sample is taken before each decision (Bush and Mosteller, 1955). Now the *proportion* of the elements in the sample conditioned to the one or the other choice determines the probability of choice. When an outcome occurs, the proportion of the elements in the entire population of elements conditioned to a choice changes and, with it, the probability of choice. Consequently, the probabilities of repeating a choice or shifting, themselves, undergo changes. This model is much closer to what we ordinarily understand by "learning."

In the linear model, the state of the subject is defined as the probability p with which he will choose S on the next play. When the outcome occurs, p will, in general, change. It is assumed that the new value of p will be a linear function of the old value. This assumption is suggested in the interest of mathematical simplicity and because it is a consequence of the above mentioned multi-element-sampling conditioning model. We now have the following type of equation governing the change in p:

$$p(t+1) = \alpha p + a, \tag{4.26}$$

where we have written p for $p(t)$ and α and a are constants independent of p and t but in general dependent on the outcome.

Defining $\lambda \equiv a/(1-\alpha)$, we can write (4.26) as

$$p(t+1) = \alpha p + (1-\alpha)\lambda. \tag{4.27}$$

Now since p is a probability, it is confined to the interval $[0, 1]$. It is easily shown that this restriction also restricts α and λ to the same interval.

Thus α and λ are the parameters of the learning process. As such, they depend on the particular outcome that instigates a change in p, if any. For instance, if the outcome is perceived as rewarding, p can be expected to increase. This will always happen if $p < 1$, $\alpha < 1$, $\lambda = 1$; for then $p(t+1) - p = \alpha p + (1-\alpha) - p = (1-\alpha)(1-p) > 0$. On the other hand if the outcome is punishing, p can be expected to decrease. This will always happen if $p > 0$, $\alpha \neq 1$, $\lambda = 0$; for then $\alpha p + (1-\alpha)\lambda = \alpha p < p$.

An intermediate situation occurs when $0 < \lambda < 1$. Then p will increase if it is smaller than λ and will decrease if it is larger than λ. In general, if the *same* outcome occurred on each play, p would tend in the limit toward the λ associated with that outcome, being ultimately fixated if $\lambda = 1$, or extinguished if $\lambda = 0$.

Actually, of course, each play of a 2×2 game does not always result in the same outcome but, instead, in any of the four possible outcomes. Each of them is, in general, associated with different values of α and λ. There are thus four pairs of these parameters, one set for each player. The recursion equations for $p(t)$ assume the following form, where $j = 1$, 2 designates the parameters and probabilities of S choices by Row and Column respectively:

$$p_j(t+1) = \alpha_j^{(1)} p_j(t) + (1 - \alpha_j^{(1)}) \lambda_j^{(1)} \text{ if } S_1S_2 \text{ occurs;} \quad (4.28)$$

$$p_j(t+1) = \alpha_j^{(2)} p_j(t) + (1 - \alpha_j^{(2)}) \lambda_j^{(2)} \text{ if } S_1T_2 \text{ occurs;} \quad (4.29)$$

$$p_j(t+1) = \alpha_j^{(3)} p_j(t) + (1 - \alpha_j^{(3)}) \lambda_j^{(3)} \text{ if } T_1S_2 \text{ occurs;} \quad (4.30)$$

$$p_j(t+1) = \alpha_j^{(4)} p_j(t) + (1 - \alpha_j^{(4)}) \lambda_j^{(4)} \text{ if } T_1T_2 \text{ occurs.} \quad (4.31)$$

The particular values of $\alpha_j^{(1)}$ and $\lambda_j^{(1)}$, presumably functions of the payoffs of the game (as well as characteristic of individuals), constitute the particular stochastic learning model for a 2×2 game.

The complexity of the linear stochastic model compared to the simple Markov chain stems from the fact that the "state space" is continuous rather than a finite set of states. If we nevertheless try to conceive of the system as being in any of the four states as originally defined (the outcomes), the transition probabilities are no longer constant but depend on the entire history of the process. Therefore, whereas the Markov chain model predicts the ultimate outcome probabilities, the linear model predicts only the probability distribution of the probabilities themselves—the probabilities "of the second order," so to say—which seriously complicates the problem of estimating the parameters from data. This complexity of the linear model makes itself felt even in the case of a single subject faced with two choices. It becomes formidable in the context of the 2×2 game, where the subject is a "two-headed" one with the heads in constant interaction.

Both the Markov chain and the linear stochastic learning model have been used as models of the iterated 2×2 game, the latter, however, only very roughly with recourse to computer simulation rather than to mathematics. The testing of both the static and of the dynamic models will be discussed in chapters 23 and 24.

5

Method

Experiments with 2×2 games can be categorized by three principal dichotomies:

1. one-play vs. iterated plays;
2. noncooperative vs. cooperative games;
3. experiments with two bona fide players vs. experiments with one programed player.

The One-play Experiment

If the subject has an opportunity to play a game only once, he must base his decision exclusively on his assessment of the situation as it is represented by the game matrix. This is all the more so if he does not know who the other player is, for then he cannot even assess the likelihood of what the other will choose, except on the basis of the structure of the game. Therefore, in one-play situations, the game matrix and the psychological characteristics of the player are the principal determining factors of decisions.

The advantage of single-play experiments is that, in them, interaction between the players (an important complicating factor) is eliminated. A disadvantage is that the experiment uses only a small fraction of the time during which an experimental subject is normally available and for that reason is "inefficient." If fifteen to thirty minutes is spent introducing the subject to the experimental setup and instructing him, the "returns" in the form of data from a single play are very low. This difficulty can be overcome by having a subject play *several* games only once. However, if the result of each play is announced to the subject (as is usually done in iterated plays), learning is likely to occur. Although we cannot say exactly what the subject will learn if the successive games with which he is presented are of various species, as long as some form of learning is at all possible, the pure decision situation of the one-play experiment is confounded with results of experience. Therefore, it is advisable to conduct one-play experiments "without feedback," that is, without announcing the outcomes of each play. If the experiment is conducted in this manner, there is no need to pair subjects. Each can be given a booklet or a set of cards with a different game matrix on each page or card. Each can be assigned a role (Row or Column) and asked to mark his choice in each game. Some hundreds of choices can easily be obtained from each subject in this way. To make the game "real," the subject is told that, after he has marked all his choices, a randomly selected "other" subject's stack of cards will be matched with his, and that he will then get the payoffs which would have resulted if he and the other subject had been actually paired.

One undesirable feature of this method is that the subject may recognize games of the same or closely related species and will make the same choice in all of them. Then, if the object of the experiment was to assess the pressures generated by different numerical payoffs in games of the same species, the difference in pressures will be obscured. Therefore, the games represented in the set should be as far apart as possible on the taxonomic tree. If many games are used, so that some are bound to be structurally similar, then similar games should be widely separated in the sequence of presentation in order to minimize the chances that "recognition" will elicit a stereotyped choice. In short, everything should be done to make the choices by the same player in different games as independent of each other as possible.

In matching the decisions of two subjects, it is essential, of course, that the games be rearranged in the same order. Moreover, in asymmetric games, the subject who played Row should be matched with the same games in which the matching subject played Column. To ensure correct matches, subjects and games can be numbered so that even-numbered subjects will always play Row in even-numbered games and play Column in odd-numbered games; odd-numbered subjects will always play Row in odd-numbered games and play Column in even-numbered games.

The data from one-play experiments comprise only the set of single decisions that the subjects made in each of the respective games. Taking proper precautions mentioned above, the same species of a game can appear in several variants, and even the same variant can be replicated a few times. Increasing the number of presentations is not costly (the subject can be asked to make several hundred decisions) and has the advantage of providing information on the subject's consistency in replicated games. If the decisions are not consistent, the inconsistencies can be interpreted as results of opposite pressures or as weak rather than strong preferences for the one or the other decision. Clearly, in evaluating the results statistically, it must be borne in mind that the same subject's decisions in replications are probably not independent. Whether a subject's decisions in games of different type are independent is an open question. Of course, decisions of different subjects (who do not interact in any way in one-play experiments) can safely be considered to be independent.

Iterated Noncooperative Play

By far the most common experiment involves iterated plays of the same game. In a noncooperative game with bona fide subjects, care must be taken to prevent explicit communication between them. This is best accomplished by physical separation. A simple arrangement comprises two booths open toward the experimenter. The subjects see the experimenter but not each other. At each play, the subjects signal their decisions to the experimenter. In the absence of apparatus, signaling can be done by raising the right or the left hand, or by pointing to one of two cards. A simple apparatus provides the subjects a choice of one of two buttons to push. The outcome of each game is announced to the subjects by one of four lights representing the four possible outcomes. An alternative is a display of four lights in a square. The lighting of both lights on the left represents the choice of strategy S by both subjects; both lights on the right, the simultaneous choice of strategy T; each kitty-corner pair represents the two disparate choices.

A relatively simple apparatus can include automatic recording of the outcomes. It is a good idea to provide the subjects with score sheets on which they also record the outcomes and the payoffs. This recording serves to emphatically call subjects' attention to each outcome.

In the experience of the authors, iterated plays of this sort can be conducted at the rate of about one play per five to ten seconds, thus of several hundred plays per hour. It turns out that, at comparatively small cost of time, the data returns can be greatly multiplied, ensuring greater statistical stability; so there is little or no advantage in economizing on the length of runs. If one is interested in the performance before experience has accumulated, the first plays can always be examined separately. There is no need to neglect taking advantage of frequently important information that can be obtained from long plays. The only question in this connection is whether the subjects' knowing that the run will be a long one influences the early phases. We do not believe that this is likely, since a fairly long run (say, twenty to fifty plays) is probably practically infinite in the mind of the subject. At any rate, the subjects need not be informed in advance about how long the run is to be.

Runs are sometimes made short in order to avoid the effect of "boredom." In our opinion, boredom is hardly ever a problem in game experiments. The fact that the statistics of protocols show great sensitivity to comparatively minute changes in payoffs seems to us to be ample evidence that the subjects get rather involved. One of us has conducted many experiments with 300-play runs and some with as many as 700 plays (Rapoport and Chammah, 1965).

The possibility of very long runs raises the question of whether it is worthwhile to have a pair of subjects in a single experimental session play several different iterated games rather than just one game. Each method has its advantages and disadvantages. In comparing behavior in different games or in different variants of the same game, the advantage of assigning several games to the same pair is that the subjects can serve as their own controls. The effects of experience can be confounded by randomizing or systematically varying the order in which the games are played. However, this sort of design introduces a "contagion effect" mentioned above, which masks differences between games or variants. In iterated games, the contagion effect may be magnified by the interactions between players.

Suppose, for example, it is desired to compare several variants of Prisoner's Dilemma. To have the subjects serve as their own controls, we can subdivide a very long run into several subruns and assign a variant of a game to each run, randomizing the order in which the variants are played. If the same pair of subjects is kept throughout the total run, a tacit coalition may develop and persist throughout the run, thus "erasing" the differential effect of the different payoff matrices. To some extent, this can be made less probable by shifting the partners in the subruns. Still, the subjects may learn the essential feature of the particular game, decide on some strategy of playing it, and keep to it throughout; then again, the differential effect may be masked. For this reason, if several games are mixed in a single experimental session, it is advisable to choose games of widely different structures, such as games belonging to different classes or orders.

The pacing of iterated plays may have a significant influence on the results. For instance, in games where cooperative and noncooperative choices are clearly defined (as in Prisoner's Dilemma), the frequency of cooperative choices seems to be related inversely to the speed of pacing. What effect pacing has on other games is not known.

Extremely fast pacing is made possible by an apparatus developed by M. Guyer and H. Gollub. The equipment includes a PDP-8/L computer, subject-to-computer interfaces, digital/analog converters, and a large Fairchild oscilloscope that displays payoff information to the players. The subjects have two choices each, as in a usual 2 × 2 game experiment. However, a choice—that is, moving a lever to one or the other position—represents a choice of an alternative "until further notice." The computer records the corresponding strategy at the rate of ten plays per second. Switching the lever to the other position produces an iteration of the other strategy at the same rate. Through the computer-controlled oscilloscope display, subjects are shown their cumulative payoffs in the form of two bars side by side. If the game contains both positive and negative payoffs, the heights of the bars may increase or decrease, depending on the pair of choices during a time period. Thus, the apparatus not only increases the pace of plays by a factor of perhaps 100 but also calls the attention of the players to the rates of change (positive or negative) of their respective cumulated payoffs and to a direct comparison between the two. A dynamic model of this format of play would be constructed more appropriately on the basis of a time-continuous, rather than a time-discrete, stochastic process. It would also bring out the role of latency in the interactions between players.

The way payoff information is displayed may also influence results by calling attention to specific aspects of the situation. If the payoffs are displayed as a 2×2 matrix, the subjects may be more likely to compare their "average" payoffs resulting from the one or the other choice, assuming the co-player's choices equally probable. This comparison may be less likely in the commonly used display, shown in table 5.1.

TABLE 5.1

If I choose	And he chooses	I get	He gets
A_1	A_2	a_1	a_2
B_1	A_2	b_1	c_2
A_1	B_2	c_1	b_2
B_1	B_2	d_1	d_2

In this display, the greater emphasis is on how the payoffs of both players depend on both their choices. Another type of display emphasizes the *control* that one player has over the payoffs of the other. However, this latter format can be used only in a class of 2×2 games called separable (Hamburger, 1969).

Consider a 2×2 game in which

$$a_1 - b_1 = c_1 - d_1; \qquad (5.1)$$

$$a_2 - b_2 = c_2 - d_2. \qquad (5.2)$$

Such a game can be represented by 5.1

	A_2	B_2
A_1	a_2+f a_1+e	a_2+h a_1+g
B_1	c_2+f b_1+e	c_2+h b_1+g

5.1

Accordingly, the players can be asked to choose between the alternatives shown in table 5.2.

TABLE 5.2

	Row's alternatives			Column's alternatives	
	Give me	Give him		Give me	Give him
1)	a'_1	a'_2	1')	f	e
2)	b'_1	c'_2	2')	h	g

The outcomes shown in 5.1 are obtained by apportioning the pay-offs as directed by both Row and Column.

Equations (5.1) and (5.2) imply that in a separable game both players must have a dominating strategy. The converse, however, is not true. Of the twenty-one games of order D_2, where both players have dominating strategies, only ten are separable, namely #1, #3, #6, #9, #11, #12, #14, #17, #19, and #21.

Games with One Programed Player

Introducing a programed player provides an opportunity to study the behavior of a subject under standardized conditions—the chosen strategy of a stooge. Here the danger arises that the subject will play a "game against nature." This will happen if the subject learns the stooge's strategy, for then he faces only the problem of finding an optimum counterstrategy, and the situation ceases to be a genuine two-person game. Several authors have found that in Prisoner's Dilemma the subject's behavior is not sensitive to changes in the stooge's noncontingent, randomized strategies (cf. chapter 17). For instance, the frequency of cooperative responses by a subject playing against a stooge who uses a randomized strategy with 80 percent cooperative responses is not much different from that of a subject playing against a stooge who uses a randomized strategy of 20 percent cooperative responses. If we suppose that a subject has become aware of the *fixed* nature of the stooge's strategy (which is, more-over, independent of his own), we can conclude that the subject will play entirely uncooperatively, because, in Prisoner's Dilemma under the assumption of maximizing one's own payoff, the completely un-cooperative strategy is best against *any* noncontingent strategy of the other player. For this reason, contingent strategies of the stooge are to be preferred. For then the subject, becoming aware of the con-tingencies, uses his choices to influence the behavior of the stooge.

If the stooge's strategy is complex, containing contingencies of high order (for instance, dependencies on several past plays), the fixed nature of the strategy is difficult to discover, and we can expect that the subject behaves as he would against a bona fide player. Then the programed player can be a useful tool for "standardizing the environment" without sacrificing the genuine game situation.

Example. In an experiment on a Threat game (#19), one of the strategies assigned to Row as a programed player was the following: "Choose S unless Column has chosen S three consecutive times. After the third consecutive choice of S by Column, switch to T and keep choosing T until Column switches to T; then switch to S." In other words, the stooge playing Row "tolerates" Column's acquisition of the maximum payoff but no more than three times in succession. A large proportion of subjects playing Column discovered this strategy and optimized by playing the pattern SSTSSTSST. . . . In this way, they prevented Row from ever using the T strategy, and so maximized their gains, but their protocols revealed nothing except the fact that they "solved the problem." In the light of this experience, Row's programed strategy was changed in a later experiment to a contingent probabilistic one. This time, Row's "impatience" was reflected in an increasing probability of shifting to T_1 as Column kept repeating S_2 (cf. p. 273). Thereby, the trivialization of the results of discovering the optimal strategy by the real subjects was avoided. It must be emphasized that a principal motivation for experimenting with noncooperative two-person games is in the circumstance that, in iterated plays, an "optimal" strategy cannot be unambiguously prescribed to the individual player, and therein lies the psychological interest of these situations.

The Cooperative Game

In the cooperative game the players are allowed to communicate. Presumably, the object of the communication is bargaining with a view of arriving at a *joint* (coordinated) choice of strategies. (Clearly, bargaining is irrelevant in a constant-sum game, because *jointly* the players are indifferent among the four outcomes, their individual interests being diametrically opposed.)

In experiments with cooperative games, it is useful to be guided by Nash's conception of this type of game as a two-phase noncooperative game (cf. p. 55). The first phase consists of a simultaneous, independent (hence, noncooperative) choice of a threat strategy by both players, which may be either one of the available pure strategies or a mixed strategy. The outcome of that choice is announced. In the second phase, each player makes a bid for a point on the negotiation set. This bid amounts to a mixture of strategies spanning the negotiation set or a portion of it. The bids are compatible either if the two points coincide, or if each player's bid is closer to the other's best outcome than to his own. If the bids are compatible, each player can get what he bid for; if they are not, each player gets the payoff associated with the pair of threat strategies.

This method has certain advantages, for it allows one to break up the play of a cooperative game into components and to study each component separately. It also permits a two-way comparison of the players' behavior with the prescriptions of game theory. For instance, it may be of interest to answer the question of whether the players choose the threat point prescribed by the theory. Whether or not their choice coincides with the game-theoretic prescription, the threat point chosen can be assumed to be the status quo point of a simple bargaining game (cf. p. 51). Then the question arises as to whether, given that status quo point, the players bid in such a way as to effect the prescribed solution (maximizing the product of the gains).

Additionally, the extent of communication allowed can be varied. For instance, communication and bargaining may be permitted prior to choosing a threat point, but not in the second phase. Or the threat point may be required to be chosen without communication, but then made the "basis of negotiation" in choosing a point on the negotiation set. Finally, communication and bargaining may be allowed throughout.

Perhaps the most serious difficulty in testing experimentally the game-theoretic solutions of cooperative games is that of making the subjects understand the uses of mixed strategies. Clearly, if the subjects do not even know the meaning of a mixed strategy, they cannot be expected to "choose" one, whereas the choice of such a strategy is just what game theory prescribes in many games. On the other hand, if the subjects are first thoroughly informed about the meaning and the implications of mixed strategy choices, they are no longer "naive," and the opportunity of comparing game-theoretic prescriptions with "ordinary" people's behavior in game situations is lost.

This problem was attacked in various ways by one of the authors in experiments to be described in chapter 22. Of the different methods employed, the most promising seems to us to be the following. Assume that the game presented calls for mixed threat strategies and also for a coordinated mixture as a solution. The subjects are asked first to play the original game in a long iterated sequence, being informed, however, that their average payoff in this preliminary sequence is not to be cashed in, but rather is to serve as the status quo point in the bargaining to follow. That is, if in bargaining for the final outcome they cannot agree, *then* each will get the payoff associated with that threat point. Thus it should become apparent that maximization of one's own payoff is not the object of the preliminary run. The object is rather to threaten the co-player with as small a payoff as possible (in case of deadlock) while at the same time keeping one's own payoff not too low so as not to impose an excessive risk upon oneself (again, in case of deadlock). Thus the threat point is essentially determined by mixed strategies if the frequencies of choices in the preliminary run are interpreted as probabilities (cf. p. 58).

The next, "bargaining," phase also consists of an iterated sequence. In this sequence, however, each player chooses not between his two alternatives but between the four *outcomes* of the game, the choices being independent on each play. If both choose the same outcome, that outcome obtains; if they choose different outcomes, each gets the payoff associated with the threat outcome. Although the actual choices are made independently, the players can avoid discrepant choices by making a (nonenforceable) agreement on a particular choice before each play. The solution will then be determined by the relative frequencies with which any of the outcomes is chosen. Note that bargaining can continue throughout the second phase; for, if one player insists on an excessive frequency of his most preferred outcome, the other can always "refuse to cooperate," thus bringing about the threatened outcome in an effort to make the first player "more reasonable."

Admittedly, this format "educates" the subjects rather thoroughly, but the amount of information given didactically is flexible. For instance, explanation of the effect of the threat point on the situation can be omitted if subjects play more than one game. They may learn by themselves, probably quite quickly, that it does not necessarily pay to maximize payoffs in the preliminary run. For instance, in game #21, if Row maximizes his payoff in the preliminary run, S_1S_2 becomes the threat point, and Row has no bargaining leverage whatsoever. In the bargaining phase, Column can always insist on S_1S_2 as the final outcome, and he will get it whether Row agrees or not, for S_1S_2 is also the threat point. The rate at which subjects learn these "facts of life" may be in itself an interesting subject of investigation.

Payoffs

Money is the simplest wherewithal of payoffs. The sizes of the stakes will be determined largely by the experimenter's budget. In iterated games, a fraction of a cent per unit of payoff can add up to wins or losses of a dollar or two per session for each subject. In our experience, this amount has been found to be a sufficient incentive for the players to play "seriously." However, experiments using "imaginary" money also usually give good results. Typically, the subjects become involved in the game and play "seriously" even without money stakes. Nevertheless, it is desirable to have the stakes as high as the budget can bear.

The numerical payoffs should be so designed that there is little likelihood that the player will end up "in the red." Conventionally, subjects are paid a fixed fee for participating in the experiments, their winnings or losses being added to or subtracted from this amount. The possibility of a subject losing his whole fee and even more presents some ethical, even legal, problems which can be bypassed if the losers are given an opportunity to win the money back in some other "game" specifically designed so that no money can be lost. Of course, the subjects should not be given the prospect of this "make-up" game at the beginning of the session. On the contrary, they should be under the impression that they may lose more than they earn.

Experiments reported have used two ways of avoiding the impression that the stakes are trivial. One is by giving big payoffs (in dollars) in accordance with the result of one play, randomly selected from the protocol of iterated plays. Subjects motivated to win money will then attempt to maximize the frequency of outcomes in which payoffs accruing to them individually or jointly are largest. Another way is to announce that a bonus will be paid to the subject who will make the largest point score among the population of subjects participating in an experiment. Note, however, that such a bonus introduces an extra competitive dimension into the game, for now it is in the interest of each player to keep the payoff of the other down as well as to bring his own payoff up.

There have not been many attempts to use a wherewithal of payoff other than money. Imaginary money has been the most common substitute, but its use, one suspects, has been dictated by budgetary considerations rather than by intentions of making systematic comparisons between experiments with real and imaginary money. Some conditions of an experiment do not permit the use of money. It may be awkward to use money when the subjects are children. On occasions, experiments have been conducted with inmates of prisons as subjects and, money being prohibited as incentive, cigarettes were used. The problem with at least some of the substitutes is that none (except possibly cigarettes paid to prisoners) can be as safely assumed to have utilities linear in the amounts as is probably the case with small amounts of money.

In some cases, electric shocks have been used as the "punishing" payoff. Because the present authors are opposed to the use of painful physical stimuli except in physiological experiments, we shall not discuss the use of such "payoffs."

Teams as Players

The two players in a 2 × 2 game need not be singles. Each "player" can be a team of individuals. However, if the game is to remain a 2 × 2 game, the players on the same team should all have the same interests. An easy way to satisfy this condition is to make payoffs to the team as a whole, requiring the amount to be divided equally among the team members.

The "team" player provides an opportunity to study the decision process in the choice of strategy. For instance, if each team consists of three individuals, decisions may be made by majority vote. The "strength" of the decision can then be assessed as to whether it was made by all three or by only two players. The idea can be extended by enlarging the teams, but the availability of subjects is a severe limiting factor in experiments of this sort. Typically, great numbers of subjects are required in order to assess the statistical features of an iterated game. Multiplying this number by the number of individuals on the team aggravates the problem and makes the additional information rather costly.

The voting within a team may be by either secret ballot, or open, such as raising hands. (The two procedures may give different results.) Or consensus may be required for each decision. In that case, it is natural to allow intrateam communication (this, of course, does not make the game a cooperative game if interteam communication is not allowed); then experimenters interested in the decision processes involved in playing a game of partial opposition can record the discussions to get whatever information is provided on this score.

Another way of getting at the decision process is to ask the players to record how they think their partner-opponents will choose on each play. This record will also provide information on how well players guess the intentions of others. It should be apparent, however, that eliciting this information can also influence the results by inviting the player to put himself in the other's shoes, at it were, or, in fact, by its slowing down the pace of decision making.

In summary, the different formats of game experiments should, in general, be assumed as different experimental conditions. As such, they raise serious difficulties in comparing results obtained by different experimenters who have presumably asked "the same question." Such difficulties pervade the entire field of experimental social psychology.

6

Variables

The principal data from experiments with 2×2 games are the choices made by the subjects. However, there are other data of varying interest to different experimenters; for example, subjects' guesses about how the co-player will choose, or answers on questionnaires administered before or after the experiment. These data and other data to be described may give information about the subjects' motivations, their conceptions of the game, attitudes toward the partner-opponent, etc.

If only the choices are of interest, then with 2×2 games a subject's choice between two alternatives on a particular play is the only datum relevant to that play produced by that subject. In a population of subjects, the fraction of subjects choosing one of the strategies becomes the only datum of the experiment. Hence, we have in the latter case a single dependent variable, and the purpose of any experiment or sequence of experiments is to observe how the fraction of subjects choosing a particular strategy varies with each of the independent variables that the experimenter decides to introduce.

In iterated games, the relative frequencies of the two choices by each subject are the simplest and most prominent dependent variable. Since the frequencies are complementary, the frequency of choices of one of the two strategies is a one-dimensional variable. It characterizes the protocol of responses of each subject. The massed frequency in a population of subjects characterizes the population.

Because of the "psychological overtones" associated with the strategies in the various 2 × 2 games, these frequencies often have been interpreted as indices of a particular type of behavior.

The great majority of experiments with 2 × 2 games have been with game #12, Prisoner's Dilemma.

6.1
GAME #12
PRISONER'S DILEMMA
IN STANDARD FORMAT

Undoubtedly, the suggestive interpretation of choice frequencies in that game has been a principal factor in singling it out as an experimental tool. The pressure to choose the dominating strategy in Prisoner's Dilemma has two components. On the one hand, if the co-player chooses T, the choice of S awards the other player his largest payoff. This pressure is, therefore, suggestive of "greed." On the other hand, if the co-player chooses S, the other's choice of S avoids the smallest payoff. This pressure is suggestive of "fear." Because S is the dominating strategy, it would seem that there is no pressure to choose T. However (and this is the essence of the dilemma), both players benefit if they choose T rather than S. To reap the benefit, they must "cooperate," that is, choose T *jointly*. For this reason, the cross pressures of Prisoner's Dilemma have been interpreted as those of "cooperation" and "competition."

Note that, from the point of view of the ordinal taxonomy which singles out the outcome S_1S_2 as the point of reference, there is no competitive pressure in this game, because either player, in shifting unilaterally from the *natural outcome* S_1S_2, suffers a competitive *dis*advantage. Seeing competitive pressure in Prisoner's Dilemma amounts to taking T_1T_2 rather than S_1S_2 as the point of reference, for T_1T_2 is the "cooperative" outcome; a unilateral shift from it (resulting in competitive advantage for the shifting player) is interpreted as "defection." It is this interpretation that suggested the labels C (for "cooperation") and D (for "defection") for the dominated and the dominating strategies respectively, and these labels have become more or less standard in the literature on experimental games.

In game #66 (Chicken), the strategy containing the natural outcome has been labeled C and has also been interpreted frequently as "cooperation." Yet the choice of C in this game has a meaning different from that in Prisoner's Dilemma, for C is actually *best* against the other player's D. In choosing it (while the other chooses D), a player does not necessarily exhibit voluntary cooperation in preference to "competition." He may be simply submitting to the other's preemption of D, which is lucrative if not "punished."

In game #19, an asymmetric game, again "cooperation" has entirely different meaning for the two players who play different roles. For Row to "cooperate" means to "submit" or to trust in Column's good intentions; for Column to "cooperate" means to share with Row. Thus Row cooperates if and only if he chooses S_1. Column, on the other hand, can be said to "cooperate" if he alternates between S_2 and T_2.

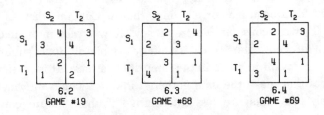

6.2
GAME #19

6.3
GAME #68

6.4
GAME #69

In games #68 and #69, a reasonable interpretation of cooperation is an alternation between outcomes S_1T_2 and T_1S_2, which requires *coordination* of the players' choices. In common usage, "coordination" is often a near synonym for "cooperation." From our analysis of 2×2 games, however, we find that coordination sometimes is and sometimes is not a necessary component of cooperation.

In short, while the frequency of choice of one of the strategies is a perfectly well-defined statistic of a protocol, one must keep in mind the variety of "psychological" interpretations of this statistic.

The next category of dependent variables are the frequencies of the four outcomes of which three are independent. From these frequencies the interdependence of the players' choices can be estimated. If the two players make their choices entirely independently of each other, the probabilities of the four outcomes, reflected in their relative frequencies, ought to be the products of the corresponding probabilities of strategy choices. In general, this will not be true. In particular, in Prisoner's Dilemma there is a strong correlation between the frequencies of C choices of the two subjects in iterated play. Consequently, the frequency of C_1C_2 will, as a rule, be considerably greater than the product of the C frequencies. Likewise, the frequency of D_1D_2 will be, in general, greater than the product of the D frequencies. In other games, this is not necessarily the case. On a priori grounds, one might even conjecture that in Chicken the probability of C choices ought to be *negatively* correlated, since C is best against D, and D is best against C. As we shall see, this conjecture is not borne out.

In some games, the sign of the correlation coefficient is even more difficult to guess on a priori grounds. To take an example, should the choices of S in game #19 be positively or negatively correlated? An argument for a positive correlation is that, if Row "submits," Column has no motivation to share, while if Column is "adamant," Row will eventually see the futility of resorting to "threat" (choosing T_1). An argument for a negative correlation is that, if Column "shares," i.e., chooses T_2 with considerable frequency, Row is not motivated to "revolt" (to choose the "threat" strategy), while if Row "submits," Column may want to share in the interest of fairness. It is these ambivalences that make the data gathered in 2×2 games informative (obviously, the data are less informative if their nature can be guessed in advance).

The interdependence of the players' choices can be measured in two ways: within protocols and across protocols. The former singles out a measure of influence that co-players exert on each other in the course of iterated plays. The latter method singles out a measure of correlation across pairs of players between their leanings toward the one or the other choice.

A measure of the tendency to imitate the choices of the co-player can be derived as follows. We define

$\sigma_i = \Pr(S_i \mid S_j)$, the probability that player i chooses S_i on play $t + 1$ after player j chose S_j on play t.

$\tau_i = \Pr(T_i \mid T_j)$, the probability that player i chooses T_i on play $t + 1$ after player j chose T_j on play t.

Note that σ_i and τ_i together are a measure of the tendency to use a Tit-for-tat strategy (cf. p. 122).

As a measure of across-protocol interdependence, we shall use the

Pearson product moment coefficient $\rho_{S_1 S_2}$. Note that $\rho_{S_1 S_2} = \rho_{T_1 T_2}$, since $(T_i) = 100 - (S_i)$. However, σ_i and τ_i can be independent of each other since the tendency to imitate the co-player's S choice need not imply a tendency to imitate his T choice, or the opposite. Further, while high values of σ_i and τ_i in a pool of protocols imply high values of $\rho_{S_1 S_2}$, the converse need not be true. A player's overall preference for S may induce the same preference in the co-player, but not necessarily a tendency to imitate from play to play.

Parameters σ_i and τ_i are related to the repetition frequencies α_i, β_i, γ_i, and δ_i, as follows. We set

$$
\begin{aligned}
\Pr(S_1' \mid S_2) &= \frac{\Pr(S_1, S_2)}{\Pr(S_2)} \\
&= \frac{\Pr(S_1 \mid S_1 S_2)\Pr(S_1 S_2) + \Pr(S_1 \mid T_1 S_2)\Pr(T_1 S_2)}{\Pr(S_2)} \\
&= \frac{\alpha_1 \Pr(S_1 S_2) + (1 - \beta_1)\Pr(T_1 S_2)}{\Pr(S_2)}.
\end{aligned}
\tag{6.1}
$$

Thus, an estimate of σ_1 is

$$
\hat{\sigma}_1 = \frac{\alpha_1(S_1 S_2) + (1 - \beta_1)(T_1 S_2)}{(S_2)}.
\tag{6.2}
$$

Similarly,

$$
\hat{\sigma}_2 = \frac{\alpha_2(S_1 S_2) + (1 - \beta_2)(S_1 T_2)}{(S_1)}
\tag{6.3}
$$

$$
\hat{\tau}_1 = \frac{(1 - \gamma_1)(S_1 T_2) + \delta_1(T_1 T_2)}{(T_2)};
\tag{6.4}
$$

$$
\hat{\tau}_2 = \frac{(1 - \gamma_2)(T_1 S_2) + \delta_2(T_1 T_2)}{(T_1)}.
\tag{6.5}
$$

Given a population of protocols obtained from several subjects playing an iterated game, the "average" conditional frequencies can be calculated in two ways. One way is by averaging the conditional frequencies of each player; another, by identifying the "average" conditional frequency with that observed in the entire pool of protocols. The two "averages" will, in general, not be equal because in the latter case the frequencies of the conditioning outcomes act as "weights" in the average, whereas in the former, they do not. As an example, consider two protocols, one with 10 S_1S_2 outcomes, the other with 100. Suppose that, in the first, each player chose S following S_1S_2 half the time, in the second, 80 percent of the time. The averaged value of α is 0.65. In the pooled protocol, however, S_1S_2 occurred 110 times and S was chosen following S_1S_2 $5 + 80 = 85$ times. The pooled value of α is therefore $85/110 = 0.77$.

Which "average" is used as an index characteristic of the game, of the experimental conditions, or of the subject population will depend on whether one chooses to view the pooled behavior as an average of individuals' (or pairs') performances or as the behavior of the population considered as an abstract "subject."

Length of Runs

Consider the runs of some particular outcome, say, of the C_1C_2 outcome in Prisoner's Dilemma. This outcome represents "established cooperation" between the players. Our interest is in the distribution of the durations of these "lock-ins." Assume for a moment that the protocol of each player is a Bernoulli process, that is, a sequence of choices, C or D, whereby the probability p of occurrence of C is fixed and independent of preceding outcomes. Then the probability of D is $q = 1 - p$. Under these assumptions, the probability that a run of C's is exactly k plays long is $p^k q$. Similarly, the probability that a run of C_1C_2 outcomes is exactly k plays long is $p^{2k}(1 - p^2)$. In other words, the probability of a run of a given length will be a decaying exponential function of the length of a CC run. The probability of a run of *at least* k plays long will be $1 - \sum_{j=0}^{k-1} p^{2j}(1 - p^2) = p^{2k}$, also a decaying exponential function of the length of the run.

Whatever be the nature of the stochastic process governing the distribution of run lengths, the probability of a run of at least a given length must be a monotone nonincreasing function of the length; in general, a decreasing function. Accordingly, we write a continuous approximation of this function as

$$\Pr(R \geqslant t) = e^{-f(t)}, \tag{6.6}$$

where R denotes the random variable representing the length of a CC run, t denotes "time," i.e., number of plays, and $f(t)$ is an appropriately chosen nonnegative function of t.

In the case just considered, $f(t) = at$; hence, the second derivative $f''(t) = 0$. The other two possible cases are those where $f''(t) < 0$ and where $f''(t) > 0$. (We shall not consider the case where $f''(t)$ changes sign in the course of the play.) The first case suggests that repetitions of the outcome in question are self-enhancing: the more times it has been repeated, the more likely are repetitions to continue. The second case suggests that repetitions are self-inhibiting: the more repetitions occur, the more likely is the run to be broken.

Self-enhancing and self-inhibiting runs suggest psychological interpretations. We might expect that, in Prisoner's Dilemma, runs of C_1C_2 may well be self-enhancing, since it is reasonable to suppose that the longer a cooperative pattern has persisted, the less likely it is to be broken. In the case of DD runs, arguments can be made either way. On the one hand, we might suppose that a "lock-in" reflecting mutual "distrust" might be self-enhancing. On the other hand, the cumulating losses associated with D_1D_2 outcomes may make these runs self-inhibiting. In Chicken, it is quite likely that D_1D_2 runs are self-inhibiting, since the outcome is severely punishing for both players and a "way out" is open to either through a shift to C, i.e., "submitting."

In a game with a threat-vulnerable natural outcome, e.g., game #19, the interesting question is whether runs of T_1S_2 are self-enhancing or self-inhibiting. In favor of the former conjecture would be a growing reluctance on the part of Row to "give up" his revolt against Column, while Column persists more and more in S on the assumption that the mounting losses will force Row to give up. In favor of the self-inhibiting conclusion is the possibility that mounting losses do exert increasing pressure on Row to give up, or Row's continued revolt exerts an increasing pressure on Column to "yield."

The nature of the process is determined by the second derivative of $f(t)$, characterizing the exponential. The problem is to estimate this function, or at least the sign of its second derivative. One way of doing it would be to combine all the protocols of several experiments involving several pairs of subjects and to plot the cumulative frequencies of runs of given lengths. Since a run of at least k plays long includes all the runs at least $k-1$ trials long, the number of runs of at least a given length will be nonincreasing (in general, decreasing) with the length of the run. We can next try to fit the plot with a decaying exponential curve and estimate the best fitting f(t). Our conclusion concerning the type of run will depend on the sign of the second derivative of f(t).

It must be borne in mind, however, that the corresponding "psychological interpretation" based on this procedure may be misleading, as will appear from the following example.

Assume that each pair of subjects is characterized by a particular value of p, hence, of a. In other words, the parameter a is now a random variable characterizing the subject population. Let the frequency distribution of a be h(α). Then, if we combine all of the protocols and plot the cumulative frequency of runs of at least a given length against that length, we shall observe

$$\Pr[R \geq t] = e^{-f(t)} = \int_0^\infty e^{-at} h(\alpha)\, d\alpha. \qquad (6.7)$$

Unless h(α) is a spike function at $\alpha = a$ (i.e., unless every subject is characterized by the same α) f(t) will not be linear in t. If f(t) has a second derivative, therefore, it will be either positive or negative (not zero), and we shall be tempted to conclude that the runs are self-enhancing if $f''(t) < 0$, or self-inhibiting if $f''(t) > 0$, whereas in reality the probability of breaking a run is independent of the length of the run for every subject.

In general, if data represent a pooling of several stochastic processes, all of the same type but with different parameters, the pooled process will not be representable by a stochastic process of the same type. This circumstance seriously impairs the usefulness of some simple stochastic process types as models of mass phenomena.

If we have reasonable confidence that our model applies to each individual subject (possibly with a different parameter), then the frequency distribution of the parameter in the population can be determined from (6.7).

To illustrate, let the *observed* f(t) be a$\sqrt{t}$, a > 0 (which is what is actually observed in some data). On the face of it, since $f''(t) < 0$, the corresponding run appears to be self-enhancing: the longer it lasts, the more likely it is to last still longer. In some cases this conclusion is tempting. Suppose, for instance, the run in question is a C_1C_2 run in Prisoner's Dilemma. If the run is self-enhancing, this means that the longer the two players cooperate, the more "firmly" is their tacit collusion established. However, the observed f(t) can also be obtained if the C_1C_2 run is a Bernoulli run for every pair (with equal termination probability at every play), provided the parameter is distributed in the population in a certain way. Solving (6.7) as an integral equation for the unknown function $h(a)$, we obtain

$$h(a) = \frac{\bar{a}a^{-3/2}}{2\sqrt{\pi}} \exp \left\{\frac{-\bar{a}^2}{4a}\right\}, \tag{6.8}$$

where $\bar{a}$ is the mean of a. It turns out that $\int_0^\infty h(a)da = 1$, so that $h(a)$ is indeed a frequency distribution, albeit not one commonly observed. If, however, we compute the distribution of $b = a^{-1}$, the mean length of the run in question, we obtain

$$g(b) = \frac{\bar{a}b^{-1/2} e^{-\bar{a}^2b/4}}{2\sqrt{\pi}}, \tag{6.9}$$

which is a well-known distribution of the "gamma" type.

Hence, the observed frequency distribution of runs is compatible with the hypothesis that for each player the process is a Bernoulli process but that the mean "longevity" of a run is distributed in the population in accordance with the frequency distribution given by (6.9).

Consider now the way a run of some outcome *ends*. For instance, a run of S_1S_2 outcomes may end in S_1T_2 or T_1S_2 or in T_1T_2. Comparisons of the relative frequencies of outcomes that follow a run of a given type also suggest psychological interpretations. Take a run of S_1S_2 outcomes in game #19. If it ends by a shift to T_1S_2, this indicates that Row's "patience" has been exhausted. If it ends by a shift to S_1T_2, this indicates that Column has finally decided to share with Row. If it ends in T_1T_2, in the absence of coordinating communication between the players, we must assume that the probability of the double shift is simply a product of the probabilities of the two unilateral shifts. The ratio of the above two probabilities that the run ends with T_1S_2 or S_1T_2 indicates the relative strengths of pressures on Row and Column. This ratio can, in fact, be calculated; it is given by $\frac{\tilde{\alpha}_1\alpha_2}{\alpha_1\tilde{\alpha}_2}$.

Another interesting ratio is one connected with runs of unilaterally cooperative outcomes in Prisoner's Dilemma, i.e., C_1D_2 and D_1C_2.

These so-called martyr runs can end either in D_1D_2 or in C_1C_2 or in a switch in roles. (The latter effect must be considered as an accidental result of simultaneous shifts.) If the run ends in D_1D_2, the "martyrdom" was a failure; the exploiter did not become "converted" into a cooperator, and the erstwhile "martyr" gave up. If a martyr run ends in C_1C_2, a "conversion" has occurred, and the martyrdom was a success. The ratio of failures to successes is represented by

$$\frac{\tilde{\beta}_1\gamma_2}{\beta_1\tilde{\gamma}_2}.$$

The Independent Variables

The independent variables used in game experiments fall roughly into three classes. Those of the first class are intrinsic to the game itself: they are the payoffs and the structure of the game, and are easiest to specify precisely and to manipulate at will.

The second class of variables involves the manipulation of the *conditions* under which the game is played. Most typical are manipulations of the behavior of the stooge player—the other player who is a confederate of the experimenter. Manipulations of other aspects of the player's environment include attempts to put the subject in one or another "state of mind," whether by instructions, by information given him about the "nature" of the other player, by messages fed to him during the course of the play, and the like.

The third class of variables includes conditions that, strictly speaking, are not manipulated experimentally but taken "from real life." For the most part, these are the "personality variables." Players can be selected from distinct populations (e.g., by sex, age, background) or selected for independently assessed personality characteristics.

Understandably, the independent variables selected for an experiment will reflect the interests of the investigator. The bulk of experimentation on games has been conducted by psychologists, principally social psychologists interested in factors affecting interpersonal relations and in behavior as a reflection of personality. As a result, a great deal of attention has been paid to independent variables related to the personality of the players. The games were used as a sort of projective test, the basic assumption being that different kinds of people play the same game in different ways, perhaps reflecting their personalities in their style of play. The attraction of these studies is in the apparent opportunity they provide to extend laboratory methods to the study of behavior rooted in "truly" psychological soil.

At the other extreme are investigators whose interests are more closely related to game theory in its own right. They picture the *game* rather than the player as the object of study. Ideally, they expect different people to behave the same way in the same game. Variability of individual behavior is for them "noise" rather than the object of interest. From this point of view, the logical choice of independent variables falls on the structural variables (primarily the payoff configuration) of the game.

As is usual in all psychological investigations, there is a trade-off between "hard" investigations and "soft" ones. The former can be more easily organized into a theory. The latter seem to be more relevant to the interests of psychologists.

Payoffs

Payoffs enter as independent variables in two ways: as "stimulus magnitudes" and as determinants of the game structure (species) by the way they are placed in the game matrix. The effects of both of these uses of payoffs as independent variables can be studied separately. By varying the *locations* of each player's payoffs in the cells of the matrix, the effect of game structure can be examined. Alternately, the species of the game can be kept constant while the numerical magnitudes of the payoffs vary within the limits imposed by the species.

Of special interest are changes in payoff magnitude effected by positive linear transformations. In chapter 3, we held the usual game-theoretic assumption that games obtained by positive linear transformations of the payoffs of a given game are strategically equivalent, even if independent transformations are applied to the payoffs of each player. But the fact that such games are strategically equivalent in the sense of game theory does not, by any means, warrant the assumption that the behavior of the players will be the same in all such games. As an example, consider the games represented by 6.5 and 6.6:

6.5

6.6

Row's payoffs in 6.6 were obtained from 6.5 by the transformation $x' = 2x + 20$; Column's, by the transformation $y' = y + 7$.

These games are "strategically equivalent," yet they look different, and there is no reason to suppose that, on the average, players will behave in the same way in the two games. Hence, an opportunity is provided to test the behavioral relevance of strategic equivalence. If there are systematic differences in the behavior of the players in two strategically equivalent games, the next step is to look for the sources of the discrepancy.

Consider now two games obtained from each other by the *same* linear transformation of the payoffs of each player. Recall that linear transformation involves the multiplication by a constant and the addition of another constant. The two operations can be applied separately to investigate their effects. In the game represented by 6.7 and 6.8, the payoffs to both players have been multiplied by 2.

6.7

6.8

Matrix 6.9 is obtained from 6.7 by adding 12 to all payoffs.

	S_2	T_2
S_1	17 / 12	12 / 17
T_1	11 / 10	10 / 11

6.9

Will the games represented by matrices 6.7 and 6.8 be behaviorally the same or different? Will the difference, if any, be smaller or larger than the difference, if any, between the game displayed as 6.7 and the game displayed as matrix 6.9?

The great variety of games species, and variations in payoffs that can be introduced within a species, make payoffs an extremely flexible independent variable. It is also the most precisely specifiable and, therefore, most promising from the point of view of theory construction.

Time

In iterated play, time is usually interpreted as a quantized independent variable measured by the number of plays (or "trials," as experimental psychologists usually call them). However, the distinction between quantized time and clock time may be important. Its effects can be brought out by varying the pacing of the plays.

Once the structure of a 2×2 game is understood by the players, and once they have played a few times, thus actually having experienced the particular structure, they tend to make their choices rather quickly. One can expect a choice in five to six seconds. The actual timing is at the discretion of the experimenter. The pace can be slowed by asking players to do things between plays (for instance, to record their choices and the outcomes, or to indicate their guesses about the other's choice). Pacing can thus become an independent variable.

Knowledge on the part of the subjects about the length of the run may affect behavior if the runs are short. To take an extreme example, if the subjects know that they are to play a game exactly twice, this knowledge may affect their decision on the first play: a subject may decide upon a strategy, "I shall choose strategy S on the first play; then, depending on how the other chooses, I shall make my decision on the second play." In other words, the subject may view his decision on the first play as a *signal* to the other and may make his decision on the second play contingent on how the other responds to the signal. If there are no more than two plays, this contingent decision may be explicit in the subject's mind. It can also be fairly explicit in somewhat longer runs, so that the entire strategy is thought through to the end of the run.

The difference between a finite and an infinite run might be crucial if the subjects were able to think a strategy through to the end of a finite run. As an example, consider Prisoner's Dilemma played 100 times by two subjects, each of whom has thought his strategy through to the end on the basis of individual rationality. For such subjects, the outcome of the last play is a foregone conclusion. Since no play follows the last play, there is no need to "signal" a cooperative intent to the other, because the possible reward of this signal (a cooperative response by the other) cannot be reaped. It follows that a subject guided by individual rationality will choose noncooperatively on the last play. Moreover, he knows that the other, likewise guided by individual rationality, will also choose noncooperatively; so that even if a player wanted to follow an impulse to cooperate as a matter of principle, he would decide that it is useless to do so on the last play; an attempt on his part to cooperate would only yield him the smallest payoff. Consequently, as far as these two players are concerned, the last outcome is bound to be a double defection, *regardless* of what happened before. This matter being decided, the ninety-ninth play becomes the "last play," and the same reasoning applies to it. And so two players individually motivated and "thinking their strategies through to the end" must come to the conclusion that *every* play must have a noncooperative outcome.

If the run is "infinite," this reasoning does not apply, because there is no "last play." In practice, all runs are, of course, finite, but long runs are more like "infinite" runs than short ones. The practical question is how short a run must be in order to be perceived as a finite run. Our guess is that it would have to be no longer than about five plays. Therefore, if one is interested in the effects of "finite runs," one should make them no longer than about five plays. Experiments with short runs then have a purpose, namely to investigate the effects of perceived finiteness. If runs are longer than that, in our opinion, they may as well be "very long."

Instructions

Since the instructions given to the subjects are an input by the experimenter, they constitute an independent variable. For most experimenters this variable presents only a problem of control, namely to make sure that instructions do not confound other independent variables in which the experimenter is interested. For some investigators, however, the influence of instructions is of intrinsic interest.

The most direct and clearly observable effect on results is produced by instructions that induce the players to strive for one or another goal. For instance, in Prisoner's Dilemma, the players may be instructed to try to make as many points as possible, each for himself without regard for the score achieved by the other player. This is the "individualistic" orientation. Or the subjects may be instructed to try to make as many points as possible *jointly* (the "cooperative" orientation). Or they may be instructed to make as many more points than the other player as they can (the "competitive" orientation). The results associated with these three conditions can be expected (and have been observed) to be widely different, but they demonstrate little more than that the subjects in an experiment tend to follow instructions.

Somewhat less trivial are the effects of differences in instructions related to how much of the strategic structure of the game is explained to the subjects. If attention is called to the "dilemma" in a Prisoner's Dilemma game, the overall frequency of cooperative responses may be increased, because the "insight" that ordinarily comes to some subjects only in the course of iterated plays, and to other subjects not at all, is provided at the start. Similar considerations apply to game #19. If the strategic structure of that game is explained in detail, Row comes to understand "what he can do" to try to force Column to share, which is by no means obvious, since a shift by Row from S_1S_2 to T_1S_2 does not thereby make a shift to T_2 more attractive to Column. The effect of "revolt" is only indirect, depending (as it does) on Column's perception of the fact that, if he shifts from T_1S_2 to T_1T_2, he will give Row the opportunity to shift to S_1T_2 and so satisfy his demand for a share. If all this is explained to the players, they may see right from the start that Row's cooperation (continued choice of S_1) can be ensured by Column's alternation between S_1S_2 and S_1T_2. In other words, explanatory instructions tend to "solve" the game for the players and so shut off the information that may be of principal interest: how players in a noncooperative nonconstant-sum game achieve equitable Pareto-optimal solutions, if at all.

In another type of instructions, attempts are made to induce subjects toward a certain goal without specifying how to achieve it. For instance, players of a Prisoner's Dilemma game may be told that the score they achieve is positively related to "intelligence," or the like. The question then is whether these players will behave differently from the "controls," in particular, whether they will "cooperate" more or less. Either hypothesis is reasonable. If the emphasis on the relation between score and intelligence "motivates" the players to get more points, this motivation may press for either more cooperation or more competition.

In our opinion, instructions make little difference in the behavior of players in a 2 × 2 game unless they actually instruct the players to choose one way or another; in which case, the results are hardly interesting. Also, if the impact of the instructions is made in a "subtle," masked way, then, it seems to us, the effect will not survive beyond the first few plays. Players get involved in the game, and it is the outcomes that are the most important determinants of sequential choices.

Information Given during Iterated Plays

This independent variable seems to be of great importance. In iterated plays, the standard procedure is to inform the players of the outcome after each play. If this information is withheld, a repeated experiment becomes in effect an experiment on a single play.

One way to reduce information without changing an iterated game into a single play is by omitting the explanation of the rules of the game but providing feedback about outcomes. Subjects are simply told that each has a choice of two alternatives and that the outcomes of each play will be determined by both choices. In the course of iterated plays, each subject will notice that there are *two* payoffs associated with each of his choices. If he remembers the instructions, he will conclude that the particular one of the two payoffs is determined by the choice of the other. Thus the game matrix can, in principle, be inferred by each subject. However, the absence of the game matrix, or equivalent, in front of him might make a substantial difference in the results (see p. 287).

In some experiments, information about the co-player's payoffs is withheld. To some extent, a player can infer or conjecture the *relative* magnitudes of the payoffs to the other. In fact, he can "experiment" to obtain this information by sticking now to one choice, then to another. The problem for each player then becomes analogous to the "two-armed bandit" problem cited in discussions of Bayesian statistical inference, except that the 2 × 2 game analogue to this problem is much more involved in that the probabilities of choices of the other player cannot be assumed to stay constant as they do in the "two-armed bandit" problem.

Supplying false information about the other's payoffs provides further opportunities of using information as an independent variable. If information about the other's payoff is either withheld altogether or is falsified, provisions must be made for giving feedback to each player independently. This necessitates using apparatus that otherwise can be dispensed with in experiments with "true" feedback, since "true" feedback can be simply announced by the experimenter.

Experimenters interested in effects of variables extraneous to the game itself have used "information about the other player" as an independent variable. The other player can be depicted as "cooperative" or "uncooperative," "submissive" or "aggressive," etc. Usually this information is given in experiments where the other player is a stooge (plays a prescribed strategy). Thereby, the behavior of the other player can be "kept constant" while information about him can vary.

Strategy of Other

Controlling the strategy of one player appears to be the most direct way of keeping an important aspect of a game constant in order to study the effects of other independent variables. It should be noted, however, that the introduction of a programed player *theoretically* converts a 2×2 game into a game against nature. For, if the choices of the other player are in principle predictable, the only problem faced by the bona fide player is that of discovering the "law" of the other's behavior and choosing a strategy which is "best" against it. Even if the behavior of the other is predictable only probabilistically, the situation is the same, because it is still possible to make choices so as to maximize expected gain. This kind of situation is quite different from the one defined by a genuine 2×2 game: there the "law" of the other's behavior may not be ascertainable for the reason that the other is "free" to change it as a consequence of its being discovered.

In actual practice, whether the bona fide subject discovers the programed strategy or not depends on its complexity. The situation is complicated by the fact that, in the last analysis, the behavior of the bona fide player is governed not by whether he has actually discovered the programed strategy, but by whether he *believes* that he has discovered it. What he "believes" is difficult to infer from his behavior. Nor is it easy to solicit this information from a post-session questionnaire. Strategies over repeated plays are not easy to describe precisely. Questions about what the strategy of the other has been usually elicit only vague answers—e.g., "to make as many points as possible"—which give no information. "Strategy," in its game-theoretic sense, is a rather sophisticated mathematical concept.

Strategies over repeated plays fall naturally into two categories: noncontingent and contingent. These can be further subdivided into deterministic and probabilistic strategies.

Noncontingent Strategies

A noncontingent deterministic strategy simply prescribes the choice on each play. Clearly, if such prescription is made entirely unsystematically, the strategy is practically impossible to discover. For this reason, it may well be used as "the constant behavior" of the other player against which to test the behavior of different players as other independent variables vary. The disadvantage of a noncontingent and deterministic but unsystematic strategy is that it cannot be usefully quantified. Quantification is desirable if the effect of an independent variable is to be theoretically interpreted. Hence, strategies of this sort are useful only as measures of control, not as independent variables.

If a noncontingent deterministic strategy is systematized, it can be readily quantified. But the more systematic it becomes, the more readily can it be discovered. For example, strategies consisting of repetitive patterns like STSTST . . . or SSSTSSSTSSST . . . soon become apparent and will often determine an obviously optimal sequence of plays by the subject.

Noncontingent probabilistic strategies are more difficult to discover. Typically, strategies of this sort involve random sequences of choices but with the relative frequency of choices fixed. Thus, each choice is determined with a fixed probability, independent of past outcomes.

Although subjects cannot be expected to state with any substantial degree of accuracy the relative frequencies of choices by the programed player, they can, nevertheless, be expected to adjust their choices to these frequencies. The situation resembles learning experiments with probabilistic reinforcements of responses. Stochastic learning theory deals with situations of this sort; it assumes various "models" of learning, which lead to different predictions of choices as functions of the reinforcement schedules (cf. chapter 4). Whether the models are applicable to 2×2 game experiments is an open question. One conjecture is that stochastic learning theory is applicable in varying degrees to games of different types.

The important difference between the 2×2 game situation and a game against nature is that in the 2×2 game information is available about the interests of the other. Consequently, not only the other's probability of choice, but also the motivation behind it may be what the subject takes into account in making his own choice. As an example, consider a varying noncontingent probabilistic strategy of the other in a Prisoner's Dilemma game. The variable is the frequency of C choices. On the surface, it seems that this variable is an index of "cooperativeness" of the other player. A reasonable hypothesis is that the C frequencies by the bona fide subject will be a monotone function of the frequency of C choices by the stooge. Whether this function will be monotone increasing or decreasing cannot be guessed a priori. On the one hand, a more "cooperative" other player may increase the pressure for cooperation, as a positive response to "cooperativeness." On the other hand, he may invite "exploitation."

What is not taken into account in such conjectures is that whether a player perceives the other as "cooperative" may depend not so much on the frequency with which the other cooperates as on the frequency with which he *responds* to cooperation. But a noncontingent strategy, whether it is predominantly cooperating or defecting, is essentially nonresponsive. This nonresponsiveness creates the impression that one is not playing against a rational player and, under this impression, the motivation to cooperate may disappear. After all, the best counter strategy to *any* noncontingent strategy in Prisoner's Dilemma is one of complete noncooperation. Whatever pressure for cooperation exists stems from the hope that the other may be "brought around" to cooperate by one's own cooperative choices and also, be it noted, may be "turned off" (from cooperation) by one's own defecting choices. It would not be surprising, therefore, to find that the frequency of C responses in a Prisoner's Dilemma game, averaged over a population of players, shows little or no systematic variation with the frequency of C responses in the programed non-contingent strategy.

Contingent Deterministic Strategies

In contingent deterministic strategies, the stooge's choice is dependent on preceding outcomes. In the simplest case, only the immediately preceding outcome will determine this choice. But the choice also can be made a function of any number of preceding outcomes.

The simplest contingent deterministic strategies are the so-called Tit-for-tat and Tat-for-tit strategies ("Tit-for-tit" and "Tat-for-tit" would be a more logical designation). In a Tit-for-tat strategy, the stooge chooses S if the bona fide player chooses S on the preceding play; otherwise, T. In a Tat-for-tit strategy, the stooge chooses the oppositely designated alternative. The best counter strategy against either of these is obvious. Thus, in Prisoner's Dilemma, the best counter strategy against the Tit-for-tat is 100 percent C, possibly ending in one or more defections toward the very end of the run. (If the total number of plays is known, the optimal number of final defections can be determined.) The best counter strategy against Tat-for-tit is clearly 100 percent D. In game #19, on the other hand, with some numerical values of the payoffs, it may be advantageous for Row to alternate between S and T in response to either the Tit-for-tat or the Tat-for-tit strategy.

These simplest contingent strategies seem to be very easy to discover. However, subjects may not be aware that they have discovered them, even though they behave as if they had. It is difficult to ascribe the choices of the other player to one's own choices. Subjects questioned about the strategy of a programed Tit-for-tat player seldom give evidence that they have become aware of the pattern.

When contingent deterministic choices can be made to depend on more than one previous outcome, they can be made progressively more complex and difficult to discover. They can also be varied according to the way the stooge responds to the last outcome on several subsequent plays. For instance, the stooge may always choose S following S by the subject. However, if the subject chooses T, the stooge may play two, three, etc., T's consecutively, regardless of how the subject chooses, after which he again takes into account the subject's last choice. If one strategy constitutes a reward for the subject and the other, punishment, the generosity of the reward and the severity of the punishment can be graded accordingly.

A direct way of comparing the effects of deterministic contingent and deterministic uncontingent strategies is by the use of the so-called yoked strategy. A contingent strategy is used against one player, and the resulting protocol of the stooge's choices is then used unconditionally, i.e., as a noncontingent deterministic strategy against another player. The performances of the players in each such pair are then compared.

Contingent Probabilistic Strategies

In the simplest of these, probabilities are assigned to the choices by the stooge following each of the four outcomes. Each of these strategies is thus described by four parameters. Some of the probabilities may be zero or one. (If all of them are either zero or one, the strategy reduces to a contingent deterministic one.) Variation in the conditional probabilities provides the opportunity for "grading" the programed strategy. As an example, consider the following two strategies in Prisoner's Dilemma with Row in the role of stooge:

$$\text{Strategy 1.} \quad P(C_1 \mid C_1C_2) = 1; \quad P(C_1 \mid C_1D_2) = 0.5;$$
$$P(C_1 \mid D_1C_2) = 1; \quad P(C_1 \mid D_1D_2) = 0.5.$$
$$\text{Strategy 2.} \quad P(C_1 \mid C_1C_2) = 0.5; \quad P(C_1 \mid C_1D_2) = 0;$$
$$P(C_1 \mid D_1C_2) = 0.5; \quad P(C_1 \mid D_1D_2) = 0.$$

It can be seen that both strategies are modifications of the Tit-for-tat strategy. In strategy 1, the modification is in the direction of "leniency": a cooperative response of the other is always rewarded by a cooperative response of the stooge on the next play, but a defecting response of the other is punished only half the time by a defecting response on the next play. In strategy 2, the modification is in the direction of greater "severity": a defecting response is always punished, but a cooperating response is rewarded only half the time.

Among the contingent strategies with dependencies on more than one preceding outcome are those where the probability of a response is a monotone increasing function of the number of times a particular strategy has occurred consecutively. For example, in Prisoner's Dilemma, while three of the probabilities conditional on the last response outcome are kept constant, the probability of C can be made to increase with each consecutive occurrence of C_1C_2. Once the run of C_1C_2 outcomes is broken, the probability of C following C_1C_2 can return to some constant value. Such a strategy gives the appearance that the stooge "learns to cooperate," being more willing to continue cooperating as the cooperative "lock-in" continues.

Strategies of this sort may be useful in simulating the one or the other player in game #19. Assume that the stooge plays Row. Row can be expected to "tolerate" a certain number of S choices by Column. But as the number of such consecutive choices increases, Row can be expected to become more and more disgruntled. Thus the following contingent probabilistic strategy can be assigned to Row.

After a single S choice by Column, Row always plays S_1 simulating an expectation that Column will alternate between S_2 and T_2, thus sharing with Row. Following two consecutives S_2 responses, Row chooses T_1 with some probability, say, 0.25. If, after choosing S_2 twice, Column chooses S_2 again, the outcome may be S_1S_2 or T_1S_2, depending on what choice was prescribed to Row by the random device. If the outcome is again S_1S_2, Row chooses T_1 with higher probability, say, 0.5, and so on.

The rate at which Row's probability of choosing T_1 increases with the number of consecutive S_1S_2 outcomes is a measure of Row's "impatience" with Column's unwillingness to share. Similarly, probabilities can be assigned to Row's choice of S_1 following given numbers of consecutive T_1S_2 outcomes. The greater the rate of increase of this probability, the greater is Row's tendency to "give up" his revolt if Column stands pat. In the extreme case, if Row always chooses T_1 following T_1S_2, this indicates that Row is determined to continue to refuse "cooperation" until Column gives in.

Although in Prisoner's Dilemma the assignment of 100 percent choice of one or the other alternative to the stooge may seem ,not quite "credible" to the subject, leading instead to suspicion that the other player is "fixed," in the case of game #19 and some other games, these constant strategies are more credible. For instance, a Row who always chooses S_1 does not seem unreasonable. He appears simply to have resigned himself to his position as underdog. The use of such "nonresisting" strategy by the underdog will reveal the extent to which the real player in the role of top dog will *voluntarily* share.

Similarly, a Column who chooses S_2 all the time does not seem unreasonable. He is simply taking advantage of his top-dog position. The use of this strategy will reveal to what extent Row players will refuse to cooperate even if their "revolt" is ineffective. (Actually, a considerable fraction of real players have been observed to choose S all the way through a run, both in the position of Row and of Column.)

In games of complete opposition, a natural strategy to assign the programed player is the maximin (or minimax) strategy prescribed by game theory. However, it must be kept in mind that, if a player chooses this optimal strategy in a 2×2 zerosum game, the expected payoff to the other player is independent of his chosen strategy (cf. p. 40). Thus the failure of the real player to respond with the maximin strategy proves nothing about his "rationality." All strategies are equally good against the maximin strategy. To see how the behavior of a real player varies with the choice of a mixed strategy by the other in a zerosum game, one should prescribe nonoptimal mixed strategies to the programed player. To any such nonoptimal mixed strategy, the best counter strategy is one or the other pure strategy. Thus, the frequency with which the particular optimal *pure* strategy is used is a measure of the real player's ability to take advantage of the situation.

The Player as an Independent Variable

Psychologists who are interested in experimental games as projective tests naturally focus on the player as the principal independent variable. "Who plays how?" is the central question in this approach. Considering the rich variety of even 2×2 games, it seems that the proper posing of this question should be "Who plays *what game* how?" Yet, as has already been noted, the concentration on just a very few games, Prisoner's Dilemma being by far the most frequent choice for "projective testing," has so far failed to provide the opportunity of systematically investigating the relation between personality and the particular pressures operating in a particular game.

Categorization of subjects is easiest, of course, if the categories

represent obvious differences. Thus, one can compare the game behavior of men and women, of children and adults, of mental patients
and others, etc. In some cases, clear differences in behavior will be
observed. It is hardly necessary to point out that it is hazardous to
draw conclusions from the observed differences about psychological
characteristics of the persons in the various categories. We have
already cautioned against taking seriously the designations of choices
in 2 × 2 games as "cooperative" or "competitive," and the like. For
one thing, as has been pointed out, "cooperation" in one game may
mean something quite different in another. Even more dangerous is
the assumption that people's behavior in an experimental game necessarily reflects their tendencies to behave analogously in seemingly
similar real-life situations. In fact, the opposite may be the case.
People may behave in experimental games in just such ways as they
do *not* behave in real-life situations. A further assumption that the
game offers an outlet for suppressed forms of behavior is no better
and no worse than the assumption that the game reflects tendencies
to behave in like manner in real life.

Another hazard is failing to take into account the interaction of
players in iterated plays. For instance, it has been frequently observed that, in sufficiently long runs of Prisoner's Dilemma, women
playing against women choose C considerably less frequently than
men playing against men. In short runs, this difference is nowhere
as clear, in fact, it is seldom observed at all. Moreover, in long runs
when a man is pitted against a woman in Prisoner's Dilemma, no significant differences are observed in the respective frequencies of C
choices. The conclusion suggests itself that the interactions in the
course of iterated play "submerge" whatever differences exist between men and women in their propensities to "cooperate" in iterated Prisoner's Dilemma. The conclusion is further corroborated by
the fact that in short runs differences are not usually observed. It
seems that the woman's intrinsic propensity to cooperate is the same
as the man's. Only in the process of interaction (and then with a
woman, not with a man) does this tendency lag behind the man's.

Nor should it be necessary to point out that subjects for psychological experiments are recruited preponderantly from university or
college students. Sex differences observed in these populations may
or may not reflect corresponding differences in the general population.

The asymmetric games offer much better opportunities to study differences between subject populations. For instance, game #19, with its top-dog and underdog roles, offers the opportunity to pit men against women in either role: woman as underdog against man as top dog or vice versa.

The possibilities of shifting roles in an asymmetric game suggests that personality types emerge from the game itself. Consider the four possible styles of play in game #19.

1. There may be a class of players who choose S predominantly, both in the role of Row and in the role of Column. If the style of play reflects real-life tendencies, then we can describe this {SS} class of players as follows: When they are in the position of underdog, they submit; when in the position of the top dog, they exploit—the syndrome of the bureaucrat, or of one who has adjusted properly to an authoritarian hierarchy.

2. The next class of players {ST} predominantly choose S in the role of Row and T in the role of Column.[1] That is, when they have no power, they submit; when they have power, they do not abuse it —the syndrome of the gentle or timid person.

3. The third class of players {TS} predominantly choose T_1 in the role of Row, but S_2 in the role of Column. They do not submit to power when they do not have it and they use it without hesitation when they do—the syndrome of the aggressive person.

4. The fourth class {TT} are those who predominantly choose T whether they are Row or Column. In other words, they do not submit to power when they do not have it and do not abuse it when they have it—the syndrome of a "fairminded" person.

Possibly these styles of play could be correlated with various categories of players, particularly players with different national, cultural, or social backgrounds.

Personality, as determined by psychological tests, is another possible independent variable. Its main use would be in validating the games as projective tests by comparing the game behavior of subjects with expectations based on the "personality profiles" revealed by the test. A very large number of personality tests have been used as independent variables in gaming experiments.

---

[1] A "predominant" choice of T_2 in this game means with a frequency approaching 50 percent (cf. pp. 189–90).

Not all those tests were used in conjunction with 2×2 game experiments. Many have, and some have been used in conjunction with both 2×2 games and other gaming situations, in simulations of international relations, for example. We shall survey some of the results in chapter 19.

The caveats in connection with using clearly recognizable categories of subjects apply with equal, perhaps greater, force to using "personality" as revealed by tests as independent variables. Probably the only way to avoid confounding personality variables with the effects of interaction between players is to use "personality" as an independent variable in single play experiments. This was done by K. W. Terhune, whose work will be described in chapter 19.

Individual vs. "Compound" Player

It is interesting to compare the behavior of individuals making autonomous decisions with that of teams making collective decisions. Here, too, an artifact that may mask the meaning of results must be taken into account. Consider the player represented by a team of three individuals who make choice decisions by majority vote, and suppose that all three individuals are "psychologically identical." Suppose further that each would choose S with probability p and that the choices of teammates are independent. The probability that S receives majority vote is given by

$$P = p^3 + 3p^2(1 - p). \tag{6.10}$$

Now, if $0 < p < 1/2$, it is easy to see that $P < p$, for then we have

$$P - p = p^3 + 3p^2 - 3p^3 - p = -p(2p^2 - 3p + 1), \tag{6.11}$$

which is negative, since

$$2p^2 - 3p + 1 > 0, \text{ if } 0 < p < 1/2. \tag{6.12}$$

This means that as long as the probability that a single subject chooses a particular alternative is less than one half, the probability that this alternative is chosen by a team of three is even smaller. Mutatis mutandis, if $p > 1/2$, the probability is enhanced that the corresponding alternative is chosen by the team. Thus, under these assumptions, the choices made by the team will be "more definite" than the corresponding choices made by the individual members, even if all are "psychologically identical." This effect, however, is a formal mathematical consequence of the decision procedure (in this case, decision by majority vote) and should not be ascribed to any peculiarity of "group psychology." On the basis of this result, one would predict that, when the probability of choosing a particular alternative is less that one half, this alternative should be chosen less frequently by a "compound" player (with decision rules as described) than by an individual player, and vice versa.

On the other hand, if experimental results are in the opposite direction, the effect could possibly be ascribed to "group psychology" since the purely *formal* team bias is in favor of the more probable choice.

Animal Subjects

As far as we know, no gaming experiments have been conducted with animal subjects. The technique of such an experiment should not be prohibitively difficult, since many animals will "work" for food pellets or other rewards and can differentiate between alternatives that give larger or smaller rewards. Since "punishments" meted out for responses may interfere with the conditioning, it is best to use time delays as differential payoffs whereby the shortest delay in delivering a food pellet corresponds to the largest payoffs. Experiments with nonhuman subjects have the advantage of permitting iterated games of practically any length and also of reflecting behavior which is probably motivated by nothing other than the payoffs.

Part II

Introduction to Part II

The point of departure in starting work on this book was a paper published by two of us (Rapoport and Guyer, 1966) in which the rich variety of structures of 2×2 games was pointed out. Part II of this book was to be devoted to discussion of experiments where the species of a game determined by its structure alone is at the center of attention.

In order to focus attention on the structure alone, everything else should be kept constant. This could be done by designing a "standard experiment," say, on the iterated games. In a series of such experiments, the subjects would be drawn from the "same population" and randomly assigned to each game. Also the numerical payoffs of all games should be from the same set, differing only in the way they are placed in the cells of the game matrix. Better still, since the ordinal taxonomy defines the payoffs only on the ordinal scale, numerical payoffs could be replaced by ordinal designations: for instance, t, s, r, and p from the largest to the smallest.

All these considerations, however, occurred to us only as the book was being written. To take them into account would have meant redoing the 12 iterated game experiments reported here, in which 240 subjects were involved. We have not done this, leaving the task, along with others, for a revised edition, if the reception of this book warrants one. Instead, we used experimental data already available and added to it so as to achieve only very roughly standard experimental conditions. In particular, in the single play experiment reported in chapter 7, the payoffs of all games were from the set 10, 1, −1, −10. These same payoffs were used in games #12 and #66 (chapter 9). These experiments were performed when the plan of the book was already projected. In the remaining experiments, the approximate standard conditions are reflected in the format: 300

plays of each game by 10 pairs of male subjects recruited from university students by advertisement. All subjects received approximately the same base fees, and points were converted into monetary winnings or losses at approximately the same rate.

The experiments reported in chapters 7 and 9 were performed in 1972 and 1973 by O. Frenkel and J. Perner at the University of Toronto. The remaining experiments were performed from 1968 to 1972 by M. Guyer and D. Gordon at the University of Michigan.

Since the statistical significance of the findings was not evaluated, these experiments do not constitute tests of hypotheses. The findings are simply compared with the expectations of some very primitive hypotheses; in the case of single plays, with expectations concerning the stability of the natural outcome; in the case of iterated games, with the repetition hypothesis, H_r (cf. p. 74) and with the shift hypothesis, H_s (cf. p. 74). Further, the interdependence of choices is roughly estimated by the Pearson product moment correlation coefficient and/or by certain conditional frequencies reflecting the tendency to play Tit-for-tat or Tat-for-tit. Occasionally, time courses are examined for evidence of learning trends.

On the whole, the purpose of Part II is simply to "take a look" at the way the fictitious "average subject" (from our populations) chooses in each of the seventy-eight games of the ordinal taxonomy in single plays and in twelve games, selected for certain interesting features, in long iterated runs.

7

Stability of the
Natural Outcome

O. Frenkel (unpublished) obtained data on single plays of all the seventy-eight games in the ordinal taxonomy using essentially the method described on p. 91.

Male students at the University of Toronto served as volunteer paid subjects. Each was paid $2.00. Additionally, prizes were offered to subjects who accumulated the largest numbers of points: first prize—$15; second and third prizes—$10 each; five prizes of $5 each.

Each subject was given a booklet of 320 pages with a 2×2 game in matrix form on each page. First, the rules of the 2×2 game were explained to the subject and questions were asked to test his understanding. He then took the booklet with him, having been promised $2 if he returned it completed within 48 hours, i.e., with his choice indicated on each page. Of the completed booklets returned by 112 subjects, 96—randomly selected—were used in the interest of equalizing cells in the analysis of variance. The remaining data were "spares," used as described below.

The booklet contained each of the asymmetric games four times; each of the symmetric games twice; of some games, three to five variants (once each); and exact replications of some games (once each). The purpose of the exact replications was to eliminate data by "unconscientious" subjects, in a way to be presently described. Aside from the variants, the payoffs in every game were the same:

135

10, 1, −1, and −10. These points were not converted into money; the incentive for accumulating points was presumably the prizes offered.

As stated, aside from the variants and replications, each subject played every symmetric game twice, once as Row, once as Column, and every asymmetric game four times, twice as Row and twice as Column. Thus, he was in exactly the same situations, strategically speaking, exactly twice. The presentations, however, were different: they were randomly selected permutations of rows and/or columns. The purpose of presenting each situation twice was to compare the relative consistency of choices in the different game species.

Aside from the forty-eight-hour deadline for returning the booklets, the subjects were told to take as much time as they wished in making their decisions and to consult with others if they desired. They were told, further, that each page presented a generally different decision problem, as they would find out if they considered their decisions carefully.

It was anticipated that in spite of these instructions some subjects would be "unconscientious," that is, would mark the pages either haphazardly or follow some fixed pattern unrelated to the structure of the games. Such performances were discovered by two pieces of "circumstantial evidence," namely an unusually low consistency between the two presentations of the same situation and by unusually low consistency in the randomly placed *exact* replications of some of the matrices. Six such performances were discovered. Two of the subjects involved volunteered the information that they had lost interest and played haphazardly (thus corroborating Frenkel's method of detection). They refused or returned the $2.00 compensation. Their booklets and the remaining four were simply removed from the data pool and replaced by randomly selected booklets from the "spares."

Table 7.1 shows the frequencies of the S_1S_2 outcomes in the seventy-eight games in the decreasing order of frequency, rounded off to the nearest percentage point.

Figure 7.1, like figure 2.4, represents the taxonomic tree of phylum N (the no-conflict games). At the end points the mean frequencies of the natural outcome observed in each category have been entered.

TABLE 7.1

Frequency of S_1S_2 %	Game #'s	Frequency of S_1S_2 %	Game #'s
99	5, 3	71	20, 13
98	4	70	49
97	60, 41, 29, 14, 7, 2	69	6
96	30, 16, 9, 8, 1	66	65, 27
95	28, 19	65	58
94	32, 10	64	56, 22
93	45	62	55
92	43, 42	61	53
91	17, 11	57	26
90	18	52	71
89	46	51	57
87	31	48	76
85	37, 36, 25, 21, 12	47	73, 61
84	47	45	72
83	44, 40, 15	44	78
82	48	38	34
81	35	36	33
79	59, 52	29	70
78	75, 64	26	38
77	77, 50	22	74, 66
76	39, 23	21	63, 62
75	54, 51	14	68
73	69	12	67
72	24		

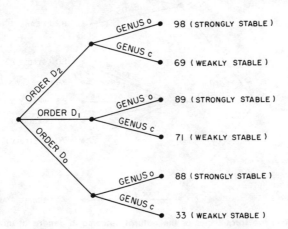

Fig. 7.1. Average frequencies of the natural outcome in genera of no-conflict games.

The strong effect of competitive pressure is conspicuous in all three orders. There is also an order effect in the expected direction, D_2 games having, on the average, the most stable natural outcomes and D_0 the least stable.

The taxonomic tree of phylum M (mixed-motive games) with average frequencies of the natural outcome in each game is shown in figures 7.2–7.4.

Again we see that genus o has the largest frequencies of the natural outcome, and again the effect of order is in the expected direction. The effect of the subclass is also apparent. Comparing the frequencies of the natural outcome in analogous orders and genera of the two subclasses of class E (order D_0, genus o), we see that they are smaller when the natural outcome—although an equilibrium— is not Pareto-optimal.

The games of class e are all of order D_0, hence, can be compared only to the games of the same order in class E. However, the latter order contains only the genus f, which class e does not contain; so the effect of class alone cannot be assessed. If we disregard order and compare the effect of class in analogous genera, we see that the frequencies of the natural outcome in genus o of class e (70, 74) are lower than those of genus o in class E (93, 80, 85).

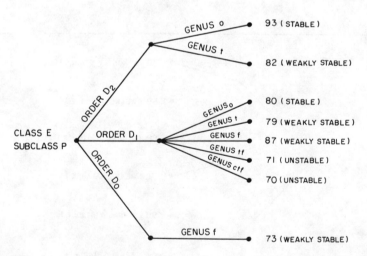

Fig. 7.2. Average frequencies of the natural outcome in genera of mixed-motive games.

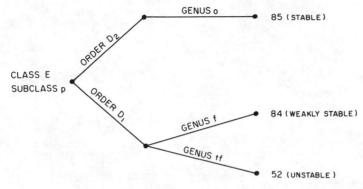

Fig. 7.3. Average frequencies of the natural outcome in genera of games of complete opposition.

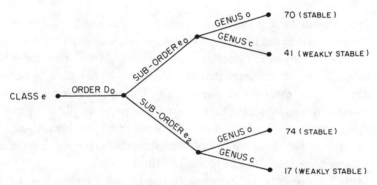

Fig. 7.4. Average frequencies of natural outcome in mixed-motive games with Pareto-deficient equilibria.

Disregarding genera and comparing analogous orders, we see that the average natural outcome frequency in class e is lower than in class E. However, the effect can be attributed to genus alone, since class e, order D_o, contains genus c, whereas class E, order D_o, does not.

Figure 7.5 shows the taxonomic tree of phylum Z with associated frequencies of the natural outcome.

The difference between D_2 and D_1 is in the direction opposite to the expected and cannot be accounted for. The reduced frequencies of the natural outcome in order D_o, genus c, can be attributed to genus as well as to order.

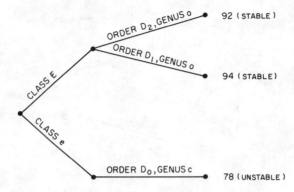

Fig. 7.5. Average frequencies of natural outcomes in genera of games of complete opposition.

The immediate impression obtained from the results of Frenkel's experiment is that the effects of subclass, order, and genus are, on the whole, in the expected direction. The effect of class alone cannot be assessed for want of games that are otherwise in the same subcategories. Nor can the relative importance of the several categories be assessed, although it seems that competitive pressure plays a prominent role. In Part IV, which is devoted to testing specific mathematical models of performance in experimental games, the results of this experiment are subjected to closer scrutiny.

Table 7.2 presents the games with the largest frequencies of the natural outcome (> 95) and the smallest (< 30). We find that without exception all fourteen of the former are of genus o (without competitive pressure). Besides, in eleven of the games with the largest $[S_1S_2]$, both players have dominating strategies; in two games, one player, and in only one, neither. In seven of the games with the smallest frequencies $[S_1S_2]$, neither player has a dominating strategy, in three, one player has. Finally, seven of the fourteen "most stable" games are no-conflict games; only two of the eleven "least stable" games are of that phylum. The expected effects of phylum, order, and genus are thus observed clearly in the extremes.

We turn to another measure of "instability," namely the fraction of the players who chose inconsistently on the two presentations of the same game in the same role. These are presented in table 7.3.

The eight "most stable" games are those where no inconsistent plays were observed in the roles shown. The eight "least stable"

TABLE 7.2

Games with largest S_1S_2				Games with smallest S_1S_2			
Game #	Phylum	Order	Genus	Game #	Phylum	Order	Genus
5	N	D_2	o	34	M	D_1	c
3	N	D_2	o	33	M	D_1	c
4	N	D_2	o	70	M	D_0	c
60	N	D_0	o	38	M	D_1	c
41	M	D_1	o	74	M	D_0	c
29	N	D_1	o	66	M	D_0	c
14	M	D_2	o	63	N	D_0	c
7	M	D_2	o	62	N	D_0	c
2	N	D_2	o	68	M	D_0	c
30	M	D_1	o	67	M	D_0	c
16	M	D_2	o				
9	M	D_2	o				
8	M	D_2	o				
1	N	D_2	o				

TABLE 7.3 The individual player's consistency of choice.
         Dom.: Did the player have a dominating strategy?
         Comp.: Was the player under competitive pressure
         to shift to T?

Games where 100% of the players indicated chose S on all four presentations					Games where 30% or more of the players chose inconsistently on various presentations				
Game #	Player	Phylum	Dom.	Comp.	Game #	Player	Phylum	Dom.	Comp.
41	C	M	No	No	73	R	M	No	Yes
38	C	M	Yes	Yes	72	C	M	No	No
32	C	M	Yes	No	71	C	M	No	No
30	C	N	No	No	70	R	M	No	Yes
14	R	M	Yes	No	70	C	M	No	No
8	C	M	Yes	No	57	C	M	No	No
4	C	N	Yes	No	49	C	M	No	No
2	R	N	Yes	No	68*	--	M	No	Yes
					67	C	M	No	Yes

*Symmetric game.

games are those where thirty or more players in the role shown played inconsistently.

We note that on the whole the availability of a dominating strategy and/or the absence of competitive pressure contribute to stability. Also three of the "most consistent" eight games are of phylum N. None of the "least consistent" are in that phylum. In none of the "least stable" games did the inconsistent player have a dominating strategy.

In addition to the individual player's ambivalence with respect to the choice between S and T, it is also interesting to observe the "global" ambivalence of each game, that is, the extent to which it divides the population of players into those who consistently play S and those who consistently play T. The product $[S_1S_2][T_1T_2]$ is an appropriate measure of "global ambivalence." Table 7.4 presents the games with $[S_1S_2][T_1T_2] > 1000$.

TABLE 7.4   Inconsistency of choice
             in the population of players.

Game #	Player	Phylum	Dom.	Comp.
73	R	M	No	Yes
67	R	M	No	Yes
63*	--	N	No	Yes
62	C	N	No	Yes
61	C	N	No	Yes
56	R	M	No	No
53	C	M	No	No

*Symmetric game.

In all eight games, the "splitting" players, i.e., those who played either S on both presentations or T on both presentations, had no dominating strategy. In six, they were subjected to competitive pressure. It is interesting to observe that three of these "most bimodal" games were no-conflict games with no dominating strategies and with competitive pressure. Note that these three games, #61, #62, and #63, do not appear among the most ambivalent with respect to the *individual* players (cf. table 7.3). These, then, can be viewed as the games that most effectively split the players into "cooperators" and "competitors."

The games in which the entire population in at least one player role chose S with perfect consistency are very numerous (33 out of the 78 games). In many cases, players in both roles did so. In all but four, there was no competitive pressure on the player in question. The four exceptions are games #37, #38, #51, and #53. In all of these, however, the "consistent" player has a dominating strategy.

The game that falls into the "least stable" category on all three counts, that is, with the smallest frequency of the natural outcome, the largest individual inconsistency, and the largest global inconsistency, is game #67. Games #66 and #68 barely fail to reach this criterion. All three games are so-called preemption games, #66 ("Chicken") being the typical representative. Preemption games will be examined in greater detail in chapter 10.

8

Two No-Conflict Games

In this chapter we examine performances on two iterated games of phylum N, #6 and #61.

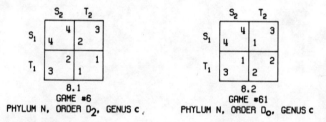

8.1
GAME #6
PHYLUM N, ORDER D$_2$, GENUS C

8.2
GAME #61
PHYLUM N, ORDER D$_0$, GENUS C

In both games, the players can get their largest payoff if both choose S. Therefore, if both were guided by "individual rationality," the natural outcome S_1S_2 would occur exclusively. However, competitive pressure is present in both games. A unilateral shift from the natural outcome gives the shifter more than the player who persists in the natural outcome. Hence, the occurrence of other than the natural outcomes can be attributed to a competitive orientation in both games.

The only respect in which the two games differ is that in game #6 both players have a dominating strategy, whereas neither player has a dominating strategy in game #61. Hence, differences in performances on these two games can be attributed to their orders.

The variants of the two games used in the experiments to be discussed are shown in 8.3 and 8.4.

144

	S_2	T_2
S_1	28 \ 28	20 \ 12
T_1	12 \ 20	-10 \ -10

8.3
GAME #6
VARIANT V

	S_2	T_2
S_1	28 \ 28	20 \ -10
T_1	-10 \ 20	12 \ 12

8.4
GAME #61
VARIANT II

Note that, whereas game #6 has one equilibrium, game #61 has two. It is therefore possible in game #61 for both players to get "trapped" in T_1T_2 of 8.4. If a player attempts to get out of this trap by a unilateral shift, he punishes himself and rewards the other. To be sure, he thereby creates a motivation for the other to shift to S and so establish the Pareto-optimal natural outcome. If, however, a player has reason to suppose that the other is competitively oriented, he has no assurance that his own shift from T to S will be reciprocated. By the same reasoning, we see that the equilibrium in S_1S_2 of 8.4 is weakened if each player *suspects* the other of being competitively oriented. For, if the other shifts from S to T in response to competitive pressure, a shift to T is justified by "self defense."

The outcome frequencies for game #6 are shown in table 8.1.

TABLE 8.1   Frequencies of the four
            outcomes in Game #6.

Pair	(S_1S_2)	(S_1T_2)	(T_1S_2)	(T_1T_2)
1	93	04	03	01
2	91	00	09	00
3	100	00	00	00
4	100	00	00	00
5	100	00	00	00
6	100	00	00	00
7	99	01	00	00
8	100	00	00	00
9	36	28	17	18
10	100	00	00	00
Means	92	03	03	02

From table 8.1, we see that the natural outcome occurs exclusively, or nearly so, in nine of the ten pairs. Only one performance (of pair 9) is erratic.

There is some evidence that some learning has occurred in the course of the performance. Table 8.2 shows the frequencies of S_1S_2 by fifty-play blocks.

TABLE 8.2   Time course of S_1S_2 in Game #6.

Plays	1-50	51-100	101-150	151-200	201-250	251-300
(S_1S_2)	89	89	93	92	92	96

Examining the individual protocols, we observe that in pairs 1 and 2, where the frequency of S_1S_2 is less than 100, (S_1S_2) increased respectively from 84 in the first block to 98 in the last and from 82 in the first block to 96 in the last. As for pair 9, their performance appears haphazard in the first five blocks, but they settle down to the exclusive choice of S in the last 25 plays.

Because of the very small frequencies of something other than the natural outcome, conditional frequencies cannot be meaningfully estimated, except in pair 9. The repetition propensities for this pair are given in table 8.3.

TABLE 8.3   Repetition propensities
in Pair 9 (Game #6).

α_1	β_1	γ_1	δ_1	α_2	β_2	γ_2	δ_2
84	38	52	52	52	46	60	52

Except for α_1, all the conditional repetition frequencies are sufficiently close to 50 to suggest haphazard play. Evidently Row tried to preserve the Pareto-optimal natural outcome but was prevented from doing this by Column's erratic choices. This "muddy" performance can perhaps be attributed to boredom, considering that a no-conflict game in principle presents no challenge to the players. Still, the fact that only one performance of the ten reflects a lack of motivation is encouraging. As we shall see, the performances of volunteer paid subjects in 300-play iterations of 2 × 2 games on the whole reflect quite faithfully the structure of the games and so give evidence of sufficient motivation, unperturbed by boredom effects.

From table 8.4. we see that game #61 represents an altogether different picture.

TABLE 8.4 Outcome frequencies in Game #61.

Pair	(S_1S_2)	(S_1T_2)	(T_1S_2)	(T_1T_2)
1	86	04	01	09
2	84	01	04	11
3	15	29	14	42
4	92	02	02	04
5	22	03	04	71
6	96	01	02	01
7	29	27	15	29
8	11	11	25	53
9	92	01	04	04
10	100	00	00	00
Means	63	08	07	22

In contrast to game #6, only one pair (pair 10) cooperated fully to preserve 100 percent occurrence of the Pareto-optimal natural outcome most preferred by both players. In five other protocols (pairs 1, 2, 4, 6, and 9), S_1S_2 occurred over 80 percent of the time. In the remaining four protocols (S_1S_2) was less than 30, and in three of them, the largest frequency is that of T_1T_2, evidence of "entrapments" in the Pareto-deficient equilibrium.

The overall time course of (S_1S_2) and (T_1T_2), shown in figure 8.1, suggests that while (S_1S_2) quickly increases already after fifty

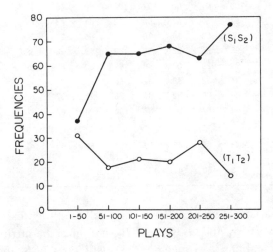

Fig. 8.1.   Time courses of (S_1S_2) and (T_1T_2) in game #61.

plays, (T_1T_2) also increases from about the fiftieth to the two hundred fiftieth play, reflecting the entrapment of some pairs in the Pareto-deficient equilibrium. In the last block, however, all but one of the "noncooperating" pairs switch to cooperation. Note also that after about one hundred plays about 90 percent of the outcomes are either S_1S_2 or T_1T_2, i.e., the two equilibria.

The repetition propensities of game #61 can be interpreted as follows.

α: The tendency to preserve the outcome most preferred by both players; essentially, cooperation.

β: The tendency to preserve competitive advantage.

γ: The tendency to repeat the outcome in which one gets the smallest payoff. In itself, this tendency is not rational. However, it can be defended in terms of the expectation that the other will shift, which he is motivated to do by an immediate gain.

δ: Avoiding the smallest payoff in the expectation that the other, also wishing to avoid it, will not shift from T_1T_2; hence, a reflection of entrapment in the Pareto-deficient equilibrium.

TABLE 8.5   Repetition propensities in Game #61.

Pair	α_1	β_1	γ_1	δ_1	α_2	β_2	γ_2	δ_2
1	100	00	57	89	100	86	00	89
2	100	91	50	97	100	50	45	83
3	57	55	43	60	43	81	43	73
4	100	60	14	58	100	86	20	75
5	95	85	22	96	100	89	38	96
6	98	20	100	48	99	00	80	25
7	91	33	38	67	66	77	36	53
8	89	85	53	96	66	47	32	72
9	99	67	00	82	100	100	67	64
10	100	--	--	--	100	--	--	--
Unweighted Means	93	55	42	77	87	68	40	70
Weighted Means	98	60	41	82	95	73	38	78

Since the variant of game #61 is numerically symmetrical, the differences between α_1 and α_2, β_1 and β_2, etc. must be attributed to statistical fluctuations. As expected, the fluctuations in β_i and γ_i are considerably larger than those in α_i and δ_i, since the frequencies of the outcomes associated with the former are considerably smaller than those associated with the latter. Combining the repetition propensities characterizing Row and Column respectively, we obtain the values shown in table 8.6.

TABLE 8.6 Combined repetition
propensities in Game #61.

	α	β	γ	δ
Unweighted Means	90	62	46	74
Weighted Means	96	66	40	80

Our hypothesis H_r (cf. p. 74) prescribes the inequality

$$\alpha > \beta > \delta > \gamma.$$

From table 8.6, we observe $\alpha > \delta > \beta > \gamma$.

The discrepancy can be ascribed to the fact that T_1T_2, the outcome associated with δ, is an equilibrium, while T_1S_2 and S_1T_2, outcomes associated with β_1 and β_2, are not. Note, however, that $\beta > \gamma$, as required by H_r.

For our variant of game #61, H_s prescribes the inequality

$$\tilde{\gamma} > \tilde{\beta} > \tilde{\alpha} > \tilde{\delta}; \text{ hence } \delta > \alpha > \beta > \gamma.$$

We observe $\alpha > \delta > \beta > \gamma$. The discrepancy is attributable to the strong attraction of S_1S_2 as the Pareto-optimal natural outcome.

The product moment correlation $\rho_{S_1S_2}$ turns out to be 0.93 in game #6 and 0.98 in game #61, suggesting strong positive interdependence of choices in both games. However, examining the individual protocols we see that we cannot have much confidence in the high value of $\rho_{S_1S_2}$ in game #6, because this high value is entirely accounted for by the single erratic pair (pair 9), which produced the only low values of both (S_1) and (S_2). On the other hand, from Table 8.2 we see that we can have somewhat more confidence in the high value of $\rho_{S_1S_2}$ in game #61.

Because S_1S_2 is virtually the only outcome in seven out of ten pairs in game #6, the intraprotocol measures of interdependence would be devoid of meaning in that game. Therefore, it only remains to calculate these measures for game #61. These are shown in table 8.7.

If $\sigma_i > (S_i)$, this is evidence of a positive imitation bias $(+)$, i.e., a tendency to play "Tit-for-tat." If $\sigma_i < (S_i)$, this is evidence of a negative imitation bias, i.e., a tendency to play "Tat-for-tit." The same applies to τ_i in relation to (T_i).

We observe that a positive tendency to imitate both the co-player's S choices and his T choices is suggested in practically all pairs.

TABLE 8.7 Imitation propensities in Game #61.

Pair	σ_1	(S_1)	Bias	τ_1	(T_1)	Bias	σ_2	(S_2)	Bias	τ_2	(T_2)	Bias
1	100	85	+	90	10	+	99	88	+	72	13	+
2	99	90	+	84	15	+	98	85	+	80	12	+
3	51	44	+	59	56	+	27	29	-	69	71	-
4	98	94	+	65	06	+	98	94	+	77	06	+
5	81	25	+	95	75	+	89	26	+	94	74	+
6	97	97	0	34	03	+	99	98	+	22	02	+
7	83	56	+	65	44	+	45	44	+	57	56	+
8	38	22	+	91	78	+	60	36	+	73	64	+
9	96	93	+	13	08	+	99	96	+	49	05	+
10	100	100	0	--	00	-	100	100	0	--	--	-

9

Competition and Cooperation

The two games used most extensively in laboratory experiments are game #12 (Prisoner's Dilemma) and game #66 (Chicken) shown in standard notation in matrices 9.1 and 9.2.

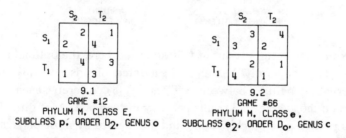

9.1
GAME #12
PHYLUM M. CLASS E,
SUBCLASS p, ORDER D_2, GENUS o

9.2
GAME #66
PHYLUM M. CLASS e,
SUBCLASS e_2, ORDER D_o, GENUS c

In game #66, this is also the format conventionally used, in which the "cooperative" upper left outcome is also the natural outcome. In game #12, however, the natural outcome is not the "cooperative" one. Conventionally, this game is represented with rows and columns interchanged, and the strategies are labeled C (cooperative) and D (defecting).

In game #12, the natural outcome is a Pareto-deficient equilibrium and is the only equilibrium. Game #66 has two equilibria, the asymmetric outcomes S_1T_2 and T_1S_2, neither of which is the natural outcome. The common feature of both games is that the cooperative outcomes, S_1S_2 in Chicken and T_1T_2 in Prisoner's Dilemma, are not equilibria. To achieve cooperation, both players must "resist the

151

temptation" to shift away from the cooperative outcome in pursuit of the largest gain, and each must trust the other not to do it. The games differ in that in game #12, if one player defects, the other gains by retaliating and defecting in turn, whereas, in game #66, retaliation is more costly than "submission." Besides, in game #12, there is no competitive pressure on the natural outcome; there is in game #66. On these grounds, therefore, one would expect that the natural outcome would be more stable in game #12. On the other hand, the natural outcome in game #12 is Pareto-deficient, whereas it is Pareto-optimal in game #66. On this ground, one might expect the natural outcome to be more stable in game #66.

The variants used in our experiment are shown in matrices 9.3 and 9.4.

9.3
GAME #12
VARIANT III
PRISONER'S DILEMMA

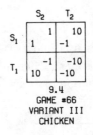

9.4
GAME #66
VARIANT III
CHICKEN

Note that in the variant of Chicken used here, the optimal collective (i.e., cooperative) strategy in iterated play is not S_1S_2 but an alternating pattern between S_1T_2 and T_1S_2, whereby each player gets on the average 4.5 points per play instead of 1. As it turned out, this pattern was quickly found and adhered to by most players.

The frequencies of the four outcomes in game #12 are shown in table 9.1.

The pairs were numbered in descending order of (T_1T_2) so as to show the large, in fact, almost the largest possible, spread between "cooperating" and "noncooperating" pairs. Although ten pairs are too few to give a true picture of the distribution in a large population, bimodality is strongly suggested. The tendency is for pairs to lock in either on T_1T_2 or on S_1S_2. The tendency is clearly seen in the protocols and is manifested in the small frequencies of the asymmetric outcomes.

In pair 8 we observe a "martyr." The large frequency of T_1S_2 and the very low frequency of S_1T_2 indicates that Row was trying hard to achieve cooperation "by setting an example," but without much

TABLE 9.1 Frequencies of the four
outcomes in Game #12.

Pair	(S_1S_2)	(S_1T_2)	(T_1S_2)	(T_1T_2)
1	01	01	01	97
2	07	01	01	92
3	14	01	02	83
4	04	05	05	86
5	21	04	03	72
6	24	05	05	66
7	54	12	07	27
8	34	02	52	11
9	58	25	05	12
10	83	09	04	03
Mean	30	07	08	55

success.

The average frequency of C choices in this experiment was 62, higher than is usually observed in this variant (cf. p. 233). This point will be discussed in chapter 14.

The time courses of (C) and of (D_1D_2) are shown in figure 9.1.

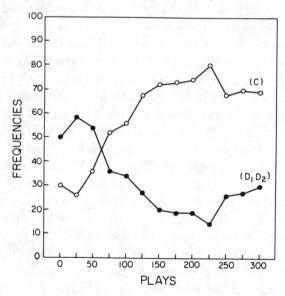

Fig. 9.1. Time courses of (C) and (D_1D_2) in game #12. The late decline in (C) and rise in (D_1D_2) is a consequence of "giving up" on the part of some persistent unilateral cooperators. This effect was also observed by Rapoport and Chammah (1965).

The initial short decline of C is worth noting. It is a typical observation in iterated Prisoner's Dilemma. Usually the decline lasts considerably longer—30–50 plays—than it appears here. In fact, in early experiments with Prisoner's Dilemma, in which the runs were rarely longer than 25–50 plays, the finding was interpreted as evidence not only of the absence of "learning to cooperate" but of actually learning *not* to cooperate. This is what seems to occur in the early stages. The reason is fairly clear. The usual initial frequency of C, the cooperative choice, is roughly around 50. Thus, about half of the initial outcomes will be either C_1D_2 or D_1C_2. In all of the outcomes, the unilateral cooperator will suffer a loss, while the unilateral defector will get the largest payoff. We can expect, therefore, that the unilateral cooperator will switch to D, whereas the unilateral defector will remain with D, and so the frequency of C choices will decrease. Also the frequency of D_1D_2 outcomes will increase. To the extent that the players realize that C_1C_2 is better for both than D_1D_2, attempts to initiate cooperation will be made and, if reciprocated, will eventually lead to predominantly C_1C_2 responses. From figure 9.1 we see that a peak of (D_1D_2) is reached early in the process after which the "recovery" occurs. This recovery was not observed in the early short-run experiments.

The motivations for repetition in game #12 are the following:

α: The player is deterred from shifting away from the natural outcome both because a unilateral shift reduces his payoff from -1 to -10 and because staying with S gives him the largest payoff (10) if the other shifts. In the literature on Prisoner's Dilemma, $1 - \alpha = \tilde{\alpha}$ is often designated by w. This propensity suggests "trust," that is, willingness to shift away from the mutually punishing outcome, trusting that the co-player will do likewise. Thus α could be called "mistrust."

β: In repeating the choice which has just led to the smallest payoff (unreciprocated attempt at cooperation) the player is manifesting "forgiveness," or "martyrdom," or "teaching by example." This propensity has also been called y in the literature.

γ: In repeating the choice that has just led to successful defection and with it the largest outcome, the player is exploiting the co-player. The complement of γ, $1 - \gamma = \tilde{\gamma}$ has been called z. This propensity suggests "repentance" or responding to the other's initiative to cooperate. Thus, γ could be called "failure to respond" or a tendency to exploit.

δ: In repeating the choice that has just led to a cooperative outcome, a player manifests resistance to the temptation to shift away in pursuit of the largest payoff. He "does not rock the boat" and allows the tacit cooperation to continue. He is showing "trustworthiness." Often this probability is designated also by x.

The repetition propensities are shown in table 9.2.

TABLE 9.2 Repetition propensities in Game #12.

Pair	α	β	γ	δ
1	00	50	37	99
2	95	50	50	100
3	93	25	92	100
4	58	57	44	99
5	92	46	85	98
6	94	18	40	98
7	83	16	77	88
8	88	50	50	68
9	92	55	46	60
10	94	25	84	65
Unweighted Means	79	39	61	88
Weighted Means	90	52	78	96

H_r prescribes $\gamma > \delta > \alpha > \beta$. From both the unweighted and weighted means, we observe $\delta > \alpha > \gamma > \beta$. That is, γ is "demoted" from first to third place. As we shall see in chapter 16, this is typically observed in Prisoner's Dilemma. Recall that γ is the propensity to repeat the "defecting" choice after a successful defection. Since the defection is more likely to be "penalized" by the co-player's retaliation, repetition can be expected to be inhibited. On the other hand, since repetition of the cooperative choice after successful cooperation (δ) tends to be reciprocated, this repetition is reinforced. Hence the high value of δ. However, the value of α is also high, in spite of the "punishment" in S_1S_2. Here we have the manifestation of the lock-in effect on S_1S_2.

H_s prescribes for variant III, $\alpha = \gamma > \delta = \beta$. The observed inequalities suggest that δ is "promoted" from third place to first, reflecting the reinforcement of repeated successful cooperative choices.

The outcome frequencies of game #66 are shown in table 9.3.

TABLE 9.3 Frequencies of the four
outcomes in Game #66.

Pair	(S_1S_2)	(S_1T_2)	(T_1S_2)	(T_1T_2)
1	01	49	49	01
2	02	49	49	01
3	02	47	45	05
4	01	49	48	02
5	01	42	46	11
6	02	42	47	09
7	04	39	36	21
8	27	30	28	16
9	05	46	39	10
10	03	39	35	22
Means	05	43	41	10

The heavy predominance of the asymmetric outcomes, S_1T_2 and T_1S_2, with nearly equal frequencies suggests that the subjects in this experiment quickly found the "alternating" cooperative solution of the game, consisting of the pattern S_1T_2 T_1S_2 S_1T_2, etc. This solution is available in this particular variant because of the inequality 2a $< b + c$, a condition usually not present in variants of Chicken used in experiments. (With one exception, noted in chapter 16, we have never seen such a variant in any of the experiments reported.) Our reason for choosing this variant will be discussed in chapter 14.

Because the alternating cooperative solution in this variant is clearly Pareto-optimal in iterated play, whereas S_1S_2 is not, the frequency of the latter cannot be used as an index of cooperation. Instead, the following index suggests itself:

$$K = (S_1T_2) + (T_1S_2) - | (S_1T_2) - (T_1S_2) |. \qquad (9.1)$$

The value of this index is 100 if S_1T_2 and T_1S_2 occur exclusively *and* with equal frequencies. The latter criterion is important since a predominance of one of the asymmetric outcomes represents dominance of one of the players over the other, hence, submission on the part of one rather than "cooperation." Actually the index is not quite satisfactory, because it does not distinguish between a protocol with 100 percent S_1S_2 and one with 100 percent T_1T_2, although the former is clearly the more "cooperative" one. A more satisfactory index would take into account both the frequency of S_1S_2, which represents cooperation of sorts (refraining from preempting the outcome with the largest payoff), and the alternating solution. The relative value to the players of the two solutions depends on the payoff matrix and, consequently, the index would have to include some weighted combination of the two solutions. In the present case, it is not worth while to apply such an index because of the very small frequencies of S_1S_2 observed.

Evidence that the alternating cooperative solution was quickly learned can be seen in table 9.4 which shows the means of K in successive fifty-play blocks.

TABLE 9.4 Time course of K in Game #66.

Plays	1-50	51-100	101-150	151-200	201-250	251-300
K	78	89	89	98	98	99

The repetition propensities in game #66 suggest the following interpretations.

α: In repeating S after S_1S_2, a player manifests "trustworthiness." He resists the temptation to shift away in the pursuit of the largest payoff which accrues to the unilateral shifter. In this way, α is analogous to δ in game #12. There is a difference, however: in Prisoner's Dilemma, retaliation is quite likely to follow a unilateral shift from T_1T_2, because the nonshifter *gains* by retaliating, whereas, in Chicken, after a unilateral shift from S_1S_2 retaliation might not follow, because the retaliator gets his lowest payoff in T_1T_2. The designation "trustworthiness" is, therefore, more justified in Chicken than in Prisoner's Dilemma: in the latter, refraining from breaking the cooperative pattern may be simply a matter of avoiding retaliation.

β: The player who repeats T after getting the largest payoff exploits the co-player. He has successfully preempted the most preferred outcome, and the co-player is faced with the choice of either "submitting," contenting himself with the next to the smallest payoff, or retaliating and risking getting the smallest. The name of Chicken is derived from this situation: the persistence of an asymmetric outcome reveals one of the players as "bold and ruthless," the other as timid.

γ: Repeating the disadvantageous asymmetric outcome has the opposite connotation. In contrast to β in Prisoner's Dilemma, where cooperation in the face of exploitation is "voluntary" (hence has the flavor of "martyrdom"), in Chicken γ has the connotation of submission or timidity.

δ: Repeating T following T_1T_2 is a manifestation of stubbornness. One is willing to continue taking punishment as long as the co-player is taking it. The rationale is "sticking it out," outlasting the other, in the hope that the other will eventually "give up" and retreat to S, thereby allowing the more stubborn player to get the largest payoff.

Table 9.5. shows the repetition propensities in game #66 averaged in each pair over both players.

TABLE 9.5   Repetition propensities in Game #66.

Pair	α	β	γ	δ
1	25	00	00	00
2	53	01	00	50
3	67	02	00	57
4	67	00	00	58
5	50	11	04	67
6	57	07	01	55
7	50	88	82	75
8	52	23	37	45
9	40	08	02	38
10	40	10	02	75
Unweighted Means	50	15	13	52
Weighted Means	51	13	11	57

H_r prescribes $\beta > \alpha > \gamma > \delta$. From table 9.5 we see that H_r is conspicuously violated. However, no psychological conjectures are justified on this score, because the predominant protocol pattern (alternation between S_1T_2 and T_1S_2) is most naturally explained by assuming that practically all pairs sooner or later found the alternating cooperative solution. Observe that the value of K in the last block of plays is practically 100. The consistently low values of β and γ are, of course, due to the alternations.

Thus the "preemptive" nature of Chicken is not brought out in this experiment. We shall have occasion to discuss both Prisoner's Dilemma and Chicken in many other contexts in chapters 15–19.

10

Preemption and Procrastination

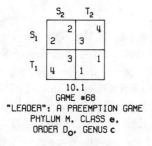

10.1
GAME #68
"LEADER": A PREEMPTION GAME
PHYLUM M. CLASS e,
ORDER D$_o$, GENUS c

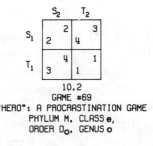

10.2
GAME #69
"HERO": A PROCRASTINATION GAME
PHYLUM M. CLASS e,
ORDER D$_o$, GENUS o

In both of these games, the natural outcome is not an equilibrium and is Pareto-deficient. Each of the two Pareto-optimal outcomes, T_1S_2 and S_1T_2, results in consequence of a unilateral shift by one or the other player. Therefore, either unilateral shift is in the interest of both players. In Leader, the player who shifts unilaterally from the natural outcome gets the largest payoff. In this respect the game is similar to Chicken, and the shifting player can be said to "preempt" his most preferred outcome, because once it obtains, the other player loses by shifting in turn. In Hero, on the contrary, it is the nonshifter who gets the largest payoff if the other shifts. He can be said to get his largest payoff by "procrastinating," i.e., letting the other be the hero. There is also a pressure to shift in Hero, because the hero also gets a larger payoff in the outcome that results from his unilateral shift than in the natural outcome. Nevertheless, in Hero, each would prefer the other to do the mutually beneficial

159

shifting. In this sense, therefore, Leader and Hero reflect opposite pressures. Both games differ from Chicken in that the unilateral shift benefits both instead of only the shifter, as in Chicken.

In both Leader and Hero, cooperation between the two players would be achieved by alternation between S_1T_2 and T_1S_2. Such alternation requires coordination of choices.

The variants of the two games used in the experiment to be described are shown in 10.3 and 10.4.

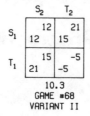

10.3
GAME #68
VARIANT II

10.4
GAME #69
VARIANT III

Tables 10.1 and 10.2 show the frequencies of the four outcomes.

Interpreting as a symptom of cooperation a large majority of S_1T_2 and T_1S_2 outcomes with approximately equal frequencies, we see that in game #68 cooperation appears to have been achieved by five pairs (1, 6, 7, 8, and 9) and in game #69 also by five pairs (6, 7, 8, 9, and 10). It is somewhat disturbing to find that in game #68 (S_1T_2) is larger than (T_1S_2) in all ten pairs. Since the payoffs were symmetric, the a priori probability of the ten inequalities in the same direction is only .002, which leads us to suspect that there may have been bias in the way the game was displayed. No such asymmetry appears in game #69. Another curious finding is that, with one exception, the cooperating pairs are all those who played last, which leads to the suspicion that information about the nature of the game and how to "beat it" might have leaked out. On the other hand, improbable events are bound to be observed at one time or another.

Examining the protocols, we find that in game #68 four of the five cooperating pairs for the most part alternated in successive plays, while one pair (pair 9) alternated in successive twenty-five-play blocks. (Recall that in the standard experiment a pause was introduced after each block of twenty-five plays.) In game #69, three of the cooperating pairs alternated successively, one in twenty-five-play blocks, and one in blocks of four or five plays.

TABLE 10.1 Outcome frequencies in Game #68.

Pair	(S_1S_2)	(S_1T_2)	(T_1S_2)	(T_1T_2)
1	03	44	40	14
2	10	52	33	05
3	01	76	11	12
4	05	55	10	30
5	17	41	14	29
6	04	48	45	02
7	03	48	47	02
8	02	49	48	00
9	00	49	46	05
10	14	41	21	23
Mean	5.9	50.3	31.5	12.2

TABLE 10.2 Outcome frequencies in Game #69.

Pair	(S_1S_2)	(S_1T_2)	(T_1S_2)	(T_1T_2)
1	32	52	16	00
2	94	02	04	00
3	23	29	46	01
4	23	29	48	00
5	09	39	51	00
6	10	45	40	05
7	01	49	49	01
8	05	47	46	01
9	00	50	50	00
10	15	43	42	01
Means	21.2	38.5	39.2	0.9

As expected, the frequency of S_1S_2 is larger in game #69 than in game #68. The difference reflects the stronger pressure to shift from S_1S_2 in game #68, since in game #69 "procrastination" provides a counter pressure.

In game #68, the motivations for repetitions are the following:

α: Prudence or timidity—persistence in the Pareto-deficient natural outcome in view of the danger that T_1T_2 may result if both shift; being content with the prospect of second largest payoff if the other shifts.

β: Preemption—persistence in the most preferred outcome in the hope or expectation that the other will not dare to shift for fear of T_1T_2.

γ: Acceptance of the next to the largest payoff, while the other gets the largest.

δ: Adamance—persistence in the least preferred outcome in the expectation or hope that the other will "yield" and so effect the most preferred outcome. This propensity is similar to the analogous one in Chicken.

Interpretations of the repetition propensities in game #69 are the following.

α: Procrastination—the propensity to repeat S_1S_2 motivated by the hope that the other will shift; also avoidance of the risk of (T_1T_2).

β: Acceptance of the "hero's reward."

γ: Confidence—propensity to repeat the most preferred outcome on the assumption that the other will be satisfied with the "hero's reward."

δ: Yielding—allowing the other to get the largest payoff by shifting.

Tables 10.3 and 10.4 show the repetition frequencies in the two games.

H_r implies the following inequalities for Leader:

$$\beta > \gamma > \alpha > \delta.$$

From the estimated values (cf. table 10.3) we get

$$\delta > \alpha > \beta > \gamma \text{ (individual) and } \delta > \alpha > \beta > \gamma \text{ (pooled)}.$$

Hence, "adamance" seems to play an important role in this game. Note also that the estimated value of δ (58–67) is compatible to that observed in Chicken (cf. p. 158). On the other hand, the value of α in Leader is smaller than that of the analogous propensity in Chicken. Note that, in Leader, the pressure to shift from S_1S_2 stems from both the competitive and the cooperative aspects of this game (the "leader" benefits both himself and the other), whereas, in Chicken, preemption is a purely competitive or exploitative act.

Still, in Leader, the relative magnitude of α is larger than that predicted by H_r. A plausible explanation is in terms of the depressed value of γ and β. Since these are the repetition propensities for S_1T_2 and T_1S_2 respectively, their lowered values indicate a propensity to alternate between these two outcomes, which, as we have seen, is apparent in the protocols.

TABLE 10.3 Repetition frequencies in Game #68.

Pair	α_1	β_1	γ_1	δ_1	α_2	β_2	γ_2	δ_2
1	22	05	05	54	89	12	03	100
2	94	100	99	87	26	85	88	13
3	60	00	78	47	60	86	03	97
4	43	84	88	74	79	96	50	87
5	69	50	51	36	39	63	38	87
6	69	01	07	57	00	01	00	29
7	89	00	01	67	44	03	02	33
8	86	00	01	00	43	00	00	00
9	--	96	97	93	--	98	95	79
10	48	24	47	41	12	42	08	67
Unweighted Means	64	36	47	56	44	49	29	59
Weighted Means	65	32	50	55	34	52	28	80

				α	β	γ	δ
Combined Means of Row & Column		(unweighted)		54	42	38	58
		(weighted)		50	42	39	67

TABLE 10.4 Repetition propensities in Game #69.

Pair	α_1	β_1	γ_1	δ_1	α_2	β_2	γ_2	δ_2
1	98	96	100	--	83	90	98	--
2	97	00	20	--	99	00	75	--
3	57	22	05	25	89	02	42	00
4	73	87	100	100	80	86	100	00
5	76	97	100	00	79	95	99	00
6	45	85	89	07	81	74	75	93
7	33	01	01	50	100	01	00	50
8	71	02	05	33	71	03	04	67
9	--	00	00	--	--	00	00	--
10	73	90	100	100	80	94	99	50
Unweighted Means	69	48	52	45	85	45	59	37
Weighted Means	85	49	54	27	90	50	53	70

				α	β	γ	δ
Combined Means of Row & Column		(unweighted)		77	47	55	41
		(weighted)		87	49	54	48

For Hero, H_r predicts

$$\gamma > \beta > \alpha > \delta,$$

whereas the observed inequalities suggest

$$\alpha > \gamma > \beta > \delta.$$

This discrepancy is entirely accounted for by the "promotion" of α, the propensity to repeat the natural outcome, i.e., a reluctance to shift. Recall that in Hero, this reluctance is a result of two sources of pressure: the unwillingness to risk T_1T_2 and the hope that the other will be the "hero." As expected, δ has the smallest value in this game. However, the observed numerical value of its mean cannot be considered reliable because the conditioning event, T_1T_2, occurs with very small frequencies in this game.

For the variant of game #68 used here, H_s prescribes

$$\tilde{\delta} > \tilde{\alpha} > \tilde{\beta} > \tilde{\gamma}; \text{ hence, } \gamma > \beta > \alpha > \delta.$$

The estimated values are seen to be in completely reversed order from those observed. This result could be taken as a strong disconfirmation of H_s.

For the variant of game #69 used here, H_s prescribes

$$\tilde{\delta} > \tilde{\alpha} > \tilde{\beta} > \tilde{\gamma}; \text{ hence, } \gamma > \beta > \alpha > \delta,$$

the same rank order as in game #68. Therefore, the promotion of α ("procrastination") brings the observed value into accord with H_s as well as with H_r.

The time courses of K in games #68 and #69 are shown in figure 10.1. It seems that "learning to cooperate" is more pronounced in Hero than in Leader. Figure 10.2 shows the tendencies under greater resolving power. Actually, the average combined frequencies of the equilibrium outcomes S_1T_2 and T_1S_2 are about equal in the two games, as can be seen also from tables 10.1 and 10.2. However, the "dominance" component of K, $|(S_1T_2) - (T_1S_2)|$, practically disappears in Hero but remains fairly constant in Leader. It is this difference that is responsible for the apparently more pronounced increase in cooperation in Hero.

The larger "skewness" in Leader may be a consequence of the stronger pressure to preempt in that game. In this experiment, how-

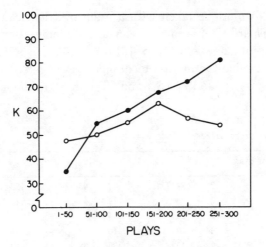

Fig. 10.1. Time courses of K in games #68 and #69 (after Guyer and Rapoport, 1969).

o———o Game #68; •———• Game #69.

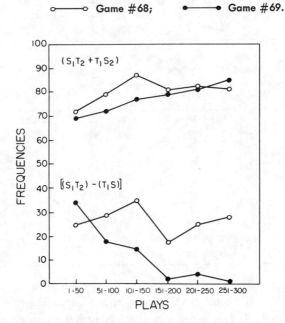

Fig. 10.2. Time courses of the components of K in games #68 and #69 (after Guyer and Rapoport, 1969).

o———o Game #68; •———• Game #69.

ever, the result must be taken with a grain of salt because of the anomalous disparity between the behavior of average Row and average Column in game #68 (cf. p. 161).

Next, we examine the intraprotocol measures of interdependence of choices, σ_1, σ_2, τ_1, and τ_2. (S_i) and (T_i) are shown alongside for comparison.

TABLE 10.5   Imitation propensities in Game #68.

Pair	σ_1	(S_1)	Bias	τ_1	(T_1)	Bias	σ_2	(S_2)	Bias	τ_2	(T_2)	Bias
1	.90	47	+	.85	54	+	.88	43	+	.98	58	+
2	.22	62	-	.06	38	-	.17	43	-	.12	57	-
3	.97	77	+	.25	23	+	.15	12	+	.98	88	+
4	.25	60	-	.34	10	-	.10	15	-	.73	85	-
5	.60	58	+	.44	43	+	.36	31	+	.80	70	+
6	.89	52	+	.91	47	+	.83	49	+	.97	50	+
7	.99	51	+	.99	49	+	.94	50	+	.95	50	+
8	1.00	51	+	.99	48	+	.98	50	+	1.00	49	+
9	.03	49	-	.11	51	-	.05	46	-	.12	54	-
10	.65	55	+	.48	46	+	.34	35	+	.35	65	-

TABLE 10.6   Imitation propensities in Game #69.

Pair	σ_1	(S_1)	Bias	τ_1	(T_1)	Bias	σ_2	(S_2)	Bias	τ_2	(T_2)	Bias
1	.67	84	-	.00	16	-	.38	48	-	.02	52	-
2	.98	96	+	.32	04	+	.99	98	+	.25	02	+
3	.91	52	+	.93	47	+	.94	69	+	.57	30	+
4	.32	52	-	.00	48	-	.45	71	-	.01	29	-
5	.40	48	-	.00	51	-	.19	60	-	.01	39	-
6	.21	55	-	.11	45	-	.36	50	-	.32	50	-
7	.98	50	+	.98	50	+	.98	50	+	.99	50	+
8	.95	52	+	.94	47	+	.93	51	+	.98	48	+
9	1.00	50	+	1.00	50	+	1.00	50	+	1.00	50	+
10	.27	58	-	.02	43	-	.25	57	-	.02	44	-

Although, for the most part, σ_i and τ_i are larger than the corresponding S_i and T_i frequencies in both games, we cannot say that there is a consistent tendency to play Tit-for-tat. In both games, σ_i and τ_i showed excesses in the protocols of six pairs and deficiencies in four. A perfect Tit-for-tat protocol would consist of either 100 percent S_1S_2 or 100 percent T_1T_2 or a perfect alternation between S_1T_2

and T_1S_2. In Leader and in Hero, the alternating pattern would reflect perfect cooperation. We see from table 10.5 that pairs 1, 6, 7, and 8 who achieved a high degree of cooperation (cf. p. 166) also showed excesses in σ_i and τ_i. On the other hand, pair 9 who also achieved almost perfect cooperation—$(S_1T_2) = 49$; $(T_1S_2) = 46$—nevertheless showed deficiencies in σ_i and τ_i. However, we have already seen the reason for this. Pair 9 alternated not play-by-play but in twenty-five-play blocks. The long runs of S_1T_2 and T_1S_2 outcomes made for low values of σ_i and τ_i.

In game #69, the cooperating pairs 7, 8, and 9 showed excesses in σ_i and τ_i. Pairs 6 and 10 who also achieved a high level of cooperation showed deficient σ_i and τ_i. But we have seen that these two pairs also alternated in blocks instead of play-by-play (cf. p. 160). On the other hand, pair 2, who showed an excess of σ_i and τ_i, hardly cooperated at all: (S_1S_2) was 97 in this pair, showing a high level of procrastination, which is also reflected in high σ_i. Thus, the interpretation of intraprotocol interdependence in these two games is beset with ambiguities.

11

A Stable and a Vulnerable
Natural Outcome

The two games to be compared are game #36 and game #64.

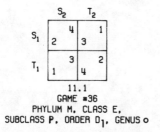

11.1
GAME #36
PHYLUM M. CLASS E.
SUBCLASS P. ORDER D_1, GENUS o

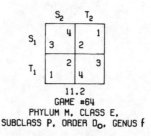

11.2
GAME #64
PHYLUM M. CLASS E.
SUBCLASS P. ORDER D_o, GENUS f

In both, Row gets less than Column in the natural outcome, a
Pareto-optimal equilibrium. The natural outcome is most preferred
by Column, and the diagonally placed T_1T_2 is most preferred by
Row. Row, the disgruntled player, has recourse to T_1S_2, which is
punishing for both players. In game #36, however, the natural outcome is neither threat-vulnerable nor force-vulnerable. It is not
threat-vulnerable because Column gets more in T_1S_2 than in S_1T_2,
and so is not motivated to shift "voluntarily" to S_1T_2 in order to forestall T_1S_2. Nor is the natural outcome force-vulnerable, because it is
not to Column's immediate advantage to shift to T_2, even after Row
has shifted to T_1S_2. According to our categorization, therefore, the
natural outcome in that game is a stable equilibrium.

In game #64, the natural outcome is not threat-vulnerable, and, at
any rate, it is not to Row's immediate advantage to have Column

shift to S_1T_2. The natural outcome is, however, force-vulnerable, because it is to Column's immediate advantage to shift to T_2 *after* Row has shifted unilaterally to T_1, effecting T_1S_2. It appears, therefore, that the natural outcome in game #64 is less stable than in game #36. In neither game, however, does the unilateral shifter gain competitive advantage.

"Cooperation" between the two players in both games would be an alternation between S_1S_2 and T_1T_2, which involves a synchronization of shifts. Since Column is "top dog" in both games in the sense that he gets the largest payoff in the natural outcome, cooperation is more to Row's advantage than to Column's. In game #64, Row has some leverage in inducing Column to cooperate; in game #36, he has little or none. A variant of game #64 was used by R. B. Braithwaite (1955) to illustrate his method of arbitrating a cooperative two-person non-constant-sum game.

The variants of the two games used in the experiments to be discussed here are shown in 11.3 and 11.4.

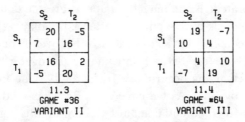

11.3
GAME #36
-VARIANT II

11.4
GAME #64
VARIANT III

Tables 11.1 and 11.2 show the frequencies of the four outcomes in the two games.

TABLE 11.1 Outcome frequencies in Game #36.

Pair	(S_1S_2)	(S_1T_2)	(T_1S_2)	(T_1T_2)
1	98	00	02	00
2	84	00	16	00
3	49	01	01	49
4	96	00	03	00
5	100	00	00	00
6	70	09	06	15
7	32	22	25	21
8	86	00	14	00
9	97	00	03	00
10	94	01	05	00
Means	80	03	08	09

TABLE 11.2 Outcome frequencies in Game #64.

Pair	(S_1S_2)	(S_1T_2)	(T_1S_2)	(T_1T_2)
1	42	08	37	13
2	76	02	12	09
3	49	01	00	49
4	35	02	09	55
5	50	05	30	15
6	87	04	08	01
7	33	08	19	40
8	47	03	07	42
9	42	04	07	47
10	28	01	43	28
Means	49	04	17	30

The difference between the mean frequencies of the natural outcome in the two games is large and in the expected direction. Hence in this respect, our categorization of natural outcomes by stability is amply corroborated. Examining the data in greater detail, we find that in the protocols of five out of the ten pairs playing game #36, the natural outcome occurs almost exclusively (over 90 percent of the time). In two pairs the natural outcome occurs over 80 percent of the time, the remaining occurrences being all T_1S_2, an indication of *futile* "revolts" by Row. As we have seen, Row has neither a threat potential nor a force potential against Column in this game. In only one pair (pair 3) is there equal sharing, which can be reasonably attributed to Column's goodwill, since Row has no leverage in this game. An interesting question is whether more pairs would have achieved equal sharing if the two Pareto-optimal outcomes were symmetric in the payoffs. (Note that an alternation between S_1S_2 and T_1T_2 would give more to Row than to Column.) We note also that in another pair (pair 6), Column, the top dog, gets his way 70 percent of the time and Row, the underdog, 15 percent of the time, the remaining 15 percent of the outcomes being split between S_1T_2 and T_1S_2. The performance of pair 7 is erratic. Although the most frequently occurring outcome is still S_1S_2, the distribution does not differ significantly from a uniform distribution.

Game #64 presents a different picture. In this game, too, Row is the underdog. But five of the pairs (3, 7, 8, 9, and 10) share almost equally, and in one case (pair 4), the underdog gets actually significantly more than the top dog. (Note that a sufficiently resolute underdog can make a top dog yield, if the latter is not too adamant, so as to effect a predominance of T_1T_2.) On the average, the top dog gets his way 49 percent of the time and the underdog 30 percent of the time, the difference being considerable but not excessive, as it is in game #36. However, the underdog must "work" for his share, as is seen in the average 17 percent occurrence of T_1S_2, which is Row's "leverage" against Column. In one case (pair 10), the frequency of T_1S_2 is as high as 43. The frequency of the "irrelevant" outcome, S_1T_2, is for the most part negligible, as in game #36.

In table 11.3, the cooperative indices in the two games are compared (cf. p. 156).

TABLE 11.3   Cooperative indices
$$K=(S_1S_2)+(T_1T_2) - |(S_1S_2)-(T_1T_2)|$$
in Games #36 and #64 compared.

Pair	Game #36	Game #64
1	0	36
2	0	18
3	98	98
4	0	70
5	0	30
6	30	02
7	42	60
8	0	84
9	0	84
10	0	56
Means	17	54

In game #36, the motivations for repetitions are the following:

α_1: Row submits to Column's dominant position.

α_2: Column expects to continue getting the largest payoff.

β_1: Having "revolted," Row persists, hoping that Column "gets the message" and shifts to T_2 to allow Row to get the largest payoff. The "revolt" has no leverage for Row, since it is not to Column's immediate interest to shift from T_1S_2 to T_1T_2. The only thing Row can hope for is that Column, in order to prevent T_1S_2, will cooperate in establishing an alternating pattern between S_1S_2 and T_1T_2. In our variant, however, such a pattern is not to Column's advantage; he gets more by simply ignoring Row's "revolts." An alternation between S_1S_2 and

T_1T_2 in this game can be attributed only to a sense of "fairness" on Column's part. We have already observed that only one of the ten pairs achieved the alternation.

β_2: Column's repetition of T_2 following S_1T_2 cannot be justified by individual rationality. The only plausible reason for it is to allow Row to get the largest payoff by shifting to T_1T_2. Therefore, β_2 is a measure of Column's "altruism" or "fairness."

γ_1: Row expects Column to shift to S_2, since S_2 is Column's dominating strategy. Therefore, he repeats S_1 to avoid -5 in T_1S_2.

γ_2: Column does not yield to Row's pressure, as indeed there is no need to in this game. Since Row's pressure has no real "punch," γ_2 is not, properly speaking, a measure of Column's "adamance" (see the analogous propensity in game #64 below). It might be construed as a measure of Column's imperviousness to Row's protest.

δ_1: Row gets the largest payoff and expects to continue getting it, which is not a realistic expectation in this game.

δ_2: Column allows Row to continue to get the largest payoff, perhaps to make up for several previous occurrences of S_1S_2.

Interpretations of α_1, α_2, β_2, and γ_1 are the same in game #64 as in game #36. However, because of Row's leverage in game #64, the suggested psychological "meanings" of the remaining propensities are different. Specifically, in game #64, the following interpretations are suggested:

β_1: Row persists in his revolt in the not unreasonable expectation that Column will shift to T_2, this being to Column's immediate advantage.

γ_2: Column does not yield to Row's pressure, in spite of the fact that it is to his immediate advantage to do so. Here γ_2 is an appropriate measure of Column's "adamance."

δ_1: Row's expectation that he can get the largest payoff in T_1T_2 again has some justification, since T_1T_2 is an equilibrium in this game.

δ_2: Column yields to Row's "victory" in T_1T_2.

Tables 11.4 and 11.5 show the repetition propensities in games #36 and #64.

H_r implies the following inequalities for game #36:

$$\delta_1 > \gamma_1 > \alpha_1 > \beta_1;$$
$$\alpha_2 > \gamma_2 > \delta_2 > \beta_2.$$

TABLE 11.4 Repetition propensities in Game #36.

Pair	α_1	β_1	γ_1	δ_1	α_2	β_2	γ_2	δ_2
1	98	14	--	--	100	--	100	--
2	85	21	--	--	100	--	100	--
3	01	100	100	01	01	00	00	01
4	98	30	00	--	100	00	90	--
5	100	00	--	--	100	--	00	--
6	73	24	96	00	70	04	53	00
7	52	44	62	55	54	42	61	45
8	90	40	00	--	100	00	100	--
9	97	12	100	00	99	00	100	00
10	97	36	100	--	99	00	93	--
Unweighted Means	79	32	65	14	82	07	70	12
Weighted Means	86	34	73	14	89	29	79	12

TABLE 11.5 Repetition propensities in Game #64.

Pair	α_1	β_1	γ_1	δ_1	α_2	β_2	γ_2	δ_2
1	69	63	54	79	94	37	73	39
2	95	57	50	100	99	12	70	79
3	01	00	50	00	00	50	100	00
4	89	74	80	97	97	20	59	94
5	66	69	40	31	78	07	76	11
6	97	42	62	100	97	08	75	00
7	88	68	71	99	88	17	27	72
8	06	05	00	02	13	40	60	01
9	95	57	45	98	94	55	57	93
10	81	88	100	99	98	00	91	87
Unweighted Means	69	52	55	70	76	24	69	47
Weighted Means	70	67	57	64	75	25	72	55

From table 11.4 we see that the individual means of the repetition propensities satisfy the predicted inequalities for Column, although the ranks of δ_2 and β_2 are interchanged in the pooled means. Row's inequalities, however, are severely violated by both individual and pooled means ($\alpha_1 > \gamma_1 > \beta_1 > \delta_1$). In particular, the observed value of δ_1 is smallest instead of largest as predicted. To be sure, this observed value is hardly reliable, being undefined in the protocols of six pairs. In three of the remaining four pairs, δ_1 is virtually zero.

Note that in pair 3, δ_1 is near zero because of almost perfect alternation between S_1S_2 and T_1T_2. In view of the complexity of the factors affecting δ_1 and the sparsity of observations from which its mean can be estimated, no conjecture is warranted concerning the pressures on Row as they are reflected in the inequalities among his repetition propensities.

H_s prescribes the following inequalities for game #36 in the variant used:

$$\tilde{\beta}_1 > \tilde{\delta}_1 > \tilde{\gamma}_1 > \tilde{\alpha}_1; \text{ hence } \alpha_1 > \gamma_1 > \delta_1 > \beta_1,$$
$$\tilde{\beta}_2 > \tilde{\delta}_2 > \tilde{\gamma}_2 > \tilde{\alpha}_2; \text{ hence } \alpha_2 > \gamma_2 > \delta_2 > \beta_2.$$

For Column, the inequalities are the same as those prescribed by H_r, and they are satisfied by the unweighted means. Also, H_s turns out to be a better predictor than H_r of Row's repetition propensities, the only discrepancy being in the relative magnitudes of δ_1 and β_1.

In game #64, H_r prescribes

$$\delta_1 > \alpha_1 > \gamma_1 > \beta_1;$$
$$\alpha_2 > \delta_2 > \gamma_2 > \beta_2.$$

From table 11.5, we observe

$$\delta_1 > \alpha_1 > \gamma_1 > \beta_1 \text{ (unweighted means)};$$
$$\alpha_1 > \beta_1 > \delta_1 > \gamma_1 \text{ (weighted means)};$$
$$\alpha_2 > \gamma_2 > \delta_2 > \beta_2 \text{ (unweighted means)};$$
$$\alpha_2 > \gamma_2 > \delta_2 > \beta_2 \text{ (weighted means)}.$$

Because of the large discrepancies in the rank orders of Row's repetition propensities between unweighted and weighted means, Row's situation is not clear. Column's rank order satisfies H_r except for the "promotion" of γ_2, the top dog's "adamance," which we shall have occasion to observe in other games (cf. chapter 13). In game #64, because of Row's leverage, there is a considerable amount of "sharing," reflected in the alternation between S_1S_2 and T_1T_2. In perfect alternation between these outcomes, we would have $\alpha_1 = \alpha_2 = \delta_1 = \delta_2 = 0$. The question, therefore, arises why both the α's and the δ's are fairly large. Examining the protocols provides the answer. Sharing is not always effected by simple alternation between S_1S_2 and T_1T_2. Some pairs achieve sharing by blocks. In the standard experiment, there is a brief pause following each block of twenty-five plays, during which the subjects add up their gains and losses.

Among our protocols of game #64 we find some where S_1S_2 predominates during one twenty-five-play block and T_1T_2 during the next. If alternation is achieved in this way, both the α's and the δ's, of course, will be large.

We turn to H_s. For game #64, our variant of this hypothesis implies the inequalities

$$\tilde{\beta}_1 > \tilde{\delta}_1 > \tilde{\gamma}_1 > \tilde{\alpha}_1; \text{ hence } \alpha_1 > \gamma_1 > \delta_1 > \beta_1;$$
$$\tilde{\beta}_2 > \tilde{\gamma}_2 > \tilde{\delta}_2 > \tilde{\alpha}_2; \text{ hence } \alpha_2 > \delta_2 > \gamma_2 > \beta_2.$$

The order of δ_2 and γ_2 is reversed in Column's propensities, again suggesting the effect of "adamance." Since Row's inequalities of weighted and unweighted means are inconsistent, no conjecture is justified.

We next examine the average time courses of the cooperative index K (cf. figures 11.1 and 11.2). As expected, there is no evidence of increase in game #36; rather the frequency of the natural outcome (favoring Column) tends to increase. In game #64, K increases by some 20 percentage points from the beginning to the end of the run. Except for the reversal in the middle, there is some evidence that the average pair is learning to cooperate.

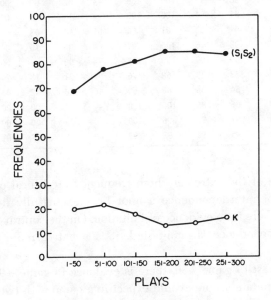

Fig. 11.1.   Time courses of K and of (S_1S_2) in game #36.

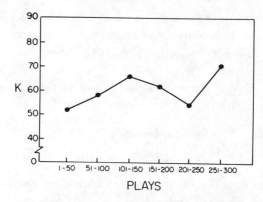

Fig. 11.2.   Time course of K in game #64.

The interprotocol measures of interdependence are strongly positive in both games: $\rho_{S_1S_2} = .97$ and $.72$ respectively in games #36 and #64. Imitation propensities in that game are shown in table 11.6.

TABLE 11.6   Imitation propensities in Game #36.

Pair	σ_1	(S_1)	σ_2	(S_2)	τ_1	(T_1)	τ_2	(T_2)
1	98	98	100	100	--	02	00	00
2	84	84	100	100	--	16	00	00
3	01	50 -	01	50 -	01	50 -	03	50 -
4	98	96 -	100	99 +	--	03	10	00 +
5	100	100	100	100	--	00	--	00
6	73	79 -	62	76 -	01	21 -	13	24 -
7	54	54	48	59 -	46	46 +	42	43 -
8	86	86	100	100	--	14	00	00
9	97	97	96	100 -	--	03	00	00
10	95	95	98	99	00	05 -	07	01 +

Because of the extremely high frequency of natural outcomes, a measure of interdependence cannot be meaningfully deduced. At any rate, there is no evidence of imitation. On the contrary, wherever an interdependence is manifested, it is negative more often than positive.

In contrast to game #36, there is evidence in game #64 of a tendency to imitate, as one would expect in a game with two equilibria on the main diagonal (cf. table 11.7).

TABLE 11.7   Imitation propensities in Game #64.

Pair	σ_1	(S_1)	σ_2	(S_2)	τ_1	(T_1)	τ_2	(T_2)
1	54	52 +	89	79 +	38	50 -	64	21 +
2	89	78 +	99	88 +	10	21 -	72	11 +
3	01	50 -	01	49 -	01	49 -	00	50 -
4	76	37 +	96	44 +	94	64 +	89	57 +
5	67	55 +	79	80 -	38	45 -	56	20 +
6	90	91 -	96	95 +	50	09 +	67	05 +
7	66	41 +	87	52 +	87	59 +	57	48 +
8	89	50 +	85	54 +	09	49 -	09	45 -
9	87	46 +	90	49 +	95	54 +	88	51 +
10	39	29 +	98	71 +	96	71 +	90	29 +

12

Two Forbearance Games

In this chapter we shall compare experimental results on games #48 and #72.

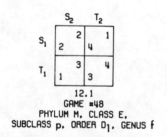

12.1
GAME #48
PHYLUM M. CLASS E.
SUBCLASS p. ORDER D_1. GENUS f

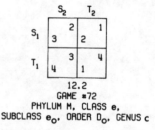

12.2
GAME #72
PHYLUM M. CLASS e.
SUBCLASS e_0. ORDER D_0. GENUS c

The variants used in the experiments are shown in 12.3 and 12.4.

12.3
GAME #48
VARIANT V

12.4
GAME #72
VARIANT IV

The games are far apart on the taxonomic tree since they belong to different classes: in game #48 the natural outcome is a deficient equilibrium (class E, subclass p), whereas game #72 has no equi-

178

librium (class e). Nevertheless, the two games are related as will appear in the analysis of their structures.

In game #48 (T_1T_2) is Pareto-optimal, indeed preferred by both players to the natural outcome, but (T_1T_2) is not an equilibrium. In this respect game #48 resembles Prisoner's Dilemma; in another respect it differs. To illustrate, assume that the players of Prisoner's Dilemma are "trapped" in the natural outcome S_1S_2. Both realize that they would be better off in T_1T_2. To get there both must shift. In the absence of communication, each could be induced to shift if he were sure that the other would shift at the same time or, in iterated play, at least shortly thereafter. In Prisoner's Dilemma, when a player shifts unilaterally, he thereby awards the co-player the largest payoff and so removes at least the latter's immediate motivation to shift. The fear of being left "holding the bag" is an additional deterrent against trying to escape from the trap in S_1S_2. The situation in game #48 is different. Whereas Column is in the same position as either player in Prisoner's Dilemma, Row's position in game #48 allows him to take the initiative in breaking out of the trap. For if Row shifts unilaterally, he gets the smallest payoff in T_1S_2, to be sure, but he thereby creates a motivation for Column to shift to T_2, since Column's largest payoff is in T_1T_2. Once (T_1T_2) occurs, Row gets his next to the largest payoff.

How the game proceeds thereafter is up to Row. If Row is satisfied with getting his next to the largest payoff, T_1T_2 will persist, which is better for both players than the natural outcome. But if Row takes the opportunity offered by T_1T_2 to shift to S_1T_2, where he gets his largest payoff, he thereby creates a motivation for Column to return to S_2 and so to restore the natural outcome, which is better for Column than S_1T_2, but worse for both players than (T_1T_2). Thus, the persistence of T_1T_2, which is best for Column and almost the best for Row, can be assured if (i) Row takes the initiative to escape from (S_1S_2), suffering a temporary loss in the process, and (ii) if Row is content to leave well enough alone after T_1T_2 has been reached. Because the pressures are on Row only, game #48 could be called a "one-sided" Prisoner's Dilemma.

Consider now game #72. The natural outcome is not an equilibrium, because Row can get a larger payoff by shifting unilaterally to T_1. If the outcome is T_1S_2, Column can get a larger payoff by shifting unilaterally to T_2. Similarly, T_1T_2 offers Row an opportunity to get more by shifting to S_1, and S_1T_2 offers a similar opportunity to Column. If each player pursued his immediate advantage (assuming unilateral shifts), the successive outcomes of game #72 would be a counter-clockwise cyclic progression. For this reason, game #72 was categorized in the earlier taxonomy as a "cycle game" (cf. Rapoport and Guyer, 1966).

Suppose now that the outcome is T_1S_2, and Column does *not* shift. Row has no motivation to shift, because he gets the largest payoff. To be sure, Column gets only his next largest payoff. However, if Column is satisfied with it, the game can persist in (T_1S_2) which is a "good" outcome for both players, analogous to (T_1T_2) in game #48.

As in game #48, this cooperative "solution" is up to one player, in this case, Column. In this way game #72 is similar to game #48. We have called these two games "forbearance games," because in both games a decision of one of the players not to try to get the largest payoff stabilizes the game in a satisfactory outcome.

The frequencies of the four outcomes of game #48 are shown in table 12.1.

TABLE 12.1   Outcome frequencies in Game #48.

Pair	(S_1S_2)	(S_1T_2)	(T_1S_2)	(T_1T_2)
1	17	04	07	72
2	07	25	11	56
3	99	01	00	00
4	26	01	01	72
5	86	07	06	01
6	0	13	0	87
7	79	0	18	02
8	0	0	0	100
9	06	0	0	94
10	45	07	04	44
Means	37	06	05	53

From table 12.1 we see that in five of the ten protocols the Pareto-optimal outcome, T_1T_2, occurred over 70 percent of the time, but in three of the protocols the natural outcome prevailed. In one, the frequencies were about equally divided between T_1T_2 and S_1S_2. In one (pair 2), although the majority of the outcomes were T_1T_2, the frequency of S_1T_2 was rather large, indicating that Row did not "abstain" from pursuing his largest payoff. In pair 7, it seems that Row's "initiative" was in vain, as shown by the relatively high frequency of (T_1S_2) but a very low frequency of (T_1T_2). Examining the protocol of this pair reveals dramatically the futility of Row's efforts, as shown in table 12.2.

TABLE 12.2 Time course of outcome frequencies in Pair 7, Game #48.

Plays	(S_1S_2)	(S_1T_2)	(T_1S_2)	(T_1T_2)
1-25	17	04	71	08
26-50	0	0	92	08
51-75	28	0	60	12
76-100	100	0	0	0
101-125	100	0	0	0
126-150	100	0	0	0
151-175	100	0	0	0
176-200	100	0	0	0
201-225	100	0	0	0
226-250	100	0	0	0
251-275	100	0	0	0
276-300	100	0	0	0

In the first twenty-five plays, Row was very persistent in trying to effect T_1T_2, as shown by the very high frequency of T_1S_2. The mutually advantageous outcome T_1T_2 did occur a few times (8 percent). But evidently Row did not resist the temptation of shifting to S_1T_2 (note that S_1T_2 occurred with frequency 04), so that (T_1T_2) did not last. In the next twenty-five plays, Row was even more persistent, effecting T_1S_2 92 percent of the time. Again T_1T_2 occurred a few times. These times, Row either did not shift to (S_1T_2) or, if he did, he was anticipated by Column, who also shifted, thus restoring the status quo. The picture was similar in plays fifty one to seventy five. Apparently Column no longer trusted Row to avoid S_1T_2 where Column suffers a loss. Accordingly, either Column never switched to T_2 following T_1S_2, or, if he did, he switched to S_2 immediately after T_1T_2, since S_1T_2 never occurred. Thereafter, Row "gave up" and the two were trapped in S_1S_2. Had Row refrained from switching to S_1 from T_1T_2, he might have established Column's trust, and both would have been comfortable in T_1T_2 thereafter. It seems that the game persisted in the deficient natural outcome because Row failed to practice forbearance in the early phases.

In game #48, the motivations for repetitions are the following:

α_1: Row accepts the payoff in the natural outcome. Note that, in the variant of the game used in this experiment, the payoffs to Row and Column in S_1S_2 are numerically as well as ordinally equal. They are unequal in other outcomes. Perhaps the equality of the payoffs made the natural outcome more attractive to Row (the "active" player) than it would have been if Row got less than Column.

β_1: The main motivation for persisting in T_1S_2 is to force Column to shift to T_1T_2. A Row player who is both "active" and "prudent" aims to keep the game in T_1T_2.

γ_1: Row is satisfied with the largest payoff.

δ_1: Persistence in T_1T_2 is a measure of Row's "forbearance." He refrains from pursuing the largest payoff and thereby keeps Column "happy." By forbearance, Row maximizes his long term gains.

α_2: Persistence in S_1S_2 is certainly rational for Column. The only motivation for shifting is in anticipation of Row's shift to T_1, which, however, cannot be expected a priori on any particular play. Only after Row has shifted does it make sense for Column to shift to T_2.

β_2: Persistence in S_1T_2 makes no sense for Column. The only motivation for not shifting is in anticipation of Row's shift, which, in this outcome, is hardly justified.

γ_2: Persistence in T_1S_2 is hardly justified. Clearly, Row's choice of T_1 is motivated by the intention to effect the Pareto-optimal outcome T_1T_2, which is most preferred by Column. The only counter pressure against shifting from T_1S_2 is the apprehension that Row will follow by shifting to S_1, effecting S_1T_2, Column's least preferred outcome. In other words, γ_2 is a measure of Column's distrust of Row's intentions.

δ_2: Column is satisfied with the largest payoff and does not anticipate a shift by Row. The conditional probability δ_2 is a measure of Column's reliance on Row's "forbearance."

Table 12.3 shows the repetition frequencies of game #48.

H_r prescribes

$$\gamma_1 > \delta_1 > \alpha_1 > \beta_1;$$
$$\delta_2 > \gamma_2 > \alpha_2 > \beta_2.$$

From the means of repetition frequencies, we observe

TABLE 12.3 Repetition propensities in Game #48.

Pair	α_1	β_1	γ_1	δ_1	α_2	β_2	γ_2	δ_2
1	96	33	00	100	83	42	86	98
2	68	42	27	74	68	64	21	96
3	100	--	100	--	99	00	--	--
4	99	40	00	100	97	54	100	100
5	94	00	81	50	94	29	89	100
6	--	--	59	93	--	97	--	100
7	99	95	--	100	100	--	89	100
8	--	--	--	100	--	--	--	100
9	94	--	--	100	100	--	--	100
10	94	38	40	91	95	65	85	99
Unweighted Means	93	61	44	90	92	50	78	90
Weighted Means	97	55	41	88	96	57	75	99

Weighted	Unweighted
$\alpha_1 > \delta_1 > \beta_1 > \gamma_1$	$\alpha_1 > \delta_1 > \beta_1 > \gamma_1$
$\delta_2 > \alpha_2 > \gamma_2 > \beta_2$	$\alpha_2 > \delta_2 > \gamma_2 > \beta_2$

The observed order of the mean conditional frequencies can be obtained from the prescribed order by "demoting" γ_1 and γ_2 and "promoting" α_1 and α_2.

Recall that γ_1 is a measure of Row's attempt to repeat S_1T_2, where he gets the largest payoff. A reduction of γ_1 can be attributed to the fact that Row does not foresee a repetition of S_1T_2—a justified expectation, since S_1T_2 is least preferred by Column; so Column can certainly be expected to shift. In fact, Column *does* shift with high probability, as shown by the low value of β_2, Column's persistence in S_1T_2.

Recall next that γ_2 is a measure of Column's distrust of Row. Its "demotion" in the rank order can, accordingly, be attributed partly to Column's trust of Row's intentions, but partly also to the immediate advantage to be gained by Column shifting from T_1S_2 to T_1T_2.

H_s prescribes the following inequalities:

$$\tilde{\beta}_1 > \tilde{\delta}_1 > \tilde{\gamma}_1 > \tilde{\alpha}_1, \text{ hence } \alpha_1 > \gamma_1 > \delta_1 > \beta_1;$$
$$\tilde{\beta}_2 > \tilde{\gamma}_2 > \tilde{\delta}_2 > \tilde{\alpha}_2, \text{ hence } \alpha_2 > \delta_2 > \gamma_2 > \beta_2.$$

The observed rank order of means can be obtained from the prescribed order by "promoting" δ_1 and δ_2. This modification is in accord with our general observation that a tendency to cooperate is usually responsible for the discrepancies between the observed orders of the conditional probabilities and those prescribed by the "short-sighted" hypotheses H_r and H_s.

The outcome frequencies of game #72 are shown in table 12.4.

TABLE 12.4 Outcome frequencies in Game #72.

Pair	(S_1S_2)	(S_1T_2)	(T_1S_2)	(T_1T_2)
1	19	11	53	18
2	37	17	30	16
3	31	13	36	20
4	36	23	25	15
5	20	02	75	02
6	53	20	19	08
7	59	04	35	02
8	04	01	86	09
9	10	01	88	01
10	25	08	54	13
Means	30	10	50	10

Note the similarity of the distributions in games #48 and #72. In both, the "cooperative" Pareto-optimal outcome has the highest frequency, the two frequencies being about equal (53 percent and 50 percent). The natural outcomes have the next highest frequency. It is somewhat larger in game #48, and it is tempting to attribute the difference to the fact that in game #48 the natural outcome is an equilibrium, whereas in game #72 it is not. However, the difference is probably not statistically significant. Still, the protocols with the highest frequencies of the natural outcome (99 percent, 86 percent, and 79 percent) are all in game #48. The two outcomes with lowest frequencies in both games are those where one of the players gets a negative payoff and thus has a strong motivation to shift.

The repetition propensities in game #72 are shown in table 12.5.

In a "cycle game" like game #72, one player is motivated to shift (whatever the outcome) in pursuit of immediate advantage. Hence, shifts can be expected whatever the outcome unless "higher order" considerations are taken into account. The "reasonable cooperative solution" in (T_1S_2) would be stable in view of such "higher considerations." As has been pointed out, the stability of this solution de-

TABLE 12.5 Repetition propensities in Game #72.

Pair	α_1	β_1	γ_1	δ_1	α_2	β_2	γ_2	δ_2
1	58	94	56	47	40	12	78	27
2	62	53	68	64	83	34	63	60
3	54	74	63	53	71	61	73	29
4	63	47	66	47	51	40	75	33
5	39	86	86	00	93	29	97	17
6	72	27	70	12	74	31	79	33
7	84	77	92	33	94	08	95	33
8	83	100	00	89	75	00	91	07
9	40	90	100	00	100	00	100	00
10	66	92	61	47	82	26	78	20
Unweighted Means	62	74	67	43	77	25	83	26
Weighted Means	65	83	67	42	76	33	86	30

pends on Column's "forbearance"—in this game, on the magnitude of γ_2.

The measure of Column's forbearance in game #72 is quite high (83 percent to 86 percent), though not as high as the analogous measure of Row's forbearance in game #48 (92 percent to 95 percent). It exceeds either player's tendency to preserve the Pareto-optimal outcome in Prisoner's Dilemma (70 percent to 90 percent).

H_r prescribes the inequalities

$$\beta_1 > \alpha_1 > \gamma_1 > \delta_1;$$
$$\delta_2 > \gamma_2 > \alpha_2 > \beta_2.$$

From table 12.5, the unweighted means of the repetition frequencies are ordered as

$$\beta_1 > \gamma_1 > \alpha_1 > \delta_1;$$
$$\gamma_2 > \alpha_2 > \delta_2 > \beta_2.$$

The weighted means are ordered as

$$\beta_1 > \gamma_1 > \alpha_1 > \delta_1;$$
$$\gamma_2 > \alpha_2 > \beta_2 > \delta_2.$$

Row's observed inequalities can be obtained from the prescribed by "promoting" γ_1. Column's observed inequalities can be obtained from the prescribed by demoting δ_2. The latter modification is easy to explain, since Column cannot realistically hope that T_1T_2 will persist: Row is very likely to shift because he gets his smallest payoff in T_1T_2. In fact, the relatively low value of δ_1 (43 percent to 50 percent) justifies this expectation. The high value of γ_1 can be attributed to Row's (justified) expectation that Column will shift ($\tilde{\beta}_2 = 67$ percent to 75 percent) and so will increase Row's payoff from five to fifteen. But, if Row anticipates Column's shift from S_1T_2, it would make good sense for him to shift likewise and so achieve the Pareto-optimal outcome T_1S_2. Evidently Row's far-sightedness does not reach that far.

H_s prescribes the inequalities

$$\tilde{\delta}_1 > \tilde{\alpha}_1 > \tilde{\beta}_1 > \tilde{\gamma}_1, \text{ hence, } \gamma_1 > \beta_1 > \alpha_1 > \delta_1;$$
$$\tilde{\beta}_2 > \tilde{\gamma}_2 > \tilde{\delta}_2 > \tilde{\alpha}_2, \text{ hence, } \alpha_2 > \delta_2 > \gamma_2 > \beta_2.$$

Comparing these with the observed inequalities, we see that the latter can be obtained by promoting γ_1 and γ_2, except that in the case of Column's weighted frequencies a "demotion" of δ_2 is also required, as in comparison with H_r. Promotion of γ_2 means giving more weight to Column's forbearance, i.e., to a tendency to cooperate, as was noted in previous comparisons.

Comparing the values of the α's in games #48 and #72, we note that they are larger in the former, as would be expected since the natural outcome is an equilibrium in game #48 but not in game #72. After all, in game #72, Row's unilateral shift from S_1S_2 benefits both players, and Row can reasonably expect that Column will "stay put" so as to reap the benefit of Row's shift. That the average Row player does not shift more often from S_1S_2 may be attributed to Column's low "staying power" in T_1S_2, which discourages Row from seeking that outcome.

A possible reason for Column's smaller forbearance in game #72, compared with Row's in game #48, is that in game #72 Column gets less than Row in both the natural outcome and in T_1S_2. Perhaps this repeated experience with a relatively smaller payoff spurs Column to shift from T_1S_2 in pursuit of the largest payoff. In game #48 (at least in the variant used here) this situation does not obtain; in the natural outcome both players get the same payoff.

In taking the initiative by shifting to T_1S_2, Row *deliberately* accepts a temporary loss in order to effect the cooperative outcome T_1T_2 (at least those Row players who take this initiative can be expected to be so motivated). Therefore, once T_1T_2 is reached, Row refrains from shifting. He is the "active" player throughout.

All these conjectures are, of course, pure speculation. We hope, however, that some of the ideas that occur in the analysis of game experiments may stimulate further studies designed to answer some of the specific questions raised here.

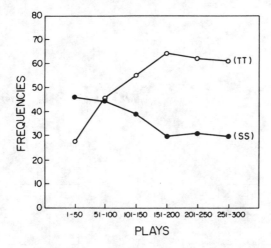

Fig. 12.1.   Time courses of outcome frequencies in game #48. There is evidence of learning: the frequency of the "cooperative" outcome (T_1T_2) increases at the expense of the frequency of the natural outcome.

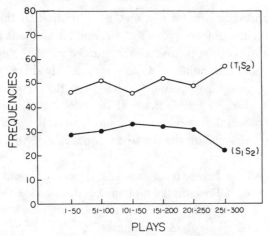

Fig. 12.2.   Time courses of outcome frequencies in game #72. There is no evidence of learning except for possible slight overall increases in the frequency of the "co-operative" outcome at the expense of the natural outcome.

13

Two Threat Games

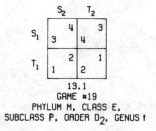

13.1
GAME #19
PHYLUM M. CLASS E.
SUBCLASS P. ORDER D_2. GENUS †

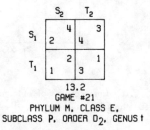

13.2
GAME #21
PHYLUM M. CLASS E.
SUBCLASS P. ORDER D_2. GENUS †

The characteristic feature of a threat game is that in the natural outcome one of the players (Row) is disgruntled and that the other player (Column) can "appease" the disgruntled player by occasional shifts from S_2 to T_2. In doing so, Column effectively shares a portion of the largest payoff with Row. On his part, Row must continue choosing S_1 in order to get his share. If Row does so, the proportion of the largest payoff that will accrue to him is entirely up to Column, since Column can regulate the relative frequencies of S_1S_2 and S_1T_2 as he pleases.

Recourse to T_1 is Row's threat against Column. Should Column refuse to share or if Row thinks he is not getting enough, Row can shift to T_1. If T_1S_2 results, Column will get less than he would have gotten in S_1T_2, i.e., if he shared "voluntarily."

In effecting T_1S_2, Row punishes himself as well as Column—in fact, himself more than Column on the ordinal scale. However, in switching to T_1, Row "tells" Column that he is not satisfied with his share. Column can "square things" with Row by shifting to T_2. If T_1T_2 results, Column gets even less than in T_1S_2, but he thereby gives Row the opportunity to effect S_1T_2, where he (Row) gets the largest payoff and Column the second largest. However, once Row has shifted to S_1, Column has the opportunity to reestablish the natural outcome by shifting to S_2.

Column can avoid outcomes T_1S_2 and T_1T_2 by sharing "voluntarily," thus removing Row's grievance and, presumably, his motivation to shift to T_1.

Note that in both game #19 and game #21 both players have a dominating strategy, S. The two games differ in the positions of Row's next to largest and next to smallest payoffs on the main diagonal.

On the ordinal scale, the discrepancy between Row's and Column's payoffs in S_1S_2 is larger in game #21 than in game #19. For this reason, we might expect that (S_1S_2) would be smaller in game #21, either because of the more frequent uses of the threat strategy by Row or because of more generous sharing by Column or both. We might also conjecture that T_1T_2 will occur more frequently in game #21, because Row might at times decide to be satisfied with the next-to-largest payoff, as in game #48 (cf. p. 179). However, this conjecture seems to be a tenuous one, in view of the fact that Column's payoff is smallest in T_1T_2. We can, perhaps, expect that Column might repeat T_2 following T_1T_2 in order to allow Row to get the largest payoff in S_1T_2. But if Row does not avail himself of this opportunity, Column can hardly be expected to let T_1T_2 continue.

The variants of games #19 and #21 used in the experiment are represented in 13.3 and 13.4.

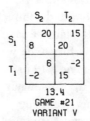

13.3
GAME #19
VARIANT VII

13.4
GAME #21
VARIANT V

The outcome frequencies in game #19 are shown in table 13.1. We observe equal sharing with no recourse to threat in only one

TABLE 13.1 Outcome frequencies in Game #19.

Pair	(S_1S_2)	(S_1T_2)	(T_1S_2)	(T_1T_2)
1	95	01	04	00
2	75	07	14	04
3	84	00	16	00
4	40	01	53	07
5	95	04	01	00
6	46	22	19	12
7	99	00	01	00
8	81	17	02	00
9	37	34	16	13
10	50	50	00	00
Means	70	14	13	03

pair (pair 10). Approximately equal frequencies of S_1S_2 and S_1T_2 occur also in pair 9. In pair 6, Row's share of the largest payoff is about one-third. In both pairs 6 and 9, however, Row must "work" for his share, as is seen in the relatively high frequencies of T_1S_2 and T_1T_2. In pair 8, the underdog gets about one-sixth, apparently given by Column, for the most part voluntarily, since (T_1S_2) is small. In the remaining pairs, Row gets a mere pittance, if anything. In three pairs (2, 3, and 4) Row resorted to his threat: in one instance with minimal success (a share of one-twelfth), in the other two instances, in vain. Note the sad lot of Row in pair 4, who resorted to T_1 60 percent of the time only to receive a share of one-fortieth. Finally, we observe three instances of almost complete submission by Row players in pairs 1, 5, and 7; they did not try to put pressure on Column and got next to nothing.

The outcome frequencies in game #21 are shown in table 13.2.

In these performances we observe an anomaly. In pair 3, Column, the top dog, submitted completely to Row, the underdog, giving him 100 percent of the largest payoff. (It might be pointed out that this is the only such performance we have observed among over 100 pairs playing either game #19 or game #21 in various experiments.) Pair 3 accounts for the somewhat lower average frequency of S_1S_2 and somewhat higher frequency of S_1T_2 in game #21, compared with game #19. Otherwise, the performances in the two games are rather similar. Approximately equal sharing occurs in pairs 1 and 10 (in pair 10, the underdog actually gets S_1T_2 44 percent of the time and

TABLE 13.2 Outcome frequencies in Game #21.

Pair	(S_1S_2)	(S_1T_2)	(T_1S_2)	(T_1T_2)
1	38	29	20	12
2	94	01	05	00
3	00	100	00	00
4	100	00	00	00
5	61	22	11	05
6	48	27	17	08
7	90	01	09	00
8	97	00	03	00
9	65	19	13	03
10	30	44	15	10
Means	62	24	09	04

more than one-half of the total largest payoffs). In three instances, the underdog gets one-third to one-fourth (pairs 5, 6, and 9) and in four instances, next to nothing. In all cases, except the anomalous one, Row had to "work" for his share at about the same rate as in game #19, that is, to resort to T_1 about 15–30 percent of the time.

Games #19 and #21 belong to the same class, order, and genus, so their structures are practically identical. Accordingly, the same interpretations of the repetition propensities are suggested in both games.

α_1: Row submits to Column's dominance or cooperates with Column.

β_1: Having "revolted," Row persists in his threat.

γ_1: Row is satisfied with the largest payoff. However, repeating S_1 after S_1T_2 also allows Column to restore the natural outcome. If Column shares "fairly," γ_1 reflects Row's cooperation.

δ_1: Row "distrusts" Column. Following T_1T_2, presumably effected by Column's "yielding" after T_1S_2, Row has the opportunity to get the largest payoff by shifting to S_1, provided Column allows S_1T_2 by repeating T_2. Therefore, Row's *failure* to shift to S_1 following T_1S_2 may be a reflection of distrust. By repeating T_1 after T_1T_2, Row restores the "threat" outcome T_1S_2 if Column "double-crosses" him by shifting to S_2.

α_2: Column does not share the largest payoff with Row.

β_2: Repeating T_2 after S_1T_2 looks like "generosity" on Column's part. In some protocols, however, where sharing is effected by alternating blocks of plays instead of play-by-play, β_2 may indicate Column's part in effecting the cooperative patterns.

γ_2: Column's "adamance"—he does not yield to Row's threat in T_1S_2.

δ_2: Column allows Row to get the largest payoff if Row "trusts" Column and switches to S_1.

Repetition propensities in game #19 are shown in table 13.3.

TABLE 13.3   Repetition propensities in Game #19.

Pair	α_1	β_1	γ_1	δ_1	α_2	β_2	γ_2	δ_2
1	98	39	33	00	99	00	91	00
2	88	33	60	50	97	60	79	33
3	96	79	--	--	100	--	100	--
4	54	74	67	75	98	00	87	100
5	99	00	92	--	97	25	100	--
6	83	57	73	58	71	36	60	42
7	99	00	--	--	100	--	100	--
8	98	00	100	--	100	100	100	--
9	71	50	78	22	07	100	85	82
10	100	--	100	--	01	01	--	--
Unweighted Means	89	37	75	41	77	40	89	51
Weighted Means	92	61	87	47	85	48	84	67

H_r prescribes the inequalities $\gamma_1 > \alpha_1 > \delta_1 > \beta_1$ and $\alpha_2 > \beta_2 > \gamma_2 > \delta_2$. We observe $\alpha_1 > \gamma_1 > \delta_1 > \beta_1$ among the unweighted means, $\alpha_1 > \gamma_1 > \beta_1 > \delta_1$ among weighted means. Apparently H_r is fairly well corroborated by the unweighted means of Row's observed propensities (except for a reversal between α_1 and γ_1). In Column's propensities, however, β_2 is demoted. H_s, on the other hand, prescribes $\alpha_1 > \gamma_1 > \delta_1 > \beta_1$ and $\gamma_2 > \alpha_2 > \beta_2 > \delta_2$. Row's propensities corroborate H_s, and Column's unweighted propensities almost do, except for a reversal between β_2 and δ_2.

In this game, the repetition propensities of interest are β_1 and γ_2. The former reflects Row's persistence in demanding that Column shift to T_2; the latter, Column's reluctance to do so. The low value of β_1 is accounted for by H_r and the high value of γ_2 by H_s. Therefore, no "interesting" psychological conjectures are suggested at this point. In chapter 16, however, when we examine the effects of payoff changes on these parameters, we shall observe some violations of H_m that do suggest such conjectures.

It is also interesting to compare α_2 and γ_2, or rather $\tilde{\alpha}_2$ and $\tilde{\gamma}_2$. $\tilde{\alpha}_2$ reflects Column's tendency to share voluntarily with Row, that is, after Row has cooperated; $\tilde{\gamma}_2$ is Column's tendency to yield to Row's threat. In game #19, $\tilde{\alpha}_2 = 23$, $\tilde{\gamma}_2 = 11$ unweighted—an indication that Column shares voluntarily more readily than "under threat." This inequality has been observed in several experiments with game #19. We shall encounter it again in chapter 16.

The repetition propensities in game #21 are shown in table 13.4.

TABLE 13.4   Repetition propensities in Game #21.

Pair	α_1	β_1	γ_1	δ_1	α_2	β_2	γ_2	δ_2
1	79	65	92	73	27	33	77	30
2	88	40	00	100	99	50	100	00
3	--	--	100	--	--	100	--	--
4	100	--	--	--	100	--	--	--
5	80	12	88	06	69	28	88	19
6	75	28	82	39	75	53	72	30
7	97	67	100	100	100	00	07	00
8	97	00	--	--	100	--	100	--
9	87	41	96	56	88	54	82	56
10	59	50	92	16	71	70	45	65
Unweighted Means	85	38	81	56	83	48	71	29
Weighted Means	89	43	94	41	87	66	65	40

H_r prescribes $\gamma_1 > \delta_1 > \alpha_1 > \beta_1$ and $\alpha_2 > \beta_2 > \gamma_2 > \delta_2$. Among the unweighted means, we observe $\alpha_1 > \gamma_1 > \delta_1 > \beta_1$ and $\alpha_2 > \gamma_2 > \beta_2 > \delta_2$. Numerically, the mean repetition propensities are quite close in the two games, although the differences are in the expected directions: interchanging Row's payoffs in $S_1 S_2$ and $T_1 T_2$ modifies α_1 and δ_1 appropriately, but the modification is not sufficient to reverse the inequalities. In Column's propensities, however, we do observe a reversal between α_2 and γ_2. Since, in game #21, Column's payoffs are identical to those in game #19, the reversal (if real) is a consequence of an indirect effect, i.e., of changes in the other player's payoffs or strategic structure. We shall have more to say about these effects in chapter 15 and 16.

Note also the low value of δ_2 (29–40) in game #21 compared with its value in game #19 (51–67). The significance of this difference is highly questionable in view of the fact that the outcome T_1T_2 occurs with very low frequencies in these games, sometimes not at all, which leaves δ_1 and δ_2 undefined. If, however, the difference is real, one might conjecture that it is due to competitive pressure. In our variant of game #21, the difference between payoffs d_1 and d_2 is numerically quite large in Row's favor. Under competitive pressure, this difference would induce Column to oppose Row's further gains. A repetition of T_2 permits Row to get the largest payoff by shifting to S_1. Hence, the low value of δ_2 may be a reflection of Column's reluctance to allow this to happen.

Intraprotocol interdependence of choices is shown in tables 13.5 and 13.6.

TABLE 13.5   Imitation propensities in Game #19.

Pair	σ_1	(S_1)	Bias	τ_1	(T_1)	Bias	σ_2	(S_2)	Bias	τ_2	(T_2)	Bias
1	96	96		01	04	-	99	99		10	01	-
2	85	82	+	44	18	+	88	89	-	24	11	+
3	81	84	-	--	16		100	100		00	00	
4	38	41	-	70	60	+	98	93	+	23	08	+
5	99	99		10	01	-	96	96		00	04	-
6	67	68	-	38	31	+	48	65	-	01	34	-
7	98	99	-	--	01		100	100		00	00	
8	97	98	-	00	02	-	83	83		00	17	-
9	50	71	-	20	29	-	37	53	-	45	47	-
10	50	100	-	00	00		00	50	-	--	50	

TABLE 13.6   Imitation propensities in Game #21.

Pair	σ_1	(S_1)	Bias	τ_1	(T_1)	Bias	σ_2	(S_2)	Bias	τ_2	(T_2)	Bias
1	43	67	-	27	32	-	53	58	-	26	41	-
2	27	95	-	100	05	+	98	99	-	00	01	-
3	--	100		00	00		00	00		--	100	
4	100	100		--	00		100	100		--	00	
5	50	83	-	22	16	+	27	72	-	14	27	-
6	29	75	-	23	25	-	29	65	-	29	35	-
7	29	91	-	00	09	-	100	99	+	100	01	+
8	97	97		--	09		100	100		00	00	
9	68	84	-	11	16	-	65	78	-	25	22	+
10	56	74	-	10	25	-	16	45	-	59	54	+

There is slight evidence of "negative imitation" with respect to S in game #19. The evidence of the same effect is stronger in game #21. If the effect were real, this would mean that a choice of S_2 by Column is an inducement to Row to choose T_1, and a choice of S_1 by Row is an inducement to Column to choose T_2. In a way, this makes sense: Row resents Column's choice of S in excess of what seems fair; hence there is a pressure on Row to resort to his threat strategy. On the other hand, the choice of S_1 by Row is an act of cooperation and may make Column more willing to share, i.e., choose T_2.

14

Summary of Part II

Although, strictly speaking, for reasons stated in the Introduction to Part II, the performances in the twelve iterated games cannot be compared with respect to structure alone, nevertheless, certain features emerge. We see, for instance, that the performances in games #6 and #61 vary widely, and we conjecture that the difference is to be attributed to the different structures of the games rather than to the magnitudes of the payoffs. Game #6 has two dominating strategies; game #61 has none. Even though both are no-conflict games, the mean frequencies of the natural outcome were observed to be widely different.

The same contrast is observed between game #36 and game #64. There is no competitive pressure on the natural outcome in either game. However, the former has one equilibrium, whereas the latter has two.

Game #64 might be called a pseudo-symmetric game. The payoff matrix looks symmetric in the sense that the payoffs of Row and Column are interchanged in the two symmetric outcomes and in the two asymmetric outcomes. Yet, the game is not symmetric since the natural outcome awards more to Column than to Row. From the data on iterated game #64, we see that the mean frequency of S_1S_2 (one equilibrium) is larger than that of T_1T_2 (the other equilibrium), a reflection of Column's strategic advantage in that game.

Pseudo-symmetric games offer the opportunity to achieve a "co-operative solution" via alternating between the two Pareto-optimal

196

outcomes. We call such a solution an "alternating cooperative solution." In genuinely symmetric games, e.g., game #68 and game #69, such a solution is, of course, available. From the data on games #19, #64, #68, and #69, we see that, while this solution is quite frequently achieved in symmetric games, it occurs but rarely in pseudo-symmetric games, at least in noncooperative games.[1]

Our variant of game #66 also had an alternating cooperative solution and it was achieved by practically all pairs; by some, almost immediately, by others, eventually. It is also possible to design variants of game #12 with alternating cooperative solutions by making 2d < b + c, and it would be interesting to see whether the solution is found as easily as it was in our variant of game #66. The only experiment with such a variant known to us was performed by P. Worchel (cf. p. 238). Unfortunately, the protocol was not published.

On the face of it, the impression is that the simple cooperative solution of games #12 and #66 would be easier to achieve than the alternating solution, because the latter requires more coordination of choices. But our results with game #66 throw doubt on that conjecture. It is possible that the very "delicacy of balance" of alternating a solution ensures its stability. Perhaps, when the players hit upon it, the "success" is so rewarding to both that they stick to it. It has a "rhythm," which may be more attractive to the players than a monotonous repetition of a simple cooperative solution.

If the standardized payoffs of the single-play experiment, 10, 1, −1, −10, had been used throughout the experiments with iterated games, we could compare the frequencies of the natural outcome in single plays with the frequencies in corresponding iterated games. Although the standardized payoffs were not used in other than games #12 and #66, we shall nevertheless make the comparison in order to check our conjectures. It seems reasonable to assume that the frequencies of the natural outcome should be considerably larger in single plays than in iterated plays in asymmetric games, where both players have a dominating strategy and where one of the players is disgruntled in the natural outcome. This is because in a single play,

---

[1] Although the variant of game #19 in chapter 13 was not pseudo-symmetric, it can be made so by proper choice of payoffs. Such variants are examined in chapters 16, 17, and 19. See, however, the strong influence of pseudo-symmetry in cooperative games in chapter 23.

Row (who is almost always the disgruntled player in our notation) can do nothing to force Column to shift away from the natural outcome and so possibly improve his own payoff, whereas in the iterated play he may be able to do so. Games #19 and #21 are of this sort. We would expect a similar effect in game #36, because, although only Column has a dominating strategy in this game, Row's rational choice is still S_1, and so the same reasoning applies. In games #12 and #48, the natural outcome is Pareto-deficient, although S is the individually rational choice for both players; we would, therefore, expect the same effect in these two games. In games #61, #64, #66, #68, #69, and #72, neither player has a dominating strategy; so, with respect to these games, the above conjecture cannot be justified. Nor can it be justified in game #6, a no-conflict game.

Table 14.1 shows the comparison of natural outcome frequencies observed in single plays (Frenkel's experiment, chapter 7) and in the variants of the corresponding games used in the experiments cited in chapters 8–13.

TABLE 14.1   Comparison of natural outcome frequencies in single and iterated plays.

Game	$[S_1 S_2]$ single play	$(S_1 S_2)$ iterated play
#6	69	81
#12	86	30
#19	95	70
#21	85	62
#36	85	80
#48	82	37
#61	21	63
#64	79	49
#66	22	05
#68	15	06
#69	74	15
#72	46	29

We observe that our conjecture is corroborated in games #12, #19, #21, #36, and #48. In fact, the same effect—a reduced frequency of $S_1 S_2$ in iterated games compared with single plays—is observed in all but two of the games. The exceptions are games #6 and #61. Both are no-conflict games with competitive pressure on the natural outcome. The indication is that competitive pressure exerts a considerable effect in single play but is lost in iterated play where the players presumably learn eventually that two can play "to beat the opponent," to the detriment of both.

Although all of these explanations may seem reasonable, much room is left for doubt. As already pointed out, the results of the experiments in chapters 8–13 and of those in chapter 7 are not, strictly speaking, comparable, because the standardization of numerical payoffs in the single play experiment was not carried through in the iterated play experiments. In one instance where it was carried out, it introduced an artifact that must be taken into account. Namely, in game #66, the presence of the alternating cooperative solution reduced (S_1S_2) to practically zero. As we shall see in chapter 16 in variants of Chicken, without an alternating cooperative solution, frequencies of S_1S_2 (the cooperative outcome in those games) are quite high. That is to say, the *level of cooperation* in long iterated runs of Chicken are typically high. Since cooperation in some variants of this game is achieved sometimes by fixating on S_1S_2 and in others by alternating between S_1T_2 and T_1S_2, a blanket statement about relative magnitudes of (S_1S_2) in single and in iterated plays cannot be made.

Payoffs were standardized also in game #12. The variant so obtained is identical to Variant III of Prisoner's Dilemma used previously by Rapoport and Chammah (cf. chapter 16) and by several others. For some reason, the level of cooperation obtained in this game in Perner's experiment reported in chapter 9, $(C) = 62$, was considerably higher than any of the earlier results. Rapoport and Chammah observed $(C) = 47$ under apparently similar conditions (runs of 300 plays) with subjects recruited from apparently similar populations. This raises the question of whether it makes sense at all to speak of a "standard experiment" in order to establish some inherent feature of a 2×2 game. We shall return to this point.

In examining the frequencies of S_1S_2 in Frenkel's experiment (cf. table 7.1), we were impressed by the low values in games #61, #66, and #68 (Leader). The latter is especially perplexing, because [S_1S_2] is quite high in game #69 (Hero), a game that seems to be closely related to Chicken. Referring to the payoff matrices of the standardized variants of games #61, #66, and #68 used in Frenkel's experiment, we find that in all of them the natural outcome is subjected to strong competitive pressure. In contrast, there is no competitive pressure on the natural outcome in game #69: the unilateral shifter suffers a competitive disadvantage.

Altogether, as will appear more clearly in chapter 23, competitive pressure plays a very important part in Frenkel's experiment, and we strongly suspect that the salience of competitive advantage was inadvertently introduced by the way the subjects were paid. Recall that each subject in that experiment filled out a booklet indicating his choice as both Row and Column in each of the seventy-eight games of the ordinal taxonomy. To decide the subject's total payoff, his performance was to be matched with another's so as to determine the outcomes. Actually, each subject's performance was matched with that of every other subject, and his total payoff was the average of accumulated points. This computation was done considerably later, after all the booklets were turned in. Thus, to get their payoffs, the subjects had to return some weeks afterward. Inevitably, it was expected that some would neglect to do so and some would become impatient, which introduced complications involving equity. It seemed less complicated to introduce incentive by offering several prizes for the highest scores achieved; that way, the prize winners could be simply contacted and paid off. At the time it did not seem that such an incentive would introduce strong competitive pressures. Presumably, as long as there were *several* prizes, it would behoove a hypothetical pair of players to try to cooperate even in single plays, at least in no-conflict games. Nevertheless, the results on the two no-conflict games, #6 and #61, suggest that competitive pressure had a telling effect. Evidently, competing even for several prizes, some of which were equal, creates the incentive to keep the opponent's score down, even at the cost of depressing one's own score, provided the "defections" hurt the other more than they hurt oneself.

To see the effects of competitive pressure under somewhat greater resolving power, Frenkel plotted the numbers of subjects who chose S with given frequencies. The distribution is shown in figure 14.1.

Bimodality is in evidence. Possibly, the secondary mode is due to the "competitors" who consistently defect even at cost to themselves if they get a competitive advantage thereby.

To see whether the prizes were indeed responsible for the bimodal distribution apparent in figure 14.1, Frenkel performed two additional pilot experiments. In the first, subjects were paid off in points

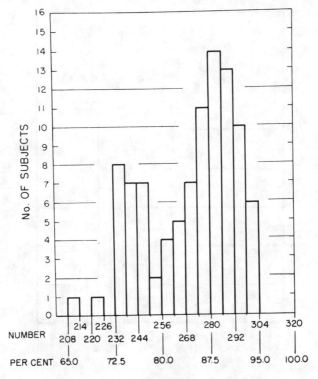

THE FREQUENCY OF CHOICE OF STRATEGY S
BY INDIVIDUAL SUBJECTS

Fig. 14.1.   Distribution of numbers of subjects choosing S the indicated number of times in Frenkel's experiment involving competitive pressure.

accumulated without the incentive of prizes. Although the number of subjects (forty) does not justify a reliable conclusion, it is nevertheless noteworthy that the secondary mode did disappear. The distribution was shifted toward the high S end, supporting the conjecture that many T choices in the original experiment were stimulated by competitive pressure (cf. figure 14.2). When, in the second pilot study, Frenkel reintroduced prizes as incentives, the distribution again showed a secondary mode.

Besides the artifact introduced by prizes, there is another aspect of Frenkel's experiment that throws doubt on the reliability of observed S frequencies as measures characteristic of the structure of the game. From the beginning, Frenkel was aware of the possibility

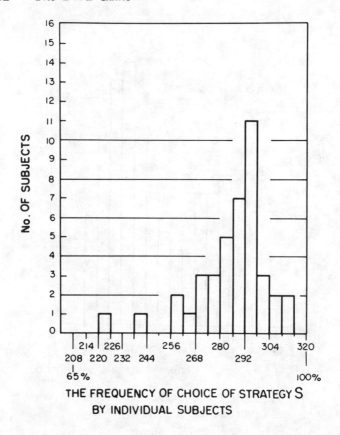

Fig. 14.2.   Distribution of numbers of subjects choosing S the indicated number of times in Frenkel's experiment not involving competitive pressure.

that the subjects would tend to make stereotyped choices dependent, to be sure, on the structure of the games, but not very sensitive to it. Examples of such stereotyped choices would be the following: (1) Always choose the maximin, that is, avoid the choice that contains −10 as one of its possible outcomes. (2) Assume that the co-player will choose either strategy with equal probabilities and choose so as to maximize expected payoffs. (3) Always choose the strategy that contains 10 as one of its possible outcomes, etc. Such stereotyped choices, though not entirely independent of the structure of the games, would preclude the complex effects of pressures and cross pressures, and this "homogenizing" of the data could be ascribed to the characteristic design of the experiment, which demands hundreds of choices from each subject. For despite having been instructed to do so, the subject could not be expected to examine each game thoroughly enough to make his choice on the basis of the particular pressures operating in it. It is far more likely that a subject would consciously or unconsciously follow some decision rule throughout the booklet. This danger was somewhat mitigated by the expectation that different subjects might design different rules. Since these rules would emerge only in the course of making successive choices, one might expect that the frequencies of the *rules* adopted would somehow reflect the influence of the game structures on choices.

Especially suspect are the S frequencies observed in game #12 and in game #19 in Frenkel's experiment. From table 7.1 we see that $[S_1 S_2]$ was 86 in game #12. Since the single choices are made entirely independently, this implies that [S] was 93. S being the "uncooperative" choice D, the frequency of the "cooperative" choice, C, was 07. In several other experiments involving single plays of Prisoner's Dilemma, [C] was quite consistently observed at around 40 (specifically, in Variant III used by Frenkel). Since in those other experiments the several games included were either other variants of Prisoner's Dilemma or no-conflict games, we conjecture that the "dilemma" remained salient, whereas in Frenkel's experiment it was "submerged" in the mixture of games with widely varying structures.

In game #19, the observed frequency of S_1 in Frenkel's experiment was 96; of S_2, 99. In another experiment involving 50 subjects, where game #19 was not "mixed" with any other, G. Harris (unpublished) obtained $[S_1] = 56$, $[S_2] = 100$. While Harris's $[S_2]$ agrees with Frenkel's and corroborates our conjecture that, in a single play of game #19, there is no rationale for playing T, there is a strong discrepancy in $[S_1]$. Apparently Harris's Rows did resort to the threat strategy, even though from the standpoint of improving their own payoffs it was absolutely useless to do so in single plays. The large number of T choices can hardly be ascribed to randomness, because Harris's *Columns* did not depart. Only the Rows in the roles of the underdog apparently chose to get a smaller payoff if in the process they could make the top dog get a smaller one too.

It is possible that the discrepancy is due to the variants of game #19 used in the two experiments. Harris's was variant III, shown on page 204 compared with Frenkel's.

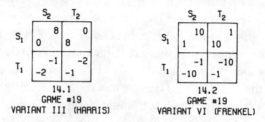

14.1
GAME #19
VARIANT III (HARRIS)

14.2
GAME #19
VARIANT VI (FRENKEL)

Note that the discrepancies between the top dog's and the underdog's payoffs in the Pareto-optimal outcomes of the two variants are comparable. However, the cost of revolt to the underdog is more severe in Frenkel's variant than in Harris's, and this may account for the much more frequent resort to T_1 by Harris's subjects. However, when we examine the T_1 frequencies in iterated game #19 in a number of experiments (to be discussed in chapters 16 and 19), we note that they are at times in the range from 40 to 50. Since Harris's frequency (44) falls within that range, we cannot say that the frequency of T_1 choices in single plays is significantly smaller than in iterated plays. Therefore, our conjecture above, to the effect that in single plays at least a dominant strategy containing a Pareto-optimal equilibrium will be chosen almost exclusively, remains an open question.

The foregoing discussion suggests that the task of determining certain behavioral regularities as functions of game structures alone is much more complex, if possible at all, than it may first appear. We confess, we entertained some hopes of affixing at least modal choice frequencies to each of the seventy-eight games of the ordinal taxonomy played under some standard conditions, either as single plays or as long iterated runs. We may have semi-consciously entertained hopes of duplicating a "table of elements," each characterized by an analogue of an "atomic weight," or something of the sort. In the light of sobering experience, it appears that obtaining these "elements" in sufficient "purity" is a formidable task.

How shall a 2×2 game be standardized? The first question is, What variant should be chosen? Clearly, if the species of the game rather than a particular variant is of interest, the two sets of four payoffs to the two subjects must be identical, so that the game species differ from each other only in the way the payoffs are placed in the matrix. But what should be the numerical value of the four payoffs? Should some be negative? Should they be equally spaced? Frenkel's choice of 10, 1, −1, and −10 was guided by the apparent symmetry of the two positive and two negative payoffs. The magnitudes were not equally spaced to allow for the supposed larger psychological difference between a positive and a negative payoff. As it turned out, this may have been a mistake in the context of the experiment. Since the subjects were not paid immediately following each choice, the salience of loss associated even with the small negative payoff may not have been felt. Consequently, the intervals between 10 and 1 and between −1 and −10 may have been perceived to be considerably larger than those between 1 and −1, which seems to be reflected in the choices attributable to competitive advantage. This effect appears to be larger when the difference between the players' payoffs in a particular outcome is 9 than when it is 2, despite the fact that in the latter case the payoffs are of opposite sign.

If the payoffs are equally spaced, then in game #66 $2a = b + c$. This means that both S_1S_2 and the alternation between S_1T_2 and T_1S_2 are equally good cooperative solutions. Is this an experimental advantage or disadvantage? On the one hand, the availability of two cooperative solutions complicates the analysis of the protocols. On the other hand, it provides the opportunity to compare the relative frequency of each solution and to test the above conjecture to the effect that the alternating cooperative solution, although possibly more difficult to achieve, would be more stable *because* it is more difficult to achieve and also because it locks the players into a rhythm instead of requiring monotonous repetition. In other words, the alternations between "giving" and "taking" may well be conducive to the "firming" of cooperation.

Possibly the only way to get at the "pure" structure of a 2×2 game is to present it with ordinal payoffs only, labeled "largest," "next-to-largest," "next-to-smallest," and "smallest," as was suggested in the Introduction to Part II. Nigel Howard, who experiments with meta-games (cf. p. 62), often insists that a decision maker faced with alternative outcomes has a clear conception only of his preference order for the outcomes, not for the *degrees* of preference. Whether this is so surely depends on the situation. It may be true whenever outcomes are distinguished qualitatively rather than quantitatively, or involve intangibles. Many decisions, however, are made in precisely defined quantitative contexts, involving amounts of money, measurable outputs, indices of efficiency, etc. In fact, statistical decision theory is based entirely on the possibility of defining utilities of outcomes at least on an interval scale. Be that as it may, for purposes of standardizing experiments with 2 × 2 games in order to examine behavior with reference to structure alone, restricting payoffs to a scale no stronger than an ordinal one is probably the indicated procedure. Except for Howard's experiments, we know of no game experiments where this is done. And even Howard's technique does not quite eliminate the impression of cardinality of payoffs, since he designates them by successive positive integers in the increasing order of preference, which may be interpreted as equally spaced numerically defined utilities.

Once the structure of the game remains as the only variable inherent to a game, the problem is still how to standardize the subject. There is, of course, no "standard subject" analogous to standard conditions of pressure and temperature in physico-chemical experiments, although the near-exclusive use of college students in game experiments amounts to an (unfortunate) tacit definition of one. The only way to create a "standard subject" is by using a sufficiently large and sufficiently representative sample of the entire human race —to date, a pipe dream. Unavoidably, we must continue to rely on whatever data are obtainable to construct a base line for comparing game species. The immediate goal is to get an idea, at least of the relative importance of the various pressures, generated in the 2 × 2 game by the interaction of strategic considerations and psychological factors.

Part III

15

Effects of Payoffs in Single Play

The most direct method of assessing the effects of payoffs on performance is by varying one payoff at a time, keeping the other seven constant. However, in the case of symmetric games it may be desirable to preserve numerical symmetry. If symmetry is to be preserved, the corresponding payoffs of the two players, e.g., a_1 and a_2, b_1 and b_2, etc., must be varied equally and simultaneously. Varying payoffs in the same game species (that is, examining performances on different variants of the game) is the most natural way of testing the monotonicity hypothesis, H_m.

H_m relates to the effect on a player's performance of changes in his own payoffs. These effects will be called *direct*. It is also possible to examine the effects on a player's choices of variations in his co-player's payoffs. These effects will be called *indirect*. We shall have occasion to examine both direct and indirect effects and to compare them.

In this chapter, we examine the effects of payoffs in single-play experiments, where the only dependent variables are $[S_1]$ and $[S_2]$, the respective fractions of populations of players choosing S as Row or Column.

At first thought, we might take as a measure of the effect of payoff changes the ratio of frequency changes ΔS_i to payoff changes Δg, where g may be a_i, b_i, c_i, or d_i ($i = 1, 2$). However, this ratio might be misleading because of the "floor and ceiling" effects of frequencies. For instance, if a frequency of 95 is observed in some variant of a game, and if a large change in some payoff pushes the frequency up to 97, the observed change of frequency per unit of payoff change will seem small, but it cannot possibly be much larger because there is very little room for the frequency to increase. We shall, therefore, transform the choice frequencies in such a way that their range—that is, the interval $(0, 1)$—will be projected on the entire real axis $(-\infty, +\infty)$. Specifically, if p is a choice frequency, we shall examine

$$q \equiv \log \frac{p}{1-p}. \tag{15.1}$$

Note that as p tends to zero, q tends to $-\infty$, and as p tends to 1, q tends to $+\infty$. Accordingly,

$$
\begin{aligned}
\Delta q &= \log\left[\frac{p+\Delta p}{1-(p+\Delta p)}\right] - \log\left[\frac{p}{1-p}\right] \\
&\log\left[\frac{p+\Delta p - p^2 - p\,\Delta p}{p - p^2 - p\,\Delta p}\right] = \log\left(1 + \frac{\Delta p}{p(1-p-\Delta p)}\right).
\end{aligned}
\tag{15.2}
$$

Since p is confined to the interval $(0, 1)$, Δp must always be less than $1-p$ if positive, and greater than $p-1$ if negative. Accordingly, for a fixed Δp, we have

$$
\begin{aligned}
\frac{d}{dp}(\Delta q) &= \frac{1}{(p+\Delta p)(1-p-\Delta p)} - \frac{1}{p(1-p)} \\
&= \frac{\Delta p(\Delta p + 2p - 1)}{p(1-p)(p+\Delta p)(1-p-\Delta p)},
\end{aligned}
\tag{15.3}
$$

where the denominator is always positive. Hence, for a fixed positive Δp, Δq increases in magnitude as p becomes large, and for a fixed negative Δp, Δq increases in magnitude as p becomes small, counteracting the ceiling and floor effects.

Recall also that if p, the fraction of S choices in a sample of plays or the fraction of a population sample choosing S, is a binomially distributed random variable, its variance is proportional to $p(1-p)$, where p is the corresponding fraction of the parent population. The variance, therefore, becomes small when p is near 0 or 1, so that small changes in p are more significant near the extreme values, which is a qualitative justification for transforming p to $\log\left[\frac{p}{1-p}\right]$.

Note further that interchanging p and $p+\Delta p$ or p and $1-p$ amounts to changing the signs of both Δp and Δq. This means that the magnitude of Δq remains invariant whether we take the larger or the smaller choice frequency as the fixed reference and whether we consider a change in S or a corresponding change in T as the dependent variable. These properties of $\log \left[\dfrac{p}{1-p} \right]$ make it a convenient dependent variable.

For our independent variable we shall take $\Delta u = \log (1 + \Delta g)$, where Δg is the change in a payoff. The logarithmic function reflects the frequent observation that the "subjective" perception of changes of stimulus suffers "diminishing returns." If we took simply the change of payoff Δg as the independent variable, we would find that when Δg is very large the effectiveness of payoff change expressed as the absolute value of ratio $\Delta q/\Delta g$ would be very small due to the "diminishing returns" effect.[1] The logarithmic transformation of Δg tends to reduce the variation of $|\Delta q/\Delta g|$ due to the "diminishing returns" effect. As we shall see, considerable variation of $|\Delta q/\Delta u|$ still remains. We can with somewhat greater justification attribute this variation to the differences in the salience of the various payoffs.

Frenkel's Experiment

A single-play experiment by O. Frenkel (cf. chapter 7) also included besides the seventy-eight games of the ordinal taxonomy some variants, namely of games #6, #12, #21, #48, and #66.

The results will be presented as follows: the numbers to the left of the upper left cell of each matrix are the observed $[S_1]$; those above the same cell are the observed $[S_2]$. In the case of symmetric games, the number at the upper left corner of the matrix represents $[S]$, the fraction of the whole population of players choosing S. Each group of matrices will be followed by a table, showing the logarithmic magnitudes of payoff changes, i.e., $\Delta u = \log(1 + \Delta g)$, the frequency of S in the first of the variants compared (always the one with the smaller payoff), the change of frequency, the change in q, and the magnitude of the effect defined as $|\Delta q/\Delta u|$. Since the variants are among those used in Rapoport and Chammah's

---

[1] The question might be raised why we do not use $\Delta g/g$ for our measure of "perceived" payoff change, by analogy with the so-called Weber-Fechner law of psychophysics. This ratio makes sense only if Δg is small relative to g. Our changes in payoffs, however, are comparable in magnitude to the payoffs themselves, and at times considerably larger.

Prisoner's Dilemma (1965) they are numbered as in that book. H_m will be considered corroborated if Δq is positive whenever a or c increases, and negative whenever b or d increases.

The analogous rule concerning indirect effects requires some elucidation. We shall suppose that, if a player's payoff changes, the co-player will assume that the first player's probabilities of choice will change in accordance with H_m. Now, if the second player has no dominating strategy, the expected change in his choice probabilities induced by the change in the first player's choice probability is clear; because, in that case, the second player's preferred choice depends on the first player's choice. This argument cannot be extended to games where the second player has a dominating strategy, for in that case he is expected to prefer this strategy regardless of the first player's choice. Therefore, in those cases, we shall adopt the following convention: the change in the second player's choice probabilities will depend on the shift hypothesis H_s. For instance, suppose S is Column's dominating strategy, but shifting away from S when Row chooses S involves a greater loss than when Row chooses T. Then, if a change in one of Row's payoffs increases the likelihood that Row will choose S, we shall suppose that the likelihood of Column's choosing S will increase, and vice versa. This analogue of H_m for indirect effects will be called $H_m{}'$.

Results of Frenkel's Experiments

Varying $(c - b)$ in Game #12

15.1
GAME #12
VARIANT IV

15.2
GAME #12
VARIANT III

15.3
GAME #12
VARIANT V

TABLE 15.1 Effects of changing (c-b) on [S] in Game #12.

VC	Δu	[S]	Δ [S]	Δq	e	H_m
IV, III	1.23	84	09	.40	.33	Yes
III, V	1.92	93	01	.07	.04	Yes

Varying d in Game #12

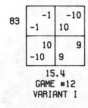

83

15.4
GAME #12
VARIANT I

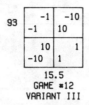

93

15.5
GAME #12
VARIANT III

TABLE 15.2 Effect of varying d on [S] in Game #12.

VC	Δu	[S]	Δ [S]	Δq	e	H_m
III, I	.95	93	-10	-.43	.45	Yes

Varying a in Game #12

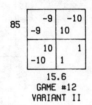

85

15.6
GAME #12
VARIANT II

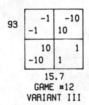

93

15.7
GAME #12
VARIANT III

TABLE 15.3 Effect of changing a in [S] in Game #12.

VC	Δu	[S]	Δ [S]	Δq	e	H_m
II, III	.95	85	08	.37	.39	Yes

Varying d in Game #66

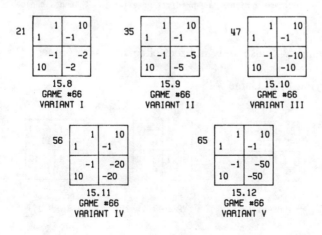

21

15.8
GAME #66
VARIANT I

35

15.9
GAME #66
VARIANT II

47

15.10
GAME #66
VARIANT III

56

15.11
GAME #66
VARIANT IV

65

15.12
GAME #66
VARIANT V

TABLE 15.4 Effects of changing d on [S] in Game #66.

VC	Δ u	[S]	Δ [S]	Δ q	e	H_m
V, IV	1.49	65	-09	-.16	.11	Yes
IV, III	1.04	56	-09	-.16	.15	Yes
III, II	.78	47	-12	-.22	.28	Yes
II, I	.60	35	-14	-.31	.51	Yes

Next, the results of Frenkel's game #21 will be examined. Here b_1 was the payoff changed, and the variants were presented only from the standpoint of Column. Therefore, the effects were indirect.

Varying a_1 in Game #21

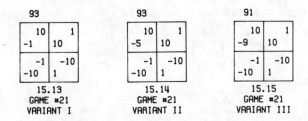

15.13
GAME #21
VARIANT I

15.14
GAME #21
VARIANT II

15.15
GAME #21
VARIANT III

TABLE 15.5 Indirect effects of changing a_1 on [S_2] in Game #21.

VC	Δ u	[S_2]	Δ [S_2]	Δ q	e	H_m'
III, II	.70	91	02	.12	.17	No*
II, I	.70	93	00	.00	.00	Yes*

*In these variants, H_s predicts <u>no</u> effect on Column's choice.

In game #48 also, only indirect effects were examined.

Varying b_1 in Game #48

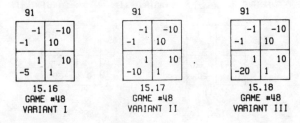

15.16
GAME #48
VARIANT I

15.17
GAME #48
VARIANT II

15.18
GAME #48
VARIANT III

TABLE 15.6   Indirect effects of changing b_1 on $[S_2]$ in Game #48.

VC	Δu	$[S_2]$	$\Delta [S_2]$	Δq	e	H_m'
III, II	1.04	91	00	.00	.00	Yes*
II, I	.78	91	00	.00	.00	Yes*

*In these variants, H_s predicts <u>no</u> effect on Column's choice.

Finally, we examine the effects of changing payoffs in game #6.
Varying b in Game #6

15.19
GAME #6
VARIANT I

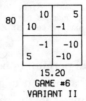

15.20
GAME #6
VARIANT II

TABLE 15.7   Effect of changing b on $[S]$ in Game #6.

VC	Δu	$[S]$	$\Delta [S]$	Δq	e	H_m
I, II	.70	83	-03	-.09	.13	Yes

Varying c in Game #6

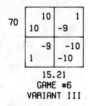

15.21
GAME #6
VARIANT III

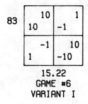

15.22
GAME #6
VARIANT I

TABLE 15.8   Effect of changing c on $[S]$ in Game #6.

VC	Δu	$[S]$	$\Delta [S]$	Δq	e	H_m
III, I	.95	70	13	.32	.34	Yes

Guyer's Experiment

The next single-play experiments were performed by M. Guyer
(Guyer and Rapoport, 1972). Here only seven games were used.
Each appeared in several variants as shown in table 15.9, and each

TABLE 15.9 Design of a single play experiment on seven games.

Game #	Number of variants	Number of permutations	Total presentations
6*	3	4	12
21	7	8	56
48	7	8	56
64	5	8	40
68*	5	4	20
69*	5	4	20
72	5	8	40

*Symmetric game. Since, in these games, relabeling the players does not produce a different permutation, there are only four permutations instead of eight as in non-symmetric games.

variant in several permutations.

Playing each asymmetric game as Row and as Column, each player found himself in the same strategic position four times. The subjects were 214 male undergraduates at the University of Michigan. Similarly as in Frenkel's experiment, each subject was given the games in the form of a stack of cards (244) which he took with him and returned filled out.

Results of Guyer's Experiment

Varying c in Game #6

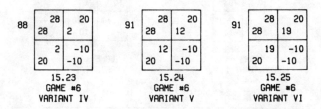

TABLE 15.10 Effects of changing c on [S] in Game #6.

VC	Δ u	[S]	Δ [S]	Δ q	e	H$_m$
IV, V	1.04	88	03	.14	.13	Yes
V, VI	.90	91	00	.00	.00	No

Varying a_1 in Game #21

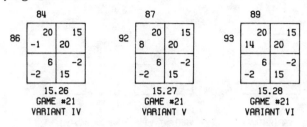

15.26
GAME #21
VARIANT IV

15.27
GAME #21
VARIANT V

15.28
GAME #21
VARIANT VI

TABLE 15.11 Direct effects of changing a_1 on $[S_1]$ in Game #21.

VC	Δ u	$[S_1]$	Δ $[S_1]$	Δ q	e	H_m
IV, V	1.00	86	06	.27	.27	Yes
V, VI	.85	92	01	.07	.08	Yes

TABLE 15.12 Indirect effects of changing a_1 on $[S_2]$ in Game #21.

VC	Δ u	$[S_2]$	Δ $[S_2]$	Δ q	e	H_m'
IV, V	1.00	84	03	.10	.10	No
V, VI	.85	87	02	.08	.10	No

Varying c_2 in Game #21

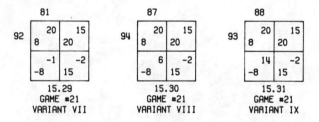

15.29
GAME #21
VARIANT VII

15.30
GAME #21
VARIANT VIII

15.31
GAME #21
VARIANT IX

TABLE 15.13 Direct effects of changing C_2 on $[S_2]$ in Game #21.

VC	Δ u	$[S_2]$	Δ $[S_2]$	Δ q	e	H_m
VII, VIII	.90	81	06	.20	.22	Yes
VIII, IX	.95	87	01	.04	.04	Yes

TABLE 15.14 Indirect effects of changing C_2 on $[S_1]$ in Game #21.

VC	Δ u	$[S_1]$	Δ $[S_1]$	Δ q	e	H_m
VII, VIII	.90	92	02	.13	.14	Yes
VIII, IX	.95	94	-01	-.07	.07	No

Varying b_1 in Game #21

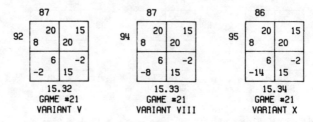

TABLE 15.15 Direct effects of changing b_1 on $[S_1]$ in Game #21.

VC	Δu	$[S_1]$	$\Delta [S_1]$	Δq	e	H_m
X, VIII	.85	95	-01	-.08	.09	Yes
VIII, V	.85	94	-02	-.13	.15	Yes

TABLE 15.16 Indirect effects of changing b_1 on $[S_2]$ in Game #21.

VC	Δu	$[S_2]$	$\Delta [S_2]$	Δq	e	H'_m
X, VIII	.85	86	01	.04	.05	Yes
VIII, V	.85	87	00	.00	.00	No

Varying b_1 in Game #48

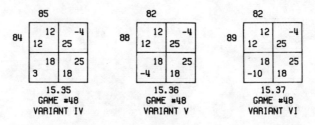

TABLE 15.17 Direct effects of changing b_1 on $[S_1]$ in Game #48.

VC	Δu	$[S_1]$	$\Delta [S_1]$	Δq	e	H_m
VI, V	.85	89	-01	-.04	.05	Yes
V, IV	.90	88	-04	-.15	.17	Yes

TABLE 15.18 Indirect effects of changing b_1 on $[S_2]$ in Game #48.

VC	Δu	$[S_2]$	$\Delta [S_2]$	Δq	e	H'_m
VI, V	.85	82	00	.00	.00	No
V, IV	.90	82	03	.09	.10	No

Varying d_1 in Game #48

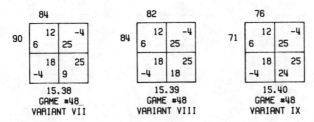

15.38
GAME #48
VARIANT VII

15.39
GAME #48
VARIANT VIII

15.40
GAME #48
VARIANT IX

TABLE 15.19 Direct effects of changing d_1 on $[S_1]$ in Game #48.

VC	Δ u	$[S_1]$	Δ $[S_1]$	Δ q	e	H_m
VII, VIII	1.00	90	-06	-.23	.23	Yes
VIII, IX	.85	84	-13	-.33	.39	Yes

TABLE 15.20 Indirect effects of changing d_1 in $[S_2]$ in Game #48.

VC	Δ u	$[S_2]$	Δ $[S_2]$	Δ q	e	H_m'
VII, VIII	1.00	84	-02	-.06	.06	Yes
VIII, IX	.85	82	-04	-.11	.13	Yes

Varying a_1 in Game #48

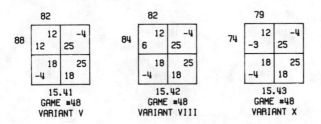

15.41
GAME #48
VARIANT V

15.42
GAME #48
VARIANT VIII

15.43
GAME #48
VARIANT X

TABLE 15.21 Direct effects of changing a_1 on $[S_1]$ in Game #48.

VC	Δ u	$[S_1]$	Δ $[S_1]$	Δ q	e	H_m
X, VIII	1.00	74	10	.27	.27	Yes
VIII, V	.85	84	04	.15	.18	Yes

TABLE 15.22 Indirect effects of changing a_1 on $[S_2]$ in Game #48.

VC	Δ u	$[S_2]$	Δ $[S_2]$	Δ q	e	H_m'
X, VIII	1.00	79	03	.08	.08	No
VIII, V	.85	82	00	.00	.00	No

Varying b_1 in Game #64

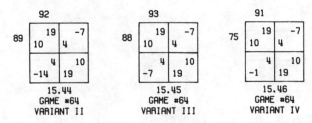

TABLE 15.23 Direct effects of changing b_1 on $[S_1]$ in Game #64.

VC	Δ u	$[S_1]$	Δ $[S_1]$	Δ q	e	H_m
II, III	.90	89	-01	-.04	.04	Yes
III, IV	.85	88	-13	-.39	.46	Yes

TABLE 15.24 Indirect effects of changing b_1 on $[S_2]$ in Game #64.

VC	Δ u	$[S_2]$	Δ $[S_2]$	Δ q	e	H'_m
II, III	.90	92	01	.06	.07	No
III, IV	.85	93	-02	-.12	.14	Yes

Varying a_1 in Game #64

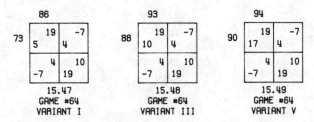

TABLE 15.25 Direct effects of changing a_1 on $[S_1]$ in Game #64.

VC	Δ u	$[S_1]$	Δ $[S_1]$	Δ q	e	H_m
I, III	.78	73	15	.43	.56	Yes
III, V	.90	88	02	.09	.10	Yes

TABLE 15.26 Indirect effects of changing a_1 on $[S_2]$ in Game #64.

VC	Δ u	$[S_2]$	Δ $[S_2]$	Δ q	e	H'_m
I, III	.78	86	07	.33	.42	Yes
III, V	.90	93	01	.07	.08	Yes

Varying b in Game #68

15.50
GAME #68
VARIANT I

15.51
GAME #68
VARIANT I

15.52
GAME #68
VARIANT III

TABLE 15.27 Effects of changing b on [S] in Game #68.

VC	Δ u	[S]	Δ [S]	Δ q	e	H_m
III, II	.78	83	-06	-.16	.21	Yes
II, I	1.08	77	-09	-.20	.18	Yes

Varying d in Game #68

15.53
GAME #68
VARIANT II

15.54
GAME #68
VARIANT IV

15.55
GAME #68
VARIANT V

TABLE 15.28 Effects of changing d on [S] in Game #68.

VC	Δ u	[S]	Δ [S]	Δ q	e	H_m
I, IV	.78	79	-02	-.05	.06	Yes
IV, II	.85	77	00	.00	.00	No

Varying b in Game #69

15.56
GAME #69
VARIANT I

15.57
GAME #69
VARIANT III

15.58
GAME #69
VARIANT V

TABLE 15.29 Effects of changing b on [S] in Game #69.

VC	Δ u	[S]	Δ [S]	Δ q	e	H_m
V, III	.78	91	-08	-.32	.41	Yes
III, I	.95	83	-07	-.18	.19	Yes

Varying c in Game #69

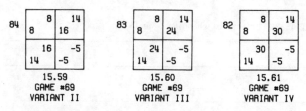

15.59
GAME #69
VARIANT II

15.60
GAME #69
VARIANT III

15.61
GAME #69
VARIANT IV

TABLE 15.30 Effects of changing c on [S] in Game #69.

VC	Δ u	[S]	Δ [S]	Δ q	e	H_m
II, III	.95	84	-01	-.03	.03	No
III, IV	.85	83	-01	-.03	.04	No

Varying a₁ in Game #72

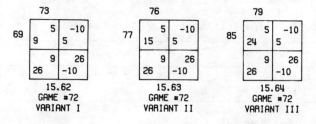

15.62
GAME #72
VARIANT I

15.63
GAME #72
VARIANT II

15.64
GAME #72
VARIANT III

TABLE 15.31 Direct effects of changing a_1 on $[S_1]$ in Game #72.

VC	Δ u	[S_1]	Δ [S_1]	Δ q	e	H_m
I, II	.85	69	08	.17	.20	Yes
II, III	1.00	77	08	.23	.23	Yes

TABLE 15.32 Indirect effects of changing a_1 on $[S_2]$ in Game #72.

VC	Δ u	[S_2]	Δ [S_2]	Δ q	e	H'_m
I, II	.85	73	03	.07	.08	Yes
II, III	1.00	76	03	.08	.08	Yes

Varying c_2 in Game #72

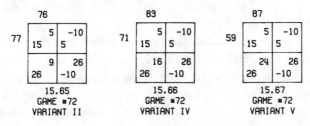

15.65
GAME #72
VARIANT II

15.66
GAME #72
VARIANT IV

15.67
GAME #72
VARIANT V

TABLE 15.33   Direct effects of changing C_2 on $[S_2]$ in Game #72.

VC	Δ u	$[S_2]$	$\Delta [S_2]$	Δ q	e	H_m
II, IV	.90	76	07	.19	.21	Yes
IV, V	.95	83	04	.14	.15	Yes

TABLE 15.34   Indirect effects of changing C_2 on $[S_1]$ in Game #72.

VC	Δ u	$[S_1]$	$\Delta [S_1]$	Δ q	e	H_m'
II, IV	.90	77	-06	-.14	.16	Yes
IV, V	.95	71	-12	-.23	.24	Yes

Single Plays of Conflict-Cooperation Games

Rapoport, et al. (1967) performed a single-play experiment using several variants of Prisoner's Dilemma, of Chicken, and of some no-conflict games. The former two species illustrate most directly the choice between conflict and cooperation. "No-conflict" games, formally speaking, involve no conflict of interests. We have seen, however, that competitive pressure often induces players to shift from the natural outcome even if both get their largest payoff there.

The experiment was performed under two conditions, "with feedback" (F) and "without feedback" (NF). The purpose of the feedback condition was to eliminate interaction between the co-players but, possibly, not the effect of experience. The subjects played successive games against unknown players, the co-player being changed at each play. In this way (it was assumed) the continuing interaction between co-players was eliminated. On the strength of this assumption, the experiment under this condition is subsumed under "single play." However, since the players were informed of the outcome of each play, it might be supposed that experience did play some part in determining choice. For instance, since several variants of the same game were presented (say, of Prisoner's Dilemma), the subjects may have learned something from the outcomes, perhaps that "cooperation does not (or does) pay in this sort of game," even though the result of each play gave less indication about the next partner's probable choice than in iterated games against the same co-player.

In the no-feedback condition, the subjects were not informed of the outcomes of the plays. This condition, therefore, was essentially the same as that in Frenkel's and in Guyer's experiments, except that the subjects made their choices in the experimental session instead of in a "take home" task.

Results of Rapoport, et al. Experiment

Varying d in Game #12 in the Feedback Condition

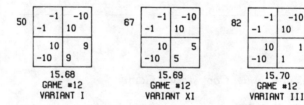

	-1	-10
50	-1	10
	10	9
	-10	9

15.68
GAME #12
VARIANT I

	-1	-10
67	-1	10
	10	5
	-10	5

15.69
GAME #12
VARIANT XI

	-1	-10
82	-1	10
	10	1
	-10	1

15.70
GAME #12
VARIANT III

TABLE 15.35 Effects of changing d on [S] in Game #12, cond. F.

VC	Δ u	[S]	Δ [S]	Δ q	e	H_m
III, XI	.70	82	-15	-.35	.50	Yes
XI, I	.70	67	-17	-.31	.44	Yes

Varying (c − b) in Game #12 in the Feedback Condition

	-1	-2
51	-1	2
	2	1
	-2	1

15.71
GAME #12
VARIANT IV

	-1	-10
82	-1	10
	10	1
	-10	1

15.72
GAME #12
VARIANT III

	-1	-50
88	-1	50
	50	1
	-50	1

15.73
GAME #12
VARIANT V

TABLE 15.36 Effects of changing c-b on [S] in Game #12, cond. F.

VC	Δ u	[S]	Δ [S]	Δ q	e	H_m
IV, III	1.23	51	31	.64	.52	Yes
III, V	1.92	82	06	.21	.11	Yes

Varying a in Game #12 in the Feedback Condition

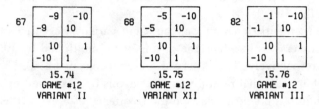

15.74
GAME #12
VARIANT II

15.75
GAME #12
VARIANT XII

15.76
GAME #12
VARIANT III

TABLE 15.37 Effects of changing a on [S] in Game #12, cond. F.

VC	Δ u	[S]	Δ [S]	Δ q	e	H_m
II, XII	.70	67	01	.02	.03	Yes
XII, III	.70	68	14	.33	.47	Yes

The analogous results in the no-feedback condition are shown in table 15.38.

TABLE 15.38 Effects of changing payoffs on [S] in Game #12, cond. NF.

VC	PC	Δ u	[S]	Δ [S]	Δ q	e	H_m
III, XI	d	.70	62	-02	-.04	.06	Yes
XI, I	d	.70	60	-02	-.03	.04	Yes
IV, III	c-b	1.23	53	09	.16	.13	Yes
III, V	c-b	1.92	62	03	.06	.03	Yes
II, XII	a	.70	60	01	.02	.03	Yes
XII, III	a	.70	61	01	.02	.03	Yes

It has been argued that the absolute magnitudes of the payoffs in Prisoner's Dilemma are important determinants of choice. That is, if all the payoffs of a given variant are multiplied by a constant, thus increasing or reducing the "stakes," the frequencies of choices are expected to change. However, there seems to be no agreement among the proponents of this view on whether "raising the stakes" (without changing their relative magnitudes) is expected to enhance or to inhibit the frequency of cooperative choices. To test the effect of multiplying all the payoffs by a constant, variant IV of Prisoner's Dilemma (cf. p. 212) was presented in two additional versions in the feedback condition. In one, all the payoffs were multiplied by 10, in the other, by 50. The S frequencies observed in the three versions were 51, 67, and 53 respectively. The comparatively high value of S in the second version seems anomalous. At any rate, no clear trend is discernible.

In the no-feedback condition, the same variant was used along with three versions in which the payoffs were multiplied by 10, 20, and 100 respectively. The observed S frequencies were 53, 53, 57, and 52. It appears that multiplying the payoffs by a constant up to a hundredfold has no clear effect on the frequency of S. Nevertheless, it should be pointed out that even the largest stakes here represent only small monetary values. Thus the maximum gains or losses in the "magnified" versions of Prisoner's Dilemma were still only 20¢ in a single play. We still do not know how a pair of millionaires would choose in a single play of this variant if a point were worth a million dollars. Unfortunately, it would be difficult to find a couple of millionaires who would agree to submit to an experiment of this sort.

In the next set of games, only competitive pressure is operative. These are borderline or "degenerate" games from the complete set, having equal payoffs to the same player in different outcomes. In these games, we define as the natural outcome the one that gives *both* players the largest payoff. Note that, given the choice of the co-player, a player concerned only with his own payoffs is indifferent between his two choices, because the resulting payoffs are equal regardless of the player's choice. However, a competitively oriented player might prefer T to S because, coupled with the other's S, this choice gives him a payoff larger than the co-player's. In contrast to Prisoner's Dilemma or Chicken, a unilateral shift from S_1S_2 does not improve the shifter's payoff; in contrast to a genuine no-conflict game, such as game #6, a unilateral shift does not impair the shifter's payoff either.

We note, below, that [S] is close to 80 in all variants. The 20 percent defection is, perhaps, a general measure of the "pure competitive pressure" in 2×2 games.

Some Results of Degenerate No-Conflict Games[2]

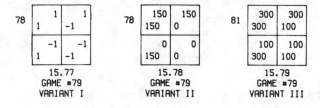

Results of single plays of Chicken are given below.

Varying d in Game #66 (Feedback Condition)

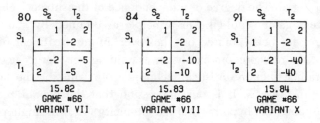

TABLE 15.39 Effects of changing d on [S] in Game #66, cond. F.

VC	Δu	[S]	Δ [S]	Δq	e	H_m
X, VIII	1.49	91	-07	-.28	.19	Yes
VIII, VII	.78	84	-04	-.12	.15	Yes

Analogous results for the no-feedback condition are given in table 15.40.

<hr />

[2] Because of equality of payoffs in different outcomes to the same player, these games are not from the ordinal taxonomy. They are numbered consecutively, game #79, etc.

TABLE 15.40 Effects of changing d on [S] in Game #66, cond. NF.

VC	Δ u	[S]	Δ [S]	Δ q	e	H$_m$
X, VIII	1.49	89	-02	-.08	.05	Yes
VIII, VII	.78	87	-04	-.14	.17	Yes

Summary and Discussion of Results

The clearest finding in all the experiments considered is a strong confirmation of H_m in single plays of 2×2 games. The shifts in [S] were in the predicted direction in sixty-one out of sixty-four comparisons. In two of the remaining three, no shift was observed. In only one comparison was the shift in the direction opposite to that predicted (corresponding to a change of c in game #69). The comparisons were independent in the sense that no inequality logically implied another.

The statistical independence of the comparisons is another matter. All we can say on that score is that the data were obtained from four separate populations of subjects: Frenkel's, Guyer's, and two of Rapoport, et al. The degree of independence of the subjects' choices in different games could be in principle ascertained by statistical means. As has been pointed out, however, in our treatment of the question, we rely predominantly on examining very large amounts of data rather than on statistical techniques of evaluating the significance of the results. It is our impression that the overall picture amply supports the hypothesis of monotonicity (H_m) in single plays.

This strong confirmation of the hypothesis in massed data is a source of both satisfaction and disappointment. On the one hand, it is somewhat encouraging to note that our abstracted "average player" behaves at least qualitatively in a predictable manner: even minute shifts of "his" choice frequencies reflect the direction of corresponding changes in payoffs. On the other hand, as has been also pointed out in the Preface, interesting psychological hypotheses would have been generated by consistent *violations* of H_m, attributable to considerations other than changes of payoffs. Since practically no such violations were observed, we resort to a rough quantitative analysis. We shall note where the effects of payoff changes were largest, that is, which payoffs in which games seem to be the most salient in the attention of our "average player."

Table 15.41 shows the sources of the ten largest effects ($e \geqslant .40$).

TABLE 15.41   Largest observed effects of payoff changes on [S]

Game #	Experimenter	Payoff changed	e
64	Guyer	a_1	.56
12	Rapoport-Chammah-Guyer	$(c - b)$	.52
66	Frenkel	d	.51
12	Rapoport-Chammah-Guyer	d	.50
12	Rapoport-Chammah-Guyer	a	.47
64	Guyer	b_1	.46
12	Frenkel	d	.45
12	Rapoport-Chammah-Guyer	d	.44
64	Guyer	a_1	.42*
69	Guyer	b	.41

*Indirect effect

We notice, first, that the largest effects were observed in all the experiments; so there is no immediate evidence that the magnitude of the effects can be attributed to particular experimental methods. Next, we observe that of the ten largest effects, nine are direct. In fact, practically all the indirect effects are quite small, even zero in several instances. Evidently, in the absence of interaction, as in single plays, the player is concerned primarily with his own payoffs. The one exception occurs in game #64, where the indirect effect of changing a_1 is large. Neither player has a dominating strategy in that game. In the absence of a clear-cut advantage of one strategy over the other, we might expect that a player will pay more attention to the other's payoffs. Finally, we observe that all of the largest effects stem from just three games, Prisoner's Dilemma, Chicken, and game #64. The first two are the most frequently chosen in experiments on 2×2 games, and the third was the subject of a whole book (Braithwaite, 1955; cf. also p. 60). On this basis, it is tempting to conclude that the payoffs of those games are the most salient. However, some of the smallest effects are also associated with those games (cf. tables 15.1, 15.37, 15.38), which makes the conjecture questionable.

Differences in the absolute values of [S] can be attributed to experimental methods. Large discrepancies of [S] in the same variants of game #12 occur between results observed by Frenkel and those by Rapoport, et al. These are listed in table 15.42.

TABLE 15.42   Comparison of Frenkel's and
Rapoport-Chammah-Guyer's
S frequencies in single plays.

Game #	Variant	Frenkel	Rapoport, et al.
12	I	83	50
12	III	93	82
12	IV	84	51
12	V	94	88
66	III	47	83

Recall that in game #12, S is the uncooperative choice. Thus the cooperative choice frequencies are all significantly higher in the Rapoport, et al. experiments than in Frenkel's. The frequency of cooperative (T) choices in the former experiment, averaged over all the variants used, was about forty.

M. Pancer (unpublished) obtained the same result in a pilot study where subjects were recruited for a one-trial game of Prisoner's Dilemma from among visitors to the Ontario Science Center. K. Terhune (1968) obtained an even higher frequency of cooperative choices in single plays of Prisoner's Dilemma (cf. chapter 19). Frenkel's average of 11.5 over all the variants of game #12 used was the lowest we have observed.

Comparisons of results in Chicken obtained by Frenkel and by Rapoport, et al. suggest the same discrepancy. In Frenkel's experiment, [S] ranged from 21 to 65 (cf. matrices 15.8–15.12). In Rapoport's, et al., [S] ranged from 80 to 91. To be sure, the defector stood to gain 9 points in Frenkel's game and only 1 point in Rapoport's, et al.; so the conclusion that in the latter experiments the subjects were "more cooperative" is not warranted. Nevertheless, the difference in [S] between, say, variant VII in Rapoport's, et al. seems excessive in the light of the results associated with comparable changes of payoffs in other games.

The only explanation that suggests itself to us is the following. In Frenkel's experiment, all seventy-eight games of the ordinal taxonomy (cf. chapter 2) were used, involving 320 choices by each subject. In the process of making his choice in game after game, a subject may well have developed some principle to guide his choices. It stands to reason that different subjects may have developed different principles, so that the entire mass of data cannot be accounted for by only *one* principle. However, if one principle guided the choices of a particular subject, so that he applied it "across the board," as it were, he would have applied it also to game #12, thus producing a contagion effect (cf. p. 91). In particular, if a subject chose the dominating strategy when he had one, he chose S in game #12, which in that game is the uncooperative choice.

On the other hand, in the Rapoport, et al. experiment, where practically all of the games were characterized by a "cooperative" versus the "uncooperative" choice, this may have become the salient issue in the minds of many subjects. In particular, in game #66 and in the "degenerate" games, the cooperative choice is also Pareto-optimal. Hence, the salience of the Pareto-optimal choice with equal payoffs may have attracted the attention of more subjects in that experiment. It is also worth noting that in Rapoport's, et al., in Terhune's, and in Pancer's experiments, the co-player was physically present (although interaction with him was not possible), whereas in Frenkel's experiment, he was not. Nor was there a co-player in Guyer's experiment. Unfortunately, in that experiment, games #12 and #66 were not used, and so there is no basis for comparison. Our conjecture is that, had those games been used in Guyer's experiment, uncooperative choices would have been predominant in those games, as they were in Frenkel's experiment.

Finally, there is a possibility that the incentive of prizes for the highest scores, rather than the incentive of the absolute scores, may have magnified the importance of competitive pressure in Frenkel's experiment. All of these conjectures can be formulated as specific hypotheses to be tested by specially designed further experiments.

16

Effects of Payoffs in Iterated Games

In iterated play, interactions between the players enter as a factor of prime importance. The nature of these interactions can be better understood if several dependent variables are examined in relation to an easily manipulatable independent variable. Here, as in the preceding chapter, it will be the payoffs, for the most part varied one at a time, sometimes two at a time in order to preserve some aspect of symmetry. The dependent variables, however, will now be several: frequencies of one player's choices, frequencies of outcomes, and repetition propensities. All of these dependent variables and others were examined in chapters 8–13, which also dealt with iterated games. There, however, only one variant of each game was examined. Here we shall examine several variants of each game. Thus the effects of payoffs can be examined while the strategic structure of the game as it is defined by its species can be kept constant.

Prisoner's Dilemma (Game #12):
Results of Rapoport and Chammah's Experiment

The results reproduced here are those obtained by Rapoport and Chammah and reported more fully elsewhere (1965).

Varying d in Game #12

16.1
GAME #12
VARIANT III

16.2
GAME #12
VARIANT XI

16.3
GAME #12
VARIANT I

TABLE 16.1 Effects of changing d on (S) in iterated P.D.

VC	Δ u	(S)	Δ (S)	Δ q	e	H$_m$
III, XI	.70	54	-17	-.30	.43	Yes
XI, I	.70	37	-10	-.20	.29	Yes

Varying a in Game #12

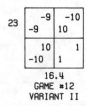

16.4
GAME #12
VARIANT II

16.5
GAME #12
VARIANT XII

16.6
GAME #12
VARIANT III

TABLE 16.2 Effects of changing a on (S) in iterated P.D.

VC	Δ u	(S)	Δ (S)	Δ q	e	H$_m$
II, XII	.70	23	18	.37	.53	Yes
XII, III	.70	41	13	.23	.33	Yes

Varying (c − b) in Game #12

16.7
GAME #12
VARIANT IV

16.8
GAME #12
VARIANT III

16.9
GAME #12
VARIANT V

TABLE 16.3 Effects of changing (c-b) on (S) in iterated P.D.

VC	Δ u	(S)	Δ (S)	Δ q	e	H$_m$
IV, III	1.23	34	20	.36	.29	Yes
III, V	1.92	54	19	.36	.18	Yes

We note that H_m is corroborated throughout. We shall now examine the effects of the same payoff changes in the same variants but in an experiment with a somewhat different design. In this experiment, every pair played all seven variants in seven blocks of fifty plays each, the order of the variants being altered from pair to pair. Thus, in this design, the subjects served as their own controls. The results are shown in table 16.4.

TABLE 16.4   Effects of changing payoffs on (S) in iterated P.D. (mixed block design).

VC	PC	Δ u	(S)	Δ (S)	Δ q	e	H_m
III, XI	d	.70	51	-17	-.31	.43	Yes
XI, I	d	.70	34	-04	-.08	.11	Yes
II, XII	a	.70	31	10	.19	.27	Yes
XII, III	a	.70	41	10	.18	.26	Yes
IV, III	c-b	1.23	33	18	.32	.26	Yes
III, V	c-b	1.92	51	10	.18	.09	Yes

Again H_m is corroborated throughout. A conspicuous feature, however, is the reduction in the values of e. This reduction is probably due to "contagion." As noted in chapter 8, the "average pair" playing a long sequence of Prisoner's Dilemma eventually learns to cooperate. Thus the frequency of cooperative T choices tends to increase, possibly regardless of the sequence of the variants of the game played. Consequently, the differences between the choice frequencies in the different variants tend to be blurred.

These differences become still more blurred if a randomly selected variant is presented on each consecutive play. In the next experiment, every pair played all seven games "mixed." On each play, one of the seven variants was presented with equal probability except that each was presented exactly 100 times (thus 700 iterations in all). The results are shown in table 16.5.

The contagion effect is manifested in the further reduction of e. In one comparison, H_m is no longer corroborated.

The mean values of T in the three experiments were 56, 60, and 62 respectively. That is, the overall "amount of cooperation" was largest in the completely randomized sequences and smallest when each pair played just one game. If the differences are significant, this sug-

TABLE 16.5 Effects of changing payoffs in (S) in iterated P.D.
(completely mixed design).

VC	PC	Δ u	(S)	Δ (S)	Δ q	e	H$_m$
III, XI	d	.70	39	-06	-.12	.17	Yes
XI, I	d	.70	33	-03	-.06	.09	Yes
II, XII	a	.70	39	01	.02	.03	Yes
XII, III	a	.70	40	-01	-.02	.03	No
IV, III	c-b	1.23	28	11	.21	.18	Yes
III, V	c-b	1.92	39	21	.37	.19	Yes

gests that most "learning to cooperate" occurred when the games were "most mixed." Perhaps the mixture facilitated the formation of the concept of "the kind of game" that was played and through it facilitated the insight which makes for cooperation in Prisoner's Dilemma. On the other hand, the effect, even if significant, was small. Moreover, it must be kept in mind that in the one game per pair experiment the number of iterations was 300, in the fifty-play block experiment it was 350, and in the randomized presentation experiment it was 700. In general, (T) tends to increase in iterated Prisoner's Dilemma. If the asymptotic bound of T is not yet reached by the three-hundredth play, the differences may simply reflect the differences in sequence length.

In table 16.6 the repetition propensities in Prisoner's Dilemma are compared across the seven variants.

TABLE 16.6 Repetition propensities in P.D.

Variant	α	β	γ	δ	Inequalities
I	70	45	55	92	δ > α > γ > β
II	68	42	47	93	δ > α > γ > β
III	85	35	66	83	α > δ > γ > β
IV	82	42	60	91	δ > α > γ > β
V	95	28	75	71	α > γ > δ > β
XI	80	44	61	85	δ > α > γ > β
XII	80	43	67	79	α > δ > γ > β

H$_r$ prescribes $\gamma > \delta > \alpha > \beta$. We observe that the value of β is indeed the lowest in all the variants. However, in no variant is γ the largest, clearly because there are no "lock-ins" on the asymmetric outcomes S_1T_2 and T_1S_2. It is the lock-ins that provide the high values of the repetition propensities, and these occur in the symmetric outcomes S_1S_2 and T_1T_2. This explains the observation that the highest values are those of α and δ. Further, α which reflects lock-ins on S_1S_2 has the highest value in the two "least cooperative" variants, III and V, reflecting a stronger tendency to lock in on S_1S_2.

The effects of payoff changes on the repetition propensities are shown in tables 16.7–16.10.

TABLE 16.7 Effects of payoff changes on α in iterated P.D.

VC	PC	Δ u	α	Δ α	Δ q	e	H_m
II, XII	a	.70	68	12	.27	.39	Yes
XII, III	a	.70	80	05	.16	.23	Yes
V, III	b-c	1.92	95	-10	-.53	.27	Yes
III, IV	b-c	1.23	85	-03	-.10	.08	Yes
III, XI	d	.70	85	-05	-.16	.23	Yes
XI, I	d	.70	80	-10	-.23	.33	Yes

TABLE 16.8 Effects of payoff changes on β in iterated P.D.

VC	PC	Δ u	β	Δ β	Δ q	e	H_m
II, XII	a	.70	42	01	.02	.03	No
XII, III	a	.70	43	-08	-.15	.21	Yes
V, III	b-c	1.92	28	07	.14	.07	Yes
III, IV	b-c	1.23	35	07	.13	.11	Yes
III, XI	d	.70	35	09	.16	.23	Yes
XI, I	d	.70	44	01	.02	.03	Yes

TABLE 16.9 Effects of payoff changes on γ in iterated P.D.

VC	PC	Δ u	γ	Δ γ	Δ q	e	H_m
II, XII	a	.70	47	20	.36	.51	Yes
XII, III	a	.70	67	-01	-.02	.03	No
V, III	b-c	1.92	75	-09	-.19	.10	Yes
III, IV	b-c	1.23	66	-06	-.11	.09	Yes
III, XI	d	.70	66	-05	-.09	.13	Yes
XI, I	d	.70	61	-05	-.09	.13	Yes

TABLE 16.10 Effects of payoff changes on δ in iterated P.D.

VC	PC	Δ u	δ	Δ δ	Δ q	e	H$_m$
II, XII	a	.70	93	-14	-.55	.79	Yes
XII, III	a	.70	79	-04	-.10	.14	Yes
V, III	b-c	1.92	71	12	.30	.16	Yes
III, IV	b-c	1.23	83	08	.32	.26	Yes
III, XI	d	.70	83	02	.06	.09	Yes
XI, I	d	.70	85	07	.31	.44	Yes

H_m is again corroborated throughout, with two exceptions. The reversals in the effects of change of a on β and γ (variants XII and II) are quite small and do not warrant suggesting a new hypothesis.

Results of Worchel's Experiment

P. Worchel (1969) examined the effects of payoff changes in five variants of Prisoner's Dilemma, one of which was identical to variant III in the Rapoport and Chammah experiments. Ten pairs of subjects, five male and five female, were assigned to each variant (16.10–16.14) and played twenty-five iterations.

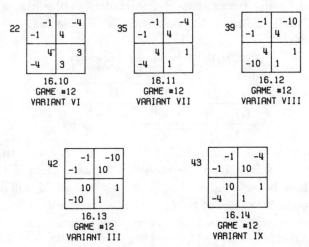

16.10
GAME #12
VARIANT VI

16.11
GAME #12
VARIANT VII

16.12
GAME #12
VARIANT VIII

16.13
GAME #12
VARIANT III

16.14
GAME #12
VARIANT IX

We observe from table 16.11 that H_m fails in one comparison. Note that variant IX is peculiar in that the asymmetric outcomes S_1T_2 and T_1S_2 give larger *joint* payoffs to the players than the symmetric "cooperative" outcome T_1T_2. This situation is usually avoided

TABLE 16.11   Effects of changing payoffs on (S) in iterated P.D. in Worchel's experiment.

VC	PC	Δ u	(S)	Δ (S)	Δ q	e	H_m
VII, VI	d	.48	35	-13	-.28	.58	Yes
VII, III	c	.85	39	03	.05	.06	Yes
VII, IX	c	.85	35	08	.15	.18	Yes
VII, VIII	b	.60	39	-04	-.07	.11	Yes
III, IX	b	.85	42	01	.02	.02	No

in Prisoner's Dilemma experiments. In fact, some authors include the condition b + c < 2d in the definition of Prisoner's Dilemma. This is done in the interest of eliminating an alternative cooperative solution of the iterated game, namely an alternation between S_1T_2 and T_1S_2, which yields a larger long-run payoff than the standard cooperative solution, T_1T_2. It would, therefore, be interesting to see whether the reversal between variants III and IX is due to such cooperative alternations, which, by reducing the frequency of T_1T_2 outcomes, results in a larger than expected value of (S). Unfortunately, the frequencies of outcomes were not reported by Worchel.

That alternation may not be the only reason for the reversal is suggested by the frequencies of first choices in the five variants which Worchel did report. These are shown in table 16.12.

TABLE 16.12   First choice S frequencies in Worchel's experiment.

Variant	VI	VII	VIII	III	IX
[S]	30	45	65	75	85

We observe that H_m is corroborated also in first choice frequencies, again, however, with one exception, between III and IX, the effectiveness being considerable (e = .20). We could still invoke alternation as the source of the reversal if we were willing to assume that some players planned alternating cooperation from the very start, but this seems unlikely.

Another explanation of the reversal is in terms of the salience of the largest payoff to the individual player. The largest payoff is, of course, always in an asymmetric outcome in all the variants of Prisoner's Dilemma. When the two payoffs are numerically equal with opposite sign, as they are in all the other variants examined here, the fact that the co-player's payoff, coupled with one's own largest, is the *smallest* may be a conspicuous feature. Thus it appears unlikely to the player that the co-player will try to effect the same outcome, and this acts as a deterrent against choosing S, the strategy that contains the largest payoff. In variant IX, the numerical inequality of the two payoffs may make the largest-smallest contrast less conspicuous. Moreover, the fact that the joint payoff is largest in an asymmetric outcome may induce the following rationalization: "There is an outcome where my payoff is largest and also the joint payoff is largest. It is, therefore, best for me and best for both of us. To effect it, I choose S." What is left out of this rationale is that the analogous decision by the co-player results in S_1S_2, where neither player gets the largest payoff and where the joint payoff is smallest.

Worchel's experiment provides an opportunity to compare the relative importance of "greed" and "fear" in Prisoner's Dilemma. These pressures are seen more clearly if we orient ourselves toward the co-operative outcome T_1T_2 (i.e., C_1C_2 in conventional notation) rather than toward the natural outcome S_1S_2 (i.e., D_1D_2) as the point of reference. Accordingly, if C_1C_2 is the initial outcome, "greed"—the hope of getting the largest payoff—exerts a pressure toward "defecting" to D. Similarly, the "fear" of getting the smallest payoff of unilateral cooperation exerts a pressure in the same direction. In Rapoport and Chammah's experiment, these two pressures could not be assessed separately since b and c, the payoffs in the unilateral outcomes, were always varied together. In Worchel's experiment, they were varied separately. Specifically, comparing variants VIII and VII, where the change was in b (the "sucker's payoff"), we observe the effect of "fear" ($e = .07$); comparing variants VII and IX, where the change was in c (the "defector's payoff"), we observe the effect of "greed" ($e = .18$). The latter appears to be larger.[1]

Worchel's results also provide an opportunity of comparing the S frequencies in variants of Prisoner's Dilemma with corresponding results obtained by Rapoport and Chammah; that is, of testing the "robustness" of payoffs as determinants of choices. As has been noted, one of Worchel's variants is variant III, used also by Rapoport and Chammah. Further, assuming invariance under positive linear trans-

---

[1] Similar results were obtained by L. G. Morehouse (1966).

formations of payoffs (cf. p. 53), we multiply the payoffs of variant VI by 3 and obtain for a, b, c, and d —3, —12, 12, and 9 respectively, that is, a variant close to variant I (cf. p. 233). The smaller a in this version of variant VI is compensated by a larger c and smaller b. Finally, variant VII is intermediate between variants IV and III (cf. p. 233), being considerably closer to IV. Comparisons are shown in table 16.13.

TABLE 16.13   Comparison of S frequencies in Worchel's (W) and Rapoport, et al. (RCG) variants of iterated P.D.

Variant	I	VI	IV	VII	III	III
Experimenter	(RCG)	(W)	(RCG)	(W)	(RCG)	(W)
(S)	27	22	34	35	54	42

On the whole, it seems that Worchel's subjects were somewhat more cooperative, considerably so in variant III. We suspect that the difference would be even larger if Worchel's runs were as long as Rapoport and Chammah's (300), for there is a tendency to learn to cooperate in long iterated runs of Prisoner's Dilemma. It may be that the main factor in producing more cooperation in Worchel's experiment was its considerably slower pace. The inter-play interval was 30 seconds (compared with 6–10 in the Rapoport-Chammah experiment) during which time the subjects not only recorded their payoffs but also predicted the co-player's choice on the next play. This procedure very likely facilitates insight into the peculiar structure of Prisoner's Dilemma and so promotes cooperation.

On the other hand, we recall that in Perner's experiment (cf. chapter 8), where the conditions were similar to those in Rapoport and Chammah's, the value of (S) in variant III was forty-five, close to Worchel's. The discrepancy cannot be attributed to the nationality of the subjects: Perner's subjects were mostly Canadians, but both Worchel's and Rapoport and Chammah's subjects were Americans. One possibility remains if one holds on to the belief in the "robustness" of payoffs as determinants of choice frequencies. Namely, Rapoport and Chammah's experiment was performed in 1962; Worchel's, presumably in 1968; Perner's, in 1972. These years span radical changes in the attitudes and perceptions of university students, from whom the subjects for these experiments were recruited. It is intriguing to imagine that this gross secular change in a cultural climate may have been reflected in behavior in a 2×2 game.

Chicken: Results of Rapoport and Chammah's Experiment

In experiments with game #66 (Rapoport and Chammah, 1966), only d was varied, again equally for both players, preserving the numerical symmetry of the variant, as shown below. Recall that in this game, d is the smallest payoff and represents the punishment meted out to the players who try to "outdare" each other. According to H_m, a decrease in d (i.e., making the punishment more severe by increasing its magnitude) should be accompanied by an increase of (S), which in this game represents cooperation or prudence.

Varying d in Game #66

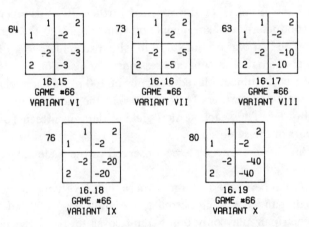

TABLE 16.14   Effects of changing d on (S) in iterated Chicken (male subjects).

VC	Δu	(S)	Δ(S)	Δq	e	H_m
X, IX	1.32	80	-04	-.10	.08	Yes
IX, VIII	1.04	76	-13	-.27	.26	Yes
VIII, VII	.78	63	10	.20	.26	No
VII, VI	.48	73	-09	-.18	.38	Yes

We observe that H_m fails in the comparison between VIII and VII. That is, we expect that as the punishment for double defection becomes less severe—passing from VIII to VII, (S) would decrease. Instead it increases. The effectiveness of the change is considerable $(e = .26)$.

We, therefore, examine a replication of the experiment with female subjects. The results are shown in table 16.15.

TABLE 16.15   Effects of changing d on (S) in iterated Chicken (female subjects).

VC	Δ u	(S)	Δ (S)	Δ q	e	H_m
X, IX	1.32	76	-19	-.38	.29	Yes
IX, VIII	1.04	57	-02	-.04	.04	Yes
VIII, VII	.78	55	14	.26	.33	No
VII, VI	.48	69	-06	-.12	.26	Yes

We observe here also that a reversal occurs in the same place. Its effectiveness is even larger than in the male subjects $(e = .33)$.

To test the "reality" of the reversal further, R. Wilson (unpublished) conducted two experiments on Chicken, using the same five variants. The first was a pilot study in which six male and six female subjects participated in separate sessions. Each session consisted of 500 plays: each subject played five runs of 100 plays each, changing both variants and partners (among those in the same group) in randomized order. Thus each session yielded data on fifteen (overlapping) pairs of the same sex.

This time a small reversal was observed in the male subjects but none in the females.

Wilson then performed a larger experiment, involving twenty male and female pairs, confining herself to variants VII, VIII, and X, and having each pair play only one variant so as to avoid the possible contagion effect which may have blurred the results (cf. p. 93). This time the reversal was again observed in the pooled data.

Tables 16.16–16.19 show the effect on the repetition propensities of changing d in the male population.

It is interesting to compare these results with analogous ones in Prisoner's Dilemma (tables 16.7–16.10). There H_m is corroborated in twenty-two out of twenty-four comparisons. That is to say, H_m remains virtually corroborated when examined "under stronger resolving power," so to say: changes in payoffs have the same effect on conditional as on unconditional probabilities of choice. Here in

TABLE 16.16 Effects of changing d on α in iterated Chicken
in Wilson's experiment (male subjects).

VC	Δ u	α	Δ α	Δ q	e	H_m
X, IX	1.32	90	-05	-.20	.15	Yes
IX, VIII	1.04	85	-07	-.19	.18	Yes
VIII, VII	.78	78	12	.40	.51	No
VII, VI	.48	90	-13	-.43	.90	Yes

TABLE 16.17 Effects of changing d on β in iterated Chicken
in Wilson's experiment (male subjects).

VC	Δ u	β	Δ β	Δ q	e	H_m
X, IX	1.32	36	-05	-.10	.08	No
IX, VIII	1.04	31	07	.13	.12	Yes
VIII, VII	.78	38	20	.35	.45	Yes
VII, VI	.48	58	-06	-.11	.23	No

TABLE 16.18 Effects of changing d on γ in iterated Chicken
in Wilson's experiment (male subjects).

VC	Δ u	γ	Δ γ	Δ q	e	H_m
X, IX	1.32	57	03	.05	.04	No
IX, VIII	1.04	60	-10	-.18	.17	Yes
VIII, VII	.78	50	03	.05	.06	No
VII, VI	.48	53	-08	-.14	.29	Yes

TABLE 16.19 Effects of changing d on δ in iterated Chicken
in Wilson's experiment (male subjects).

VC	Δ u	δ	Δ δ	Δ q	e	H_m
X, IX	1.32	50	-03	-.05	.04	No
IX, VIII	1.04	47	11	.19	.18	Yes
VIII, VII	.78	58	06	.11	.14	Yes
VII, VI	.48	64	-04	-.07	.15	No

Chicken, on the other hand, H_m is not corroborated in six out of sixteen comparisons. To be sure, the effects associated with reversals are for the most part small. Nevertheless, the fact that in Prisoner's Dilemma even the smallest effects are almost all in the expected direction raises the question why this is not so in Chicken.

Examining the effect on α of changing d (table 16.16), we observe the same reversal (VIII vs. VII) as in the gross frequencies. But the effect of changing d on other conditional frequencies varies. We observe the same reversal effect on γ (table 16.18), but also an opposite effect in X vs. IX. The patterns in the effects on β and δ are altogether different. Let us, therefore, examine the effects of changing d on the repetition propensities in the female population (tables 16.20–16.23).

TABLE 16.20   Effects of changing d on α in iterated Chicken in Wilson's experiment (female subjects).

VC	Δ u	α	Δ α	Δ q	e	H_m
X, IX	1.32	82	-10	-.25	.19	Yes
IX, VIII	1.04	72	07	.16	.15	No
VIII, VII	.78	79	09	.29	.37	No
VII, VI	.48	88	-06	-.21	.44	Yes

TABLE 16.21   Effects of changing d on β in iterated Chicken in Wilson's experiment (female subjects).

VC	Δ u	β	Δ β	Δ q	e	H_m
X, IX	1.32	48	04	.07	.05	Yes
IX, VIII	1.04	52	12	.18	.17	Yes
VIII, VII	.78	64	-04	-.07	.09	No
VII, VI	.48	60	-09	-.16	.33	No

TABLE 16.22   Effects of changing d on γ in iterated Chicken in Wilson's experiment (female subjects).

VC	Δ u	γ	Δ γ	Δ q	e	H_m
X, IX	1.32	66	-11	-.20	.15	Yes
IX, VIII	1.04	55	-07	-.12	.12	Yes
VIII, VII	.78	48	-04	-.07	.09	Yes
VII, VI	.48	44	07	.12	.25	No

The reversal effect on α is still observed in VIII vs. VII (table 16.20), but so is an additional reversal in IX vs. VIII. Again the remaining patterns are different, H_m being corroborated in only ten of the sixteen comparisons. The number of corroborations is the

TABLE 16.23 Effects of changing d on δ in iterated Chicken
in Wilson's experiment (female subjects).

VC	Δ u	δ	Δ δ	Δ q	e	H_m
X, IX	1.32	48	03	.05	.04	Yes
IX, VIII	1.04	51	10	.18	.17	Yes
VIII, VII	.78	61	03	.06	.08	Yes
VII, VI	.48	64	-03	-.05	.10	No

same as in the male population, but they are in different comparisons. Here the discrepancies suggest hypotheses. Ignoring the question of the significance of the small effects (to be tested in subsequent experiments), we might conjecture the following. In the male population, the reversal noted in the gross frequencies stems from an "opposite" effect of a change in d on α and γ. The first reflects a greater tendency to preempt more as the loss associated with double preemption increases (moderately); the second reflects a tendency to yield less, that is, to retaliate if the co-player preempts. In the female population, the reversal stems from an opposite effect on α and β, that is, on the tendency to preempt more and on the tendency to continue preempting if the co-player yields. We note further that as the punishment for double preemption becomes excessively severe in variant X, another reversal occurs in the male but not in the female population—from IX to X. β increases instead of decreasing (that is, there is more adamance if the co-player yields); γ decreases instead of increasing (that is, there is less yielding, more retaliation, if the co-player preempts); δ increases instead of decreasing (that is, there is more lock-in on the mutually punishing outcome T_1T_2).

In reading tables 16.16–16.23, note that the changes in the propensities are given as we pass from X to IX, etc., that is, in the opposite direction.

The above example illustrates the "generation of hypotheses" by data that violate "common sense expectations."

A Threat Game: Results of Guyer and Gordon's Experiment

M. Guyer and D. Gordon (unpublished) examined performances in iterated game #19 using five variants shown below. Eighteen pairs of subjects were randomly assigned to each of the variants to be played

100 times. In each session, the subjects played also against six programed strategies. Some of the latter data will be examined below, and again more fully in chapter 17. Here we confine discussion to the performances of bona fide pairs.

Varying a_2 and c_1 in Game #19

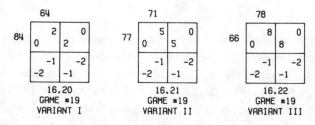

| | 16.20 GAME #19 VARIANT I | 16.21 GAME #19 VARIANT II | 16.22 GAME #19 VARIANT III |

Changing both a_2 and c_1 simultaneously changes the discrepancy between the top dog's and the underdog's payoffs while preserving the apparent symmetry of the game matrix. Actually, of course, the game is asymmetric, with Row in the role of the underdog, but it has a symmetric feature in that Row's and Column's payoffs are interchanged in the two columns.

TABLE 16.24 Effects on changing a_2 and c_1 on (S_2) in iterated Game #19.

VC	Δu	(S_2)	$\Delta (S_2)$	Δq	e	H_m
I, II	.60	64	07	.12	.20	Yes
II, III	.60	71	08	.18	.30	Yes

TABLE 16.25 Effects of changing a_2 and c_1 on (S_1) in iterated Game #19.

VC	Δu	(S_1)	$\Delta (S_1)$	Δq	e	H_m
I, II	.60	84	-07	-.20	.33	No
II, III	.60	77	-11	-.24	.40	No

According to H_m, both (S_1) and (S_2) should be largest in variant III and smallest in variant I. We observe that this is so in the case of (S_2), but that the opposite is true in the case of (S_1). Here, then, is another definitive disconfirmation of H_m. The result can be attributed to indirect effects. Although increasing values of c_1 are expected to make S_1 more attractive to Row, the equally increasing values of a_2 accentuate the discrepancy in favor of Column in the natural outcome, which predominates. Consequently, Row, becoming increasingly more disgruntled, is more motivated to "revolt" by resorting to his threat strategy. Moreover, as a_2 increases, S_2 becomes increasingly more attractive to Column. Consequently, he shares with Row less frequently, aggravating Row's discontent.

Next we examine the effect of changing b_1, which is the cost to Row of resorting to the threat strategy.

Varying b_1 in Game #19

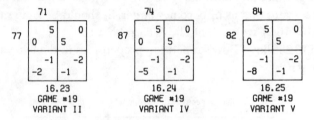

TABLE 16.26   Direct effects of changing b_1
in iterated Game #19.

VC	Δ u	(S_1)	Δ (S_1)	Δ q	e	H_m
V, IV	.60	82	05	.17	.28	No
IV, II	.60	87	-10	-.30	.50	Yes

TABLE 16.27   Indirect effects of changing b_1
in iterated Game #19.

VC	Δ u	(S_2)	Δ (S_2)	Δ q	e	H_m'
V, IV	.60	84	-10	-.26	.43	Yes
IV, II	.60	74	-03	-.06	.10	Yes

In table 16.26 we observe a reversal with a fairly large e in the comparison of variants V and IV. Even though the use of threat is more costly to Row in V, he resorts to it more frequently than in IV. In the comparison between II and IV, however, H_m is corroborated:

the more the revolt costs, the less frequently it is used. Possible explanations of this reversal will be discussed below.

In considering indirect effects we shall modify somewhat our definition of H_m'. Recall that in single plays H_m' was defined in terms of H_s, because in the absence of iterations a player could consider only the *consequences* of the co-player's shift from S. He could do nothing to *prevent* or *encourage* such a shift. In iterated play, on the other hand, interaction plays a foremost role, and changes in the co-player's payoffs affect the choices calculated to modify the co-player's behavior. Thus, consider a change in b_1 in game #19 which makes T_1 more attractive to Row. We would expect Column to be indirectly affected by this change in the direction of larger (T_2), hence smaller (S_2), in the process of "appeasing" Row so as to forestall the presumably more likely revolt. Our present version of H_m', therefore, states that as b_1 becomes larger, S_2 should become smaller. From table 16.27 we see that H_m' is corroborated.

Table 16.28 shows Row's repetition propensities in the five variants of game #19.

TABLE 16.28   Row's repetition propensities in Game #19.

Variant	α_1	β_1	γ_1	δ_1	Inequalities
I	90	51	94	58	$\gamma_1 > \alpha_1 > \delta_1 > \beta_1$
II	84	52	88	42	$\gamma_1 > \alpha_1 > \beta_1 > \delta_1$
III	80	65	80	50	$\gamma_1 = \alpha_1 > \beta_1 > \delta_1$
IV	96	68	98	56	$\gamma_1 > \alpha_1 > \beta_1 > \delta_1$
V	86	38	91	44	$\gamma_1 > \alpha_1 > \delta_1 > \beta_1$

Our repetition hypothesis H_r prescribes inequalities $\gamma_1 > \alpha_1 > \delta_1 > \beta_1$ which, except for reversals between δ_1 and β_1, is corroborated. The effects of payoff changes are shown in tables 16.29–16.32.

We observe substantial reversals of β_1 and δ_1 in variants II, III, and IV. In these games, the discrepancy between Row's and Column's payoffs in the natural outcome are large and they evidently are reflected in the large values of β_1, Row's persistence in continuing the use of the threat strategy T_1 in T_1S_2. In variant V, the discrepancy is also large, but the cost to Row in T_1S_2 is excessive, as reflected in the significantly reduced value of β_1.

TABLE 16.29   Effects of changing payoffs on α_1
in iterated Game #19.

VC	PC	Δu	α_1	$\Delta \alpha_1$	Δq	e	H_m
I, II	a_2, c_1	.60	90	-06	-.23	.38	No
II, III	a_2, c_1	.60	84	-04	-.12	.20	No
V, IV	b_1	.60	86	10	.59	.98	No
IV, II	b_1	.60	96	-12	-.64	1.07	Yes

TABLE 16.30   Effects of changing payoffs on β_1
in iterated Game #19.

VC	PC	Δu	β_1	$\Delta \beta_1$	Δq	e	H_m
I, II	a_2, c_1	.60	51	01	.02	.03	No
II, III	a_2, c_1	.60	52	13	.23	.38	No
V, IV	b_1	.60	38	30	.58	.97	Yes
IV, II	b_1	.60	68	-16	-.29	.48	No

TABLE 16.31   Effects of changing payoffs on γ_1
in iterated Game #19.

VC	PC	Δu	γ	$\Delta \gamma$	Δq	e	H_m
I, II	a_2, c_1	.60	94	-06	-.33	.55	No
II, III	a_2, c_1	.60	88	-08	-.26	.44	No
V, IV	b_1	.60	91	07	.69	1.15	No
IV, II	b_1	.60	98	-10	-.82	1.37	Yes

TABLE 16.32   Effects of changing payoffs on δ_1
in iterated Game #19.

VC	PC	Δu	δ_1	$\Delta \delta_1$	Δq	e	H_m
I, II	a_2, c_1	.60	58	-16	-.28	.47	Yes
II, III	a_2, c_1	.60	42	08	.14	.23	No
V, IV	b_1	.60	44	12	.21	.35	Yes
IV, II	b_1	.60	56	-14	-.25	.42	No

Next we note that α_1 decreases from variant I to variant III, while β_1 increases. Both trends reflect Row's growing dissatisfaction with the discrepancy between his payoff and Column's in S_1S_2. In variants II, IV, and V, on the other hand, the trends in α_1 and β_1 are not monotone. As the cost of "revolt" to Row increases from II to IV to V, we would expect α_1 to increase. It does so significantly from II to IV, but drops also significantly from IV to V. The effectiveness of payoff change in these variants is very large. For instance, comparing II and IV, we observe $e = 1.07$ in the expected direction, whereas, comparing IV and V, we observe $e = .98$ in the direction opposite to that expected.

In view of these results, we see the following picture. Increasing discrepancy between Row's and Column's payoffs in the natural outcome has a consistent effect on Row's propensity to "revolt" ($\tilde{\alpha}_1$) and on his propensity to stick to the threat strategy (β_1), increasing both. On the other hand, increasing the cost of revolt to Row *at first* seems to have a "deterrent" effect, reducing his propensity to "revolt." But as the cost of revolt increases further, the propensity to revolt *increases*. Increasing cost of revolt has the opposite effect on the persistence of revolt. At first, increasing cost increases the propensity to persist in T_1S_2 ($e = .48$); as the cost becomes excessive, however, persistence drops ($e = .97$).

The behavior of α_1 is similar to that of γ_1. The two rise and fall together. This is not surprising in view of the fact that both α_1 and γ_1 reflect an accommodating attitude on the part of the underdog. As for β_1 and δ_1, both reflect a hostile attitude. Repetition of T_1 following T_1S_2 reflects persistent protest against the "inequity" of the natural outcome; repetition of T_1 following T_1T_2 reflects Row's distrust of Column's willingness to allow Row to obtain the largest payoff by switching from T_1T_2 to S_1T_2. We would, therefore, expect the changes in β_1 and δ_1 to be in the same direction. However, we observe a discrepancy in the comparison between I and II.

The question arises whether these violations of monotonicity (H_m) in Row's choice frequencies can be attributed entirely to Row's perception of the game or whether Row's interactions with Column need also be taken into account. Probably both are contributing factors. We are, however, in a position to examine Row's choice frequencies independently of interactions with Column. We do this by matching Row against a programed Column player (stooge) who always plays S_2. In game #19, this "adamant" strategy on the part of Column is not incredible. In fact, several bona fide players have been observed to use it. Table 16.33 shows Row's repetition propensities against Column's 100 percent S strategy.

TABLE 16.33 Row's repetition propensities against Column's 100% S_2 strategy in iterated Game #19.

Variant	I	II	III	IV	V
α_1	96	93	88	96	97
β_1	79	79	82	83	47

We observe that α_1 still decreases from I to II to III, again reflecting Row's increasing dissatisfaction with the increasing discrepancy. β_1 does not increase from I to II but does from II to III. Both effects, therefore, are still observed, though considerably reduced in magnitude. The reversal in α_1 from IV to V is no longer observed. Apparently, with interaction eliminated, the "deterrence" of increasing cost of revolt is effective. In β_1, however, we still observe the same reversal: β_1 increases from II to IV (in spite of rising costs of persistence in T_1S_2) and drops precipitously from IV to V as the cost becomes excessive. Since in the absence of interaction the reversal in β_1 from II to IV is less pronounced and the reversal of α_1 from IV to V is altogether eliminated, we have reason to suppose that both Row's perception of the game in which he is the underdog and his interactions with Column are contributing factors to the effects of payoff changes.

Table 16.34 shows Column's repetition propensities.

TABLE 16.34 Column's repetition propensities in Game #19.

Variant	α_2	β_2	γ_2	δ_2	Inequalities
I	49	14	71	33	$\gamma_2 > \alpha_2 > \delta_2 > \beta_2$
II	60	11	73	21	$\gamma_2 > \alpha_2 > \delta_2 > \beta_2$
III	72	08	82	23	$\gamma_2 > \alpha_2 > \delta_2 > \beta_2$
IV	69	15	79	28	$\gamma_2 > \alpha_2 > \delta_2 > \beta_2$
V	85	12	75	15	$\alpha_2 > \gamma_2 > \delta_2 > \beta_2$

H_r prescribes the inequality $\alpha_2 > \beta_2 > \gamma_2 > \delta_2$, which is definitely violated in all five variants. H_s prescribes $\tilde{\beta}_2 > \tilde{\delta}_2 > \tilde{\gamma}_2 > \tilde{\alpha}_2$, hence $\alpha_2 > \gamma_2 > \delta_2 > \beta_2$, which is more nearly reflected in the data. Nevertheless, neither hypothesis prescribes the highest value to γ_2, which we observe in four variants. Recall that γ_2 represents Column's resistance to Row's "demand" reflected in the $T_1 S_2$ outcome. In fact, the persistence of $T_1 S_2$ is a measure of the "battle of wills" between the two players.

The effects of payoff changes on Column's propensities are shown in tables 16.35–16.38.

TABLE 16.35   Effects of changing payoffs on α_2 in iterated Game #19.

VC	PC	Δu	α_2	$\Delta \alpha_2$	Δq	e	H_m or H_m'
I, II	a_2, c_1	.60	49	11	.19	.32	Yes
II, III	a_2, c_1	.60	60	12	.23	.39	Yes
V, IV	b_1	.60	85	-16	-.41	.68	Yes
IV, II	b_1	.60	69	-09	-.17	.28	Yes

TABLE 16.36   Effects of changing payoffs on β_2 in iterated Game #19.

VC	PC	Δu	β_2	$\Delta \beta_2$	Δq	e	H_m or H_m'
I, II	a_2, c_1	.60	14	-03	-.12	.20	Yes
II, III	a_2, c_1	.60	11	-03	-.15	.25	Yes
V, IV	b_1	.60	12	03	.12	.20	No
IV, II	b_1	.60	15	-04	-.16	.27	Yes

TABLE 16.37   Effects of changing payoffs on γ_2 in iterated Game #19.

VC	PC	Δu	γ_2	$\Delta \gamma_2$	Δq	e	H_m or H_m'
I, II	a_2, c_1	.60	71	02	.04	.07	Yes
II, III	a_2, c_1	.60	73	09	.23	.38	Yes
V, IV	b_1	.60	75	04	.10	.17	No
IV, II	b_1	.60	79	-06	-.14	.23	Yes

TABLE 16.38 Effects of changing payoffs on δ_2
in iterated Game #19.

VC	PC	Δu	δ_2	$\Delta \delta_2$	Δq	e	H_m or H_m'
I, II	a_2, c_1	.60	33	-12	-.27	.45	Yes
II, III	a_2, c_1	.60	21	02	.05	.08	No
V, IV	b_1	.60	15	13	.34	.57	Yes
IV, II	b_1	.60	28	-07	-.16	.27	No

We note that α_2 increases monotonically from I to II to III. That is to say, as the discrepancy between the payoffs in the natural outcome increases, Column becomes progressively more reluctant to share "voluntarily" with Row. Also γ_2 increases monotonically from I to II to III. Not only is Column more reluctant to share "voluntarily," but also more reluctant to yield to Row's threat. Next we see that α_2 increases monotonically from II to IV to V; that is, as the cost of revolt to Row increases, Column tends to share less voluntarily. Column's "adamance" (γ_2) also increases from II to IV. From IV to V, however, we see a reversal: as the cost of revolt to Row becomes excessive, Column tends to yield more to Row's threat. Can it be that Column's sense of fairness is finally aroused as he sees Row take a large punishment in order to protest the inequity of the natural outcome? To see the situation in a simpler context, we examine Column's behavior against a completely "passive" Row, a stooge who always plays S_1, that is, never "revolts." The results are shown in table 16.39.

TABLE 16.39 Column's S_2 frequencies against
Row's 100% S_1 strategy
in iterated Game #19.

Variant	I	II	III	IV	V
(S_2)	75	82	76	84	78

Here we no longer see any monotonicity: α_2 increases from I to II, reflecting Column's greater reluctance to share as the discrepancy becomes larger; however, it decreases from II to III as the discrepancy becomes excessive, reflecting a larger propensity to share. Next,

α_2 increases from II to IV as the cost of revolt to Row increases, but it drops from IV to V as the cost of revolt to Row becomes excessive. We must remember, however, that in this situation the "cost of revolt to Row" is seen only on paper, because, in fact, Row (a stooge) never revolts. Admittedly, it is somewhat far-fetched to imagine that Column shares more in variant V in order to forestall a revolt by Row which is costly to *Row* but not to Column. If such an effect can be established, however, it is all the more intriguing for being quite unexpected. Note, finally, that the decrease of α_2 in variant V is not observed when Column is playing against a bona fide Row. This throws some doubt on our conjecture that, as the cost of revolt to Row becomes excessive, Column "shows consideration" by sharing, thus forestalling excessive costs to Row. It is barely possible that Column shows "concern" when Row never actually resorts to T_1, but not when he does. Clearly, to establish the reality of this rather subtle result, more data are required.

Guyer and Gordon's experiment included also two variants of game #50. This game is similar to game #19, differing from it only in that it is to Column's immediate advantage to yield when Row revolts, since Column's payoff is larger in T_1T_2 than in T_1S_2.

Varying c_2 in Game #50

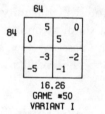
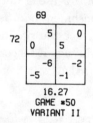

16.26
GAME #50
VARIANT I

16.27
GAME #50
VARIANT II

TABLE 16.40   Direct effect of changing c_2 on (S_2) in iterated Game #50.

VC	Δu	(S_2)	$\Delta (S_2)$	Δq	e	H_m
II, I	.60	69	−05	−.10	.17	No

TABLE 16.41   Indirect effect of changing c_2 on (S_1) in iterated Game #50.

VC	Δu	(S_1)	$\Delta (S_1)$	Δq	e	H'_m
II, I	.60	72	12	.31	.52	Yes

As the cost to *Column* of Row's revolt increases, we expect Row to revolt more, since the revolt is expected to have a greater effect on Column. This expectation is corroborated by the decrease in S_1 from variant I to variant II—a pronounced indirect effect ($e = .52$). The direct effect of the increase in the cost to Column is, however, in the direction opposite to that expected. Column yields *less* in variant II than in variant I. Again we see evidence for the conjecture that resentment at the loss caused by the co-player's choice may override pecuniary considerations.

To see the situation under a stronger resolving power, we turn to the repetition propensities, shown in tables 16.42–16.43.

TABLE 16.42 Row's repetition propensities
in iterated Game #50.

Variant	α_1	β_1	γ_1	δ_1	Inequalities
I	86	45	95	39	$\gamma_1 > \alpha_1 > \beta_1 > \delta_1$
II	80	54	85	50	$\gamma_1 > \alpha_1 > \beta_1 > \delta_1$

TABLE 16.43 Column's repetition propensities
in iterated Game #50.

Variant	α_2	β_2	γ_2	δ_2	Inequalities
I	51	16	67	31	$\gamma_1 > \alpha_2 > \delta_2 > \beta_2$
II	66	19	65	37	$\alpha_2 > \gamma_2 > \delta_2 > \beta_2$

For Row, H_r prescribes inequalities $\gamma_1 > \alpha_1 > \delta_1 > \beta_1$, and H_s prescribes $\gamma_1 > \alpha_1 > \beta_1 > \delta_1$. For Column, H_r prescribes $\alpha_2 > \beta_2 > \delta_2 > \gamma_2$, and H_s prescribes $\alpha_2 > \delta_2 > \gamma_2 > \beta_2$. Row's propensities corroborate H_r in both variants, except for one reversal, and H_s completely. Column's propensities corroborate neither H_r nor H_s. The discrepancies can be attributed in both variants to the "promotion" of γ_2, again reflecting the "battle of wills" characteristic of threat-vulnerable games.

The effects of payoffs on the propensities are shown in tables 16.44 and 16.45.

From table 16.44, we see that the reversal in the effect of changing c_2 on Column's choice frequencies is due entirely to the change in

TABLE 16.44   Direct effects of changing c_2 on
Column's repetition propensities
in iterated Game #50.

Propensity	Δq	e	H_m
α_2	-.27	.45	No
β_2	-.09	.15	Yes
γ_2	.04	.07	Yes
δ_2	-.12	.20	Yes

TABLE 16.45   Indirect effects of changing c_2 on
Row's repetition propensities
in iterated Game #50.

Propensity	Δq	e	H_m'
α_1	.19	.33	Yes
β_1	-.13	.22	Yes
γ_1	.53	.88	Yes
δ_1	-.19	.32	Yes

α_2. That is, in variant II, where the cost to Column of Row's resort to T_1 is larger, Column becomes somewhat more ready to repeat S_1T_2, where Row gets the largest payoff, somewhat less adamant (reflected in the smaller value of γ_2), somewhat more ready to allow Row to switch to S_1T_2 from T_1T_2 (reflected in the larger value of δ_2). All these are symptoms of greater cooperativeness on Column's part. However, Column becomes very much less willing to share "voluntarily" with Row when the latter can hurt him more, as is reflected in the large increase in α_2 ($e = .45$).

The Largest Effects of Payoff Changes

In iterated games, we can examine the effects of payoff changes both on the gross choice frequencies and in the repetition propensities. Of the former, the eight equal to or larger than .40 are listed in table 16.46. The picture is quite similar to that in single plays (cf. p. 229).

The ten largest effects of payoff change on repetition propensities are shown in table 16.47.

TABLE 16.46   Largest observed effects of payoff changes on (S).

Game #	Experimenter	PC	e
12	Worchel	d	.58
12	Rapoport-Chammah	a	.53
50	Guyer-Gordon	c_2	.52
19	Guyer-Gordon	b_1	.50
12	Rapoport-Chammah	d	.44
12	Rapoport-Chammah	d	.43
19	Guyer-Gordon	b_1	.43*
19	Guyer-Gordon	a_2, c_1	.40**

*Indirect effect
**Reversal of H_m

TABLE 16.47   Largest observed effects of payoff changes on repetition propensities.

Game #	Experimenter	PC	Propensity affected	e
19	Guyer-Gordon	b_1	γ_1	1.37
19	Guyer-Gordon	b_1	γ_1	1.15**
19	Guyer-Gordon	b_1	α_1	1.07
19	Guyer-Gordon	b_1	α_1	.98**
19	Guyer-Gordon	b_1	β_1	.97
66	Rapoport - Chammah	d	α	.90
19	Guyer-Gordon	c_2	γ_1	.88*
12	Rapoport-Chammah	a	δ	.79

*Indirect effect
**Reversal of H_m

We observe that the largest effects of payoff change on repetition propensities are about twice as large as the largest effects on gross choice frequencies. The latter are weighted averages of the repetition propensities over the two outcomes associated with each choice. We see, therefore, that the largest effects of payoff changes are highly selective, being concentrated on one of the two outcomes associated with each choice. It is interesting to note, however, that in all cases but one the concentration is *not* on the outcome associated with the payoff changed. For instance, in game #12, the largest effect of a change in a is on δ, not on α; in game #66, the largest effect of a change in d is on α, not on δ etc. We can think of no explanation for this apparent anomaly.

Effects of Absolute Payoff Magnitudes

Payoffs, as they are conceived in game theory, are supposed to represent utilities on an interval scale, which is invariant with respect to positive linear transformations (cf. p. 52). If the payoffs in an experimental game indeed represent utilities, then the results should not be affected if all the payoffs are multiplied by a positive constant. On the whole, experimental evidence supports this hypothesis. We have seen in the preceding chapter that, in single plays, the fraction of subjects choosing a particular strategy remains practically unchanged in no-conflict games and in Prisoner's Dilemma when the payoffs are multiplied by a factor as large as twenty (cf. variants I and V of game #79, p. 227). Although variants II and III of game #79 are not obtained by multiplying the payoffs of variant I by a constant, they are nevertheless of the same species, and yield maximum payoffs 300 times those of variant I. Yet, the frequencies of choices in the five variants differ by at most four percentage points.

S. Oskamp and C. Kleinke (1970) have reviewed analogous experiments with iterated games. On the whole, the results are similar to those with single plays. By way of exception, McClintock and McNeel (1966) found in a no-conflict game with competitive pressure that increasing the payoffs from 0.2¢ to 2¢ per point elicited a higher level of cooperation. The result is hardly surprising in an iterated no-conflict game. Since such a game presents no "problem," boredom may become a factor in iterated play, leading to defections, which can be expected to be the more frequent the smaller is the reward associated with the natural (cooperative) outcome.

Results on Prisoner's Dilemma are more interesting since there is no a priori reason to believe either that bigger payoffs enhance cooperation or that they stimulate competition.

Evans (1964) reported no difference in performance in short runs between games played for imaginary money and those played for points to be added to the subjects' examination scores.

Radlow (1965) used high payoffs ($5.00 in the cooperative outcome). However, the payoffs were determined for a *single* play chosen at random from a run of ninety-eight plays. Hence, strictly speaking, the game was played for an expected payoff of about 5¢ per play in the cooperative outcome. Radlow reported that the level of cooperation in this experiment was "higher than usually observed." However, since the magnitude of the payoffs was not manipulated in the experiment, a basis of comparison is lacking.

In a systematic study of the effects of payoff magnitudes undertaken by Oskamp and Kleinke (op. cit.), the following variants of Prisoner's Dilemma were used.

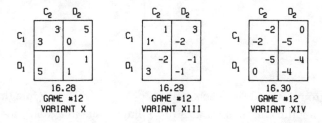

Variant X was used in three conditions with payoffs in dollars, dimes, and pennies, respectively. The payoffs of variants XIII and XIV were in pennies. Note that these variants are obtained by subtracting 2 and 5 points respectively from variant X. Hence, all variants are strategically equivalent from the game-theoretic point of view.

Actually, the multiplication of payoffs by factors of 10 and 100 was only apparent, as in Radlow's experiment above, because in the dimes and dollars conditions only the *means* of points earned per ten plays and per play respectively were converted to money. Thus the total amount to be earned by perfect cooperation was $3.00 in both conditions. Therefore, the results shown in table 16.48 still do not reflect significant manipulation of payoff magnitudes.

TABLE 16.48 Effects of changing payoff units on (C) in iterated Prisoner's Dilemma in Oskamp and Kleinke's experiment.

Subjects	Variant X dollars	Variant X dimes	Variant X pennies	Variant XIII pennies	Variant XIV pennies	Means
Males	28	32	23	22	61	33
Females	22	26	21	34	23	25
Means	25	29	22	28	42	29

We note that the differences in performance are slight and show no trend. The relatively high level of cooperation in variant XIV is accounted for entirely by the male subjects.

In their next experiment, however, the manipulation of payoff magnitudes was genuine. The variant of Prisoner's Dilemma used is shown in 16.31.

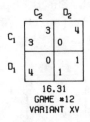

16.31
GAME #12
VARIANT XV

One group of male subjects was paid in poker chips (imaginary money), another in pennies, a third in dimes. The imaginary money group achieved an overall average level of cooperation (30 plays) of 44; the pennies group, 36; the dimes group, 34. The higher level achieved by the imaginary money group is accounted for by a "recovery" following the initial typical drop in cooperation level (cf. p. 154), whereas in the pennies and dimes groups the level of cooperation declined through the 30 plays.

The subjects of this experiment were high school juniors. In the pennies group, a cooperating pair could earn 90¢ each; in the dimes group, they could earn $9.00, which, the authors remark, is "an extremely large sum in the minds of high school juniors, for them to earn for a half hour of enjoyable work." On the strength of these findings, there is no evidence that payoff magnitudes have a discernible effect on strategy choices in Prisoner's Dilemma.

17

Strategy of Other

S. Oskamp (1971) published a comprehensive review of the experiments on mixed-motive games where the strategy of one of the players was an independent variable. In this chapter, we shall reproduce some of the findings of that review, along with some others, and comment on their significance for a behavioral theory of 2×2 games. In the definitions to be given, we follow Oskamp's terminology.

The *strategy of the other* is a preprogramed sequence of plays used by one of the players in an iterated game.

As a rule, the real subject is not supposed to be aware that he is playing against a programed sequence. Logically, if the real player is aware that he is playing against a program, the identity of the co-player should be of no importance, for then the only problem for the real player (assuming that his goal is to maximize his own payoff) is to discover the program and the best strategy against it. However, whether the identity of the programed co-player makes a *psychological* difference is an open question. It may well be that, if the stooge is the experimenter himself, the subject might be more strongly (or less strongly) motivated to "compete," i.e., to play so as to maximize payoff differences, than if the other player is a "fellow subject" constrained to play according to the program, or if the player is a computer.

Aside from these psychological overtones related to the identity of the co-player, there is a fundamental difference between playing against a bona fide subject and playing against a programed stooge.

In the latter case, nothing that the real subject can do can make the co-player change his strategy. This is not to say that the real subject can do nothing to influence the stooge's *choices*, for a programed strategy can be a contingent one where the stooge's choices depend on the subject's. What cannot be changed is the fixed program itself. The psychological effect of this determinacy depends on the complexity of the contingencies. In principle, a program can include also changes of contingencies, so that it may *seem* that the co-player "learns" and hence can be influenced to "change his strategy." In the last analysis, then, the difference between playing against a real co-player and playing against a stooge is in the impression made on the real player—on the subject's *belief* about the extent to which the co-player can be influenced by his choices.

Experiments with programed strategies are of two types. In one, a programed strategy is used throughout the iterated sequence of plays, the object being to see the differential effects of two or more programed strategies on the real-player's performance *against these strategies*. In this type of experiment, the effects are called *concurrent*. In the other type, a programed strategy is used in a preliminary sequence of plays, followed by a sequence of plays to be scored, the latter of which may be against another programed strategy or between two bona fide players. The object here is to compare the effects of different preliminary programed strategies on the *subsequent* performance of the subject. The effects compared in this type of experiment are called *delayed*.

Oskamp summarized the results of some sixty experiments with programed strategies in respect to the following features:

1. The type of game used. The types included are Prisoner's Dilemma (numerically symmetric), Prisoner's Dilemma (numerically asymmetric), Chicken, and some games from the complete set.

2. Whether the effects studied were concurrent or delayed.

3. The type of programed strategies compared. The noncontingent strategies were designated by 85 percent C, 15 percent C, 0 percent C, etc., referring to C frequencies (e.g., in Prisoner's Dilemma or in Chicken) in randomized sequences. Of the contingent strategies, the most commonly used was Tit-for-tat (cf. p. 122).

4. Plays scored. Where concurrent effects are studied, plays are scored from the first; where delayed effects are studied, beginning with the onset of the phase tested.

5. Comparison of C scores, the dependent variable associated with the programed strategies compared. (Note the concentration of attention on this particular variable and see our remarks in chapter 20 in this connection.)

6. The level of significance of the differences of C scores (if reported).

7. Whether the interaction of the programed strategy with other independent variables was examined and whether the effects were significant.

In the footnotes of Oskamp's summary table some details of the experimental conditions are given (Oskamp, op. cit., pp. 234, 241).

Prisoner's Dilemma

Concurrent effects of randomized noncontingent mixed strategies. "Pure" noncontingent strategies, i.e., 100 percent C and 100 percent D, will be discussed separately below. On the whole, the results in this group of studies are least conclusive. Predominantly, "cooperative" programed strategies generally elicit somewhat more cooperation from the real player than the predominantly noncooperative ones. For the most part, however, the effects are slight and in many cases statistically not significant. For example, Bixenstein, Potash, and Wilson (1963) examined thirty-play sequences, comparing the performance of the real player against 83 percent C and against 17 percent C strategies. The respective frequencies of C choices by the subject were 33 and 29. Swingle and Coady (1967) compared performances against even larger extremes—96 percent C and 4 percent C—and found C frequencies of 40 and 30 respectively. Knapp and Podell (1968) found (C) = 43 against 80 percent C and (C) = 32 against 20 percent. This difference was statistically significant. However, in that experiment, the programed strategies were preceded by a preliminary sequence of 50 percent C in both cases. Thus, for one group of subjects, the tested programed strategy represented a change in the direction of "more cooperation" by the co-player, whereas, for the other group, the tested strategy represented a change toward "less cooperation" by the co-player. Therefore, the difference in performance can be attributed to the direction of change rather than to the absolute value of cooperation in the programed strategies compared.

Gahagan, Long, and Horai (1969) found a significant difference in the performance against 50 percent C and 10 percent C. However, in that experiment the procedure included occasional threats of loss of points if the subjects did not cooperate on the next play.

Gahagan and Tedeschi (1969) found practically no difference, (C) = 42 vs. (C) = 43, in performances against 75 percent C vs. 50 percent C, although their procedure also included communication; for example, occasional promises to subjects that the "co-player" would cooperate on the next play.

The diversity of experimental conditions (cf. the footnotes in Oskamp's table) makes difficult an overall evaluation of results. Still, the impression is preserved that the effects of varying noncontingent randomized strategies in Prisoner's Dilemma are rather weak. In view of our discussion (cf. p. 121), this was to be expected. A co-player using a *noncontingent* randomized strategy appears nonresponsive. Since the principal motivation for choosing C in iterated Prisoner's Dilemma is to get the co-player to cooperate, the futility of these attempts when playing against a noncontingent strategy removes the motivation. The "best" strategy against a noncontingent strategy in Prisoner's Dilemma being 100 percent D, one would expect the performances to stay on a rather low level of C frequency.

Concurrent effects of pure noncontingent strategies. The differences in performance against 100 percent C and 100 percent D strategies are consistently more definitive than those against noncontingent mixed strategies. Sermat (1967) observed (C) = 40 against a pure cooperative strategy and (C) = 15 against a pure defecting one in 30 plays. Lave (1965) observed (C) = 90 and (C) = 28, respectively, in 15 plays. Wilson (1969) observed (C) = 06 against 100 percent D and (C) = 56 against 100 percent C in 120 plays.

As has been pointed out, in experiments with programed strategies the question arises as to what extent the subjects realize that they are playing against a stooge. It would seem that a pure strategy would be more suspect than a randomized one, but the results of most experiments do not warrant this conclusion. Apparently, a 100 percent C strategy is attributed to a "completely cooperative" co-player and a 100 percent D strategy to a "completely uncooperative" one. For the most part, the response to 100 percent D strategy has a very low C frequency. The average response to a 100 percent C strategy has a C frequency in the neighborhood of 50. A closer examination of the protocols reveals that the distribution of performances suggests bimodality. Roughly, one half of the subjects respond to a "completely cooperative" strategy with almost complete cooperation, while the other half "exploits" the "completely cooperative" player. We shall encounter this sort of bimodality also in other contexts.

Concurrent effects of contingent strategies. The amount of cooperation elicited by the Tit-for-tat strategy is consistently larger than that elicited by other strategies compared with it. Crumbaugh and Evans (1967) compared Tit-for-tat with an identical pattern of choices independent of the subject's and found $(C) = 65$ in response to the former, $(C) = 44$ in response to the latter. Oskamp (1970) compared Tit-for-tat with performances of bona fide pairs and found $(C) = 81$ vs. $(C) = 68$ in one experiment, $(C) = 49$ vs. $(C) = 27$ in another. All differences were significant at $p = .05$ level.

The Tit-for-tat strategy can be defined in terms of the following conditional frequencies with the stooge as Column: $Pr(C_2 \mid C_1C_2)$ $= 1$; $Pr(C_2 \mid C_1D_2) = 1$; $Pr(C_2 \mid D_1C_2) = 0$; $Pr(C_2 \mid D_1D_2) = 0$. Thus, the strategy can be modified either in the direction of more cooperation or less cooperation. For example, the following contingent strategy could be called a "semiforgiving" Tit-for-tat: $Pr(C_2 \mid C_1C_2) = 1$; $Pr(C_2 \mid C_1D_2) = 1$; $Pr(C_2 \mid D_1C_2) = .50$; $Pr(C_2 \mid D_1D_2)$ $= .50$. Analogously, the following strategy could be called "semiresponsive" Tit-for-tat: $Pr(C_2 \mid C_1C_2) = .50$; $Pr(C_2 \mid C_1D_2) = .50$; $Pr(C_2 \mid D_1C_2) = 0$; $Pr(C_2 \mid D_1D_2) = 0$.

A. M. Chammah (1969) compared performances in Prisoner's Dilemma against five strategies: 100 percent C, "semiforgiving" Tit-for-tat, "semiresponsive," and 100 percent D. The results are shown in table 17.1.

TABLE 17.1   C frequencies observed against five programmed strategies in iterated Prisoner's Dilemma.

Strategy	100% C	Semi-forgiving	Tit-for-tat	Semi-responsive	100% D
Male Subjects	39	53	70	33	16
Female Subjects	51	38	75	10	06

From the foregoing results it appears that the "responsiveness" of the co-player is a major factor in eliciting cooperative choices in

Prisoner's Dilemma. "Responsiveness," however, could be perceived not merely in terms of the probabilities of choice conditioned by a single preceding outcome, but also in terms of changes of these probabilities. For example, the "lock-in" on C_1C_2, which accounts for most of the cooperation observed in iterated Prisoner's Dilemma, may depend on the fact that the probability of C choices increases as the number of consecutive C_1C_2 outcomes accumulates. To test this conjecture, Amnon Rapoport and A. Mowshowitz (1966) compared performance in Prisoner's Dilemma against two contingent strategies. One was determined by fixed conditional probabilities of C choice, dependent only on the preceding outcome. In the other, the probabilities of C choices following C_1D_2, D_1C_2, and D_1D_2 were the same as in the first, but the probability of C_2 following C_1C_2 increased monotonically with the length of uninterrupted C_1C_2 runs.

Specifically, the following fixed conditional probabilities were used:

$$\Pr(C_2 \mid C_1C_2) = .79; \Pr(C_2 \mid C_1D_2) = .33;$$
$$\Pr(C_2 \mid D_1C_2) = .44; \Pr(C_2 \mid D_1D_2) = .20.$$

The original intent was to duplicate the mean conditional C frequencies observed in variant XII by Rapoport and Chammah (cf. p. 235). However, because of a mistake in the program, the values of $\Pr(C_2 \mid C_1D_2)$ and of $\Pr(C_2 \mid D_1C_2)$ were interchanged.

We shall now compare four performances in variant XII of Prisoner's Dilemma, namely (*i*) by bona fide players in Rapoport and Chammah's experiment; (*ii*) by bona fide players in the Amnon Rapoport and Mowshowitz experiment; (*iii*) against the contingent strategy described above; (*iv*) against the same contingent strategy where the subjects were informed that they were playing against a computer that was simulating a human performance. This last condition was used by Amnon Rapoport and Mowshowitz as an added control. The comparisons are shown in table 17.2.

If we fix our attention on (C), it appears that bona fide play is considerably more cooperative than play against a programed strategy, even though the programed conditional probabilities of C choices are approximately equal to the corresponding mean conditional frequencies in bona fide play. However, some aspects of the experiment caution against this conclusion. The values of x, y, z, and w in the performances against the programed strategy are aver-

TABLE 17.2   Comparison of performances by bona fide
players (Exp. I, II) and by subjects against
fixed contingent strategies (Exp. III, IV)
in iterated Prisoner's Dilemma.

Experiment	(C)	(CC)	(DD)	x	y	z	w
I	59	*	*	79	44	33	20
II	59	49	31	81	43	37	22
III	36	19	45	75	29	36	20
IV	31	16	49	71	32	38	18

*In this experiment, the values of (CC) and (DD)
in each variant separately are not available.

TABLE 17.3   Comparison of subject's and stooge's
propensities in Exp. III and IV in
iterated Prisoner's Dilemma.
(Subject is Row; stooge is Column).

Experiment	x_1	x_2	y_1	y_2	z_1	z_2	w_1	w_2
III	73	76	34	25	26	36	19	22
IV	70	72	38	26	34	42	13	22

ages of the corresponding values of the subject and of the stooge. These are given separately in table 17.3.

Note that in the subject's performance, $y > z$, but in the stooge's performance $z > y$—the consequence of the erroneous interchange of conditional probabilities in the program. Next, observe that in both experiments x_2 is considerably smaller than the assigned value of $Pr(C_2 \mid C_1C_2) = .79$. The reason for the discrepancy is that x_2 represents the actually occurring conditional frequency, which is subject to the statistical fluctuations in the table of random numbers according to which the stooge's choices are determined. Since x_2 here is calculated as the unweighted mean over the runs, this fluctuation is considerable. In view of this lowered value of x_2 in the programed strategy, we cannot be sure whether the considerably lower value of (C), compared with that observed in bona fide play, is due to the fixedness of the programed strategy or to the accidentally smaller values of x_2. Note, nevertheless, that except for the reversal in y, due to the program error, the real subject's propensities are considerably lower than the stooge's and lower than the mean propensities observed in bona fide play. The results, therefore, are quite consistent with the conjecture that the programed strategy elicits less cooperation than bona fide play for reasons other than the accidentally lowered values of x_2.

As for the performances in experiments III and IV, they are quite similar, suggesting that awareness of the co-player as a "human performance simulating computer" makes little difference in performance against programed strategy.

In the next experiment, subjects played against a programed strategy where y_2, z_2, and w_2 had the same values as before but where x_2 increased with the number of consecutive C_1C_2 outcomes.

Specifically, the stooge "learned" in accordance with the linear stochastic model (cf. p. 87), namely, in accordance with the following recursion equation:

$$x(t+1) = \begin{cases} \alpha x(t) + (1 - \alpha)\lambda & \text{if the outcome on the} \\ & (t-1)\text{th play is } C_1C_2; \\ x_0 & \text{otherwise, where } x_0 \text{ is} \\ & \text{the initial value of x.} \end{cases}$$

In choosing x_0, α, and λ as the parameters of the model Amnon Rapoport and Mowshowitz were guided by an attempt to find a reasonable simulation of bona fide play. For x_0, y_0, z_0, and w_0, they chose the median values of the bona fide pairs, namely 91.6, 41.1, 36.1, and 17.1 respectively. For the learning parameters, they took $\alpha = .700$, $\lambda = .985$. A Monte Carlo simulation with these parameters yielded (averaged over six runs of 300 plays) $(C) = 61$, $(C_1C_2) = 51$, $(D_1D_2) = 30$, close to the corresponding values in experiment II.

In experiment V, subjects played against the "learning" program described above. Table 17.4 presents a comparison between the performance of bona fide players (experiment II), of subjects (i.e., Row only) in experiment V, and subjects in experiment IV.

Comparing the performance against a "learning" program with

TABLE 17.4 Comparison of performances by bona fide players (Exp. II), subjects playing against a "learning" program (Exp. V), and subjects playing against a fixed contingent program (Exp. IV).

	(C)	x	y	z	w
Experiment II	59	81	43	37	22
Experiment V	49	69	30	36	18
Experiment IV	31	70	38	34	13

that against a program with fixed conditional probabilities, we see that more cooperation is elicited in the first. However, the propensities of the subjects are not consistently higher in experiment V than in experiment IV. We can only conclude, therefore, that the higher value of (C_1) is due to the assigned value of x_2 $(= 92)$ being higher in V than in IV $(x_2 = 79)$. The high trustworthiness of the stooge produces a higher value of (C_2); and, because the mean trustworthiness of the real subject is also rather high, the level of (C_1) goes up also. To be sure, x_1 in experiment V is seen to increase in successive fifty-play blocks $(x_1 = 43, 54, 65, 69, 67, 71)$. Unfortunately, the time courses of x_1 in experiments III and IV were not reported, so that the "learning of trustworthiness" by the subject cannot be attributed to the "learning of trustworthiness" by the stooge.

Comparing the results of experiment V with those of experiment II (bona fide players), we see that the level of cooperation elicited by the "learning program" is lower on all counts, even though the median value of x_1 in II, to which x_2 in V was equated, is considerably higher than the mean value of x_1.

In view of these results, we suppose that the interactions between bona fide players are more complex than those captured by even a learning program of the sort described. We have seen that a Tit-for-tat strategy usually elicits more cooperation in Prisoner's Dilemma than any other programed strategy, and even more than bona fide play. On the other hand, there is little or no evidence of consistent Tit-for-tat play by bona fide players. Perhaps there are only occasional bursts of Tit-for-tat in bona fide play, and it is these that establish temporary (C_1C_2) runs, interrupted by defections, leading to D_1D_2 runs; then, perhaps, to unilateral attempts to reestablish cooperation, etc. In other words, choices may be determined, not so much by random events with fixed probabilities defined by immediately preceding outcomes or even by a fixed number of preceding outcomes (as assumed in stochastic models "in discrete time," cf. p. 404), but rather by short term strategies projected over a few plays, the *duration* of these strategies being essentially a continuous random variable. We shall have more to say about this model in chapter 24. Here we shall only note that the failure in simulating a bona fide performance via a program characterized by estimated parameters of a contingent strategy may be inherent in the finite time-discrete nature of these programs. Whether or not the subjects realize it, the program does not feel "human enough" to them, and so elicits, in general, less cooperation than does a bona fide co-player. The Tit-for-tat strategy is a notable exception in that it elicits the most cooperation. But the success of Tit-for-tat need not be attributed to a realistic simulation of a human co-player; it may be simply most efficient in conditioning the C choice.

Delayed effects. Most of the experiments aimed at examining the delayed effects of programed strategies failed to yield any clear results. Among the few where significant delayed effects of initial strategy were noted are those of Scodel (1962), Harford and Hill (1967), and Harford and Solomon (1967). Scodel compared 10D, followed by 40C, with 50C and noted that the subject responded with significantly more C choices from the twelfth to fiftieth play when the first fixed strategy was used. One might interpret this result as suggesting that the initial D choices by the stooge establish a "credible threat," which elicits more C choices than "unconditional cooperation." Another reasonable interpretation is that the *change* from an uncooperative to a cooperative strategy is regarded by the subject (who may have been trying to establish cooperation) as an indication that the co-player has *learned.* The "gratification" of having successfully taught the co-player to cooperate may be a stronger incentive to continue cooperation than the second stooge's inherent "virtue."

Harford and Hill compared 6D, 3C, 7 Tit-for-tat with 6C, 10 Tit-for-tat, scoring plays 10 to 16, and found that the subjects responded with (C) = 52 against the former and with (C) = 37 against the latter strategy. Again, the change from D to C seems to have had the same effect as in Scodel's experiment. It is observed again in Harford and Solomon's experiment, where 3D, 3C, 7 Tit-for-tat elicited (C) = 47 in plays 7–30, whereas 3C, 27 Tit-for-tat elicited only (C) = 32. All differences were significant at p = .05 or less.

Chicken

Results with noncontingent strategies in Chicken are similar to those in Prisoner's Dilemma. McClintock, Harrison, Strand, and Gallo (1963), using 85 percent C, 50 percent C, and 15 percent C in 60 plays, observed corresponding C frequencies of 36, 41, and 38 respectively. Sermat (1964), using 80 percent C, 60 percent C, 40 percent C, and 20 percent C, observed respectively (C) = 42, 41, 43, and 33 in 50 plays. In the next 60 plays of the same experiment, Sermat observed (C) = 38 and 34 against 90 percent C and 10 percent C respectively.

The relative ineffectiveness of changing C frequencies in noncontingent strategies is somewhat more surprising in Chicken than in Prisoner's Dilemma, inasmuch as Chicken has no dominating strategy, so that C is best against D and vice versa. One would think that, if the subject "sizes up" the co-player by estimating the probabilities with which he will play C or D, he can guide himself accordingly in Chicken. However, observations do not support this conjecture.

When the programed strategies are pure, significant differences between performances are observed, as in Prisoner's Dilemma. Results obtained by Sermat are presented in table 17.5.

TABLE 17.5 Comparison of performances against pure strategies in iterated Chicken in Sermat's experiments.

Experiment	Strategy	Subject's (C)	Number of plays	Significance of difference
1964, Exp. 3	100% D	58	100	.001
	100% C	29	100	
1967, Exp. 1	100% D	48	30	N.S.
	100% C	45	30	
1967, Exp. 2	100% D	50	30	.001
	100% C	20	30	
1967, Exp. 4	100% D	56	30	Yes (level not reported)
	100% C	32	30	

We observe that in all experiments the differences are in the expected direction: the subject tends to yield to the "adamant" co-player and tends to exploit the "submissive" one. The protocols of Sermat's experiments are not available to the authors. We would conjecture, however, that the distribution of C frequencies against the 100 percent C strategy is roughly bimodal, as in Prisoner's Dilemma, reflecting a partition of subjects into "cooperators" and "exploiters." Possibly the frequencies of C choices against the 100 percent D strategy is also bimodal reflecting a partition of subjects into "submitters" and "resisters." However, if many players attempt to "resist" against

100 percent D and eventually give up, the bimodality of the distribution may be submerged.

Sermat (1967) also examined the delayed effects of 100 percent C and 100 percent D strategies in Chicken. 30C followed by 200 Tit-for-tat elicited (C) = 66 in trials 31–230, whereas 30D followed by 200 Tit-for-tat elicited (C) = 39. It is interesting to note that these results are opposite to analogous ones in Prisoner's Dilemma: initial C followed by a more retaliatory strategy elicits more C choices than initial D. Recall, however, that in Chicken the best response to C is D and vice versa. We would expect, therefore, that a change toward a more "severe" strategy calls for accommodation, while a change toward a less severe strategy may invite exploitation. However, in two other experiments by Sermat, using the same programed strategies, no significant differences in delayed effects were observed.

No-Conflict Games

Five experiments with no-conflict games are cited in Oskamp's review. The games were from the complete set, being borderline between game #6 and game #63.

Wilson and Wong (1968) noted that 0 percent C, 90 percent C, and 1C, 19 Tit-for-tat elicited (C) = 24, 36, and 38 respectively in 20 plays. Gallo, Irwin, and Avery (1966) observed (C) = 78 vs. Tit-for-tat, (C) = 50 vs. 80 percent C, a and (C) = 49 vs. 100 percent C. Scodel (1962) observed no significant difference, (C) = 85 and 83 vs. 10D, 40C, and 50C respectively. Cowan (1969) studied the interaction between the effects of strategies and the so-called Machiavellianism scores of subjects, the dependent variable being the *change* in the subjects' C frequencies. He found that 15C followed by 15D elicited more change than 15D followed by 15C in subjects with low "Mach" scores than in subjects with high scores. In the fifth experiment, (Kaufmann, 1967), the independent variable was induced perception of the co-player rather than a programed strategy, so that this experiment does not belong in the review. The results of the foregoing experiments confirm the effectiveness of Tit-for-tat in games with clearly defined cooperative and competitive aspects.

In what follows, we examine the effects in two asymmetric games of programed strategies on several dependent variables in addition to choice frequencies.

A Threat Game

M. Guyer and D. Gordon (unpublished) examined performances of subjects in five variants of game #19 against a stooge employing different programed strategies. Each subject played 100 times in each of the following conditions:

1. as Row against an "adamant" strategy;
2. as Row against a "tight" strategy;
3. as Row against a "semi-yielding" strategy;
4. as Column against a "passive" strategy;
5. as Column against a "modest" strategy;
6. as Column against a "demanding" strategy.

In addition, each subject played 100 times

7. as either Row or Column against a bona fide player.

For each subject, the seven conditions appeared in a different permutation chosen at random from the 5040 permutations. The variants of the game were those examined in chapter 16, reproduced here for convenience.

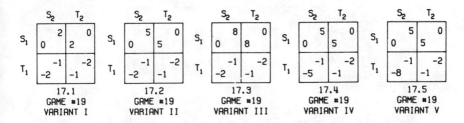

The strategies were programed as follows:

1. Column's "adamant" strategy: 100 percent S_2.
2. Column's "tight" strategy: following Row's choice of S_1, S_2 with probability .75; following Row's T_1, always S_2.
3. Column's "semi-yielding" strategy: following S_1, always S_2; following T_1, S_2 or T_2 with equal probabilities.
4. Row's "passive" strategy: 100 percent S_1.
5. Row's "modest" strategy: following a single S_2 (i.e., after a break in a T_2 run), always S_1; following two consecutive S_2's, S_1 or T_1 with respective probabilities .75, .25; following three consecutive

S_2's, S_1 or T_1 with equal probabilities; following four or more S_2's, T_1; following T_2, always S_1.

6. Row's "demanding" strategy: following a single S_2 or T_2, always S_1; following two consecutive S_2's, S_1 or T_1 with equal probabilities; following three or more S_2's, always T_1.

The "adamant" and the "passive" strategies are self-explanatory. Column's "tight" strategy amounts to Column's willingness to share .25 of the largest payoff with Row and a refusal to yield in response to Row's use of the threat strategy. Column's "semi-yielding" strategy amounts to a refusal to share "voluntarily" and a tendency to yield to Row's threat with probability .5. Row's "modest" strategy reflects a gradual increase in Row's impatience with Column's coopting of the largest payoff; his "demanding" strategy represents a more rapid increase of impatience.

Table 17.6 shows the frequencies of Row's T_1 choices when playing against each of Column's programed strategies. The corresponding frequencies in bona fide games are shown for comparison.

TABLE 17.6   Row's T_1 frequencies against Column's various programmed strategies in iterated Game #19. (Corresponding frequencies in bona fide play are shown for comparison).

Var.	I	II	III	IV	V	Means
Column's Strategy						
Adamant	18	23	40	19	05	21
Tight	15	19	38	19	09	20
Semi-yielding	21	24	45	21	09	24
Bona fide	16	23	34	13	18	21

Evidently, the effect of Column's strategy on the frequency of Row's revolts is slight, but the observed differences are suggestive. As expected, Row revolts more frequently against Column's semi-yielding strategy than against the other two; the use of the threat strategy is absolutely ineffective against either the adamant or the tight strategy but it does induce Column to "yield" (with probability .5) when he uses the semi-yielding strategy. Further, we would expect Row to resort to his threat strategy less frequently when playing against the tight strategy than when playing against the adamant strategy since, in the former, Column appears to share "voluntarily" about a quarter of the time. We observe differences in the expected direction in variants I, II, and III; no difference in variant IV, and a reversal in variant V. The reversal cannot be readily explained. Note further that, regardless of the programed strategy, (T_1) increases from variant I to II to III (as Row becomes more disgruntled), then decreases as the cost of revolt increases in variants IV and V.

It is also interesting to compare the observed (T_1) with the optimal frequencies, given the various programed strategies. Obviously, against both the adamant and the tight strategies, Row's optimal strategy is 100 percent S_1. The observed T_1 frequencies are excessive. Against the semi-yielding strategy, Row's optimal strategy is again 100 percent S in variants I, IV, and V, and again (T_1) is excessive. In variants II and III, however, Row's optimal strategy is an alternation between S_1 and T_1, i.e., 50 percent T_1. This frequency is approached only in variant III.

Table 17.7 shows the frequencies of Column's T_2 strategy when playing against each of Row's programed strategies.

TABLE 17.7   Column's T_2 frequencies against Row's various programmed strategies in iterated Game #19. (Corresponding frequencies in bona fide play are shown for comparison.)

	Var.	I	II	III	IV	V	Means
Row's Strategy							
Passive		20	15	19	15	11	16
Modest		34	26	32	32	15	28
Demanding		33	29	34	29	22	29
Bona fide		36	29	16	25	16	24

Here the results are more definitive. Column shares considerably more when Row plays the modest strategy than when he plays the passive strategy. The increase of (T_2) is seen in all five variants. On the other hand, Row's demanding strategy evokes practically no increase of (T_2) on the average, and there are decreases in two of the five variants. The results suggest that, while Column may be willing to "give in" to "reasonable" demands by Row, excessive demands do not wrest more and may sometimes be counter-productive.

Column's optimal strategy against Row's passive strategy is, of course, 100 percent S_2. The observed departure can be interpreted either as "goodwill" (voluntary sharing) or as attempts to forestall

Row's use of threat. Against Row's modest and demanding strategies, Column's optimal strategy is an alternation between S_2 and T_2; hence the observed T_2 frequencies are consistently smaller than optimal.

The effects of programed strategies on the conditional repetition frequencies are shown in tables 17.8 and 17.9. Of particular interest are the effects of Column's strategies on $\tilde{\alpha}_1$ and β_1, for these represent respectively Row's propensity to revolt and to persist in the use of T_1; also the effects of Row's strategies on $\tilde{\alpha}_2$ and $\tilde{\gamma}_2$, for these represent respectively Column's propensity to share voluntarily and to yield to Row's pressure.

TABLE 17.8 Effects of Column's strategies on $\tilde{\alpha}_1$ in iterated Game #19.

	Var.	I	II	III	IV	V	Means
Column's Strategy							
Adamant		04	07	12	04	03	06
Tight		09	14	15	03	06	09
Semi-yielding		15	24	34	13	06	18
Bona fide		10	16	20	04	14	13

TABLE 17.9 Effects of Column's strategies on β_1 in iterated Game #19.

	Var.	I	II	III	IV	V	Means
Column's Strategy							
Adamant		79	79	82	83	47	.94
Tight		66	52	81	91	49	1.82
Semi-yielding		50	43	60	51	34	1.43
Bona fide		51	52	65	68	38	1.67

Note that in variants I, II, and III, $\tilde{\alpha}_1$ tends to be larger when Row is playing against the tight strategy than when he is playing against the adamant strategy. Yet, against both of these strategies, resort to T_1 is totally ineffective. Why, then, should Row resort to it more frequently when playing against the tight strategy *in spite* of the fact that in this condition he gets a share of the largest payoff (about one-fourth), whereas he gets nothing when Column plays adamant? We surmise that Row attributes Column's occasional sharing to his (Row's) occasional resort to threat and is therefore encouraged to do so. The T_1 frequencies in variants IV and V are too small to warrant comparison.

Turning to the effects on β_1, we see that the tight strategy evokes less "persistence" in the use of T_1 than the adamant strategy, in variants I, II, and III. Thus, the reduced *unconditional* frequency of T_1 against the tight strategy (cf. table 17.9) is due to the reduced *persistence* in T_1S_2 rather than to increased frequency of shifts from S_1 to T_1. We surmise, therefore, that when playing against the tight strategy Row resorts to *short* runs of T_1, followed by return to S_1. We would expect this behavior if Row believed that his occasional resorts to threat were effective (as they seem to be against the tight strategy). In effect, he uses occasional "bursts" of T_1 to keep Column in line.

It is interesting to note the reversals of this trend in variants IV and V. In these two variants, the cost of revolt to Row is large. We surmise that only strongly disgruntled Row players resort to T_1 with considerable frequency in these variants. For such players, occasional sharing by Column may seem not enough; so they are encouraged to persist even more when such sharing occurs than when Column is adamant. At any rate, we have here examples of suggested reversal effects that deserve further investigation.

The large reductions in β_1 in the semi-yielding condition can be explained simply. In that condition, Column is likely to shift to T_2 following T_1S_2 with probability .5. If Row learns to anticipate such shifts, he will shift to S_1 simultaneously so as to get the largest payoff without going through T_1T_2. The increased frequency of these anticipatory shifts is reflected in the smaller values of β_1.

The clearest results are those related to the effects of passive and modest strategies on $\tilde{\alpha}_2$, i.e., on Column's tendency to share "voluntarily" (table 17.10). Row's "modest" demands evoke on the average twice as much sharing as completely passive acceptance of Column's top-dog position. If we assume that following S_1T_2 Column shifts back to S_2 (which he does in these two conditions with probability of about .95), then he shares in effect $\tilde{\alpha}/(1 + \alpha)$ of the largest payoff. This amounts to about .17 when Row is passive and about .31 when Row is modest. Of course, the payoffs of both players are reduced when the threat strategy is used. (Below we shall see whether Row's modest strategy actually "pays" in comparison with the passive one.) Next we note that Row's demanding strategy does not evoke significantly more voluntary sharing by Column than does the modest strategy. There may be an upper limit on how much the top

TABLE 17.10 Effects of Row's strategies on $\tilde{\alpha}_2$ in iterated Game #19.

	Var.	I	II	III	IV	V	Means
Row's Strategy							
Passive		25	18	24	16	22	21
Modest		58	38	52	46	30	45
Demanding		60	44	60	41	27	46
Bona fide		51	40	28	31	15	33

TABLE 17.11 Effects of Row's strategies on $\tilde{\gamma}_2$ in iterated Game #19.

	Var.	I	II	III	IV	V	Means
Row's Strategy							
Modest		24	26	29	28	20	25
Demanding		20	33	25	28	30	27
Bona fide		29	27	18	21	25	24

dog is willing to share under any conditions; or else Row's "impatience" as manifested in the demanding strategy may evoke Column's resentment.

From table 17.11 we see that the demanding strategy is hardly more effective in wresting concessions from Column after the use of threat than is the modest strategy.

Finally, comparing the magnitudes of $\tilde{\alpha}_2$ and $\tilde{\gamma}_2$ (tables 17.10 and 17.11), we see that the former is larger throughout. That is, Column is more likely to share "voluntarily" than following the use of threat. Nevertheless, it must be kept in mind that, when the threat strategy is not used *at all*, Column shares even less "voluntarily" than following the use of threat *when* it is used. In this respect, the threat strategy corresponds to the sort of real threats that lose effectiveness once they are used but depend for their effectiveness on occasional use. Blackmail and kidnapping are extreme examples: once the threats are carried out in *particular* instances, they lose all effectiveness for *that* instance; but to be effective they must have been carried out in other instances.

Let us now look at the effectiveness of the several programed strategies with respect to the average payoffs associated with them. We can imagine that the programed player is playing against an "average human player" and so assess the relative effectiveness of the

TABLE 17.12 Payoff accruing to Column using various strategies in iterated Game #19.

	Var.	I	II	III	IV	V	Means
Column's Strategy							
Adamant		1.47	3.60	4.41	3.87	4.70	3.61
Tight		1.15	2.89	3.43	2.96	3.46	2.78
Semi-yielding		1.19	2.60	2.70	3.30	4.31	2.82
Bona fide		.85	2.37	3.52	3.09	3.27	2.62

TABLE 17.13 Payoffs accruing to Row using various strategies in iterated Game #19.

	Var.	I	II	III	IV	V	Means
Row's Strategy							
Passive		0.41	0.77	1.53	0.76	0.56	0.81
Modest		0.96	0.23	1.60	0.07	-0.70	.43
Demanding		0.02	0.33	1.66	-0.56	-2.41	-.19
Bona fide		0.37	0.77	0.65	0.66	-0.13	0.46

strategies by comparing the average payoffs that accrue to the player using them. These are shown in tables 17.12 and 17.13. The payoffs accruing to the bona fide player are shown for comparison.

From table 17.12 we see that Column's optimal strategy against the "average human player" (naturally, sampled from the particular population used) is the adamant strategy. The tight and semi-yielding strategies are on the average about equally effective. From table 17.13 we see that Row's optimal strategy against the average player (from the same population) is the passive one. Recall that the modest strategy elicited more T_2 choices from Column but, given the payoffs of the variants used, the modest strategy "did not pay." The demanding strategy did worst of all on the average, but was slightly more effective than the modest strategy in variants II and III.

Game #50

Guyer and Gordon's experiment included also two variants of game #50 played under the same conditions as game #19. As shown in 17.6 and 17.7, in this game the natural outcome is both threat- and force-vulnerable, hence, less stable than in game #19.

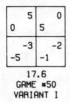

17.6
GAME #50
VARIANT I

17.7
GAME #50
VARIANT II

We have already seen (cf. chapter 16) that this lower stability is reflected in greater frequencies of T choices in bona fide play.

The effects of strategies in the two variants of the game are shown in tables 17.14–17.17.

TABLE 17.14 Effects of Row's strategies on $\tilde{\alpha}_2$ in iterated Game #50.

	Var. I	II	Means
Row's Strategy			
Passive	50	27	38
Modest	58	48	43
Demanding	61	47	54
Bona fide	49	34	42

TABLE 17.15 Effects of Row's strategies on $\tilde{\gamma}_2$ in iterated Game #50.

	Var. I	II	Means
Row's Strategy*			
Modest	31	77	54
Demanding	36	68	52
Bona fide	33	35	34

From tables 17.14 and 17.15 we see that increasing pressure by Row appears to elicit more voluntary sharing ($\tilde{\alpha}_2$) and more yielding ($\tilde{\gamma}_2$) from Column in variant I. In variant II, however, the effect of increasing pressure from "modest" to "demanding" is in the opposite direction. The reversal again raises the question of possible "psychological" effects. Does Column's severe loss in T_1S_2 of variant II evoke resentment against Row and make Column more "stubborn" as Row becomes more demanding?

From tables 17.16 and 17.17 we see that in variant I more voluntary sharing (the tight strategy) and more yielding (the semi-yielding strategy) elicits from Row a larger propensity to revolt but de-

TABLE 17.16 Effects of Column's strategies on $\tilde{\alpha}_1$ in iterated Game #50.

	Var. I	II	Means
Column's Strategy			
Adamant	15	13	14
Tight	19	09	14
Semi-yielding	30	25	27
Bona fide	14	20	17

TABLE 17.17 Effects of Column's strategies on β_1 in iterated Game #50.

	Var. I	II	Means
Column's Strategy			
Adamant	81	83	82
Tight	62	79	70
Semi-yielding	46	47	46
Bona fide	45	54	48

creases his persistence in the use of the threat strategy, an effect observed in variants, I, II, and III of game #19. In variant II of game #50, we note one reversal.

Tables 17.18 and 17.19 show the average payoffs accruing to the users of the programed strategies.

TABLE 17.18 Payoffs accruing to Row using various strategies in iterated Game #50.

	Var. I	II	Means
Row's Strategy			
Passive	1.72	1.09	1.41
Modest	.73	.90	.82
Demanding	.73	.72	.73
Bona fide	.98	.00	.49

TABLE 17.19 Payoffs accruing to Column using various strategies in iterated Game #50.

	Var. I	II	Means
Column's Strategy			
Adamant	1.50	.38	.94
Tight	2.10	1.54	1.82
Semi-yielding	1.73	1.22	1.48
Bona fide	2.22	1.02	1.62

Evidently, in game #50 the passive strategy is still optimal for Row. While putting pressure on Column generally wrests concessions, the cost of revolt in the variants used is too large to be compensated. However, Column's optimal strategy in game #50 is no longer the adamant strategy. The tight strategy yields more against the "average player." From tables 17.18 and 17.19 we see that the tight strategy elicits fewer revolts and less persistence on the part of Row than the adamant strategy in variant II. In variant I, although it elicits more revolts, it substantially reduces persistence. Because of the higher costs to Column in T_1T_2 in game #50, the tight strategy turns out to be the more effective one.

The reduction of persistence by the tight strategy is the interesting effect. Actually, Column is as "adamant" in this strategy as in the adamant one when the outcome is T_1S_2. However, the occasional sharing in the tight strategy here may lead Row to believe that only short "bursts" of T_1 are required "to keep Column in line" (as was conjectured on p. 277).

18

Information and Communication

Game theory was originally conceived as a theory of rational decision in conflict situations, where rationality is manifested in the ability to utilize all available information in arriving at a decision. In formal game theory, "available information" is understood as "information accessible according to the rules of the game." Thus, in chess, the disposition of the pieces on the board is visible to both players throughout the game. The rules being precisely defined, the options open to each player in every situation are also available information. Therefore, *in principle,* a chess player can know all possible future positions that may occur in the course of the game. *One* of his strategies comprises the set of all decisions that he can make, each decision being associated with each of the possible positions. The set of all his strategies is the set of all such sets. This latter set, although not infinite, is unimaginably large. Nevertheless, knowledge of this set is formally "available" to the player. A "rational" chess player, as defined in game theory, is one who selects from this huge set a "best" strategy, the existence of which is guaranteed by a theorem on so-called games of perfect information. Chess is an example of such a game.

In card games, some strategically relevant information is, in general, not available; for example, the initial distribution of hands among the players. Some information about this distribution usually becomes available by inference; for instance, what cards are *not* held by other players, because one sees them in one's own hand or because they have already been played. All this inferrable information is also considered to be "available" to the player.

Not available as information are the *strategies* selected by other players. These decisions are in the players' minds, and in general the rules of games of strategy do not require the players to disclose them. Note that, even after another player has made all of his moves, his chosen *strategy* is not necessarily inferrable, because many different strategies may have led to the same choice of moves. To know another's strategy, one must know how he *would* have moved in any situation that might have arisen.

In a 2 × 2 game played once, each player has only two strategies. The rules of the game specify the outcomes that result from each of the four combinations of strategy choices, and that constitutes the total of information available to each player initially. In the usual experiment with an iterated game, the choices made on each play become known to both players, and from this information a player might make inferences about how the other will choose on subsequent plays; but these are not inferences deduced from the structure of the game, since the rules do not prescribe particular choices of available strategies in iterated play. If such inferences are made, they are made on grounds that incorporate certain assumptions about the co-player's mental processes. The use of a programed player is, in fact, an attempt to manipulate the inferences the subject can make by imposing a pattern on the successive decisions of the programed player. This sort of manipulation is effected via increasing the information available to the subject, since the imposed pattern is, in general, more easily discernible than the unrestricted choices of the co-player.

In an experiment with an iterated game, information available to the subject can be restricted, for instance, by not disclosing the choices made by the other player. If the payoff matrix is known, the only way to conceal the choices of the co-player is by not announcing the outcomes of the successive plays, since the choices of the co-player can be inferred immediately from the outcomes resulting from one's own choices. If the outcomes of iterated play are not announced, the iterated game becomes a succession of single plays. In such a sequence, we can logically expect that a player who has decided that one of his strategies is better than the other will always choose the same strategy since, without feedback information on the outcomes, there is no reason for him to change. On the other hand, if the player has no clear preference between his two strategies, he may play a mixture. In fact, in a game of complete opposition without an equilibrium outcome, we would expect a rational player to play a mixture even if information about outcomes is withheld.

This expectation suggests the following experiment with a zerosum 2×2 game without dominating strategies. Assuming that in such a game at least some players will play mixtures of strategies, we can compare the mixtures chosen in iterated games where no payoff feedback is given with iterated games where feedback is provided. The former represent the players' "solution" of a zerosum game in the game-theoretic sense; the latter represent the result of interaction between the two players.

Another way of restricting information is by not displaying the game matrix and providing only payoff feedback in an iterated game. In principle, this does not constitute *actual* restriction of information, since the payoff matrix of a 2×2 game can be easily inferred from the payoff feedback, there being only four outcomes to associate with four paired choices. However, we may find that when information about the game matrix must be inferred, instead of being directly available, the experimental results will differ markedly from those when the game matrix is displayed.

Effects of Information

Rapoport and Chammah (1965) conducted experiments with Prisoner's Dilemma with the game matrix not displayed. Otherwise, the conditions were the same as those in the experiment described on p. 232. The seven variants are shown below and on the page following, with corresponding C frequencies.

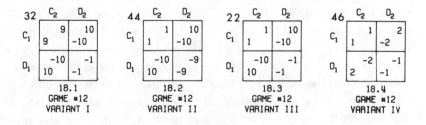

| | 18.1 GAME #12 VARIANT I | 18.2 GAME #12 VARIANT II | 18.3 GAME #12 VARIANT III | 18.4 GAME #12 VARIANT IV |

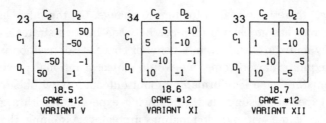

18.5
GAME #12
VARIANT V

18.6
GAME #12
VARIANT XI

18.7
GAME #12
VARIANT XII

We note first that, in comparisons of variants XI and I and variants III and V, H_m is not corroborated, in contrast to all experiments with matrices displayed, where H_m is corroborated almost without exception (cf. tables 18.1–18.2). Here there are practically no differences among the C frequencies, except for the markedly low (C) in variants III and V and the high (C) in variants II and IV. In III and V, unilateral cooperation is most severely punished and unilateral defection most highly rewarded. In IV, the "sucker's" punishment is mildest. In II, double defection is most severely punished. On the other hand, increasing reward for bilateral cooperation seems to have no effect. A reasonable explanation is that with a low level of (C), hence a still lower level of (C_1C_2), there is little opportunity to learn that "cooperation pays." In previous experiments, even if the initial level of cooperation was low, the displayed matrix *called attention* to the mutually advantageous cooperative outcome C_1C_2. We suspect that in the absence of the game matrix the players, on the whole, did not infer the payoff structure of the game and were guided in their choices only by the immediate positive and negative reinforcements. Comparison of C frequencies in the two conditions, with and without displayed matrix, are shown in table 18.1. Propensities α, β, γ, and δ when the matrix was not displayed are shown in table 18.2.

Note the predominance of α as the largest repetition propensity when the matrix is not displayed. This variable is an index of the extent of fixation on D_1D_2—the "trap" in Prisoner's Dilemma. The extent of fixation on C_1C_2, the cooperative solution of the game, is reflected in δ. While this frequency is largest in four of the seven variants when the matrix is displayed (cf. table 16.6), it is in third place in five of the seven games when the matrix is not displayed, and highest in none. Only with regard to one repetition propensity are the two experiments in full agreement: β is smallest throughout.

TABLE 18.1 Comparison of C frequencies in iterated P.D.
with and without displayed game matrix.

Var.	I	II	III	IV	V	XI	XII
Matrix displayed	73	77	46	66	27	63	59
Matrix not displayed	32	44	22	46	23	34	33

TABLE 18.2 Repetition propensities in iterated P.D.
without game matrix displayed.

Var.	α	β	γ	δ	Inequalities
I	86	36	75	66	$\alpha > \gamma > \delta > \beta$
II	75	34	72	70	$\alpha > \gamma > \delta > \beta$
III	91	37	80	68	$\alpha > \gamma > \delta > \beta$
IV	78	33	68	75	$\alpha > \delta > \gamma > \beta$
V	92	33	76	67	$\alpha > \gamma > \delta > \beta$
XI	84	34	66	72	$\alpha > \delta > \gamma > \beta$
XII	89	40	78	69	$\alpha > \gamma > \delta > \beta$
Means	85	35	74	70	$\alpha > \gamma > \delta > \beta$

That is, the least propensity is that of repeating the outcome associated with the "sucker's payoff."

The results of the experiment just described raise the question as to what extent the "understanding" of a mixed-motive game contributes to the way it is played. This question, in turn, raises another: What does it mean to understand the deeper aspects of the strategic structure of a mixed-motive game? In Prisoner's Dilemma, a "deeper" understanding is naturally identified with the realization that by establishing implicit cooperation, even without a binding agreement, both players can do better than in being guided by "individual rationality," which dictates the choice of D.

R. E. Knox and R. Douglas (1968) performed an experiment in which the independent variable was the instructions given to the subjects. One group was instructed in the usual manner: only enough information was provided to ensure that the subjects knew the correspondence between their paired choices and the payoffs. Another group was given "comprehensive" instructions in which they were encouraged to think out their choices. These instructions contained statements like "on the basis of our previous studies, we feel that there are two important aspects involved in understanding a situation: (*i*) understanding *how* to go about making your choice, and (*ii*) understanding *why* you might want to make that particular choice"; or, "because the consequences of your choices are quite important in terms of the different amounts of money that you can make on a trial, it should be obvious to you that it is a good idea to try to figure out just what choice the other person is likely to make before you decide to choose . . . ," etc.

The variant of Prisoner's Dilemma used is shown in matrix 18.8.

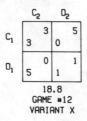

18.8
GAME #12
VARIANT X

Another independent variable used, in addition to the instructions, was the exchange rate of the points gained—namely, one cent per point in one group of subjects and one dollar per point in another. Table 18.3 shows median C frequencies in the four conditions.

TABLE 18.3 Effects of instructions and of payoff units on median numbers of C choices (out of maximum 20) in iterated P.D. in Knox & Douglas's experiment.

	Instructions	
	Traditional	Comprehensive
Payoff units		
Cents	6.70	5.50
Dollars	7.00	5.50

The differences between performances favor traditional instructions but are not statistically significant. However, the shortness of the runs (ten iterations) prevents a definitive conclusion. Note also that the rate of exchange makes little or no difference, as was noted in chapter 16 (cf. p. 259). Comparison of the *variances* of the number of C choices shows a different picture (table 18.4).

The ratio of the variances for the exchange variable is significantly different from unity by the F test at $p \leqslant .02$. The ratio of the variances on the instructions variable does not quite reach significance at the 0.1 level. However, *if* the effect of comprehensive instructions

TABLE 18.4 Effects of instructions and payoff units on
variance of the number of C choices by pairs of
players in iterated P.D. in Knox & Douglas's exp.

| | Instructions | |
	Traditional	Comprehensive
Payoff units		
Cents	2.16	11.29
Dollars	20.25	30.47

on the variance of C frequencies is real, this may indicate that call-ing the players' attention to the intricacies of the situation tends to produce opposite effects in different players. The same can be said about increasing the stakes. That is to say, in consequence of more extensive deliberations suggested by either the higher stakes or the instructions, some players are induced to cooperate more consis-tently, while others, on the contrary, are induced not to cooperate. Such a polarization would tend to produce larger variances.

An effect of this sort is in accord with the nature of Prisoner's Dilemma. There is no "right" solution to this game. Careful "reason-ing" can lead to the conclusion that the "rational" choice is C and equally well to the conclusion that the "rational" choice is D. What comprehensive instructions and larger stakes seem to do is to bind the subjects more firmly to the conclusions that they would have arrived at on the basis of what aspect of the game is more salient to them. This is the same effect that is observed in *long* sequences of iterated Prisoner's Dilemma. Eventually, the average level of cooper-ation tends to increase. But even more, the variance of C choices tends to increase as more and more pairs get locked in on the one or the other of the symmetric outcomes. Evidently, more elaborate in-structions and higher stakes produce the same effect more quickly.

A similar experiment was performed by Wrightsman, et al. (1968). This time the "treatments" were three levels of instructions. At the minimum level, only an abstract description of the game was given. At the middle level, "two illustrated examples showed concretely the intersection and payoffs when both subjects chose blue [i.e., C] and when both chose red [i.e., D]." In the maximum level condition, "simulated trials were played in addition to the illustrated examples and the abstract description of the mechanics of the game play. Here each subject was shown under simulated conditions how much money he would win in each of the four joint-choice combinations."

The time course of the number of cooperative choices per trial block are shown in figure 18.1.

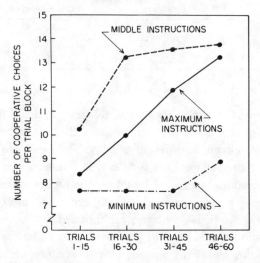

Fig. 18.1. Mean cooperation scores for different instruction levels and trial blocks (after Wrightsman, et al.).

The effect of the instructions was statistically significant ($p < .01$). However, contrary to expectations, the middle level produced the most cooperation. The authors suggest a plausible explanation. Since in the middle level illustrations were confined to the symmetric outcomes C_1C_2 and D_1D_2, of which clearly the cooperative one is preferred, it is not unlikely that the attention of the subjects may have been directed toward the value of cooperating in the Prisoner's Dilemma game. The subjects may even have taken this illustration as a cue about what was expected of them.

There are certain dangers in using instructions as an independent variable in gaming experiments. It is, naturally, a variable of great interest to psychologists since it supposedly represents a way of controlling the subject's mental set or attitude. If, however, the instructions have a *direct* bearing on the performance itself, the purpose of the experiment may be defeated in the sense that the data will simply answer the question as to what extent the instructions were followed by the subjects.

In one of the early experiments on Prisoner's Dilemma, conducted by M. Deutsch (1958), three groups of subjects were given different "orientations" toward the game. One group was given a "cooperative" orientation, one an "individualistic," and one a "competitive" orientation, induced "by verbal instructions to the subjects which characterized for them the objectives they were to have in playing the game and the objectives they could assume their co-player to have" (Deutsch, op. cit.). The actual instructions were not reproduced in the report of the experiment, but one could well imagine them to be somewhat as follows. The "cooperative" group may have been told that the objective of the game is to maximize the joint payoff; the "individualistic" group, that the objective was to maximize one's own payoff without regard to the payoff of the other; the "competitive" group, that the objective was to maximize the difference between one's own and the co-player's payoff. If this was the case, then it is clear that the "cooperative" subjects were in effect told to choose C, for the joint payoff is maximized in the C_1C_2 outcome, and the "competitive" subjects were in effect told to choose D, for the difference between payoffs is maximized in C_1D_2 and D_1C_2 in favor of the D chooser. As for the "individualistic" group, they could not readily translate the instructions into specific choices because of the inherent dilemma of the game. The results clearly reflect such explicit or implicit instructions. The proportions of subjects choosing C in single plays of Prisoner's Dilemma are shown in table 18.5.

TABLE 18.5 Effects of instructions on [C] in single play Prisoner's Dilemma in Deutsch's experiment.

Instructions	[C]
Cooperative	89
Individualistic	36
Competitive	13

Had the orientations been induced by some oblique method not having a direct bearing on the actual game, the very substantial difference in the results would have been impressive.

We note in passing that the fraction of C choosers among the individualistically oriented subjects is quite close to that observed in the single-play experiments described on p. 224.

Introducing "indirectly" induced orientations presents its own difficulties. In an iterated game, players get involved in the game process and are most strongly affected by the interactions that characterize the process. It is doubtful that under these circumstances a "subtle" differential in instructions will have a lasting effect.

Positive differential effects induced by different motivations not directly related to how to play were observed by D. Wallace and P. Rothaus (1969). Their subjects were male volunteers from two open wards of the Houston Veterans Administration Hospital, whose diagnoses ranged from anxiety reactions to schizophrenic reactions. The subjects were divided in two ways, according to instructions and according to matching.

The instructions varied in offering different incentives. In one set, the individual reward condition (IR), the subjects were told that the individual who obtained the highest total point score would be awarded $2.00 in addition to his winnings. In the group reward condition (GR), the subjects were told that each individual from the *ward* that got the highest total point score would be awarded $2.00 in addition to his earnings.

The matching varied according to whether the players were paired with co-players from the same ward (intragroup) or from the other ward (intergroup). Thus there were four groups (six pairs each):

1. individual Reward Intragroup;
2. individual Reward Intergroup;
3. group Reward Intragroup;
4. group Reward Intergroup.

Note that the reward condition per se can be expected to orient the player either toward maximizing his own score (IR) or toward maximizing the combined score of his ward (GR). However, the group-cooperative orientation can be geared to cooperative behavior in the game only when an individual plays against a member of his own group (his ward). When he plays against a member of the other ward, the group reward condition, instead of providing a co-operative incentive vis-à-vis the co-player, actually strengthens the *competitive* incentive, because in this condition the player competes not only for himself but also for his group.

The variant of Prisoner's Dilemma used is shown in 18.9.

The runs were ten plays long. The frequency of C choices in the four conditions are shown in table 18.6.

18.9
GAME #12
VARIANT XVI

TABLE 18.6   Effects of matching and of individual vs. group rewards on (C) in iterated Prisoner's Dilemma in Wallace & Rothaus's experiment.

| | Matching | | |
	Intra-group	Intergroup	Means
Individual rewards	83	55	69
Group rewards	93	23	58
Means	88	39	

Comparing the performance of the intragroup and intergroup pairs, we find a large, highly significant difference ($p < .01$) in favor of the intragroup pairs. The experimenters point out that "both wards develop cohesive patient groups, enabling the study of behavior between strangers and intergroup members."

Comparing the performances of the IR and GR groups without regard to the matching condition, we find that the frequency of C choices in the latter is actually smaller (though not significantly). This finding would be contrary to expectation on the basis of the instructions alone, but examining the performance of intragroup and intergroup plays we see the true picture: Instructions orienting toward group solidarity are effective only in intragroup matching. From table 18.6 we see both the positive and negative effects of the GR condition. The interaction (Intra-Inter) x (IR-GR) was found to be significant at the .05 level. Thus the group-reward condition significantly intensified the difference between intragroup and intergroup performances.

We observe, in passing, that in spite of the shortness of the runs, the frequencies of C choices in the intragroup condition are very high, even considering the "mildness" of the game used ($T - R = 1$; $R - P = 8$), which may be evidence for the "cohesive patient groups" developed within the hospital wards.

One form of information as an independent variable is information given to a player about the personality or attitude of the other player. For instance, in games of competition-cooperation, information about the "cooperativeness" of the co-player may induce not only assumptions about the choices he is likely to make but also an attitude, say, a preference to cooperate or, contrarily, a propensity to exploit. In a game with bona fide players, the effect of the attitudinal set can be considerable even if information about the attitude of the co-player is given to only one of the players, because the induced attitude manifested in the informed player's choices may influence the choices of the other, which may, in turn, reinforce the induced attitudes or inhibit them. If, on the other hand, the co-player is programed, the influence of the attitudinal set can be studied without the additional complication of induced interactions.

In experiments with stooges, "information about the other" can be given to the subject implicitly via the co-player's prescribed choice patterns. Such studies were subsumed under the rubric "Strategy of Other" and were discussed in the preceding chapter. In what follows, we examine the effects of information about the co-player given explicitly, that is, information about his propensities, attitudes, race, background, etc.

In an experiment by G. W. Baxter, Jr. (1969), white female freshmen at George Peabody College played variant XVI of Prisoner's Dilemma (see 18.9, p. 293) against the same programed strategy, namely 27C and 3D, the D choices always falling on the sixth, fourteenth, and twenty-second play.

Before the experimental session, each subject was introduced to the supposed co-player, one of two female accomplices, one white, the other black, who could be taken for college freshmen. In addition, each subject was given either no information about the co-player or information in the form of answers to certain questions. One set of answers was judged by independent raters to give the impression of "cooperativeness"; the other, of "competitiveness." Lastly, the subjects were grouped into those from northern regions of the United States and those from southern regions. The choices in the three ten-play blocks were analyzed separately. Thus the design of the experiment was $3 \times 2 \times 2 \times 3$ factorial, representing information given (3), race of other (2), geographical region (2), and block of plays (3). Analysis of variance failed to reveal differences approaching significance with respect to either the block of plays or geographical region or interactions of these with the other conditions. Of interest, therefore, are the effects of information concerning race and concerning "cooperativeness" of the other player. The results are summarized in table 18.7.

TABLE 18.7 Effects of information about co-player on (C)
in iterated P.D. vs. a fixed programed strategy
in Baxter's experiment.

Supposed attitude of co-player	Supposed race of co-player		Means
	Black	White	
Cooperative	64	80	72
Unknown	60	64	62
Competitive	59	60	60
Means	61	68	

It turned out that the effect of information about "cooperativeness" was significant ($p \leqslant .04$) and in the expected direction: the largest number of C choices were made by the subjects who thought they were playing against a "cooperative" player; the smallest number, by those who thought they were playing against a "competitive" player; the number of C choices by subjects playing without this information was intermediate.

The overall effect of the supposed "race" of the other failed to reach the chosen criterion of significance ($p < .05$), but it was in the expected direction ($p < .09$). Moreover, the difference in (C) against the supposed *cooperative* white and the supposed *cooperative* black co-player was significant at $p < .02$. The experimenter conjectures that there was a stronger tendency to exploit the supposed cooperative black co-player.

It should be noted that in this experiment the plays were made consecutively, with the subject always choosing first. Thus a choice of C reflects predominantly "trust" rather than "trustworthiness." Recall that in simultaneous choices the two supposed factors are confounded. Apparently, information about the other had some influence on the readiness to trust her rather than on the propensity to respond to her choices one way or the other. Consequently, the smaller number of initiated C choices when playing against a supposed cooperative black co-player may indicate a stronger distrust (in comparison with the attitude toward a cooperative white player) rather than a tendency to exploit. This interpretation is conjectural, however, because it is not easy to separate "trust" from "trustworthiness" in Prisoner's Dilemma except when subjects make both first and second choices in sequential plays.

In this connection, it is interesting to examine the frequencies of C choices by the same subjects following the stooge's D choices (on the sixth, fourteenth, and twenty-second plays). Here the effect of race was significant ($p < .05$). These choices were made more frequently vis-à-vis the supposed *black* co-player. The effect of information was not significant, but the interaction of race and information was ($p < .03$), the largest number of C choices being vis-à-vis the *competitively* described black co-player. This result seems to support the "exploitation" hypothesis. Namely, whereas there is a tendency to appease the supposedly competitive *black* co-player, there is a tendency to exploit the cooperative black co-player. The result would be highly interesting if confirmed as a hypothesis stated in advance.

In the following experiments with a programed co-player, the independent variable is a strategy *available* to the co-player. Actually, the co-player never uses this available strategy, the programed strategy being 100 percent choice of the other strategy. Therefore, these experiments are subsumed under those where information given to a player, rather than the strategy of the other, is the independent variable.

P. G. Swingle (1970) used the following matrices in iterated games in which the stooge took the role of Column.

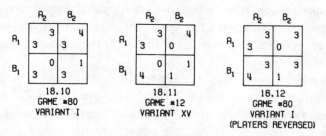

18.10
GAME #80
VARIANT I

18.11
GAME #12
VARIANT XV

18.12
GAME #80
VARIANT I
(PLAYERS REVERSED)

The stooge's strategy was always 100 percent A_2. The object of the experiment was to compare the performances of subjects who *saw* different strategies available to the co-player.

The experimenter considers this situation to be a simulation of different power relations between the subject and the co-player. Thus, according to him, the subject playing Row in 18.10 has "full power." This interpretation apparently stems from the circumstance that in this game Row can affect Column's payoffs without thereby being subjected to any influence from Column's play, because Row's payoffs are equal in all four cells. The situation in 18.12 is reversed. Here the subject perceives the co-player as having "power." Note that the two matrices differ only in the interchange of roles: 18.11 is a variant of Prisoner's Dilemma, and since this game is symmetric, it is presented as an example of a game with equal power.

Swingle's interpretation of the power relations is open to objections. "Power" is usually interpreted, not only in terms of the ability to affect the situation of others, but also in terms of the ability to affect one's own situation. From this point of view, Row in game 18.10 has no power at all, since he cannot change the magnitude of his own payoff no matter what he does. However, assuming Swingle's interpretation of the power relations, the question to be answered is with regard to the subject's tendency to exploit the "cooperative" co-player in each of the three situations: when the subject has power, but not the co-player; when both have equal power; when the co-player has power, but not the subject. As stated, the co-player always chooses A_2, which Swingle interprets as "cooperation." In view of the fact that Row's payoffs in game 18.10 are all equal, it is difficult to see why the choice of A by Column in that game is "cooperative," except to the extent that Column does not take advantage of the opportunity to get more than Row in A_1B_2 (without, however, depressing Row's payoff).

The game represented by 18.11, being a variant of Prisoner's Dilemma, needs no comment. Let us now consider game 18.12 in which Swingle assumes Row has "no power." But Row has a dominating strategy in B_1. In using it, he does not hurt Column in any way, except possibly if Column is competitively oriented. However, he benefits himself.

Swingle's hypothesis was that "subjects attempt to maximize their payoffs against an unconditionally cooperative opponent when the opponent has more power than the subject. The equal power situation would lie somewhere between the two." Following his interpretation, we assume that his hypothesis states that subjects' choice of B will be most frequent in 18.12, least in 18.10, and intermediate in 18.11. The frequency of B choices was about 80 in 18.12, about 68 in 18.11, and about 60 in 18.10.

The high frequency of B_1 in 18.12 is explained most directly by the

circumstance that in that game B_1 strictly dominates A_1, and moreover, Row's strategy choice has no effect on Column's payoffs. Hence,
Row has no reason to suppose that Column will retaliate (as he may
well do in game 18.11).

The results on 18.11 would be more revealing if the frequency
choices of individual subjects were reported. It would be interesting
to see whether the distribution is bimodal in this case, separating
players who exploit the 100 percent cooperative player in Prisoner's
Dilemma from those that cooperate with him.

The frequency of 60 of B_1 choices in 18.10 seems at first to indicate either malevolence or a strong competitive orientation on the
part of the average subject. However, another interpretation suggests
itself. Recall that the natural outcome in this game is A_1B_2. The behavior of the co-player who keeps choosing A_2 looks puzzling. Consider a subject who feels that the outcome should be A_1B_2 rather
than A_1A_2, since the two outcomes award the same payoff to him
but A_1B_2 awards more to Column—in other words, a benevolent subject. He might think that the way to get Column to play B_2 is by
choosing B_1. The outcome B_1A_2 might induce Column to switch to
B_2, since he gets 1 in B_1B_2 and 0 in B_1A_2. (Actually, the same difference in Column's payoffs characterizes the choice between A_1A_2 and
A_1B_2; but possibly Row might think that the difference is more conspicuous between B_1A_2 and B_1B_2.) Accordingly, at least some of
Row's B_1 choices may have been made in an attempt to "force" Column to choose B_2 "for his own good," as it were, in the hope of lock-
ing in on the Pareto-optimal outcome A_1B_2.

We have the impression that Swingle was misled by the labels
attached to strategies in Prisoner's Dilemma. In 18.10 and 18.12,
these labels, suggesting "cooperation" and "defection," no longer
represent the situation. They were nevertheless retained as the payoffs of Prisoner's Dilemma were changed, and so contributed to a
misunderstanding of the pressures operating in the other two games.
For this reason, we feel it is advisable to have a standard form of the
2×2 game where the natural outcome always appears in the same
position. When the structure of the game is changed by varying the
payoffs, the erstwhile natural outcome may no longer be one. In that
case, the rows and/or columns of the matrix should be interchanged
appropriately to avoid the impression that the "upper left" is always
the natural outcome, or, in games of cooperation-competition, the

"cooperative outcome," as established by the conventional notation for Prisoner's Dilemma.

M. Shubik (1962) performed an experiment with several 2×2 games in which information about the co-player's payoff was withheld. The principal purpose of the experiments was to test a number of game-theoretic solutions of nonconstant-sum games, but there is an interesting by-product of Shubik's experiment that suggests a line of investigation having considerable psychological interest which we want to point out here. After playing the iterated game, Shubik's subjects were asked to guess the rank order of the co-players' payoffs in each game. The only information available to the subjects about the others' payoffs was what could be deduced from the others' choices (which were announced to the subjects), or rather from their recollections of the others' choices. Therefore, the accuracy with which the players infer the relative magnitudes of the others' payoffs in the different outcomes is of interest. In particular, it would be interesting to see whether some games distort the perceptions of the others' preferences for outcomes more than others.

Because the number of subjects in Shubik's experiments was small (five pairs) and the runs were short (ten to twenty), statistical evaluation of the accuracy of their perceptions is not enlightening. Still, it is noteworthy that the average ranks assigned to the four payoffs of the co-player were in correct order. If we designate the most preferred outcome by 4 and the least preferred by 1, the average ratings of the four outcomes were 3.43, 2.89, 2.41, and 1.64 respectively. With larger numbers of subjects various statistical methods could be used to determine the accuracy score for each type of game. Also the performances in the *perceived* games could be compared with those in games that are actually of that species. To give an example, one of the games used by Shubik was Prisoner's Dilemma and consequently had the structure shown in 18.13 (standard format).

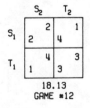

18.13
GAME #12

When we enter Row's perceived (incorrect) rank order of Column's payoffs, we get the game as Row sees it:

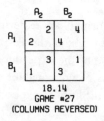

18.14
GAME #27
(COLUMNS REVERSED)

That is, Row perceives the game as a no-conflict game, and it seems to him that by choosing A_1 (actually the noncooperating strategy) he is cooperating, creating the opportunity for the largest payoff for both if only Column will choose B_2. He may interpret Column's defections to A_1A_2 as a defense against his (Row's) possible defection to B_1B_2 in pursuit of competitive advantage. If we enter Column's perceived rank order of Row's payoffs, we get

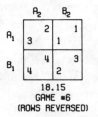

18.15
GAME #6
(ROWS REVERSED)

Here Column also perceives the game as a no-conflict game. It seems to him that *he* is cooperating and that the outcome most preferred by both would occur if only Row did the right thing and chose B_1. It would be interesting to see how frequently such "projections" of one's own uncooperative behavior on the co-player occur when the players are not informed of their co-players' payoffs.

M. Guyer and A. Rapoport (1969) investigated performances in Leader (game #68) and Hero (game #69) when information about the other's payoff was withheld. The variants of the games are shown in 18.16 and 18.17.

18.16
GAME #68
VARIANT II
("LEADER")

18.17
GAME #69
VARIANT III
("HERO")

The main variable examined was the index of cooperation defined in chapter 6, namely,

$$K = (T_1S_2) + (S_1T_2) - |(T_1S_2) - (S_1T_2)|.$$

Comparison of K in the two games and in the two conditions is shown in table 18.8.

TABLE 18.8 Effects of information about co-player's payoffs on K in iterated Games #68 and #69.

Game	I	NI
#68 ("Leader")	57	16
#69 ("Hero")	63	33

The effect on the amount of cooperation of withdrawing information about the other's payoff is clearly detrimental in both games.

Next, we examine the two components of K separately to see which is affected more strongly. Table 18.9 shows the comparison between the first components, $(S_1T_2) + (T_1S_2)$.

TABLE 18.9 Effect of information about co-player's payoffs on the asymmetry component of K, $(S_1T_2) + (T_1S_2)$ in iterated Games #68 and #69.

Game	I	NI
#68 ("Leader")	85	87
#69 ("Hero")	79	77

Evidently, information has practically no effect on the frequencies of the asymmetric outcomes. The picture looks very different when we compare the other, that is, the "dominance" components of K, $|(S_1T_2) - (T_1S_2)|$, as in table 18.10.

TABLE 18.10 Effect of information about co-player's payoffs on the dominance component of K, $(S_1T_2) - (T_1S_2)$ in iterated Games #68 and #69.

Game	I	NI
#68 ("Leader")	28	71
#69 ("Hero")	16	44

We conclude that the entire effect of information on the amount of cooperation in these games is via the "dominance" component.

Apparently, it is the realization of the fact that the positions of the players are equal that induces them to share equally in tacit collusion.

When full information about the payoff matrix is lacking, the one or the other player is likely to dominate; that is, to "have his way" more often in effecting his most preferred outcome. Let us see how this might happen.

Suppose in the course of a run one of the asymmetric outcomes, say, T_1S_2, occurs. Assuming independence of choices on single plays, the probability that one player shifts is larger than the probability that both shift simultaneously. Whichever player shifts unilaterally from T_1S_2, the payoffs of both players are reduced. Hence there is generated a pressure on both players to shift again. Again the probability that only one shifts is larger than the probability that both shift. Now the matter hinges on whether it is more likely that the player who has just shifted from T_1S_2 will shift back than that the player who did not shift will now shift. If the former event is more likely, our effect is explained; for then T_1S_2 recurs, and since the payoffs of both players have increased, the tendency to shift away again is reduced. In the extreme case, T_1S_2 will be "fixated" and, consequently, $|(S_1T_2) - (T_1S_2)|$ will be large.

Can we now justify the hypothesis that it is more likely that the shifting player will shift back than that the repeating player will shift? We conjecture that this is indeed the case, because the payoff of the shifting player has been reduced in consequence of his *own* action, whereas the payoff of the repeating player has been reduced while he was "doing nothing." It seems to us that "corrective action" is more likely to be taken by the shifting player, since he can immediately attribute the reduction of his payoff to what he just did, whereas the nonshifting player must first ascertain (or at least hypothesize) why his payoff was reduced while he did "the same as before."

Next, it seems that information has a greater effect on the "dominance" component of K in Leader than in Hero. We seek a rationale for this observation.

Dominance in both games is reduced by propensities to shift away from the asymmetric outcomes S_1T_2 and T_1S_2. Since both games are symmetric, it suffices to fix our attention on one of these outcomes, say, T_1S_2. In the information condition in Leader, the predominant pressure to shift away from T_1S_2 is on Column, who gets less than Row and who may try to effect S_1T_2, where he gets most, by shifting to T_1T_2, thus putting a very strong pressure on Row to shift to S_1T_2 (cf. 18.16). In Hero, on the other hand, when T_1S_2 occurs in the information condition, the predominant pressure to shift is on Row. When Row shifts to S_1S_2, he also puts pressure on Column to shift to S_1T_2; but this pressure, represented by $b_2 - a_2 = 6$ (cf. 18.17), is considerably smaller than the corresponding pressure in Leader, represented by $c_1 - d_1 = 20$. To be sure, the cost of shifting to the shifter is smaller in Hero than in Leader, but this cost, being associated with the shifter's own payoffs, is known in both conditions. Therefore, it is knowledge of the other's payoffs that contributes to the attractiveness of a shift from either asymmetric outcome more in Leader than in Hero. Possibly this is the effect reflected in the larger reduction of the dominance component in Leader when information about the other's payoff is available than when it is not.

In the information condition, the larger dominance in Leader (assuming the differences significant) can perhaps be explained. Leader is a preemption game; the player who takes the initiative by shifting away from the natural outcome unilaterally gets the largest payoff. Retaliation is costly. In Hero, the unilateral shifter does not get the largest payoff, and returning to natural outcome is not very costly to him. Accordingly, more returns to the natural outcome are expected in Hero. These provide inducement for the co-player to take the part of the "hero" and so to reduce dominance.

The apparently larger dominance effect of no-information in Leader remains unexplained.

A rather revealing comparison between the information and the no-information conditions in Leader and Hero is between the correlations of the components of K over the player pairs. Using Spearman's coefficient of rank order correlation, we find the values shown in table 18.11.

TABLE 18.11 Rank order correlations across pairs of players between the asymmetry and dominance components of K in iterated Games #68 and #69.

	Hero - I	Hero - NI	Leader - I	Leader - NI
Spearman's coefficient	-.398	+.472	-.736	+.524

Of these correlations, only −.736 is significantly different from zero at the .05 level (N = 10 in each category). Nevertheless, the fact that the correlations in the two information conditions are of opposite sign in both games warrants further investigation. Noting that the differences in the correlations between games are not large, we combine the data for each game and compare the correlations. These are −.673 in the information condition and +.703 in the no-information condition. Both correlations are now significant at the .01 level.

Still, there is some room for scepticism inasmuch as the range of $| (S_1T_2) - (T_1S_2) |$ is not independent of that of $(S_1T_2) + (T_1S_2)$. Thus a *positive* correlation between $| (S_1T_2) - (T_1S_2) |$ and $(S_1T_2) + (T_1S_2)$ might be an artifact since, as the sum increases, the upper bound on the absolute difference also increases. (As compensation, this circumstance makes the *negative* correlation more impressive.) To counteract the possible artifact, Guyer and Rapoport normalized the difference scores, so that they would have the same range; i.e., used

$$\frac{| (S_1T_2) - (T_1S_2) |}{(S_1T_2) + (T_1S_2)}$$

instead of the absolute difference for each pair. The correlations now become −.801 in the information condition and +.708 in the no-information condition. Both are significantly different from zero at the .01 level.

The result invites several interpretations. The most direct, it seems, is that in the information condition the dissatisfied player at a Pareto-optimal outcome will tend to permit this outcome to occur only when it is a part of an alternating sequence, that is, when he is doing his part in a cooperative run. Thus the more frequent occurrence of the asymmetric outcomes will be associated with more alternations; that is, smaller absolute differences between (S_1T_2) and (T_1S_2), hence with a negative correlation between the former and the latter.

In the no-information condition it would appear that the alternating pattern is more difficult to establish. Those pairs that do establish it may do so at the cost of increasing the frequencies of the symmetric (Pareto-deficient) outcomes. That is, the alternation is achieved stepwise, passing through T_1T_2 or through S_1S_2 rather than directly. The result would be a positive correlation between (S_1T_2) $+ (T_1S_2)$ and $| (S_1T_2) - (T_1S_2) |$.

Another explanation for the positive correlation is that high frequencies of the asymmetric outcome in the no-information condition may be mostly a result of "giving in" by one or the other player rather than to an alternating pattern. This makes for a more "skewed" protocol and so contributes to the positive correlation between the sum and the absolute difference of asymmetric outcome frequencies.

Effects of Communication

A direct comparison between performances in Prisoner's Dilemma with "level of communication" as an independent variable was made by H. Wichman (1970). The subjects were divided into four groups according to the following conditions. The *isolated* condition (I) was the standard one, where the co-players were not permitted to communicate and were visually isolated from each other. In the *see only* condition (SO), they were able to see each other but not to communicate by sound (they could make gestures). In the *hear only* condition (HO), they were permitted to speak to but not see each other. In the *see and hear* condition (S&H), unlimited communication was allowed. The time courses of median C frequencies are shown in figure 18.2.

The results are as could be expected. The level of cooperation is lowest in the isolated condition and highest in the see-and-hear condition. Moreover, the level of cooperation is higher in the hear-only condition than in the see-only condition. This result could also be expected since the effectiveness of communication depends on establishing a collusion which can be more easily proposed by explicitly verbalized offers than by gestures. Moreover, the attention of the co-player can be readily engaged by calling out, but not by gesturing, if the co-player is not looking.

The significance of the differences was established by Jonckheere's distribution-free k-sample test. The hypothesis was supported by that test at $p < .005$ level.

In the following experiment by R. Radlow and M. F. Weidner (1966), some aspects of behavior in iterated Prisoner's Dilemma were observed under conditions permitting explicit (nonenforceable) agreements between players. The variant used is shown in 18.18.

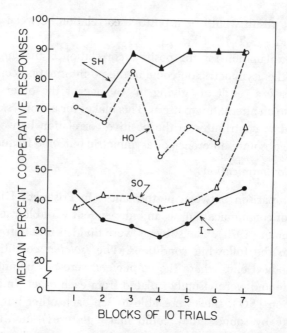

Fig. 18.2. Median levels of cooperation for four different experimental conditions: isolated (I), see only (SO), hear only (HO), and see and hear (S&H) (after H. Wichman).

18.18
GAME #12
VARIANT XVII

The players could choose among the following commitments, communicated to the co-player:

1. I will press my left button the first trial. On each following trial, I will press the button that *you* had pressed on the previous trial.

2. I will press my left button the first trial. If you had pressed your left button also, I will press my left button on the second trial. I will continue to press my left button as long as you do, but if you press your right button at any time, I will press my right button for *every* trial thereafter.

3. I will press my left button on the first trial. If you had pressed your left button also, I will press my left button on the next trial. I will continue to press my left button as long as you do, but if you press your right button, I will switch and press my right button for every succeeding trial until you press your left button for three consecutive trials as a signal that you wish to resume joint choices of our left buttons.

4. I will press my right button on the first trial. If you had pressed your left button on the first trial, I will press my left button on the second trial. Thereafter, I will continue to press my left button as long as you do, but if you press your right button at any time, I will press my right button for *every* trial thereafter.

5. I will press my right button on the first trial. On each following trial, I will press the button that *you* had pressed on the previous trial.

Each player of the sixteen communicating pairs chose one of the five options (printed on a card) and passed it to the co-player who, in turn, chose one and passed it back. The exchange continued until three pairs of options were chosen consecutively or until fifteen exchanges were made, in which case, the last choices became final. It is interesting to note that both players in nine of the sixteen pairs chose commitment 3. Both players of three pairs chose commitment 1, and both players of one pair chose commitment 5. In the remaining three pairs, the players chose different commitments (3, 1), (1, 2), and (1, 5).

Of the five commitments, 1 and 5 are announcements of a Tit-for-tat strategy. They differ only in that 1 begins with a C choice, 5 begins with a D choice. Commitments 2 and 4 are totally retaliatory. They promise to cooperate as long as the other does, but threaten total withdrawal of cooperation if the co-player makes a single defecting choice. These two differ also only in the initial choice. Commitment 3 is like 2, except that it gives the other player a chance to reestablish cooperation, evidence of intent being three consecutive C choices (a "penance").

Observe that the majority of subjects chose the harshly punishing but potentially forgiving commitment 3. Of the remainder, all but one chose the one or the other version of Tit-for-tat. Only one subject chose the initially cooperating but totally retaliatory commitment 2. (On the initial exchanges of commitments, twenty-one of the thirty-two players chose commitment 3; only three chose the harshest commitments 2 and 4; the remaining players chose Tit-for-tat.)

Now, if the commitments were considered binding by the subjects and if they acted "rationally," in consideration of these commitments the results would be entirely predictable since the commitments completely determine the sequence of outcomes. For example, any combination of commitments 1, 2, and 3 would result in runs of 100 percent C. A pair of subjects choosing 5 or 4 would have to choose D throughout. A combination of 1 and 5 would have to result in a sequence of alternating C_1D_2 and D_1C_2 outcomes, etc. However, there was nothing in the instructions indicating that the commitments were binding or not binding. Indications of how the subjects interpreted the agreements were obtained from the subjects' statements after the experiment. In some cases, the subjects asked explicitly whether the commitments were binding, in which case they were told that they were not. In four cases, the subjects' interpretations could not be ascertained.

A large majority of the subjects did not consider the commitments to be binding. In spite of this interpretation, in 24 of the 28 cases where 100 percent C protocols would have resulted under binding commitments, they did in fact occur. In the other four cases, the frequency of C choices was between 80 and 95. On the other hand, in one pair, where the result of sticking to the commitment would have been a 50 percent C run, the C frequencies were 32 and 22. In the remaining pair, where a binding commitment would have resulted in a 100 percent D run, the C frequencies were 36 and 39.

The noncommunicating pairs produced a typical Prisoner's Dilemma time course of (C) with the characteristic initial decline and a recovery after about 30 plays. The average (C) in this group was 55 compared with 90 in the communicating group (differences significant at the .001 level by the Mann-Whitney test).

R. G. Swensson (1967) examined the effect of both information about payoffs and communication in variant X of Prisoner's Dilemma played by female subjects (18.19).

One player of each pair was given complete information about the payoffs; the other was given information only about her own payoffs. The communication conditions were varied according to whether

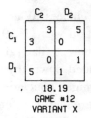

18.19
GAME #12
VARIANT X

only the informed player or only the uninformed player or both (alternately) could send a standard message prior to each play and according to the content of the message. This was either "I have chosen—" (information only), or "You choose—" (command only), or "I have chosen—; you choose—" (information and command).

Analysis of variance indicated significant effects only over blocks of plays (the usual decline of C frequency in thirty plays) and an interaction between information and blocks. The source of interaction is seen by comparing the frequency of C choices of all the informed players (pooled from all the communication conditions) with those of the uninformed players block by block. Among the informed players, (C) decreases from 48 in the first block of ten plays to 30 in the third block. Among the uninformed players, (C) is practically constant (38) in all three blocks. The small number of pairs (four or five) in each condition all but precludes observing significant differences in the effects of the variables in question. The observed differences, however, are suggestive and are worth examining in larger experiments. Thus, without communication, (C) of informed players was 31; of the uninformed players, 19. Examining the outcome frequencies in that condition, we find $(C_1 C_2) = 5$; $(D_1 D_2) = 55$. Since $(C_1) = (C_1 C_2) + (C_1 D_2)$, and $(C_2) = (C_1 C_2) + (D_1 C_2)$, we infer that in the uninformed condition $(C_1 D_2)$ was 26, whereas $(D_1 C_2)$ was 14. Apparently Row, the informed player, makes more frequent attempts to initiate cooperation than the uninformed player.

Next, we note that whenever only one player could send the message "I have chosen—; you choose—" the sender of the message made more C choices than the recipient regardless of whether the sender was informed or uninformed. Thus, when the sender was the informed player, the distribution of the outcome frequencies was (20, 25, 11, 43). Again it was the informed player (the sender) who made more unilateral cooperative choices. When the sender was the uninformed player, the distribution was (11, 9, 25, 54). Here the uninformed player also made more unilateral cooperative choices.

If these effects were "pinned down" by using appropriately large numbers of subjects, one might conclude that the opportunity to communicate outweighs the effect of information about the other's payoffs. Moreover, it is the active communicator who seems to be more motivated to initiate cooperation than the recipient of the message.

This conclusion can be deduced also from the nature of the situation and from the format of the standard message and the content. Consider the informed player. The only message that it makes sense to send is "I have chosen C; you choose C." (Since the uninformed player sees her own payoff matrix, she is not likely to obey "I have chosen D; you choose C." The other two messages, if obeyed, would bring losses to the sender.) Therefore, the sender has two options: to keep the promise in the message bidding for cooperation or to break it. Promises once broken are not likely to be believed when repeated; therefore, the rational sender is practically certain to choose C. The *recipient* of the message, however, especially if uninformed about the payoffs of the other, is not under any compulsion to obey.

Consider now the uninformed *sender* of messages. She sees only her own matrix and so may send messages which, if obeyed, will get her the largest payoff. The co-player, however, knowing her own payoffs, is not likely to obey messages that will bring losses. Only the message that promises C is likely to be obeyed. It may take some time for the uninformed player to find out that the message promising C is the only productive one. For this reason, we would expect somewhat less cooperation when the uninformed player is the sender than when the informed player is the sender. Examining the outcome frequency distributions above, we find that this is the case.

19

Who Plays How

For the psychologist, the player himself is often the most interesting independent variable in game experiments. If so, the experiment can serve either of two purposes: (i) to test hypotheses concerning how players with certain independently observed characteristics will behave in a given game, or (ii) to generate hypotheses concerning some psychological feature of a player or a category of players on the basis of their behavior in game experiments.

As an example of the first approach, the much used Prisoner's Dilemma, generally regarded as a model of cross pressures between a tendency to "cooperate" and a tendency to "compete," is presented to separate groups of subjects whose independently assessed characteristics suggest that they are motivated more strongly by one or the other pressure. In the second approach, an a priori judgment of the players' tendencies is not usually warranted. For instance, opinions differ on whether men or women are more strongly motivated to cooperate or to compete. Here the results of an experiment may give grounds for generating a hypothesis. It goes without saying that generalization of results is warranted only if the generated hypothesis is corroborated in a variety of contexts.

Sex Differences

Consistent differences in performance of men and women in Prisoner's Dilemma were observed by Rapoport and Chammah (1965).

311

In all seven variants of that game used in those experiments, women playing against women chose C considerably less frequently than men playing against men. The results are shown in table 19.1. The outcome frequencies, averaged over the seven variants are shown in table 19.2. Table 19.3 presents a comparison of the cooperative propensities.

TABLE 19.1   Comparison of C frequencies in male & female pairs playing iterated Prisoner's Dilemma.

Variant	I	II	III	IV	V	XI	XII	Means
Male pairs	73	77	46	66	27	63	59	59
Female pairs	34	27	28	48	11	55	30	33

TABLE 19.2   Comparison of outcome frequencies in iterated P.D. in male & female pairs (7 variants pooled).

	(C_1C_2)	(C_1D_2)	(D_1C_2)	(D_1D_2)
Male pairs	51	08	09	32
Female pairs	23	11	11	55

TABLE 19.3   Comparison of cooperative propensities in iterated P.D. in male & female pairs (7 variants pooled).

	x	y	z	w
Male pairs	85	40	38	20
Female pairs	75	37	26	15

The largest and statistically the most significant differences between propensities are between x and z. These two propensities relate to the tendency to respond cooperatively to the co-player's cooperative choice. We conjecture, therefore, that an important determining factor of the women's "less cooperative" performance is the weaker tendency to *reciprocate* cooperation. The comparison suggests also that women respond less cooperatively to the co-player's noncooperative choice, but the differences in the corresponding propensities (y and w) are smaller and probably not significant.

The performances of co-players in male pairs are more closely linked than those of female pairs, as can be seen from the comparison of product moment coefficients shown in table 19.4.

TABLE 19.4 Comparison of product moment
coefficients in male & female pairs
in iterated P.D. (7 variants pooled).

	Male Pairs	Female Pairs
$\rho_{C_1 C_2}$	.97	.87
$\rho_{x_1 x_2}$	.79	.34
$\rho_{w_1 w_2}$	.48	.46

Observe that all the product moment coefficients are lower in female pairs. The largest difference, however, is in $\rho_{x_1 x_2}$, while the difference in $\rho_{w_1 w_2}$ is negligible. Here we have further evidence that the "less cooperative" performance of female pairs is probably due to a weaker tendency in women to respond cooperatively to the co-player's cooperation rather than a stronger tendency to respond noncooperatively to the co-player's noncooperation.

The lock-in effect on $C_1 C_2$ can be examined in the following manner. Consider the conditional frequency of the C choices following one, two, three, etc. *consecutive* $C_1 C_2$ outcomes. A monotone increase in this propensity would indicate a progressive lock-in effect: the longer cooperation lasts, the more likely it is to continue still further. We have already pointed out, however, that the distribution of the lengths of $C_1 C_2$ runs in pooled data is not a reliable measure of the lock-in effect, because the longer runs are likely to come from more cooperative pairs; so that the lock-in effect is likely to be confounded with the "natural selection effect" (cf. p. 111). To bypass this difficulty, Rapoport and Chammah examined separately the C frequencies conditioned by progressively longer consecutive $C_1 C_2$ runs in each of the following populations: those that had runs of at least five consecutive $C_1 C_2$ outcomes, those that had runs of at least four consecutive $C_1 C_2$ outcomes, etc. The comparison of male and female pairs is shown in table 19.5

The general impression is that, whereas in male pairs the conditioned frequency of C choices rises steadily with the number of consecutive $C_1 C_2$ outcomes, no such effect is observable in female pairs.

Comparison of D choices conditioned by lengths of preceding $D_1 D_2$ outcomes is shown in table 19.6. There is slight evidence of a

TABLE 19.5 C frequencies following CC runs.
(5) averaged over pairs having CC runs
at least 5 long; (4), 4 long; (3), 3 long.

Pairs		Length of runs			
		1	2	3	4
Male	(5)	68	79	86	87
	(4)	66	78	80	
	(3)	65	75		
Mixed	(5)	74	75	85	85
	(4)	68	69	74	
	(3)	64	62		
Female	(5)	69	66	73	68
	(4)	68	61	64	
	(3)	63	53		

TABLE 19.6 D frequencies following DD runs.
(5) averaged over pairs having DD runs
at least 5 long; (4), 4 long; (3), 3 long.

Pairs		Length of runs			
		1	2	3	4
Male	(5)	69	69	71	74
	(4)	68	67	68	
	(3)	67	62		
Mixed	(5)	64	70	71	79
	(4)	62	69	67	
	(3)	60	65		
Female	(5)	69	71	72	73
	(4)	68	71	71	
	(3)	68	70		

lock-in effect in both male and female pairs, but no discernible difference.

Comparison of time courses of C frequencies in male and female pairs is shown in figure 19.1.

We observe that in the beginning both curves stay close together. Both show the characteristic decline in C frequencies. However, the women "recover" later than the men and then only slightly. Assuming that the principal factor in "recovery" is learning to respond cooperatively to the other's cooperation, we see the apparent reason for the "less cooperative" performance of the female pairs.

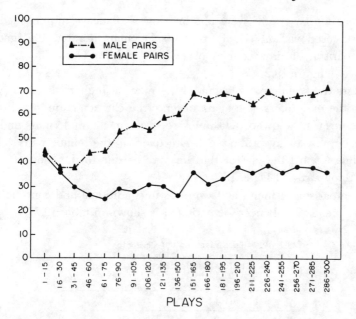

Fig. 19.1. Time courses of C frequencies in male and female pairs in Rapoport and Chammah's experiment.

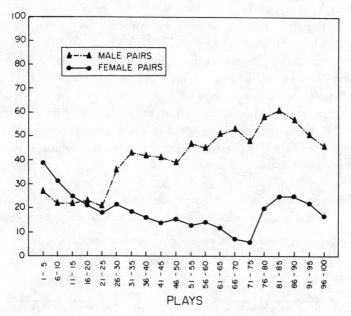

Fig. 19.2. Time courses of C frequencies in male and female pairs in Pancer's experiment.

Very similar results were obtained by M. Pancer (unpublished). Pancer used variant III of Prisoner's Dilemma iterated 100 times. Comparison of time courses of (C) in male and female pairs is shown in figure 19.2.

Here the female pairs began with somewhat higher values of (C) than the male pairs. We again observe the characteristic initial decline in (C), followed by a quick recovery in the male pairs and a considerably delayed and weaker recovery in the female pairs. The decline toward the end of the run may be due to the "end effect" (cf. Rapoport and Dale, 1966).

Comparison of men's and women's unconditional and conditional C frequencies in Pancer's experiment is shown in table 19.7.

TABLE 19.7   Comparison of C frequencies and of cooperation propensities in male & female pairs in iterated P.D. (Var. III), Pancer's experiment.

	(C)	x	y	z	w
Male pairs	42	73	27	35	15
Female pairs	19	43	25	25	15

As in Rapoport and Chammah's experiment, the differences in x and z are larger than those in y and w. The C frequencies are somewhat lower than in Rapoport and Chammah's experiment, wherein 300 iterations (C) = 46 was observed in male pairs and (C) = 27 in female pairs in the same variant.

When men and women are paired as co-players in iterated Prisoner's Dilemma, the difference between the performances practically disappears. Table 19.8 presents a comparison of the male and female player's performance in mixed pairs (Rapoport and Chammah, 1965).

The differences between the performances are very slight. Note, however, that even here the differences in cooperation propensities

TABLE 19.8   Comparison of outcome frequencies and of cooperative propensities in male and female co-player's performance in iterated Prisoner's Dilemma (7 variants)

	(C_1C_2)	(C_1D_2)	(D_1C_2)	(D_1D_2)	x	y	z	w
Male as Row	40	10	09	41	80	40	33	21
Female as Row	40	09	10	41	78	44	29	22

that favor the male co-player are in x and z as before.

The above results point up the overriding influence of experience and interaction as determining factors of performance, at least in Prisoner's Dilemma, as against some inherent propensity to make the one or the other choice. Therein may be the explanation of the failure of many investigators to find sex differences in this game. Such differences are not likely to be revealed in short runs typical of many experiments with iterated games.

Experiments with single plays of Prisoner's Dilemma provide further evidence that there are hardly any differences in the men's and women's initial inclinations to choose one way or the other. The reference is to the single-play experiments of Rapoport and Chammah discussed in chapter 15. The results of single-play experiments with no experience and no interaction (the no-feedback condition, cf. p. 223) are shown in table 19.9.

TABLE 19.9 Comparison of fractions of men and women who chose C in single plays of P.D.

Variant	I	II	III	IV	V	XI	XII	Means
[C] men	44	39	38	49	33	40	39	40
[C] women	46	41	38	45	37	40	40	41

Interesting sex differences in performances in variant II of threat game #19 were found by J. Edwards and R. Gordon (unpublished).

This asymmetric game offers the opportunity to compare the performances of men and women in both roles—Row, the underdog, and Column, the top dog—as well as in performances against a co-player of either sex in either role. Thus eight performances can be compared: four where a male player in either role is matched with a co-player of either sex, and four where a female player is similarly matched. In Edwards and Gordon's experiment, six of the eight performances were examined. The remaining two will be taken from Rapoport, Guyer, and D. Gordon's experiment for comparison. Table 19.10 summarizes the comparison of performances, where T_1 is interpreted as "threatening"; T_2, as "sharing or yielding."

We observe that the largest differences are those involving the sex of the top dog. When Column is a woman, both male and female

TABLE 19.10 Comparison of men's and women's T frequencies
in iterated Game #19 (Variant II).

Co-player	Men threatening (T_1)	Men sharing or yielding (T_2)	Women threatening (T_1)	Women sharing or yielding (T_2)
Male	23	29	31	12
Female	55	20	49	14

Rows resort to the threat strategy considerably more frequently. Other possible differences that can be stated as conjectures are the following:

1. Women underdogs "revolt" against a male top dog more frequently than do men.
2. Women underdogs "revolt" against a female top dog less frequently than do men.
3. Women "revolt" more frequently against women top dogs than do men against men top dogs.
4. Men share or yield more frequently when playing as top dog against a male underdog than when playing against a female underdog.
5. Women share less frequently with women underdogs than do men with men underdogs.

Unfortunately, not all of these conjectures can be supported by Edwards and R. Gordon's data even if all the differences were significant, because the data on male pairs stem from a different experiment. Table 19.11 shows the dangers attendant to generalization without proper controls.

TABLE 19.11 Comparison of performances on Var. II of Game #19
of four populations.

Population	(S_1S_2)	(S_1T_2)	(T_1S_2)	(T_1T_2)	Threat	Sharing
U.S. Males 1969	47	18	30	05	35	23
U.S. Males 1972	53	24	17	06	23	29
U.S. Females 1972	53	28	14	07	21	35
Canadian Females 1972	43	08	41	08	49	14

We note that the performances of United States male and female pairs (University of Michigan students) playing in 1972 are practically indistinguishable. United States males (also from the University of Michigan), playing in 1969 seem considerably more aggressive, revolting more frequently as underdogs, and sharing less frequently as top dogs. Canadian females (University of Toronto students) playing in 1972 seem to be the most aggressive, revolting most, and sharing least. It is impossible to say whether the differences (assuming significance) can be attributed to sex, nationality, or, for that matter, the political climate of two different years. At the risk of redundancy, we reiterate our caveat: no conclusions are offered in this book. Results of experiments are displayed to show that psychologically interesting conjectures can be generated by performances on 2×2 games. Many of these conjectures can be followed up by experiments especially designed and controlled to answer more reliably the questions raised.

In search of further evidence, we turn to comparison of men's and women's performances against programed strategies. The data in tables 19.12 and 19.13 are from Guyer and D. Gordon's experiment.

TABLE 19.12 Comparison of T_1 frequencies in Game #19 against Column's adamant strategy (100% S_2), U.S., 1972.

Var.	I	II	III	IV	V	Means
Men	18	23	40	19	05	21
Women	23	42	39	06	07	23

TABLE 19.13 Comparison of T_2 frequencies in Game #19 against Row's passive strategy (100% S_1), U.S., 1972.

Var.	I	II	III	IV	V	Means
Men	20	15	19	15	11	16
Women	19	30	20	13	11	19

There is little evidence that the performances of men and women (United States, 1972) playing game #19 against programed players differed significantly. On the average both revolted against an adamant top dog with about the same frequency. Both shared on the average about the same fraction of the largest payoff (1/6) with a completely passive Row; both shared progressively less as the cost of revolt to Row increased (even though he never revolted).

We have seen above that bona fide players did not reveal any marked differences either. To be sure, experiments with mixed pairs in game #19 were not performed in the United States. Therefore, the question remains open as to whether the rather interesting results obtained by Edwards and R. Gordon bearing on the interaction of sex and the role on the top-dog-underdog game can be replicated and, if so, in what settings.

Personality Differences

K. Terhune (1968) compared the performances of three populations characterized by different mixtures of three "needs" as assessed by the thematic apperception tests (TAT). Terhune describes the three categories as follows:

Those motivated by a need for achievement—the need or desire to meet a standard of excellence in accomplishment (NACHES).

Those motivated by a need for affiliation—the need to establish and maintain friendly relations with others (NAFFS).

Those motivated by a need for power—the need or desire to exert control over others (NEPOS).

If these are indeed sources of motivation in different degrees in different people, it seems reasonable to expect that, in a situation offering a choice between "competition" and "cooperation," those with different predominant motivations will show different choice tendencies. Accordingly, Terhune assumed that the NAFFS will play Prisoner's Dilemma "more cooperatively" than the NEPOS. With regard to the NACHES, Terhune was guided in formulating his hypothesis by the findings of M. Deutsch (1958). Deutsch used different sets of instructions to create different motivational sets in subjects playing Prisoner's Dilemma. As expected, the subjects instructed to try to get more than the co-player chose D predominantly; those instructed to maximize joint gains chose C predominantly; those instructed to maximize their own gains without regard to the gains or losses of their co-players produced an intermediate performance.

As has already been pointed out (cf. p. 117), these results show hardly more than that subjects tend to follow instructions. However, Deutsch's experiments yielded other somewhat more interesting findings, namely, that whereas the competitively oriented and the cooperatively oriented subjects played rather consistently across different experimental conditions, the "individualistically" oriented subjects apparently adapted their level of cooperation or competition to different conditions.

Examination of the conditions provides a simple interpretation of the results. The conditions varied according to whether the choices of the two players were made simultaneously or consecutively, and according to whether opportunities to communicate were present or absent. Now, it stands to reason that, if Prisoner's Dilemma is played "competitively" (i.e., essentially as a constant-sum game in which the payoff differences of the original game serve as the de facto payoffs), the opportunity to communicate would make no difference in the choice preferences. Note also that the use of consecutive instead of simultaneous choices amounts to allowing (limited) communication. Further, if the subjects are instructed to play cooperatively, that is, to maximize joint games, they can be expected to choose C even in the absence of an opportunity to communicate; therefore, the introduction of this opportunity cannot make much difference. It follows that the largest differences in C frequencies across the above experimental conditions will be observed in the intermediate "individualistically" oriented subjects.

Terhune, however, interpreted Deutsch's results as indicating differences in the (induced) personality characteristics rather than differences in the situation. Accordingly, he hypothesized that his NACHES, whom he took to be analogous to Deutsch's individualistically oriented subjects, would exhibit the largest variance of performance across experimental conditions.

In assessing aspects of personality by TAT, it is found that generally all three dimensions of motivation are present in most people but in different degrees. Thus, if a simple high-low dichotomy is used on each of the three dimensions, eight different patterns will be observed. In fact, it turns out that the subjects' scores on the three dimensions are fairly independent statistically except for a slight negative correlation between the need for affiliation and the need for power.

For his subjects, Terhune used those who were above the median on one of the three dimensions and below on the other two; hence, three categories: predominantly NACHES, predominantly NAFFS, and predominantly NEPOS.

Both single play and iterated versions of Prisoner's Dilemma were used. In single plays, the subjects were asked not only to choose between two alternatives but also to indicate whether they expected the co-player to choose the one or the other. In this way, the motivation to choose C or D could be more precisely defined. For instance, the subject who chooses C when he expects the co-player to do likewise exhibits both "trustworthiness" (not taking advantage of the other's attempt to cooperate) and "trust" (that the other will cooperate). The subject who chooses C while expecting the other to choose D is possibly trying to teach by example or is exhibiting a "pacifist" or "turn the other cheek" attitude. The player who chooses D while expecting the co-player to choose C is clearly behaving in an exploitative way, in contrast to the subject who chooses D while expecting the other to do likewise, for in the latter case he can justify his choice on grounds of "self-defense." (Note that these distinctions are analogous to those we have made among conditional probabilities, assuming that a player expects the co-player to repeat his choice. In eliciting the player's expectations explicitly, the interpretations are perhaps more justified.)

Terhune used the following three variants of Prisoner's Dilemma, each characterized by a "cooperative index" (CI) computed as $(R - P)/(T - P)$ (cf. p. 79).

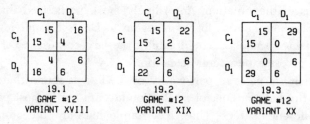

19.1
GAME #12
VARIANT XVIII

19.2
GAME #12
VARIANT XIX

19.3
GAME #12
VARIANT XX

From his results Terhune draws the following conclusions (1968, p. 17):

1. NACHES were the most trusting and trustworthy, regardless of the game matrix. As temptation to defect increased (as the CI decreased), they defected more, mainly as a defensive measure.

Seldom did they try to exploit.

2. NAFFS were highly cooperative when playing the rather "safe" game (variant XVIII, CI = .75). However, they cooperated considerably less in the more risky games and became mainly suspicious and defensive.

3. NEPOS were consistently noncooperative and tried to exploit their partners considerably more than did the other groups.

"Justification for defection" appears more clearly in table 19.14, which shows the proportion of subjects who expected C when "defecting" (hence, were exploiting their co-players) and the proportion who expected D when defecting (hence, may be said to be acting "in self defense").

TABLE 19.14 Comparison of exploitative and defensive choices of three personality types in single plays of Prisoner's Dilemma in Terhunes' experiment.

Var.	CI	Naches Expl.	Naches Defns.	Naffs Expl.	Naffs Defns.	Nepos Expl.	Nepos Defns.
XVIII	.75	0	100	71	29	62	38
XIX	.45	23	77	25	75	72	28
XX	.3]	27	73	45	55	63	37

Note that in variant XVIII with the largest CI, the NACHES defected *only* defensively. In the other two variants, large majorities of NACHES defecting also did so "in self defense." Of the NEPOS, in contrast, the majorities of those who defected in all three variants did so while expecting the co-player to cooperate; hence, they defected "exploitatively." The behavior of the NAFFS seems inconsistent.

The proportion of players expecting cooperation in single plays is shown in table 19.15.

TABLE 19.15 Proportions of players expecting cooperation in single plays of P.D.

Var.	XVIII	XIX	XX
Naches	67	69	60
Naffs	72	42	75
Nepos	75	78	75

Terhune reports that the differences across populations are not statistically significant except in variant XIX. The data suggest, however, that the NEPOS are most likely to expect the co-player to cooperate in a single play of Prisoner's Dilemma. If so, it may be because the NEPOS view their co-players as "suckers." (We have already seen that NEPOS are most likely to defect even if they expect cooperation.) It is also interesting to note that the overall proportion of players who expect the co-player to cooperate in a single play of Prisoner's Dilemma is considerably larger (>60 percent) than the proportion actually cooperating (about 40 percent, as in several other experiments). Finally, we observe that the expectations of the NAFFS are the least consistent across the variants.

The clearest differences among the performances of the three populations are apparent in figure 19.3, which shows the proportions of players who chose C when cooperation was expected and when defection was expected.

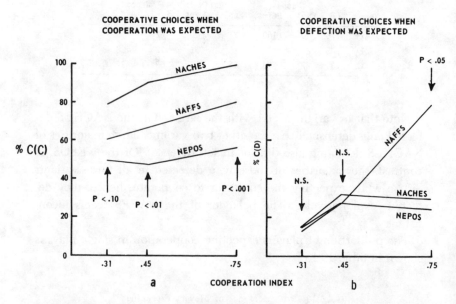

Fig. 19.3. Frequencies of cooperative choices when cooperation or defection of other was expected in Terhune's experiment (from K. W. Terhune, 1968).

We observe that when cooperation was expected the NACHES cooperated most and NEPOS least in all three variations. When defection was expected, the incidence of cooperation among the

NACHES and the NEPOS is low throughout. It is the NAFFS who "play the martyr," but only in variant XVIII with the largest CI (cf. figure 19.3).

Clear differences attributable to personality were observed by M. Deutsch (1960). The measure used was the so-called F-scale (Adorno, et al., 1969). People with high scores on that scale are said to reveal themselves as more "authoritarian." Specifically, they favor more strict child rearing practices than people who rate low on the scale; they tend to be more prejudiced against minority groups, less liberal in their political opinions, and less sophisticated intellectually.

In Deutsch's experiment, each subject played Prisoner's Dilemma (as shown in 19.4) twice. The first time, he was to choose first. The other player's choice was not revealed to him (in fact, there was no "other player"). The second time, the subject was informed that the co-player (fictitious) chose C, and he was to reply.

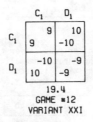

19.4
GAME #12
VARIANT XXI

Since the outcome of the first play was unknown to the subject, the second play was essentially a single play of a 2×4 game, where the subject had available four meta-strategies listed on p. 63. A choice of C by the subject indicated that he chose either strategy 1 ("choose C unconditionally") or strategy 2 ("choose same as co-player"). A choice of D indicated either strategy 3 ("choose opposite") or strategy 4 ("choose D unconditionally").

Consecutive choices permit a clearer interpretation of the attitudes associated with them. The player who chooses C when he has to make the first choice appears to manifest "trust"; that is, he places himself in a situation open to exploitation by the other in the hope that the other will not take advantage of him but will reciprocate cooperatively. The player who chooses C in response to the co-player's C exhibits "trustworthiness"; he refrains from exploiting the "trusting" player.

Table 19.16 shows that the trusting subjects tended strongly to be

TABLE 19.16   No. of subjects in each of the four
categories in Deutsch's experiment.

	Trusting	Untrusting (suspicious)
Trustworthy	24	5
Untrustworthy	4	22

TABLE 19.17   Distribution of four player types
among three personality types
in Deutsch's experiment.

	Low F	Medium F	High F
Trusting and trustworthy	12	10	2
Suspicious and untrustworthy	0	13	9
Suspicious but trustworthy	0	4	0
Trusting but untrustworthy	2	3	0

TABLE 19.18   Fractions of four player types
among the three personality types.
Here "Trusting" is a combination of
TT and TU; "Trustworthy," TT and ST, etc.

	Low	Medium	High
Trusting	1.00	.43	.22
Suspicious	.00	.57	.78
Trustworthy	.86	.47	.22
Untrustworthy	.14	.53	.78

also trustworthy and vice versa. Table 19.17 shows the distribution
of the four types among the three groups of subjects who rated,
respectively, high, medium, and low on the F-scale.

If we examine the fractions in each population group that made
each of the four categories of choices, we see a somewhat clearer
picture (cf. table 19.18).

Of some interest also is the observation that the high and low F's
were "consistent"; that is, either predominantly both trusting and
trustworthy or both suspicious and untrustworthy. The medium F's
showed the least consistency. Of course, the small number of subjects does not warrant any conclusion on this score, but it seems
worthwhile to test the conjecture further: Is consistency in this con-

text related to a certain rigidity in the personality makeup?

George W. Baxter, Jr. (1972) has reviewed the literature pertaining to the use of personality of subject as an independent variable. The studies are divided into three groups: those in which the personality characteristic used yielded positive results; those in which it yielded negative results; those in which it yielded positive results in some studies and negative ones in others. If future studies are similarly classified, clearly the last (inconclusive) category is bound to grow, and the first two to be depleted, for the sort of experiments where personality of the subject is a variable are seldom if ever performed under reasonably constant conditions, and the categorization of persons into personality types is seldom distinguished either by reliability or independent validation.

Of the studies reviewed where a personality characteristic gave positive results in game experiments, Baxter mentions only Terhune's, discussed in this chapter (cf. p. 320) and two others. The great majority of personality assessment measures gave negative results. These included such diverse tests as Allport's A-S Reaction Study of Ascendance, Chein's Anti-Police Attitudes, Rosenberg's Faith in Human Nature, the Taylor Manifest Anxiety Scale, the Buss-Durkee Verbal Hostility, etc., etc.

Among the measures that yielded inconsistent results in various experiments are the F-Scale of Authoritarianism, with which M. Deutsch had obtained positive results (cf. p. 326), various scales of Intelligence, Risktaking and Avoidance, and many others.

K. W. Terhune (1970) presented a more detailed review of the literature on game experiments relating personality characteristics to "conflict and cooperation." His summary of positive and negative findings is shown in table 19.19. (Note that several of the experiments reported involve other than 2×2 games.)

Although positive findings outnumber negative ones, it must be kept in mind that experiments reporting positive findings are more likely to find their way into print than those that yield no discernible results.

In practically all studies seeking correlations between personality traits and game performance, subjects are selected with high or low scores on the traits in question, and their performances are compared. Gerardo Marin (1973) tried the opposite tack. His subjects were college students from two private universities in Bogota, Co-

TABLE 19.19 Personality and attitudinal variables studied in relation to Conflict-Cooperation (from Terhune, 1970).[1]

Personality/attitude measure employed	Studies finding relation	Studies finding no relation
California F-scale	Deutsch (1960): Prisoner's Dilemma; Driver (1965): Internation simulation; Bixenstine and O'Reilly (1966): Prisoner's Dilemma; Wrightsman (1966): Nonzero-sum game	Gahagan et al. (1967): Prisoner's Dilemma
Tolerance for ambiguity (composite)	Pilisuk et al. (1965): Expanded Prisoner's Dilemma; Teger (1968): Allocations Game	Nardin (1967)
Rokeach's dogmatism scale (or version thereof)	Druckman (1967): Bargaining; Gahagan et al. (1967): Prisoner's Dilemma	—
Cognitive abstractness—concreteness	Driver (1965): Internation simulation	—
Authoritarian nationalism vs. equalitarian internationalism; aggressive militarism vs. nonbelligerence	Crow and Noel (1965): Internation exercise	—
Needs for achievement, affiliation, dominance	Haythorn and Altman (1967)	—
Affiliation, self-prominence orientations; Achievement orientation	Higgs and McGrath (1965): Nonzero-sum game	Higgs and McGrath (1965): Nonzero-sum games.
Gough ACL: needs for aggression, autonomy, abasement, deference	Marlowe (1963): Prisoner's Dilemma	Marlowe (1963): Prisoner's Dilemma
Gough ACL: needs for nurturance, dominance		
MMPI dominance scale	Sermat (1968): "Chicken" game	
Allport ascendence—submission	Fry (1965): Matching game	
Wrightsman's philosophies of human nature scale	Wrightsman (1966): Nonzero-sum game; Uejio and Wrightsman (1967): Prisoner's Dilemma	

Personality/attitude measure employed	Studies finding relation	Studies finding no relation
Lutzker's internationalism—isolationism scale	Lutzker (1960): "Chicken" game; McClintock, Harrison, Strand, and Gallo (1963): "Chicken" game; McClintock et al., (1965): Nonzero-sum game	Pilisuk et al. (1965): Expanded Prisoner's Dilemma
Internationalism scale (composite)	—	Wrightsman (1966): Nonzero-sum game; Daniels (1967): Bargaining study
Ideology of conciliation vs. Real politik; Christie's Machiavellianism scale	Guetzkow et al. (1960): Internation simulation; Geis (1964): "Con Game" and "Ten Dollar Game"; Uejio and Wrightsman (1967): Prisoner's Dilemma; Teger (1968): Allocations game	—
Bixenstine's flexible ethicality	Bixenstein and Wilson (1963); Bixenstine et al. (1963): both with Prisoner's Dilemma	Bixenstine et al. (1964): Nonzero-sum game
Needs for achievement, affiliation, power (TAT-measured)	Terhune (1968): Prisoner's Dilemma; Terhune and Firestone (1967): Internation game	—
"Entrepreneurial" vs. "bureaucratic" types combined with level of aspiration	Crowne (1965): Prisoner's Dilemma	—
Ager's political cynicism	Uejio and Wrightsman (1967): Prisoner's Dilemma	Wrightsman (1966): Nonzero-sum game
Kogan-Wallach risk-taking propensity	Crow and Noel (1965): Internation exercise	Pilisuk et al. (1965): Expanded Prisoner's Dilemma
Risk-aversion propensity	—	Dolbear and Lave (1966): Prisoner's Dilemma
Gore-Rotter internal—external control test	Teger (1968): Allocations game	—

1. In addition, all these variables found unrelated: (a) Guilford-Zimmerman Personality Test: questionnaire on "8 basic values" (Bixenstine et al., 1964; nonzero-sum game). (b) Rogers-Dymond Self-Acceptance; Monetary Risk Preference (Pilisuk et al., 1965: expanded Prisoner's Dilemma). (c) Buss-Durkee Verbal Hostility; Rehfisch Rigidity; Berkowitz Social Responsibility; Chein's Personal Optimism; Chein's anti-Police Attitudes; Crowne-Marlowe Social Desirability; Edwards' Social Desirability (Wrightsman, 1966: nonzero-sum game).

lumbia, half of them female. Each filled out a questionnaire prepared by the Canadian Peace Research Institute (Spanish version). Two weeks later, each subject was asked to make his choice in a single play of ten variants of Prisoner's Dilemma all with a cooperative index of 0.50 (cf. p. 322). Thus, the subjects fell into two categories, the "cooperators" (with eight or more C choices) and the "noncooperators" (with eight or more D choices). Table 19.20 shows the mean scores of the two populations on twelve components of personality presumably revealed by the questionnaire.

TABLE 19.20   Personality scores of cooperators and non-cooperators in single plays of Prisoner's Dilemma in Marin's experiment.

Scale	Cooperators		Non-cooperators	
	Mean	Standard deviation	Mean	Standard deviation
Conformity	21.27	6.33	19.83	4.44
Nationalism	24.63	3.97	23.25	4.59
Irresponsibility	18.54	6.71	17.55	3.54
Religiosity	26.81	5.80	24.51	6.89
Impulsivity	23.81	6.32	25.67	6.33
Bureacraticism	20.36	5.84	18.81	5.59
Neuroticism	18.18	5.81	21.46	5.07
Militarism	25.63	5.44	26.41	3.95
Misanthropy	20.54	3.39	22.93	5.52
Discipline	20.27	6.33	20.58	4.99
Conservatism	22.09	3.45	22.97	5.81

Marin points out that the only significant difference between the means was found in the "neuroticism" scale (cooperators less "neurotic"). The two groups were also compared with regard to their "compassion" scores, derived from their answers on the questionnaire. The cooperators' compassion score was 266.45, the noncooperators', 260.67. The difference, although in the expected direction, was not significant.

The impression is unavoidable that direct, enlightening relations between the personality of subjects, as assessed by existing personality tests, and gaming behavior are not likely to be established; certainly not, if predominantly a single dependent measure, frequency of C choices, in just one or at most very few 2 × 2 games is used as the index of behavior. Unfortunately, this has been the case in the

overwhelming majority of the studies. Nevertheless, the few definitive findings relating personality characteristics to game behavior
suggest that the question deserves further exploration. In the above
mentioned review article, Terhune discusses ways of bringing out
more effectively the role of personality as a determinant of game
behavior.

Differences Attributable to Background

In an experiment by D. P. Crowne (1966), family background as
well as motivational structure of the subjects was an independent
variable. The background was assessed as "entrepreneurial" or
"bureaucratic," according to whether the parents of the subject were
engaged in "risk taking" occupations (farmer, small business man,
lawyer, doctor, etc.) or employment in a relatively large organiza-
tion with a complex structure. The hypothesis was that the entrepreneurial group would play Prisoner's Dilemma more competitively
than the bureaucratic group, reflecting the attitudes presumably in-
culcated by parents.

The level of aspiration (motivational structure) was tested by presenting the subject with a task of skill in which he announced his
expected score before each trial of that task. From the shifts of estimates as related to the scores achieved, one of several motivation
patterns was ascribed to the subject: (i) essentially "realistic" adjust-
ments to success and failure; (ii) cautious, failure-avoiding attitudes;
(iii) essentially "unrealistically" high estimates (wishful thinking).
The variant of Prisoner's Dilemma used is shown in 19.5.

19.5
GAME #12
VARIANT XV

The runs were twenty plays long. Table 19.21 shows the mean
numbers of C choices in the six experimental groups.

Groups marked by different subscripts differ significantly. The
difference in performance between the two groups with different

TABLE 19.21 Comparison of subjects' performances in iterated P.D.
in Crowne's experiment. N: number of subjects in each
category; M: mean number of C choices in 20 plays.
(Means with different subscripts differ significantly.)

Family orientations	Level of aspiration patterns					
	Realistic		Cautious		Unrealistic	
	N	M	N	M	N	M
Enterpreneurs	21	6.05_b	12	4.42_b	11	10.91_a
Bureaucrats	15	11.67_a	14	8.64_b	3	8.33_a

family orientations is in the expected direction: bureaucrats cooperate more ($p = .06$). The difference in level of aspiration is not reflected significantly in the performance. It is noteworthy, however,
that the subjects in the "cautious" group tend to cooperate least, as
expected. Interaction between family orientation and level of aspiration is significant at the .02 level. That is, the type of level of aspiration patterns makes no difference among bureaucrats, but does
among the entrepreneurs.

When the performances of symmetrically matched pairs were examined (bureaucrats matched with bureaucrats, entrepreneurs with
entrepreneurs), the difference in the predicted direction becomes
highly significant, as shown in table 19.22.

TABLE 19.22 Comparison of numbers of C choices in
contrasting pairs in Crowne's experiment.

	Homogeneous pairs		Mixed pairs	
Enterpreneurs	5.77	$b = .01$	8.64	n.s.
Bureaucrats	10.77		9.07	

The finding is consistent with that in performances of men and
women. Sexes differ significantly in homogeneous pairs but not in
mixed pairs.

With respect to the interaction effect of family background and
level of aspiration, the experimenter offers the following conjecture:

Entrepreneurial subjects with more disturbed "irreal" LOA
[level of aspiration] patterns deviated from the exploitative
bargaining strategy of other entrepreneurs. These individuals
may represent entrepreneurial "casualties" in the sense that they
seek to avoid competition. In distinction to the other groups of

LOA patterns, the 5, 6, 8, and 9 groups are characterized by inability to deal realistically with competition. . . . The bargaining situation allows a kind of "avoidance of competition" in which cooperation occurs not for cooperative goals but as an avoidance of the painful consequences expected from competitive behavior. Competitiveness, of course, is more salient for entrepreneurs than for bureaucrats. A fruitful hypothesis is that the maladjusted LOA entrepreneurs are subjected to more external parental demands and higher goals as children. In this connection, it is interesting to note the trend toward a more frequent occurrence of maladjusted LOA patterns among the entrepreneurs.

The conjecture is interesting but contains, in our opinion, a misconception of the motivational pressures in Prisoner's Dilemma. In identifying C with cooperation and D with competition, the author envisages the game as a "bargaining" situation, where competition is manifested in "harsh bargaining" and cooperation in "avoidance of competition." As has been pointed out, it is misleading to view a noncooperative game (without communication) as a bargaining situation, since the essential elements of bargaining—threats and promises—are lacking, except possibly implicitly in the successive choices. Even then it is difficult to conceive these choices as "bargaining" acts, because of their ambivalent character. Is the choice of D an act of exploitation or of self-defense? The meaning of the C choice is clearer: it is definitely a bid for cooperation, but as such, it is highly *active* rather than a passive "avoidance of competition," as Crowne apparently interprets it. Actually, Crowne's interpretation would be considerably more relevant in Chicken, where the choice of D *is* aggressive, competitive, *and risky*—an act crowned with success if the co-player responds with C, thus *avoiding* D_1D_2, which in this game is truly the "painful consequence of competition." In Prisoner's Dilemma, on the contrary, the choice of C in the face of the co-player's D is *not* "avoidance of painful consequence": the outcome C_1D_2 is the most "painful" to Row, and D_1C_2, to Column. We see the unfortunate consequences of fixating on Prisoner's Dilemma as "the game of cooperation and competition."

It may well be that the choice of C in Prisoner's Dilemma, even in the face of noncooperation by the co-player, reflects what the author calls "irreal" aspiration levels, representative of the young who have rejected entrepreneurial values (presumably "realistic" and "cautious" aspiration levels) and with them the competitive orientation ascribed to that social group. This conjecture can certainly be followed up in experiments with other 2×2 games.

Differences Attributable to Nationality (or Background)

Performances of Danish and American subjects in a threat game (game #19) were compared by Rapoport, Guyer, and D. Gordon (1971). It must be pointed out that the populations differed in background as well as in nationality. The Danish subjects were recruited from the student body of the Technical University of Denmark; the American subjects were recruited from the student body at large of the University of Michigan. The observed differences may, therefore, be a reflection of orientations influenced by vocational preference as well as by national background. Variants I, II, and III of game #19 were used (cf. p. 246).

Each pair played six sequences of 100 plays each. Thus an experimental run consisted of 600 plays. Each subject participated in only one such experimental run, alternating between the roles of Row (the "underdog") and Column (the "top dog") in blocks of 100 plays. In each experimental run, all three variants were used in systematically changed order. Consequently, each subject played each of the three variants 100 times as Row and 100 times as Column. Table 19.23 shows the outcome frequencies in the performances of the two populations.

TABLE 19.23 Comparison of outcome frequencies in Danish and American subjects in iterated Game #19.

	(S_1S_2)	(S_1T_2)	(T_1S_2)	(T_1T_2)
DK.	70	17	11	2
U.S.	47	18	30	5

The immediately apparent difference is between the frequencies of S_1S_2 and T_1S_2. In the American population, the latter frequency is considerably larger at the expense of the former. That is, Americans in the role of the "underdog" resort more frequently to the available threat. On the other hand, there is practically no difference between the frequencies of S_1T_2; that is, Danes and Americans as top dogs "share voluntarily" in about the same degree. Comparisons of repetition propensities in the two populations are shown in tables 19.24 and 19.25.

TABLE 19.24 Comparison of repetition (or anti-repetition) propensities of Row in Danish and American subjects in iterated Game #19.

		$\tilde{\alpha}_1$	β_1	$\tilde{\gamma}_1$	δ_1
Var. I	DK.	07	49	02	28
	U.S.	15	74	12	40
Var. II	DK.	09	59	06	39
	U.S.	16	75	15	58
Var. III	DK.	09	60	05	19
	U.S.	20	75	13	54

TABLE 19.25 Comparison of repetition (or anti-repetition) propensities of Columns in Danish and American subjects in iterated Game #19.

		$\tilde{\alpha}_2$	β_2	γ_2	$\tilde{\delta}_2$
Var. I	DK.	22	05	88	83
	U.S.	29	31	84	74
Var. II	DK.	18	11	81	76
	U.S.	25	08	83	81
Var. III	DK.	27	06	82	78
	U.S.	32	10	85	73

The clearest differences between the Danish and American players are seen in the performances of Rows. The propensities are all Row's tendencies to choose T_1. All these propensities without exception are larger in American than in Danish Rows. They suggest the following conjectures.

1. Americans as underdogs tend to revolt more frequently than do Danes ($\tilde{\alpha}_1$).

2. Americans as underdogs tend to prevent the restoration of the

natural outcome (which favors the top dog) more frequently than do Danes ($\hat{\gamma}_1$).

3. Americans as underdogs tend to persist in the threat posture more than do Danes (β_1).

4. Americans as underdogs tend to distrust the top dog more frequently than do Danes (δ_1).

Examination of Column's propensities reveals no consistent difference among Column players of the two populations, except possibly in $\tilde{\alpha}_2$, which would suggest the following.

5. Americans as top dogs tend to share more frequently with underdogs than do Danes.

The very large value of American β_2 in variant I seems anomalous. It may have been caused by one or two pairs alternating between S_1S_2 and S_1T_2 in blocks of plays, rather than successively.

Since in this experiment every subject played both in the role of Row and of Column, we can compare performances with the view of seeing whether the patterns of behavior of a subject in the two roles are in any way related. Consider the following four types of players.

$\{S_1S_2\}$: These players predominantly submit to power when they are underdogs (play S_1 as Row) and wield power when they are top dogs (play S_2 as Columns). (The "authoritarian" syndrome.)

$\{S_1T_2\}$: These players predominantly submit to power when they are underdogs (play S_1 as Row) but do not abuse power when they have it (play T_2 as Column, hence share with Row). (The "non-aggressive" syndrome.)

$\{T_1S_2\}$: These players do not submit to power when they are underdogs (play T_1 as Row), but wield power when they have it. (The "aggressive" syndrome.)

$\{T_1T_2\}$: These players do not submit to power (play T_1 as Row), do not abuse power when they have it (play T_2 as Column). (The "fairminded" syndrome.)

Combining the two populations (82 subjects), we assign to each an S_1 score (the overall frequency of his S choices as Row) and an S_2 score (the overall frequency of S choices when he is Column). Individuals whose S_1 and S_2 scores are both above the median of the combined population are designated as S_1S_2 subjects; those with S_1 scores above the median and S_2 scores below are designated as S_1T_2 subjects, etc. Table 19.26 shows the distribution of the four "archetypes" in the two populations.

TABLE 19.26   Distribution of "personality
types as manifested in
underdog topdog performances
in iterated Game #19.

		Danish	American
$\{S_1S_2\}$	("authoritarian")	16	4
$\{S_1T_2\}$	("non-aggressive")	11	10
$\{T_1S_2\}$	("aggressive")	7	14
$\{T_1T_2\}$	("fair-minded")	8	12

A rough estimate of the significance of the difference in the two profiles is $p < .02$ (chi-square $= 10.35$, df $= 3$). The appropriateness of the chi-square test can be questioned, because the subjects were paired; thus the performance of one subject may well have influenced the performance of the other, contrary to the assumption of independence. However, we can investigate the question of how a subject's behavior as Row influenced his own behavior as Column. Actually, the subject's patterns of behavior in the two roles were not significantly correlated. Therefore, on this score at least, the use of the chi-square test in comparing the population profiles was justified. It stands to reason that the population profiles exhibiting both the similarities and the differences in the two populations could be more firmly established by a larger experiment.

20

Summary of Part III

The foregoing chapters were devoted to a selective survey of experimental work on 2×2 games, and as we have repeatedly remarked, the vast bulk of that work deals with Prisoner's Dilemma. Only occasionally are other games examined. The game of Chicken is usually identified, but games that are neither Prisoner's Dilemma nor Chicken often arise "by accident," as it were, when the payoffs of what was originally a Prisoner's Dilemma are varied and get outside the range of that game (cf. pp. 296–99). Most of this experimental work was done by psychologists, motivated, no doubt, by the opportunity to study "conflict and cooperation" in controlled experimental settings.

The notion of "cooperation" is most directly relevant to symmetric games of partial conflict, of which there are only four in the ordinal taxonomy: Prisoner's Dilemma, Chicken, Leader, and Hero. In the last two, cooperation is manifested in an alternation between the two asymmetric outcomes. In the first two, cooperation can be manifested in the exclusive occurrence of an outcome (T_1T_2 in Prisoner's Dilemma, S_1S_2 in Chicken) or in an alternation between S_1T_2 and T_1S_2. The latter is the more "rational" cooperative solution if $2R < T + S$. In the structurally or numerically asymmetric games, a definition of a rational cooperative solution does not readily present itself. Such definitions, however, are offered in the theory of *cooperative* games (cf. chapter 3). Since these solutions in general involve strategy mixtures, they apply at most to iterated games, where strategy mixtures

337

can be considered to be manifested in choice frequencies. Therefore, asymmetric games can be used to compare experimental data with nonobvious solutions. These comparisons will be made in Part IV.

Aside from the opportunity offered by asymmetric games to put the theory of cooperative 2 × 2 games to a test, they offer also a much richer psychological content than symmetric games because of the different roles of the two players. We have seen, for example, how game #19 suggests a plethora of relations and interactions between a "top dog" and an "underdog" in a mixed-motive conflict. We feel that the ramifications of the asymmetric 2 × 2 game should be explored much further than they have been to date.

It seems to us that another shortcoming of the work done so far is the undue emphasis given to standard procedures of experimental psychology. The so-called scientific method is often impressed on students in the field as a set of hard and fast rules, according to which an experiment is performed with a clearly specified aim—to test a hypothesis. A statistical evaluation of the data is made toward that end, as a result of which the hypothesis is corroborated (if the results are "statistically significant") or, by implication, not corroborated (if they are not). It goes without saying that this conception of research tends to focus attention only on results that have a direct bearing on the hypotheses chosen in advance. Moreover, usually only statistically significant results will be discussed, an occasional (apologetic) mention being made of results that "did not reach significance but were in the expected direction."

In work of this sort, a premium is placed on statistically significant results. Hence, a pressure develops to choose hypotheses that are likely to be corroborated at a specified level of significance. This is unfortunate, in our opinion, because corroboration of hypotheses that appear plausible on a priori or common sense grounds adds little to our knowledge or understanding. At most, such corroborations show that what we felt intuitively to be true can be demonstrated under controlled conditions. The interesting results are the *unexpected* ones, especially if they call attention to aspects of a situation that had escaped our attention (it is commonplace to find post hoc explanations of such results if they are noticed). Strictly speaking, from the point of view of statistical inference, such results cannot be treated as "findings" if they had not been anticipated as hypotheses, even if post hoc analysis indicates that the results are "significant."

Summary of Part III   339

(To take an extreme example, observing a specific license number of a car is a priori highly improbable, but if it had not been "hypothesized," the result is not indicative of anything.) Nevertheless, calling attention to a priori improbable results (even if they had not been hypothesized) is not completely worthless. Their value is as *generators* of new hypotheses, to be tested in specially designed experiments with controls appropriate to the tests. The more "surprising" these unanticipated results are, the more rigorously they should be tested. If they pass such tests, they add substantially more to our knowledge and, perhaps, to our understanding.

Therefore, if more is expected from experiments than confirmation of our expectations, another research strategy is indicated. In preliminary experiments, the "net" can be thrown far and wide in order to get some hints about what is happening. Quantitative results can be described without reference to their statistical significance, *as if* they were "real" (cf. our discussion of the results of Edwards and Gordon's experiment on p. 318). The most interesting of these *suggested* relations among the variables can then be singled out for further attention and further testing in subsequent experiments which should have a much sharper focus, concentrating, perhaps, on one variable at a time in order not to spread the available "n" (number of subjects) too thinly.[1] Many of the experiments discussed in the foregoing chapters involved quite respectable numbers of subjects but also many conditions, so that only a few subjects could be assigned to each "cell" in a factorial design, thus weakening the power of the tests.

Of the effects of payoffs on choice frequencies in 2×2 games, we find the most regularly corroborated result is one that is consistent with the monotonicity hypothesis. It is also the least interesting, because it is entirely in accord with common sense expectations. In the behavior of the "average" subject, we would expect the choice frequency of a strategy to be monotonically related to both of the payoffs associated with that strategy. More interesting are the occa-

---

[1] The use of univariate analysis of variance as a preliminary survey of possible effects is an example of "throwing the net far and wide." But here the search is confined to the effects of several *independent* variables upon a single dependent variable. We are suggesting a preliminary search for effects on several *dependent* variables, keeping the number of independent variables in an experiment minimal. Multivariate analysis is the proper tool in such procedures.

sional reversals, such as were observed in game #66 (p. 242), game #19 (p. 247), and game #50 (p. 256). It is these reversals that have triggered our speculations concerning "psychological" rather than purely strategic features of game behavior, or of features that can be explained in the light of elementary reinforcement theory. It goes without saying that such speculations do not lead to a defensible psychological theory, but they could lead to interesting theories if they were formulated as hypotheses and tested in specially designed "concentrated" experiments.

Also worth noting is the relative insensitivity of choice frequencies to absolute magnitudes of the payoffs, at least in single plays (cf. p. 226). The indications are that mathematical models relating choice frequencies to payoff structure of a game (at least, in single plays) ought to be invariant at least with respect to the same similarity transformations applied to the payoffs of each player (i.e., multiplying all eight payoffs by the same positive constant). At any rate, this assumption appears to be tenable in the context of a numerically symmetric game, where a similarity transformation preserves symmetry. In the case of transformations involving additive constants, the situation is less clear, for such transformations may change positive payoffs into negative ones and vice versa. There are vague indications (to our knowledge not systematically investigated) that the signs of the payoffs have a stronger influence on choice frequencies than their absolute magnitudes. The question is worth exploring further. Besides, general linear transformations may turn a numerically symmetric game into an asymmetric one and so radically change its "psychological dynamics." Altogether too few experiments have been carried out on numerically asymmetric variants of structurally symmetric games.

Although some results indicate that the payoffs of a numerically symmetric game played once can be multiplied by a factor of 100 without discernible differential effects, the monetary worth of these payoffs to experimental subjects remains within the range of usual compensations. The question which often arises is: What would be observed if the payoffs were sufficiently large to induce intense concern in the subjects? The question remains open; it cannot be answered in the light of what is known about "risk behavior," for we are dealing here not with games against nature, where specific magnitudes of risk can be specified or assumed, but with a radically different situation, where each of two players tries to guess what is going on in the mind of the other, and each guess is subject to the characteristic whirlpool, "He thinks that I think that he thinks . . . ." Game experiments in which subjects may lose really significant amounts (say, of the order of life savings) cannot be performed for ethical reasons. Though ethical considerations do not stand in the way of experiments where all payoffs are nonnegative, the necessarily large positive payoffs to subjects in such experiments are prohibitively expensive since, as always, the results can be evaluated only statistically and so require many replications. Recall, for example, that in Oskamp's experiment when payoffs were in dollars (cf. p. 259), the average payoff of several plays, rather than the sum, was the actual amount paid to the subjects. If questions concerning the effects of really large monetary payoffs in games of partial conflict were considered sufficiently important, it might be worthwhile to spend a great deal of money answering them. But on this score, we do not have a definitive answer.

The observation that the hypothesis of monotonicity is generally corroborated, although in itself not very interesting, leads to more substantive questions related to the *quantitative* assessments of the effects of payoffs depending on the pressures associated with them. We have attempted very rough assessments of this sort; for instance, comparing the change of choice frequencies per unit change of presumed utilities in the different cells of the game matrix. Our results were not very consistent but they did suggest a number of conjectures; for instance, that changes in R in Prisoner's Dilemma had, on the whole, larger effects on C frequencies than changes in P. The lack of consistency could be attributed to lack of control of experimental conditions or, more likely, to large variances introduced by individual differences.

The last point is worth pondering. Assume that, under constant experimental conditions, total variance in game behavior is due to two sources: the payoff structure and individual differences. Assume, further, that in iterated play some asymptotic choice frequencies are achieved. Now imagine an experiment with subject populations so large that individual differences are "washed out" in the "average player." Then the choice frequencies as a function of each of the eight payoffs of any 2×2 game could be empirically determined. The nature of these functions would suggest a psychological theory related to the relative importance of the pressures operating in these games. In particular, the effect of changes in a player's payoffs on his own choice frequencies could be quantitatively compared with the corresponding effects on the choice frequencies of the other player. In general, of course, each of these functions should be considered as a function of eight payoffs; the separate dependence on single payoffs would be only a trajectory in a cross section of a nine-dimensional space. Putting these trajectories together into a total picture would be a formidable mathematical task. However, the task may not be as hopeless as it seems, because the theory of the *cooperative* 2 × 2 game provides this function, since it indicates a method of obtaining the "threat point" and the Pareto-optimal solution for each game once the payoffs are given on an interval scale. Thus, there is a "base line" with which to compare the empirically estimated function. Here the underlying assumption is that in the very long run an iterated game would approach a "solution" of a cooperative game. Again, systematic discrepancies between the theoretical solution and the observed asymptotic frequencies and the game-theoretic "rational" solution might provide a basis for a psychological theory. The possible relevance of such a theory to "real life" situations will be discussed in the last chapter.

Turning to the experiments discussed in chapter 17, we suspect that those on Prisoner's Dilemma and Chicken were, for the most part, motivated by the question of "how to elicit cooperation" in those games by the use of appropriate strategy in sequential play. The answer is fairly clear from the results. Noncontingent randomized strategies have little or no effect, and so discorroborate the implicit hypothesis that "cooperation elicits cooperation, and competition elicits competition." The hypothesis is an attractive one and may well be corroborated in many contexts, but the context chosen is not the appropriate one because of the "unresponsiveness" of noncontingent strategies: there being no way of establishing a tacit collusion with an unresponsive co-player, the subject's choices are probably governed by a simple instrumental conditioning process, which, because of the payoff structure of Prisoner's Dilemma, would drive the subject's C frequencies down regardless of the noncontingent strategy of the co-player. In Chicken, due to the absence of dominating strategies, the situation is more complicated, but the impossibility of establishing tacit collusion remains. On the grounds of simple reinforcement theory, the subject's C frequency in Chicken should be negatively correlated with the stooge's in noncontingent strategies. We have seen no evidence for this in the data examined. It is barely possible that the reinforcement principle here counteracts a Tit-for-tat tendency, so that the opposite effects are canceled. For lack of more convincing evidence, however, we must conclude that, in both Chicken and Prisoner's Dilemma, noncontingent strategies account for very little of the total variance of choice frequencies.

The "pure" noncontingent strategies are a notable exception. These must soon be perceived as such by the subjects, so that it is meaningful to compare subjects' reactions to them. We have seen in many cases that the pure fixed strategies bring out sharp differences in the subjects' behavior. For instance, against a 100 percent C strategy in Prisoner's Dilemma, roughly one half of the subjects respond cooperatively and one half, "exploitatively"; against the underdog's 100 percent passive strategy in game #19; about one quarter of the subjects in the role of top dog respond by sharing about equally; most of the remaining subjects share little or nothing. Very few share a "modest" fraction of the largest payoff, although the solution of the cooperative game prescribes 25 percent to Row in variant I of that game. It appears, therefore, that pure fixed strategies provide an opportunity of separating the subjects into two "types." We have seen how such types are suggested in bona fide play of game #19 (cf. p. 335); they could probably be brought into sharper focus in experiments with programed strategies. Implications for further investigations of the behavior of each "type" in other games and in other situations are clear.

Of the contingent strategies, Tit-for-tat elicits consistently the most cooperation in Prisoner's Dilemma. Obviously, it would be fatuous to interpret this result as a vindication of the "eye-for-an-eye" principle. The success of Tit-for-tat may be no more than that of a simple reinforcement schedule in a two-choice situation, devoid of ethical overtones.

The general impression obtained from experiments where information or communication are the independent variables is that, in games where competition and cooperation generate cross pressures and cooperation is to the advantage of both players, information relevant to understanding the nature of the game and opportunities for communication both facilitate learning to cooperate. This is especially true in symmetric games where the cooperative solution is unique and "fair." Since this result might have been expected on common sense grounds, it is not of great interest. Of much greater interest are the effects of communication and information in asymmetric games, where the optimal cooperative solution is not obvious and, moreover, where notions of equity may be at cross purposes with the relative bargaining advantage of the players.

The use of information as an independent variable opens possibilities for using game experiments to study perception as well as behavior. Investigations of perceptions are sometimes included in such experiments in the form of questionnaires given to subjects after experimental sessions. These usually include standard sociometric items, eliciting "ratings" of the co-player on various scales—"likability," "cooperativeness," etc. The value of such questionnaires seems doubtful to us. At best, answers will indicate that a co-player who "cooperates" will be rated as "cooperative," a player who plays predominantly D in Chicken will be labeled high on an "aggression" scale, etc. Shubik's experiment (cf. p. 299) suggests an altogether different approach. Let the information about the co-player's payoffs be withheld from each player. After the experimental session, let each player rank the payoffs of the other (as he thinks they are) in the order of magnitude. Our dependent variable becomes the accuracy of this assessment. The results are objective and quantifiable. They are measures of the amount of *distortion* in the perception of the interests of the co-player introduced by a particular payoff structure or by particular payoff magnitudes. It is just these distortions rather than corroborations of common sense expectations that are most interesting. To take an example, in games #19, #21, #44, or #64, Row may be made severely disgruntled by a numerical discrepancy between his and Column's payoffs in the natural outcome. In variants of this sort, frequent shifts by Row from the natural outcome can be expected, as well as persistence in T_1S_2, in the hope of eventually effecting an outcome where Row gets a larger payoff. Suppose now Row is informed of Column's payoffs, but Column is not informed of Row's. Column may attribute Row's persistence in T_1S_2 to the larger payoff in that outcome instead of to resentment against the inequity of the natural outcome. The diversity of structures of 2 × 2 games suggest innumerable variations on this theme.

Like the effects of information, the effects of communication can be in opposite directions. As we have seen, opportunities for unlimited communication facilitate cooperative solutions of symmetric games. With asymmetric games, the situation may be radically different. For, in those games, opportunities exist for making threats as well as promises, and the effects of threats can be either productive or counter-productive. As an example, consider the following variant of game #64:

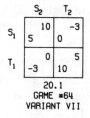

20.1
GAME #64
VARIANT VII

If limited communication is allowed, say, only a few exchanges, the players may settle on some easy solution, such as alternating between S_1S_2 and T_1T_2. If more extensive communication is allowed, Column's superior bargaining position may become clear to him but perhaps not to Row (it is easier to see one's advantage than one's disadvantage). Column may then demand his full share as prescribed by the solution of the *cooperative* game. The solution of this variant happens to be 6 to Row and 9 to Column, which may be considered grossly unfair by Row, and so cooperation may be inhibited.

Experiments with subjects as independent variables can be classified in two large categories, hypothesis testing and hypothesis generating. In the former, a population of subjects with previously assessed personality characteristics are expected to play a given game predominantly in a given way; for instance, cooperatively or noncooperatively, aggressively or passively, paying attention primarily only to his own payoffs or to both his and the co-player's, etc. Corroboration of the hypotheses establishes the game as a "diagnostic instrument," by means of which the (unknown) personality characteristics of a subject undergoing tests can be assessed from his behavior in the game. Obviously, the value of this instrument depends crucially on its reliability. Judging by the results of experiments so far performed, reliability of game behavior as an indicator of personality characteristics is not large, even if large populations of subjects are compared. Naturally, it is even smaller in the case of an individual subject. At most, therefore, game behavior can be used as merely an additional component in a battery of personality tests.

In our opinion, the hypothesis-generating experiments with subjects as independent variables are more valuable instruments of psychological research. In these experiments, a priori hypotheses about the game behavior of different categories of subjects cannot be made with any degree of confidence. There is no reason to suppose that "men cooperate more than women" or that "Americans revolt against power more frequently than Danes." Of course, formally such hypotheses may be advanced, but they can be advanced in either direction. Moreover, they are much too vague and broad, and it would be naive to expect an experiment with a 2 × 2 game to provide confirmation. What we find in fact in experiments of this sort are different results under different conditions, so that the questions posed cannot be answered by a "yes" or "no." The exploration of these conditions then becomes the main research task. Since we do not know in advance what are the important determining conditions, the preliminary broadside method of inquiry is indicated, in which results are merely suggestive. Thus, many experiments with Prisoner's Dilemma suggest that there is no discernible difference between men's and women's propensity to "cooperate" in the short run, but there is in the long run. To our knowledge, this finding was never subjected to experimental verification *specifically designed* to test it as a formally stated hypothesis. In our opinion, it would be worthwhile to do so.

The psychologist is naturally interested in more than the factual result. He wants to know *why* women seem to "cooperate" less than men, at least in long runs of Prisoner's Dilemma, and many are quick to resort to post hoc depth-psychological explanations. In our opinion, some trivial explanations must be refuted before "deeper ones" are advanced. For instance, when we compare the performance of women in Prisoner's Dilemma with the performance of men who do not see the game matrix (cf. p. 287), we find the levels of cooperation approximately equal. There is a possibility, therefore, that the low level of cooperation observed in female subjects might be due to the fact that they pay less attention to the matrix than male subjects do. If so, then the conditions of "matrix displayed" and "matrix not displayed" should make little or no difference in the level of cooperation of female subjects. If, on the contrary, the level of cooperation of female subjects when the matrix is not displayed is considerably lower than when the matrix is displayed, the "different attitudes of men and women toward the matrix" may be ruled out as a determining factor and other conjectures about the "cause" of the difference in the level of cooperation of men and women can be advanced with better justification.

Similar questions arise in connection with the "personality types" suggested by the comparison of performance of Danes and Americans in game #19 (cf. p. 336). The conjecture about distributions of these types in the two populations was an afterthought, not a hypothesis confirmed by the experiment. Therefore, tests of significance of the difference between the two distributions are not really in order. The conjecture, however, seems interesting enough to follow up. Once it becomes the principal question, appropriate experimental design is suggested. To begin with, the two populations should be much more strictly matched for other characteristics (age, background, etc.) than was done in the experiment discussed here. Next, differences would probably be more clearly brought out in play against programed strategies, specifically, against Row's "passive" strategy and Column's "adamant" one. The populations should be sufficiently large to include the "extreme" types: those who as Rows hardly ever "revolt" and as Columns hardly ever "share" {SS}; those who as Rows "revolt" with excessive frequency and as Columns hardly ever share {TS}; those who as Rows hardly ever revolt and as Columns share with frequencies approaching 50 {ST}; those who revolt frequently and share generously {TT}. The incidence of these types in the two populations can then be meaningfully compared.

The numerous conjectures concerning the differences between men and women as underdogs and as top dogs matched against coplayers of each sex, which we treated as if they were "findings" (cf. p. 318) though, of course, they were not, could be followed up in a similar fashion.

Finally, it is to be noted that the number of species of 2 × 2 games used as experimental tools is still very small. The experiments described in Part II represent a systematic attempt to collect data on games other than Prisoner's Dilemma and Chicken, which had been used almost exclusively in game experiments since they began about 1958. Each of those experiments, however, involved only one variant of each iterated game and only the "standard condition," i.e., prolonged runs with bona fide players. Whether the extension of gaming experiments in all their variety to a great many species of 2×2 games will lead to results of interest to behavioral scientists depends in great measure on how systematically such investigations are pursued "in depth."

Part IV

Introduction to Part IV

In the next four chapters we shall examine some models of behavior in 2 × 2 games that have been put to experimental test. Chapters 21 and 22 will be devoted to game-theoretic models. Game theory prescribes a definitive solution for the two-person constant-sum game, namely, the minimax strategy for each player, which is pure if the game has a saddle point, and mixed if it does not. The prescription is unique in the sense that the outcome of the game awards a unique (actual or expected) payoff to each player regardless of the prescribed strategies that are chosen (of which there may be several).

Attempts have been made to extend prescriptive game theory to nonconstant-sum games. As we have seen, these attempts are beset with difficulties. Unlike the equilibria of constant-sum games, which are all equivalent and interchangeable (cf. p. 37), those of nonconstant-sum games may be neither. Thus, if the individual players are advised to choose strategies containing equilibria, the resulting outcome need not be an equilibrium.

We have seen (cf. p. 46) that J. Harsanyi evaded this problem by singling out among the equilibria of a noncooperative game those dictated by an extended definition of individual rationality. That this extension does not remove the difficulty of a prescriptive theory can be seen in Prisoner's Dilemma. This game has a single equilibrium, which is, of course, trivially equivalent to and interchangeable with itself. Thus it constitutes the solution of the game, but it violates collective rationality. One can, of course, accept the view that collective rationality cannot operate if *enforceable* agreements cannot be made, as they cannot even in Harsanyi's modified definition of the noncooperative game. However, this is an assumption that one may choose or not choose to make.

At any rate, in the context of experimental behavioral science, the

351

game-theoretic prescriptions are relevant only to the extent that they can serve as a base with which to compare the distributions of observed outcomes. As we have seen in numerous experiments described in the preceding chapters, discrepancies between observed outcomes and equilibria, even Pareto-optimal ones, let alone Pareto-deficient ones, is as often a rule as an exception.

For cooperative games, where not only communication and bargaining but also binding agreements are possible, a number of solutions have been proposed. In chapter 3, we have examined some of them. We have seen (cf. p. 60) that Braithwaite's solution is applicable to only very few of the games in the ordinal taxonomy. Raiffa's solution has not, to our knowledge, been put to an experimental test. In what follows we shall see that, in general, neither the maximin solution of games of complete opposition nor the Nash solution of the cooperative game is experimentally corroborated (assuming that the payoffs represent the utilities of the players).

In chapters 22 and 23, we shall turn our attention to purely behavioral models. Chapter 23 will be devoted to a "static behavioral theory" of the 2 × 2 noncooperative, nonconstant-sum game. "Behavioral" is here used in the descriptive sense. The theory will attempt to account for the differences of performance in different 2 × 2 games by their payoff structure. It is a static theory, because only the overall average performance, not the process, in iterated games will be related to the game structure. The aim of the theory is to derive an "index," some tractable function of the payoffs to serve as a predictor of choice frequencies. In chapter 4, we derived some indices for Prisoner's Dilemma and for Chicken. The method will now be generalized to all 2 × 2 games.

In chapter 24, dynamic models of iterated games will be considered. The aim of these models is to predict the time courses of performances. The underlying theory is for the most part identical with the stochastic theory of learning. Following the work of P. Suppes and R. Atkinson, we shall compare the stochastic learning models with the game theoretic models in experiments with constant-sum games.

21

Testing the Maximin
Solution of the Zerosum Game

Three of the seventy-eight games of the ordinal taxonomy are games
of complete opposition, distinguishable by their orders. In game #11,
of order D_2, both players have a dominating strategy; in game
#45, of order D_1, one player has a dominating strategy; in game #75,
of order D_0, neither player has a dominating strategy. Game theory
prescribes S_1S_2 as the outcome of all variants of games #11 and #45,
as the result of choices by rational players, since S_1S_2 is the saddle
point in both games. Game #75 has no saddle point. The game-
theoretical prescription for this game is in terms of mixed strategies,
and the mixtures depend on the variant, since in this case the payoffs
must be given on an interval scale (cf. p. 52).

In a single play of a game, a mixed strategy is defined as a "probabilistic" choice, determined, say, by a chance device in which the
probabilities of the choices available to the player are fixed in accordance with the prescribed mixture. If we imagine that a player
has a device of this sort inside his head, and if all the players in a
population use the same device (i.e., with the same probabilities),
we can expect that the fraction of players choosing S in a game of
complete opposition will reflect the probability of that choice. Under
this admittedly rather far-fetched assumption, we can put the game-
theoretic model to a "test," as it were (without taking the "test" too
seriously). The comparison between the theoretical and observed

fractions of players choosing S in the three games are shown in table 21.1. Data are from Frenkel's single-play experiment (cf. chapter 7).

TABLE 21.1   Comparison of theoretical and observed
S frequencies in the three games of
complete opposition in Frenkel's experiment.

Game #	$[S_1]$ pred.	$[S_1]$ obs.	$[S_2]$ pred.	$[S_2]$ obs.
11	100	95	100	97
45	100	98	100	96
75	50	86	91	91

We note that five of the observed frequencies agree well with those predicted. Nevertheless, this agreement is not overly impressive in as much as it is confined to the instances where the predicted frequencies are extreme (100 in four cases and 91 in one). Where the predicted frequency is 50, the discrepancy between it and the observed frequency (86) is very large.

The concept of strategy mixture can be concretized much more naturally in iterated games. In fact, a player, rational in the sense of game theory, playing an iterated zerosum game without a saddle point, would randomize his choices in accordance with the prescribed mixture. Therefore, experiments with iterated zerosum games offer a rather direct opportunity to test the game-theoretic model of rational decision making.

To our knowledge, no experiments with iterated 2×2 games of orders D_2 or D_1 (with saddle points) have been performed.[1] Judging by the results observed in games with strongly stable, Pareto-optimal equilibria (e.g., game #36 discussed in chapter 10), it is unlikely that experiments with iterated variants of game #11 or game #45 would yield results very different from those observed in single plays: almost exclusive occurrences of the natural outcome. Such experiments, therefore, do not seem to be worthwhile. There remain only experiments with variants of game #75.

Only a few experiments with iterated constant-sum games of order D_0 have been performed. Moreover, with very few exceptions, they

---

[1] Experiments with 3×3 games with saddle points have been performed (e.g., Lieberman, 1960). In this book, however, we do not leave the context of 2×2 games.

involved a programed player. This programed player typically uses the optimal (minimax) mixture, the object of the experiment being to see whether the subject also uses his optimal mixture, or at least tends to learn to use it toward the end of a long run of iterations.

To our way of thinking, it is unreasonable to expect that a subject ignorant of game theory will learn to optimize his mixture by playing against a programed *optimal* mixture, at least in a 2×2 game. We have seen that in a zerosum 2×2 game, when one player plays his minimax strategy, the expected payoff of the other is the same no matter what strategy he plays. If we assume that learning in this context depends on differential reinforcement of choices (for which there is considerable evidence in other contexts), we cannot expect any learning to occur when a naive subject plays against a minimax mixed strategy. This, in fact, was a result of an experiment performed by B. Lieberman (1962). The zerosum game used is shown in 21.1.[2]

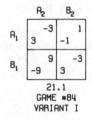

21.1
GAME #84
VARIANT I

The subject was Row; Column was the stooge. Row's optimal mixture in this game is (.75, .25); Column's is (.25, .75). The time course of A frequencies is shown in figure 21.1. Fluctuations of (A_2) are statistical: the average frequency of A_2 choices is .25. We observe that the frequency of A_1 (i.e., the subject's) choices are nowhere near the optimal frequency (75). Rather they seem to follow the fluctuations of (A_2). At any rate, there is no indication of trend toward 75, which, as we have pointed out, cannot be expected. On the other hand, the subject's apparent imitation of the stooge is understandable, since the best reply to A_2 is A_1 and the best reply to B_2 is B_1.

In his next experiment, Lieberman's stooge departed from the

---

[2] This game is not quite a variant of game #75, because of the equalities $a_1 = d_1$, $a_2 = d_2$. However, it reduces to game #75 if we change the absolute magnitudes of a_1 or d_1 by minute amounts.

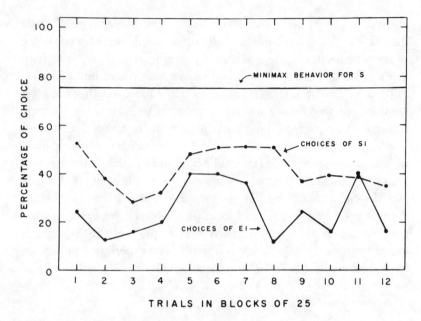

Fig. 21.1. Frequency of Subject (S₁) and Stooge (E₁) choices over successive blocks of 25 trials where stooge plays optimal mixed strategy in 21.1.

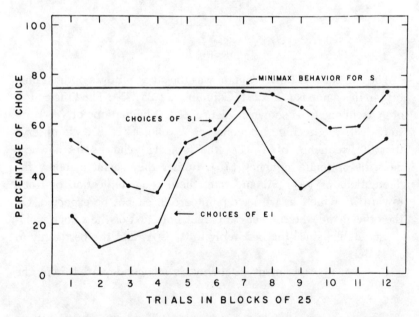

Fig. 21.2. Frequency of Subject (S₁) and Stooge (E₁) choices over successive blocks of 25 trials where stooge employs a strategy of increasing frequency of E₁ choices.

minimax strategy by playing A₂ with increasing average frequency. This time, a trend toward the minimax on the part of the subject *was* observed, as shown in figure 21.2. However, this trend is explained by the subject's imitation of the stooge, as can be plainly seen from figure 21.2 (p. 356).

J. Fox (1972) recognized the reason for the absence of learning on the part of the subject when playing against the minimax mixture in a zerosum game. Implicit in this recognition (although not explicitly stated in Fox's paper) is the hypothesis that subjects playing against a minimax strategy will choose one of the strategies with a frequency approximately constant in time. Fox's zerosum game is shown in 21.2.

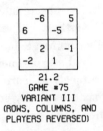

21.2
GAME #75
VARIANT III
(ROWS, COLUMNS, AND
PLAYERS REVERSED)

The stooge played his optimal mixture (3/7, 4/7). The subject's optimal mixture is (3/14, 11/14). Again the average subject missed this optimal mixture by a wide margin. Surprisingly, however, a slight trend toward the minimax mixture was observed in the subject's performance.

In Fox's next experiment, the stooge played (0.6, 0.4) instead of the minimax. The best strategy against this mixture is 100 percent A₁. A trend upward of (A₁) was in fact observed, from an initial value of about 55 to a final value of about 75. Note that in Fox's game, in contrast to Lieberman's, the subject, learning to exploit the stooge's departure from the minimax, must move *away* from his minimax, not toward it. Thus the trend toward the minimax in Lieberman's experiment can be interpreted as learning to exploit the opponent, not learning to play the minimax, as is more clearly demonstrated in Fox's experiment.

The question remains why Fox's subjects tended to approach the minimax when playing against a minimax. Fox offers the conjecture (not without reservation) that the subjects were learning "to reduce risk." It is indeed the case that in the minimax mixture the strategy involving the larger loss has the smaller frequency. Assuming the conjecture, the question arises why the subjects did not learn to reduce risk in Lieberman's experiment when they were playing against the minimax. The answer that suggests itself to us is the following. In Lieberman's experiment, the minimaxing stooge played A_2 (where Row's largest loss was situated) with probability .25, that is, comparatively rarely. In Fox's experiment, the minimaxing stooge played B_2 (where now Row's largest loss was situated) with probability .57, that is, considerably more frequently. Accordingly, Fox's subjects had more opportunity to learn to "avoid risk."

On the whole, both Lieberman's and Fox's results are roughly in accord with hypotheses usually made in theories of reinforcement learning. None of the results substantiate the normative prescriptions of game theory. Nevertheless, Lieberman's suggestion that "game theory fails to predict human behavior" is not justified in the present context, because, in the experiments performed, no opportunity was given to the subjects to learn the optimal strategy: all strategies against a minimax are equally good.

D. Gordon (unpublished) performed a single-play experiment with a zerosum game where the subjects were asked to choose a mixed strategy. The subjects were actually paired and told that their payoffs would be the weighted average of the four payoff entries, the weights being the probabilities of occurrence determined by pairs of chosen mixed strategies. Gordon used Fox's variant of game #75 (cf. 21.2). Table 21.2 presents the numbers of subjects who assigned frequencies to A_1 and A_2 in the ranges shown.

TABLE 21.2   Numbers of subjects who assigned probabilities to choices A_1 and A_2 in the ranges shown in Gordon's experiment.

Probability assigned	0-.10	.11-.20	.21-.30	.31-.40	.41-.50	.51-.60	.61-.70	.71-.80	.81-.90	.91-1.00
to A_1	29	3	2	6	9	2	5	0	0	2
to A_2	32	6	5	2	2	0	1	2	0	8

The mean probability assigned to A_1 was .29; to A_2, .27. As we have seen, minimax mixtures assign .21 to A_1 and .43 to A_2. Thus there is no evidence that the "average player" plays optimally. Instead, we observe that the largest number of players (about half) choose B_1 and B_2 as pure or nearly pure strategies. If the subjects consider themselves playing a game against nature, where nature chooses her two strategies with equal probabilities, we see that Column maximizes expected gain by choosing B_2. As for Row, his two strategies yield the same expected gain, but by choosing B_1 he minimizes risk. It has been observed that maximization of expected gain (assuming equiprobable choices by the opponent) and minimization of risk are fairly good predictors of choices in single plays, but they do not tell the whole story.

Probably the most "fair" test of the game-theoretic prescription of minimax mixture is in an iterated game with bona fide players. One might expect that even naive players may approach maximin frequencies in long runs, because, if each exploits the other's departure from the minimax, they may "zero in" on the equilibrium. To see this, consider a "mechanical" model that simulates the process.

The general 2×2 zerosum game is shown in 21.3.

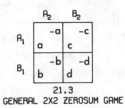

21.3
GENERAL 2X2 ZEROSUM GAME

Without loss of generality, we can assume $a \geqq d > b \geqq c$ (cf. p. 38). Let Row choose A_1 with frequency x and Column choose A_2 with frequency y, where x and y are now variable, subject to modification upward or downward in consequence of differential reinforcements. Suppose further that whenever Column plays A_2, A_1 is reinforced for Row to the extent that a is larger than b. Similarly, whenever Column plays B_2, B_1 is reinforced for Row to the extent that d is larger than c. Column's reactions are analogous. Whenever Row plays A_1, B_2 is reinforced for Column to the extent that $-c$ is larger than $-a$; whenever Row plays B_1, A_2 is reinforced to the extent that $-b$ is larger than $-d$. Embedding the process in continuous time, we can represent these assumptions by a differential equation model as shown in equations 21.1 and 21.2.

$$dx/dt = y(a - b) + (1 - y)(c - d), \qquad (21.1)$$
$$dy/dt = x(c - a) + (1 - x)(d - b). \qquad (21.2)$$

Expanding, we obtain

$$dx/dt = Dy + E, \qquad (21.3)$$
$$dy/dt = -Dx + F, \qquad (21.4)$$

where $D = a + d - b - c > 0$, $E = c - d < 0$; $F = d - b > 0$.

Consider the pair (x, y) as a point in two-dimensional space, and let us examine its motion. Note that when

$$x = F/D = \frac{d-b}{a+d-b-c}; \; y = -E/d = \frac{d-c}{a+d-b-c}, \qquad (21.5)$$

$dx/dt = dy/dt = 0$, that is, the point is at rest. But then x and y correspond exactly to the minimax mixture (cf. p. 40). Moreover, the equilibrium at that point is stable. For, suppose x deviates from the equilibrium by increasing slightly. Since the coefficient of x in the expression for dy/dt is negative [cf. (21.4)], dy/dt will become negative and, consequently, y will decrease. But the coefficient of y in the expression for dx/dt [cf. (21.3)] is positive. Consequently, when y decreases, dx/dt will become negative, and x will decrease. In short, an increase of x will bring about a "force" which will eventually cause x to decrease. The same situation holds with respect to the fluctuations of y.

However, the fact that the point $(F/D, -E/D)$ is an equilibrium does not guarantee that x and y will ever be at that equilibrium. Indeed, our model implies that this equilibrium will never actually be reached unless x and y are at it initially. To show this, let us solve the pair of differential equations for x and y as functions of t and so get the dynamic behavior of these variables.

First, we differentiate (21.3) with respect to t and obtain

$$d^2x/dt^2 = D(dy/dt). \qquad (21.6)$$

Substituting (21.4) for dy/dt, we obtain

$$d^2x/dt^2 = -D^2x + DF. \qquad (21.7)$$

The general solution for this second order differential equation is

$$x = M\cos(Dt) + N\sin(Dt) + F/D, \qquad (21.8)$$

where M and N are constants determined by the initial conditions, that is, by the initial values of x and y.

Solving for y in the same way, we obtain

$$y = M' \cos(Dt) + N' \sin(Dt) - E/D. \qquad (21.9)$$

If, when $t = 0$, $x = x_0$, $y = y_0$, the constants M, M', N, and N' turn out to be: $M = x_0 - F/D$, $M' = y_0 + E/D$, $N = -(x_0 - F/D)$, $N' = -(y_0 + E/D)$.

Substituting these values into (21.8) and (21.9), we obtain the parametric equation of an ellipse. That is to say, our model implies that the point (x,y) will move *around* the equilibrium point $(F/D, -E/D)$ without ever reaching it (unless it happens to coincide with it initially). Nevertheless, the *average* values of x and y will be F/D and $-E/D$ respectively, as can be shown by integrating x over its period, $2\pi/D$ and dividing by it. In this way, a simple "mechanical" model predicts the minimax mixed strategies for both players. To the extent that the model reflects a particular aspect of reinforcement learning—namely, that minute shifts in choice probabilities in short periods of time are proportional to the advantages gained by the shifts—we can view this model as the dynamic underpinning of the game-theoretical solution. At least we can say that the game-theoretic solution is consistent with a certain reinforcement learning model, and so an approach of naive subjects toward minimax strategies in a zerosum game can be expected on those grounds.

Malcolm and Lieberman (1965) had nine pairs of subjects play the game shown in 21.1 (cf. p. 356).

Row's optimal mixed strategy is (3/4, 1/4); Column's is (1/4, 3/4). The value of the game is zero to both players.

The observed frequencies of S_1 and T_2 (for both of which 75 is prescribed as optimal) are shown in table 21.3.

We see that Row's behavior is rather close to optimal. In fact, five of the nine Row players chose S_1 within 7 points of the optimal frequency. Column's T_2 frequencies are consistently lower than optimal.

TABLE 21.3 S_1 and T_2 frequencies in an iterated zerosum game in Malcolm & Lieberman's experiment.

Pair	1	2	3	4	5	6	7	8	9
(S_1)	60	62	82	76	76	66	64	68	70
(T_2)	51	50	61	74	62	66	44	54	52

Examining the game matrix, we can conjecture the reason for the discrepancy on intuitive psychological grounds. Row's motivation for preferring S_1 may well be dictated by prudence: in avoiding T_1, he avoids the outcome T_1S_2 where he gets the smallest payoff (-9). On the other hand, his largest payoffs are equal, so that there is no counter pressure on him to choose T_1 in pursuit of the largest payoff. Column's situation is different. To avoid his smallest payoff (-3), Column might choose either S_1 or T_2. But his largest payoff in T_1S_2 creates a pressure toward S_2, which may account for the increase of (S_2) above the optimal (.25).

On the whole, the average Column player (and eight of the nine individual players) chose T_2 with frequency larger than 50, which may be accounted for by Row's relatively more frequent choice of S_1. Note that if Row's S_1 frequency were *fixed* at a value less than 75, then Column's optimal strategy would be the pure strategy T_2. The fact that the frequencies of T_2 are far below 100 reflects the interactions in the course of the play. If Column were to choose T_2 exclusively, a rational Row would choose T_1, inflicting -3 on Column, which would induce the latter to shift to S_2. If these interactions were immediate and continuous, optimal mixed strategies would be approached.

Let us now examine the time course of choice frequencies, averaged over the nine pairs by twenty-five-play blocks, and the payoffs to Row to see whether any trends are apparent. The results are shown in table 21.4. The last column shows Row's expected payoff.

There is slight evidence that both Row and Column move toward their optimal strategy mixtures, and this is reflected in the smaller average numerical values of Row's losses in the latter part of the run. However, if learning occurs at all in this game, it occurs rather early, perhaps in the first three blocks; thereafter, the behavior of the average players is fairly constant.

TABLE 21.4   Time courses of S_1 and T_2 frequencies and of Row's average payoff per play, $g(R)$, in Malcolm and Lieberman's experiment.

Plays	1–25	26–50	51–75	76–100	101–125	126–150	151–175	176–200
(S_1)	64	68	65	76	71	70	70	71
(T_2)	40	54	54	63	62	64	58	62
$g(R)$	-.68	-.24	-.32	-.08	-.08	-.12	-.20	-.04

Becker (H. Kaufmann and G. M. Becker, 1961) observed subjects learning to play optimally in a constant-sum game without a saddle point. Five 2×2 games with the same value were used. In each game, the subjects were required to apportion their choices in 100 *imagined* iterations. The experimenter thereupon adopted a counter strategy which was optimal against the particular mixed strategy chosen by each subject, and paid the resulting expected payoff to the subject. Note that this optimal strategy is always a pure strategy except when the subject uses his maximin (or minimax) strategy, and that the payoff to the subjects was consequently the larger, the closer his mixture was to the maximin. Under these conditions, it is hardly surprising that the subjects eventually learned to approach the maximin mixture. The experiment cannot, therefore, be considered as a corroboration of the game-theoretic prescription, but simply as a demonstration of a learning process wherein the subject is reinforced to the extent that he approaches a prescribed behavioral pattern, as in operant conditioning.

22

Testing Nash's Solution of the Cooperative Game

To our knowledge, the only experiments to date aimed at testing Nash's solution of the cooperative game were performed by D. Gordon (1934–1972), whose untimely death left the work unfinished. Most of the data, however, were gathered.

Recall that Nash conceives of the cooperative game as a *noncooperative* game in *extensive* form, i.e., as a sequence of moves. This game consists of two phases between which negotiation takes place. In phase 1, each player independently chooses one of his available strategies, pure or mixed. The pair of strategies so chosen constitutes the *threat outcome* which will obtain if they fail to agree on the outcome of phase 2 (cf. Luce and Raiffa, 1957, p. 140). In phase 2, each player independently "makes his claim," that is, specifies a mixture of the Pareto-optimal outcomes that he thinks should be the final outcome of the game. If the two claims are compatible, each gets what he has claimed; otherwise, the threat outcome goes into effect. Note that, after the threat outcome has been determined, the cooperative game reduces to the simple bargaining problem (cf. p. 51).

As an example, consider game #19. To play this game "cooperatively," the players must first establish the threat outcome. For instance, Row may choose T_1 and Column S_2. This determines T_1S_2, which will go into effect if the players cannot agree in phase 2. (In the variants of game #19 so far considered, T_1S_2 happens to be the threat outcome prescribed by Nash's model. In what follows, however, we shall examine another variant where this is not the case.)

Having established T_1S_2, which neither player likes, as the threat outcome, the players can now negotiate for the "mixture" of S_1S_2 and S_1T_2 of the two Pareto-optimal outcomes.[1] Clearly, Column prefers the mixture to favor S_1S_2 as much as possible, and Row prefers it to favor S_1T_2. The threat point provides each player with a bargaining leverage. Each can point out to the other that if the other does not yield to one's proposal, he will suffer the consequences by getting the payoff associated with the threat point. (The argument, of course, runs both ways.)

Suppose now that, when the time comes to make the claims, Row claims a (.5, .5) mixture of S_1S_2 and S_1T_2, while Column claims a (.75, .25) mixture in favor of S_1S_2. These proposals are incompatible, because each claims a larger probability for his preferred outcome than the other cedes. These claims result in the threat outcome T_1S_2. Had each claimed at most as much as the other cedes to him, each would have received what he claimed. For instance, Column might have claimed S_1S_2 with probability 0.60, while Row claimed S_1T_2 with probability 0.20 (< 0.40). In that case, Column would get the expected payoff resulting from a (.6, .4) mixture, and Row would get the expected payoff resulting from the (.8, .2) mixture. (Note that this outcome, while not Pareto-optimal, is feasible; that is, the players could get these expected payoffs by choices of appropriate mixed strategies in the original game.)

Testing this model experimentally presents certain problems. The players must understand the concept of mixed outcomes, and some way must be available to them to anticipate the results of proposing and receiving mixtures of outcomes. Gordon bypassed this problem in the following way. He presented the subjects with a geometric representation of the games. Examples of such diagrams are shown in figures 22.1–22.4 (pp. 366–67). In phase 2, the players independently put a mark on the line segment (or the broken line) that

---

[1] The negotiation makes the game cooperative in the sense that the players can agree to coordinate their strategy choices so that a Pareto-optimal outcome or a mixture of Pareto-optimal outcomes results. In Nash's conception, the negotiation is tacit. It is *as if* after this tacit negotiation each player makes his "claim" independently, weighing the expected gain against the chance of incompatible claims.

represents the Pareto-optimal set. If Row's mark was not to the right of Column's (that is, if Row awarded to Column not less than Column claims, and vice versa), the claims were compatible, and each received accordingly. Otherwise, in all experiments except one (experiment 1 below) the players received the threat outcome payoffs.

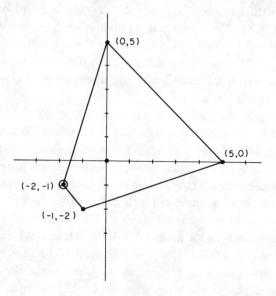

Fig. 22.1.   Geometric representation of game #19, variant II.

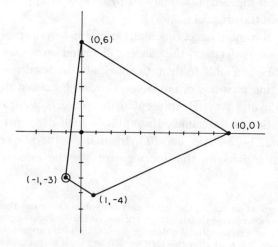

Fig. 22.2.   Geometric representation of game #21, variant XI.

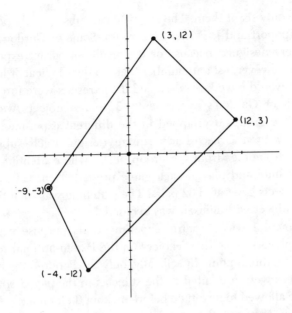

Fig. 22.3. Geometric representation of game #64, variant VIII.

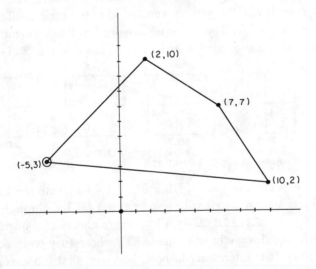

Fig. 22.4. Geometric representation of game #44, variant II.

Gordon's idea was to test the component parts of Nash's model separately, namely, the choice of threat outcome and the bargaining problem. To do this, he designed seven experiments, but was able to complete only six of them. The seventh was subsequently performed by A. Rapoport and J. Perner in Toronto. Some of Gordon's experiments were designed because of the results of earlier experiments. We shall, however, list and number them in their logical order, in the way they would have been designed if the results were foreseen.

In each of Gordon's experiments, 32 male subjects were used. Some of the groups overlapped in the different experiments in accordance with a Graeco-Latin square design. Each subject was paired with another from the group of 32, whose identity was unknown to him, and played each game presented *once*. In this way the 32 subjects generated 32 pairs. The matching was such that pairing of a subject with himself was avoided.

Experiment 1 was a control experiment. Its purpose was to see how the players make their choices on the Pareto-optimal set in the absence of a threat point. Specifically, only the Pareto-optimal sets of eight games were presented to the subjects in the payoff space, and they were allowed to negotiate before making their choices. After the negotiation, they put their marks on the Pareto-optimal set. If the choices were compatible, the rule described above determined the outcome. If not, the players were asked to try again until the choices were compatible. There was no penalty for disagreement.

The four games used in experiment 1 are shown in 22.1–22.4

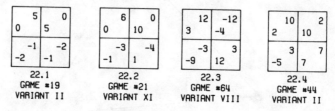

As expected, in games #19, #64, and #44, where the Pareto-optimal sets are symmetric with respect to the 45° line through the origin (cf. figures 22.1, 22.3, 22.4), the average claims of the players were nearly equal; exactly so in game #19 where they were equal in all 32 pairs. It is interesting to note, however, that the average payoff claimed in game #19 (2.42) was slightly less than the maximum possible, assuming equal division (2.50). Turning to the protocols, we see that three pairs apparently agreed to take less (in equal amounts). The players in two of the pairs took 2.0 each, in one pair, 1.0. Were there a penalty for incompatible claims, the outcome would be attributed to caution against a double cross. In the control condition, however, there was no such penalty, and discussion was permitted. Thus the reason for the three instances of a "collusion to take less than the most possible" remains unexplained.

In game #21, Row's average claim was considerably larger than Column's. There is no question about the statistical significance of the result, since Row's claims were larger than Column's in 30 out of the 32 pairs. The claims are equal in only one pair, and Column's is the larger in one. Examining the protocols, we see that in 19 of the 32 pairs Row claimed 5.00 and Column claimed 3.00. We expect, therefore, that the point (5, 3) on the Pareto-optimal line is somehow special and provides a "prominent" solution. Indeed, it is the midpoint of the Pareto-optimal line (cf. figure 22.2). Examining the claims of the players in the remaining eleven pairs, where Column claimed less than Row, we see that the outcomes also cluster around the point (5, 3). We conclude that, in the absence of a threat point, it is the *midpoint* of the Pareto-optimal set, rather than the equal payoff point, that appears to the players as the salient compromise solution.

The condition in experiment 2 was the same as that of experiment 1, except that the threat point in each game (as determined by Nash's theory) was also shown represented in the diagram presented to the subjects. No negotiation was allowed. If the players' choices were incompatible, they received the payoffs determined by the threat point.

Experiment 3 was the same as experiment 2, except that negotiation was allowed before the players made their (independent) choices on the Pareto-optimal set. Thus, both experiments 2 and 3 amount to the second phase of Nash's interpretation of the cooperative game as a game in extensive form, with and without negotiation, respectively.

Eight games were used in experiments 2 and 3: the four used in experiment 1, and the four shown in 22.5–22.8.

The purpose of experiments 2 and 3 was to see whether the predominant symmetry of the final outcome with respect to the end points of the Pareto-optimal set, observed in experiment 1, would be disturbed when the threat outcome, awarding unequal payoffs in case of a deadlock, was put into the picture; further, to see what effect, if any, could be attributed to the introduction of the negotia-

5	0
0	10
-2	-3
-5	-9

22.5
GAME #20
VARIANT II

10	0
0	10
-4	-6
-5	-9

22.6
GAME #20
VARIANT III

9	0
0	7
-8	8
-3	$\frac{13}{4}$

22.7
GAME #56
VARIANT II

16	6
7	-10
0	-2
-11	16

22.8
GAME #37
VARIANT II

tion process, during which the unequal positions of the players might be brought out. Let us, therefore, see what might be the biases introduced by the threat point and/or negotiation in each of the eight games.

In game #19, we would expect that the threat point would bias the outcome in Column's favor, since Row stands to lose more than Column in case the threat outcome $(-2, -1)$ obtains. The theoretical solution of this game awards 2 to Row and 3 to Column.

In game #21, the theoretical solution awards 7 to Row and 1.8 to Column. We can hardly expect, however, that players ignorant of this presumably "fair" solution will adopt it, although we might expect a shift in Row's favor away from the midpoint (5, 3) of the Pareto-optimal line, which was the predominant outcome in the absence of the threat point.

In game #44, the symmetrically placed corner of the Pareto-optimal set (cf. figure 22.4) was chosen by 27 out of 32 subjects in experiment 1. The Nash solution, however, favors Column. It is interesting to see whether the introduction of the threat point will shake the salience of the corner and effect a shift in that direction.

Whereas game #44 has only one equilibrium, at S_1S_2, game #64 has two, at S_1S_2 and T_1T_2. In variant VIII of that game, the slope of the Pareto-optimal line is -1. In experiment 1, the midpoint of that line segment was chosen by 20 out of 32 subjects; the remaining 12 choices were scattered symmetrically around it. However, the threat outcome of that game biases the solution strongly in Column's favor, awarding 10.50 to Column and only 4.50 to Row.

The two variants of game #20 are strategically equivalent, since variant III results when Column's payoffs in variant II are doubled. If the two games are perceived as strategically equivalent by the players, the outcome should award the same numerical payoff to Row in both games. Column's payoffs should be twice as great in variant III.

In game #56, the Pareto-optimal set is a broken line, as in game #44. However, it is not symmetric with respect to the axes, and the corner is not its midpoint. We can thus compare the effect of the corner as a "prominent" solution with the effects of other pressures in that game.

In game #37, the Nash solution awards Column his maximum payoff. We expect that this outcome will appear only rarely as the solution whether or not negotiation is permitted.

The results of experiments 2 and 3 are compared in tables 22.1–22.8. The columns denote (i) the average claim (bid) made by Row (BR); (ii) Column's average claim (BC); (iii) Row's actual average gain "g(R)"; (iv) Column's actual gain "g(C)"; (v) number of disagreements, i.e., threat outcomes out of the 32 plays (D). The last line shows the payoffs awarded by the solution. We shall now pose a number of questions, answers to which are suggested by the data.

1. Does the underdog in each game claim a smaller payoff? Strictly speaking, since the payoffs are only on an interval scale, the "underdog" should be defined as the player whose most preferred outcome on the relevant segment of the Pareto-optimal set (in case

TABLE 22.1   Average bids and payoffs in Game #19.

	BR	BC	g(R)	g(C)	D
Exp. 2	2.05	2.54	1.04	1.65	7
Exp. 3	2.34	2.57	2.31	2.54	1
Theory			2.00	3.00	

TABLE 22.2   Average bids and payoffs in Game #21.

	BR	BC	g(R)	g(C)	D
Exp. 2	4.45	2.94	1.94	1.43	12
Exp. 3	4.45	3.22	4.45	3.22	0
Theory			7.00	1.80	

TABLE 22.3   Average bids and payoffs in Game #64.

	BR	BC	g(R)	g(C)	D
Exp. 2	6.01	8.24	0.50	3.69	10
Exp. 3	6.50	8.85	4.36	7.19	4
Theory			4.50	10.50	

there is more than one segment) is furthest from the solution. We assume, however (for reasons stated below), that numerical payoffs have a stronger salience for the subjects than the distance to the solution. Therefore, we shall define the underdog as the player to whom the solution awards the smaller numerical payoff.

Examining the first and second columns of tables 22.1–22.8, we see that in experiment 2 (without negotiation) the underdog claimed

TABLE 22.4   Average bids and payoffs in Game #44.

	BR	BC	g(R)	g(C)	D
Exp. 2	5.72	7.17	1.27	5.18	12
Exp. 3	5.70	8.08	4.10	7.03	5
Theory			4.33	8.60	

TABLE 22.5   Average bids and payoffs in Game #20, Var. II.

	BR	BC	g(R)	g(C)	D
Exp. 2	3.15	3.03	0.15	1.40	10
Exp. 3	3.10	3.54	1.74	2.69	5
Theory			4.09	2.75	

TABLE 22.6   Average bids and payoffs in Game #20, Var. III.

	BR	BC	g(R)	g(C)	D
Exp. 2	4.65	5.02	0.97	2.13	10
Exp. 3	4.79	5.42	4.09	4.72	2
Theory			4.09	5.91	

TABLE 22.7   Average bids and payoffs in Game #56.

	BR	BC	g(R)	g(C)	D
Exp. 2	4.60	5.28	2.04	2.03	15
Exp. 3	4.69	4.67	4.53	4.47	1
Theory			3.63	7.20	

TABLE 22.8   Average bids and payoffs in Game #37.

	BR	BC	g(R)	g(C)	D
Exp. 2	9.20	11.55	5.29	6.06	13
Exp. 3	8.82	12.51	8.43	11.76	5
Theory			7.0	16.0	

less in all eight games. In experiment 3 (with negotiation) there was a slight reversal in game #20 variant II. The claims in game #56 were nearly equal.

2. Does the underdog actually get less on the average than the top dog?

Looking at columns three and four of experiment 2, we see a reversal in game #20 variant II and the payoffs in game #56 are almost equal, the same exceptions that were observed in the claims. In experiment 3, the same reversal occurs and the same near equality in game #56. The differences of payoffs obtained show no trend as negotiation is introduced. Although, as we shall see, the number of equal claims and equal payoff outcomes increases substantially in experiment 3, the increase must be offset by other effects in the opposite direction, perhaps by arguments on the part of the top dog which show the underdog his disadvantages. As expected, the total amounts claimed are larger in experiment 3, where agreements can ward off incompatible claims, diminishing the necessity for conservative bids (cf. p. 369). The payoffs obtained are also larger in experiment 3 since the number of threat outcomes substantially declines.

3. Is the Nash solution a good predictor of the outcome of the simple bargaining problem?

As we have seen, the solution predicts fairly well which of the (composite) players will make the bigger claim and will get more in the outcome. However, large differences in numerical payoffs awarded by the solution are not observed, at least in the format of the bargaining problem presented in experiments 2 and 3. The final average payoffs are for the most part considerably closer together than the solution predicts.

4. What, then, are the players guided by in making their claims and in negotiating the outcome?

We turn to tables 22.9–22.16 (pp. 374–75). The row entries represent the apparently salient points on the Pareto-optimal set.

P_e is the point that awards equal numerical payoffs.

P_a is the so-called point of constant relative advantage. It is obtained by drawing a 45° line from the threat outcome to the Pareto-optimal set. At the intersection, the player who would have got more (lost less) at the threat point gets as much more in the final outcome. This principle underlies H. Raiffa's "arbitrated solution" of the bar-

TABLE 22.9 Choice of salient points in Game #19.

	Experiment 2				Experiment 3			
	R	R*	C	C*	R	R*	C	C*
P_e (2.5)	7	3	7	7	17	17	17	17
P_a (2, 3)	13	13	11	7	7	7	8	7
$P_m = P_a$								

TABLE 22.10 Choice of salient points in Game #21.

	Experiment 2				Experiment 3			
	R	R*	C	C*	R	R*	C	C*
P_e (3.67)	4	4	4	4	10	10	10	10
P_a (5, 3)	8	5	10	7	8	8	8	8
$P_m = P_a$								

TABLE 22.11 Choice of salient points in Game #64.

	Experiment 2				Experiment 3			
	R	R*	C	C*	R	R*	C	C*
P_e (7.5)	5	2	4	4	13	9	10	10
P_a (4.5, 10.5)	2	2	6	2	6	6	6	4
$P_m = P_a$								

TABLE 22.12 Choice of salient points in Game #44.

	Experiment 2				Experiment 3			
	R	R*	C	C*	R	R*	C	C*
P_e (7)	9	4	11	10	11	9	9	9
P_a (2, 10)	0	0	3	0	1	1	5	1
$P_m = P_e$								

TABLE 22.13 Choice of salient points in Game #20, Var. II.

	Experiment 2				Experiment 3			
	R	R*	C	C*	R	R*	C	C*
P_e (3.33)	4	1	6	5	16	14	16	16
P_a (0.84, 4.58)	3	3	1	0	1	1	2	1
P_m (5, 2.5)	1	0	3	3	0	0	0	0

TABLE 22.14   Choice of salient points in Game #20, Var. III.

	Experiment 2				Experiment 3			
	R	R*	C	C*	R	R*	C	C*
P_e (5)	10	5	12	11	18	17	19	19
P_a (4.09, 5.91)	8	6	6	2	5	5	5	5
$P_m = P_e$								

TABLE 22.15   Choice of salient points in Game #56.

	Experiment 2				Experiment 3			
	R	R*	C	C*	R	R*	C	C*
P_e (4,8)	6	3	4	2	23	22	21	21
P_a** (5.0, 4.28)	5	5	6	3	4	4	3	3
P_m** (5.12, 4.0)								

**Because P_a and P_m are close, the choices are counted for either point.

TABLE 22.16   Choice of salient points in Game #37.

	Experiment 2				Experiment 3			
	R	R*	C	C*	R	R*	C	C*
P_e (10)	11	5	9	7	13	10	10	10
P_a (7, 16)	7	7	6	1	1	1	1	1
P_m (11.5, 7)	2	1	1	1	0	0	0	0

gaining problem, except that the latter is applied only when the payoffs of both players have been normalized on the interval (0, 1). Apparently, the "Raiffa point" has a certain salience to the players even if the payoffs are not normalized.

P_m is the midpoint of the relevant line segment of the Pareto-optimal set. In game #44, the symmetrically placed "corner" of the game diagram was so labeled.

In tables 22.9–22.16 the columns show the number of times the claim was made at each of the salient points by Row (R) and by Column (C), and the number of times the associated payoff was actually obtained by Row and Column (R*, C* respectively).

We note that the number of choices and of outcomes associated with P_e increases in experiment 3, showing the "equalizing" influence of negotiation. The salience of P_a, on the other hand, does not show an increase, except possibly in game #64. Moreover, P_a is not salient in game #44, where it is overshadowed by the symmetrically placed "corner"; nor in game #20 variant II, where it probably seems "unfair" to Row. P_m coincides with P_a in games #19, #21, and (almost) #56; in games #44 and #20 variant III, it coincides with P_e. Therefore, in games #44 and #20, we cannot tell to which of the two coinciding points salience should be ascribed. Only in games #20 variant II and #37 are all three points distinct. In neither game is P_m salient. Note, however, that in game #20, the disparity of the payoffs at the midpoint is large (appearing unfair?), while in game #37, P_a is salient even though it is an extreme point of the Pareto-optimal segment. Note, further, that the salience of this point disappears with negotiation, in spite of the fact that it coincides with the Nash solution.

In summary, it seems that equality of payoffs has a strong attraction for the players, especially after negotiation. It may simply be an "easy way to settle."

In order to give the Nash solution a "fair trial" in its competition with the "salient points," Gordon designed some games in which neither P_e nor P_a are feasible outcomes; that is, both these points are beyond one of the extremes of the Pareto-optimal set. The Nash solution sits at the other extreme. An example is shown in figure 22.5. Obviously, the midpoint of the Pareto-optimal set is always in the diagram and so cannot be eliminated. The idea of Gordon's next experiment (experiment 4) was to see which would exert the stronger "pull"—the two salient points off one end of the Pareto-optimal set or the Nash solution at the other end.

The games used in experiment 4 are shown in 22.9–22.12.

9	3	13	10	13	−11	20	0
10	−3	18	30	1	−8	0	−13
1.5	7	4	3	−9	7	−5	9
1	15	6	13	−10	4	−9	4

22.9	22.10	22.11	22.12
GAME #64	GAME #19	GAME #64	GAME #64
VARIANT IX	VARIANT VIII	VARIANT X	VARIANT XI

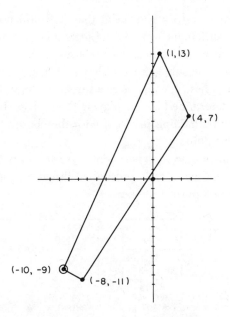

Fig. 22.5. Geometric representation of game #64, variant X.

The results of experiment 4 are shown in table 22.17.

TABLE 22.17 Average final outcomes in Gordon's Exp. 4.

Game	Final outcome g(R)	g(C)	Midpoint Coordinates		Nash solution $g^*(R)$	$g^*(C)$
#64 Var. IX	11.6	7.9	12.5	8.0	14.87	7.05
#19 Var. VIII	23.3	10.9	24.0	11.5	30.00	10.00
#64 Var. X	2.6	9.8	2.5	10.0	1.00	13.00
#64 Var. XI	1.2	13.6	2.0	14.5	0.05	19.87

It would be naive, in our opinion, to conclude from these data that the two salient points at one end and the Nash solution at the other exert "almost equal pulls" on the final outcome, thus placing it very near the midpoint of the Pareto-optimal set. A much simpler, though perhaps less interesting, explanation presents itself; namely, when the other salient points are out of the picture, the midpoint becomes salient.

So far, evidence points to the conclusion that the Nash solution of the bargaining problem has little or no salience in the minds of Gordon's subjects. In view of the rather sophisticated derivation of this solution, it is hardly surprising that it would not occur as the focal point of settlement to naive subjects ignorant of the theory.

In the next two experiments, both phases of the cooperative game were operative. The subjects were shown both the game matrix and the diagram. In phase 1, each chose a threat strategy. Thus the threat outcome was determined by the players themselves. In phase 2, they went on to the bargaining problem with the chosen threat outcome as the reference point.

The four games used in experiment 5 are shown in 22.13–22.16. In these games, the theoretically prescribed threat outcome is the intersection of the two pure strategies.

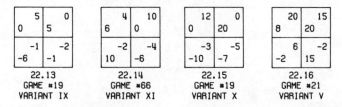

22.13
GAME #19
VARIANT IX

22.14
GAME #66
VARIANT XI

22.15
GAME #19
VARIANT X

22.16
GAME #21
VARIANT V

The experiment was designed to answer three questions. (i) Would the players choose the threat outcome prescribed by the theory? (ii) How would the final outcome compare with what the theory prescribes if the *chosen* threat outcome were the reference point of the bargaining? (iii) How would the final outcome compare with what the theory prescribes for the game, i.e., with reference to the theoretically prescribed threat outcome?

Variant IX of game #19 is "rigged" in Column's favor, in the sense that $S_1 S_2$ is predetermined if $T_1 S_2$ is chosen as the threat outcome. The same is true, of course, if $S_1 S_2$ is chosen. To be sure, if $T_1 T_2$ is chosen as the threat outcome, the solution awards 3 to Row and 2 to Column. In fact, however, this happened only twice out of 32 plays. $S_1 T_2$, which awards 5 to Row and 0 to Column, was never chosen as the threat outcome.

Variant X of game #19 looks asymmetric. However, the solution (7.5, 7.5) awards equal payoffs to the players.

In variant V of game #21, outcome $S_1 T_2$ is the solution. In other words, the game is rigged in favor of Row.

Variant XI of game #66, an asymmetric variant of Chicken, awards 4 to Row and 6 to Column if the correct threat point, $T_1 T_2$, is chosen.

The results of experiment 5 are given in tables 22.18–22.21. The columns show (1) the threat point chosen, "Th," the correct threat point being starred; (2) the number of times that the threat point was chosen; (3) and (4) Row's and Column's claims; (5) and (6) the actual average payoffs, the number in parentheses being the theoretically prescribed payoffs with respect to the *chosen* threat outcome; (7–9) the number of occurrences of the salient points. (In game #66, the "corner" in the Pareto-optimal set was assumed to be salient, but it was chosen only once.)

We first examine columns five and six, where the average gains of Row and Column are compared with those ascribed by Nash's bargaining theory on the basis of the particular threat outcome chosen.

In game #19 variant IX, we see a fair agreement only when S_1S_2 was the chosen threat outcome, that is, when Row was "helpless" vis-à-vis Column. In those cases, Row got on the average just a little more than 0, which he would have received had Column pursued his advantage to the hilt. The little he got was in consequence of the two occurrences of P_e (cf. column eight).

TABLE 22.18 Results of Gordon's Exp. 5, Game #19.

Th	N	BR	BC	g(R)	g(C)	P_e	P_a	P_m
S_1S_2	5	7.0	11.4	0.7(0)	11.4(12)	0	4	0
S_1T_2	1	20.0	7.4	20.0(20.0)	0(0)	0	1	0
T_1S_2*	24	5.9	8.6	3.5(7.5)	7.0(7.5)	3	0	1
T_1T_2	2	7.4	7.4	7.4(13.3)	7.4(4)	1	0	0
		Means		3.8(7.1)	8.0(7.75)			
		Solution		7.5	7.5			

TABLE 22.19 Results of Gordon's Exp. 5, Game #21, Var. V.

Th	N	BR	BC	g(R)	g(C)	P_e	P_a	P_m
S_1S_2	12	12.7	19.5	9.3(8)	19.5(20)	1	9	0
S_1T_2	2	17.2	16.2	17.2(20)	16.2(15)	1	0	0
T_1S_2*	17	13.8	17.7	11.8(19.8)	16.3(15.1)	4	0	2
T_1T_2	1	16.5	16.3	16.5(9.2)	16.3(19.5)	1	0	0
		Means		11.3(15.0)	17.5(16.2)			
		Solution		19.8	15.1			

It is interesting to observe that, when Row had no bargaining power, his average *claim* was for a (.5, .5) mixture in variant IX and close to it in variant X (cf. column three). In those instances, Row has (theoretically) nothing to lose whatever he claims. In several cases, he actually claimed the maximum. On the other hand, one might think that under those circumstances Row might be prudent to ask for a very small amount, appealing to Column's goodwill.

We note, further, in variant IX of game #19, that T_1S_2 and S_1S_2 were chosen with almost equal frequencies. Actually, since the solution of that game awards everything to Column, it does not matter which threat strategy Row chooses. For this reason, both S_1S_2 and T_1S_2 are starred. However, Row got somewhat more when he chose T_1S_2, where he had an *apparent* threat against Column.

On the average, in the "rigged" variant IX of game #19, where Row "deserved" 0, he got 1.2.

In game #66, there is fair agreement between Nash's prescription and the observed average gains when the correct threat point, T_1T_2,

TABLE 22.20   Results of Gordon's Exp. 5, Game #19, Var. IX

Th	N	BR	BC	g(R)	g(C)	P_e	P_a	$P_m = P_e$
S_1S_2*	14	2.5	4.4	0.6(0)	4.4(5)	2	10	
S_1T_2	0	--	--	-- (5)	-- (0)	--	--	
T_1S_2*	16	1.8	3.2	1.3(0)	2.9(5)	6	0	
T_1T_2	2	2.7	2.3	2.7(3)	2.3(2)	1	1	
			Means	1.1(0.2)	3.5(4.8)			
			Solution	0.0	5.0			

TABLE 22.21   Results of Gordon's Exp. 5, Game #66, Var. XI.

Th	N	BR	BC	g(R)	g(C)	P_e	P_a	P_m
S_1S_2	1	5.0	5.0	5.0(6)	5.0(4)	1	0	0
S_1T_2	6	4.2	7.1	2.3(0)	7.1(10)	2	3	0
T_1S_2	1	5.0	5.0	5.0(10)	5.0(-2)	1	0	0
T_1T_2*	24	4.8	5.3	4.2(4)	5.0(6)	11	5	1
			Means	3.9(3.5)	5.4(6.4)			
			Solution	4.0	6.0			

was chosen. Note, however, the frequent occurrence of P_e in those instances. When S_1S_2 or T_1S_2 was chosen, Row's advantage was not realized. In both cases the gains were equal. Of course, no conclusion is warranted on the basis of only two observations.

Column's advantage in this game, on the whole, is reflected in the average payoffs, which are not far from the prescribed solution.

Game #19 variant X shows severe discrepancies between Nash's model and the observations. Although the correct threat point was chosen in three-fourths of the cases, Column's average gain was twice Row's, whereas the solution awards equal payoffs. We offer the following explanation. As was shown, the final outcome depends on two parameters: the position of the threat points and the slope of the Pareto-optimal line. A small (or numerically large, if negative) horizontal coordinate of the threat point in the geometric representation works *against* Row. A numerically small slope of the Pareto-optimal line works *for* Row, vis-à-vis the *numerical* magnitudes of Row's payoffs. (Of course, the *mixture* representing the final outcome is invariant with respect to positive linear transformations of the payoffs.) Now, in variant X of game #19, the horizontal coordinate of the threat point (-10) is considerably smaller than the vertical (-3), pointing to Row's disadvantage. On the other hand, the slope of the Pareto-optimal line is numerically small ($-3/5$), which points to Row's advantage. In theory, these two features cancel each other in this variant. In practice, however, the position of the threat point is apparently more salient to the players than the slope of the Pareto-optimal line. This may account for Row's disadvantage in the results.

Another explanation may be the salience of the natural outcome in this game of order D_2, where both players have a dominating strategy. In S_1S_2, Row gets 0, whereas Column gets 12. This discrepancy may add to Column's advantage in the threat outcome.

In game #21, we observe the same effect as in variant X of game #19. The solution (19.8, 15.08) favors Row. Yet Column receives the larger average numerical payoff throughout, as appears from the examination of the protocols. We see again that Row is disadvantaged with respect to the threat point (-2, 6). Although he is advantaged with respect to the slope of the Pareto-optimal line ($-5/12$), apparently the former condition has the larger "weight" in determining the final outcome. In this game (of order D_2), the natural outcome also favors Column.

Turning now to the cases where one of the Pareto-optimal outcomes was chosen as the threat outcome, thus "incapacitating" one of the players, we see that in those cases the advantaged player tends to exploit his advantage, but not always. In a small minority of cases (10 percent to 20 percent), the "helpless" player gets more than the other needs to grant. In some particular cases, an equal division of payoffs is observed. These equal divisions account for the small average excess gained by the player without bargaining power. "Pittances" have been observed only very rarely.

Finally, we note that the salience of the special points, P_e, P_a, and P_m, has been reduced when the players *themselves* chose the threat strategies rather than being presented with a "ready made" threat outcome by the experimenter. This finding may be psychologically interesting. It may suggest that an *externally* imposed threat outcome is less salient in calling attention to the players' unequal bargaining positions. It may even induce some sort of "solidarity" in the minds of the players. But, when the players on their own commit themselves to a threat outcome, it competes for their attention with the salient points on the Pareto-optimal set.

In experiment 6, the players again chose the threat outcome. This time the theoretically prescribed threat outcome was an intersection of mixed strategies. The use of mixed strategies was explained to the subjects as follows. They were to imagine that the actual choice of the threat strategy is determined by a chance device. They were to choose the probability with which this device would determine strategy S (and, of course, T with complementary probability). Thus, the payoffs at the threat point would be determined as the expected payoffs resulting from the two probability mixtures.

In order to give the subjects a feeling for this procedure, they first participated in a session of playing a zerosum game used by Gordon in the experiment discussed above (cf. p. 358).

Games #20 variant II, #20 variant III, #56, and #37 were used in experiment 6 (cf. 22.5–22.8).

It was observed that, although some of the subjects did in fact use strategy mixtures in choosing threat strategies in this experiment, the majority chose pure strategies.

As above, the results of experiment 6 will be evaluated with reference to the "composite player" representing the 32 subjects. This composite player chooses one composite threat strategy mixture as Row and one as Column. The mixture is compared with the theoretically prescribed one. Next, the chosen mixture is used as the reference point in Nash's bargaining problem to determine the solution prescribed with reference to *that* point, which is then compared with the composite observed solution. The observed solution is also compared with the Nash solution of the game. The results are shown in tables 22.22–22.25.

TABLE 22.22 Results of Gordon's Exper. 6, Game #20, Var. II.

	Threat point			Solution payoffs	
	Obs.	Theo.	Obs.	Theo. w/ref. to threat point chosen	Theo. w/ref. to correct threat point
Mixture	(S_1) 70	09			
	(S_2) 95	59			
Payoffs at threat point	R -1.42	-5.66	R 2.40	3.0	4.09
	C 2.72	-1.92	C 3.80	3.5	2.95

We note from table 22.22 that the chosen threat point is considerably more "conservative" than the prescribed. This is because the natural outcome strategies are chosen with larger frequencies. In consequence, Row's theoretical advantage in this game is lost. He actually gets less than Column in the final outcome, whereas Nash's solution prescribes a larger payoff to him.

In the first two columns of the table, the chosen threat strategy mixtures and the payoffs resulting from these mixtures are compared with the theoretically prescribed mixtures and their associated payoffs. In the last three columns, the observed average payoffs of the final outcome are compared with those prescribed theoretically for the threat mixture *chosen*, "Theo.," and with Nash's solution of the game. Note, however, that the observed final outcome payoffs are not too disparate from those prescribed with reference to the (composite) threat point chosen.

Variant III of game #20 is actually strategically equivalent to variant II, since the former results when Column's payoffs in the latter are multiplied by 2. Therefore, the prescribed threat-point mixture (though not Column's payoff in it) is the same in both variants. Again we observe that the choice of threat point is "conservative,"

TABLE 22.23 Results of Gordon's Exper. 6, Game #20, Var. III.

	Threat point				Solution payoffs	
	Obs.		Theo.	Obs.	Theo. w/ref. to threat point chosen	Theo. w/ref. to correct threat point
Mixture	(S_1)	54	09			
	(S_2)	94	59			
Payoffs at threat point	R	-2.13	-5.66	R 2.84	2.36	4.09
	C	3.16	-3.84	C 7.26	7.64	5.91

although Row is somewhat more daring in this variant: he chooses
T_1 with larger probability. The observed final outcome is again quite
close to the theoretical with respect to the chosen threat point. In this
variant, Column's numerical payoff as prescribed by Nash's solution
is larger than Row's. The difference is exaggerated in the observed
final outcome. It seems, therefore, that in both variants of this game
Column's bargaining advantage is perceived by the players as larger
than it actually is.

TABLE 22.24 Results of Gordon's Exper. 6, Game #56, Var. II.

	Threat point				Solution payoffs	
	Obs.		Theo.	Obs.	Theo. w/ref. to threat point chosen	Theo. w/ref. to correct threat point
Mixture	(S_1)	67	10			
	(S_2)	69	60			
Payoffs at threat point	R	1.14	-0.18	R 3.30	3.35	3.63
	C	3.10	-0.92	C 7.90	7.80	7.20

In game #56 variant II, Row was again conservative in the choice
of threat-strategy mixture, whereas Column's mixture was close to
the theoretical. Here the observed final outcome is close to both the
theoretically prescribed on the basis of the threat point chosen and
to Nash's.

Game #37 has been rigged. Row has no bargaining power and the
Nash solution is at Column's most preferred outcome. This is also the
case with regard to the threat point chosen by the players. (Note
that in this game Row is bolder, while Column is more conservative

TABLE 22.25 Results of Gordon's Exper. 6, Game #37, Var. II.

	Threat point				Solution payoffs	
Mixture	Obs.		Theo.	Obs.	Theo. w/ref. to threat point chosen	Theo. w/ref. to correct threat point
	(S_1)	50	70			
	(S_2)	92	75			
Payoffs at threat point	R	-1.81	0.65	R 8.0	7.0	7.0
	C	7.51	9.30	C 14.0	16.0	16.0

than the theory prescribes.) The observed final outcome is close to both the theoretical and Nash's. As usual in such situations, the composite underdog gets an average "pittance" which reflects, not actual pittances ceded by the advantaged player, but rather the presence of "equalizers" among the players.

The results of Gordon's experiments suggest that, except possibly in experiment 6, the Nash solution of either the bargaining problem or of the 2 × 2 cooperative game has no discernible salience in the minds of the players. Instead, the midpoint of the Pareto-optimal set, the point of equal division, and the point of constant relative advantage seem to provide anchorages for arriving at a compromise solution, at least when the threat outcome is given (rather than chosen by the subjects). It occurred to Gordon that it was perhaps the geometric representation of the game that brought out the salience of those points. In order to verify this conjecture, the geometrical representation had to be abandoned. This was done in Gordon's last experiment, which he was not able to finish.

Gordon had designed the geometrical representation in order to avoid the "training" that had to be given to the subjects to make the concept of the "mixed outcome" meaningful to them. In this last experiment (subsequently performed by J. Perner), this problem had to be solved. Perner followed the method outlined in chapter 3. In the first phase, the subjects chose the threat point. In the four games used (the same as those of experiment 1, cf. 22.1–22.4), the threat outcome is determined by pure strategies, hence, presents no difficulty.

To simulate the final "mixed outcome," in the second phase the following procedure was used. In each of ten successive iterations, each player in turn was to propose an *outcome* (instead of choosing a strategy as in the noncooperative game). The co-player was to respond either by agreeing or disagreeing (proposing another outcome was tantamount to disagreement). In case of agreement, the outcome proposed obtained. In case of disagreement, the threat outcome obtained. The relative frequencies of outcomes agreed upon were interpreted as the mixture of the final outcome. Observe that only in game #19, 22.1 is the mixture (0.5, 0.5) salient because of the apparent symmetry of the game matrix. In the other games, this is not the case; in order to achieve equal payoffs, an unequal mixture has to be adopted. Therefore, if equal payoffs are predominant in those games, the salience of the equal payoff solution can be safely assumed.

Next, the midpoint between the Pareto-optimal outcomes is not salient without the geometrical representation. (Some knowledge of analytic geometry is needed to establish the midpoint.) Nor is the point of constant relative advantage salient for the same reason.

Free discussion was allowed before the onset and throughout the duration of the second phase. The players took turns in proposing the outcome for ten consecutive plays. Thus the possible salience of simple alternation was also avoided. In order to establish the occurrence of the two outcomes with the same frequency, each player had to agree to the other's proposed outcome ten times in succession (thus to *trust* the other to agree to his proposals an equal number of times). Of course, alternation or equal occurrence of the two outcomes, although less likely than in one-play alternation, could be established anyway. If this happened, the salience of this solution could be assumed.

Also, after every ten plays, each player had the option of asking for a new determination of the threat outcome. This was done to avoid trapping a pair of players in one of the Pareto-optimal outcomes as the threat outcome throughout the 100-play iteration. We have already seen that in single plays this leads in the majority of cases to the complete exploitation of the "helpless" player. To be sure, we do not know whether this would be the case in iterated play. However, our procedure gives us the opportunity to observe these situations, while at the same time we avoid trivial runs. With only ten pairs of subjects assigned to each of the four games, we did not want to "invalidate" any protocol because of players happening to choose initially the "wrong" threat outcome. As it turned out, whenever such a Pareto-optimal threat outcome was chosen, the bid to redetermine the outcome was always made, and the players settled down with the correct outcome after, at most, two 10-play sequences. The data to be presented are based on the entire run, for we consider the occasional choice of the wrong threat outcome as part of the dynamics of the bargaining process.

Each experiment with a cooperative game was preceded by an experiment with 100 iterations of the same game played noncooperatively. After 50 iterations, the players switched roles. The idea was to compare the overall average performances on the noncooperative and the cooperative versions in order to determine the overall effect of introducing explicit bargaining into the picture.

The results of that experiment 7 are shown in tables 22.26–22.33. The entry in the last column is "+" if the top dog gets a larger payoff, "–" if the underdog gets more, and "0" if the payoffs are equal.

We can now compare the results on games #19, #21, #44, and #64 in four conditions, namely, in two noncooperative versions and two cooperative versions, and, within these, in the iterated version (Rapoport and Perner's experiment) and the single-play geometric representation version (Gordon's experiment). We are particularly interested in comparing the underdog's and the top dog's payoffs in the four conditions. For clarity's sake, we identify the four conditions once again:

1. The noncooperative single-play geometric representation version was used in Gordon's experiment 2^2 (cf. tables 22.1–22.8).

2. The iterated noncooperative version was that used in the first part of the Rapoport and Perner experiment (cf. tables 22.26–22.29).

3. The cooperative single-play geometric representation version was that used in Gordon's experiment 3^3 (cf. tables 22.1–22.8).

4. The iterated cooperative version was that used in the second part of the Rapoport and Perner experiment (cf. tables 22.30–22.33).

The comparison is shown in table 22.34 the last column of which gives the excess of the top dog's payoff over the underdog's.

---

[2] This version is noncooperative because prior to the players' independent claims no discussion is permitted.

[3] This version is cooperative because discussion and prior agreements are permitted, although they are not binding. This definition is at variance with Harsanyi's (cf. p. 46).

TABLE 22.26   Observed average payoffs in
              iterated non-cooperative Game #19, Var. II
              in Perner's experiment.

Pair	g(R)	g(C)	Sgn (Δ)
1	-0.18	4.46	+
2	-0.03	1.91	+
3	-0.02	4.92	+
4	-0.59	1.15	+
5	0.29	1.27	+
6	0.25	2.67	+
7	1.31	2.65	+
8	-0.30	0.74	+
9	0.22	1.65	+
10	0.08	1.48	+
Mean	0.09	2.29	+

TABLE 22.27   Observed average payoffs in
              iterated non-cooperative Game #21, Var. XI
              in Perner's experiment.

Pair	g(R)	g(C)	Sgn (Δ)
1	-0.51	-2.22	+
2	-0.31	1.68	-
3	2.57	2.27	+
4	2.43	3.11	-
5	0.85	-0.14	+
6	0.46	0.43	+
7	-0.54	-1.53	+
8	5.09	-0.02	+
9	2.09	3.69	-
10	1.70	3.83	-
Mean	1.38	1.11	+

TABLE 22.28 Observed average payoffs in
             iterated non-cooperative Game #64, Var. VIII
             in Perner's experiment.

Pair	g(R)	g(C)	Sgn (Δ)
1	-0.95	2.64	+
2	-0.88	6.54	+
3	0.38	7.71	+
4	-0.75	2.40	+
5	5.54	3.48	-
6	3.48	7.89	+
7	-0.04	6.12	+
8	-0.83	1.41	+
9	2.13	10.71	+
10	1.52	2.55	+
Mean	0.66	5.14	+

TABLE 22.29 Observed average payoffs in
             iterated non-cooperative Game #64, Var. II
             in Perner's experiment.

Pair	g(R)	g(C)	Sgn (Δ)
1	3.16	7.00	+
2	1.72	9.72	+
3	1.67	8.78	+
4	3.52	6.72	+
5	1.66	5.62	+
6	1.63	5.62	+
7	1.93	6.89	+
8	1.59	5.43	+
9	4.44	6.20	+
10	6.66	6.50	-
Mean	2.80	6.94	+

TABLE 22.30 Observed average payoffs in
iterated cooperative Game #19, Var. II
in Perner's experiment.

Pair	g(R)	g(C)	Sgn (Δ)
1	1.91	2.93	+
2	1.80	3.20	+
3	2.50	2.50	0
4	-0.53	-1.01	-
5	1.75	2.50	+
6	0.06	3.00	+
7	2.43	2.49	+
8	2.43	2.49	+
9	0.99	2.17	+
10	2.50	2.50	0
Mean	1.58	2.27	+

TABLE 22.31 Observed average payoffs in
iterated cooperative Game #21, Var. XI
in Perner's experiment.

Pair	g(R)	g(C)	Sgn (Δ)
1	4.89	2.97	+
2	3.75	3.75	0
3	3.60	3.84	-
4	4.00	3.55	+
5	3.75	3.75	0
6	4.00	3.55	+
7	3.60	3.90	-
8	3.60	3.84	-
9	3.60	3.84	-
10	3.60	3.84	-
Mean	3.84	3.64	+

TABLE 22.32   Observed average payoffs in
               iterated cooperative Game #64, Var. VIII
               in Perner's experiment.

Pair	g(R)	g(C)	Sgn (Δ)
1	7.50	7.50	0
2	2.73	5.00	+
3	5.43	7.12	+
4	7.50	7.50	0
5	9.30	4.59	-
6	7.50	7.50	0
7	7.50	7.50	0
8	7.05	7.95	+
9	5.42	8.74	+
10	5.61	7.11	+
Mean	6.55	7.05	+

TABLE 22.33   Observed average payoffs in
               iterated cooperative Game #44, Var. II
               in Perner's experiment.

Pair	g(R)	g(C)	Sgn (Δ)
1	1.64	8.19	+
2	4.56	7.72	+
3	4.62	7.67	+
4	5.86	6.90	+
5	3.86	8.79	+
6	2.82	7.84	+
7	0.77	6.37	+
8	3.25	9.25	+
9	2.58	6.85	+
10	4.67	8.40	+
Mean	3.46	7.80	+

TABLE 22.34   Comparison of underdog's and top dog's
average payoffs under four conditions.

	Underdog's	Top dog's	Δ
Game #19, Var. II			
Iter. non-coop.	0.09	2.29	2.20
Gordon's Exp. 2	1.04	1.65	0.61
Gordon's Exp. 3	2.31	2.54	0.23
Iter. coop.	1.58	2.27	0.65
Game #21, Var. XI			
Iter. non-coop.	1.10	1.38	0.27
Gordon's Exp. 2	1.43	1.94	0.51
Gordon's Exp. 3	3.32	4.45	1.13
Iter. coop.	3.64	3.84	0.20
Game #64, Var. VIII			
Iter. non-coop.	0.66	5.14	4.48
Gordon's Exp. 2	0.50	3.69	3.19
Gordon's Exp. 3	4.36	7.19	2.83
Iter. coop.	6.55	7.05	0.50
Game #44, Var. II			
Iter. non-coop.	2.80	6.94	4.14
Gordon's Exp. 2	1.27	5.18	3.91
Gordon's Exp. 3	4.10	7.03	2.93
Iter. coop.	3.46	7.80	4.34

As expected, both players get larger average payoffs in the cooperative versions and the smallest payoffs in the single-play noncooperative version, where, recall, about one-fourth to one-third of the plays resulted in the threat outcome. Next, we note that the differences between the underdog's and the top dog's average payoffs are smaller in the cooperative than in the noncooperative versions. Thus discussion, by and large, does *not* seem to bring out the unequal bargaining positions of the players but rather makes equal division of payoffs more salient. Further, we note that there is no evidence for our conjecture that the salience of equal division might have been due to the geometric representation of the games in Gordon's experiments. On the contrary, the differences between the underdog's and the top dog's payoffs is, on the average, *smaller* in the iterated version of the cooperative game (where geometric representation was not used) than in Gordon's experiment 3 (where it was used).

Finally, we note that game #44 is the only one of the four games in which the difference between the players' payoffs in the iterated cooperative version is close to that prescribed by the Nash solution. Examination of the matrix of that game suggests that an equal division of payoffs could be effected in that game in two ways: either by an alternation between S_1S_2 and S_1T_2 or by repeating T_1T_2. However, when the game matrix is displayed, it is (or should be) clear to Column that he need not ever consent to accept S_1T_2, because he gets more in the threat outcome. On the other hand, equal division at T_1T_2 may not seem equitable to Column, not only because of the large discrepancy of payoffs in the threat outcome (8), but also because his payoff in that outcome is positive, whereas Row's is negative. Game #44 is the only one of the four games in the last experiment in which this is the case. Perhaps this is what makes Column's advantage so salient in this game. Column would then insist on some alternation between S_1S_2 and T_1T_2 which would give him more than 7 on the average, which he in fact gets in seven out of ten pairs.

It is also interesting to compare the results on games #20 variant II, #20 variant III, #56, and #37. These were played under the conditions of experiments 3 and 6. Both versions were single play cooperative (discussion permitted). In experiment 3, however, the players were *given* the threat outcome, whereas in experiment 6 they chose it themselves. The comparison is shown in table 22.35.

TABLE 22.35 Comparison of underdog's and top dog's payoffs in Gordon's Exps. 3 & 6.

	Underdog's	Top dog's	Δ
Game #20, Var. II			
Exp. 3	3.54	3.10	-0.44
Exp. 6	3.80	2.40	-1.40
Game #20, Var. III			
Exp. 3	5.42	4.79	0.77
Exp. 6	2.84	7.26	4.42
Game #56, Var. II			
Exp. 3	4.67	4.69	-0.02
Exp. 6	3.30	7.90	4.60
Game #37, Var. II			
Exp. 3	8.82	12.51	3.69
Exp. 6	8.00	14.00	6.00

Pooling the payoffs of the four games, we observe that, whereas in experiment 3 the average difference in the top dog's favor was 1.00, in experiment 6 it was 3.41. This leads to an intriguing psychological conjecture. Can it be that the players bargain "harder" when they themselves choose the threat outcome (experiment 6) than when the outcome is given to them by an "outside authority"? Does an external imposition of the "threat" make for solidarity between the players? Unfortunately, this conjecture is not corroborated when we compare the results on games #19 variant II, #21, #64, and #44, which were played under the condition of experiment 3 (imposed threat) and Perner's experiment (chosen threat outcome). Still, these two conditions are not quite comparable, because in Perner's experiment the cooperative game was iterated, whereas in Gordon's experiment 6 it was played once. The question, therefore, remains open. We have another "generated hypothesis" to be further tested under more rigorously controlled conditions.

23

Static Models

If a system is defined by a set of mathematically expressed variables, and its state by the values assumed by the variables at a given moment, then a *dynamic* mathematical model of a system is a set of relations among the variables (including interactions among them) that leads to the determination of the dependence of the state variables on time. A static model, on the other hand, is typically a representation of the system in equilibrium or in a steady state. For instance, in an iterated 2×2 game, we might observe that the choice frequencies tend after many iterations to constant (asymptotic) values. An expression relating these values to some independent variables of interest (e.g., payoffs, external conditions, parameters characterizing populations of players, etc.) would constitute a static model of the game. Thus a static model, describing the steady state of the system comprising the game and the players, can be derived from a dynamic one. Or the time courses of the choice frequencies could be ignored, attention being directed to their averages over the entire iteration. Relations of these averages to the independent variables would then constitute a static model of the game. Models of games played once are, by their nature, static, since time courses of the variables do not enter. As has been pointed out, in that context, choice frequencies must be interpreted as fractions of populations of players choosing the one or the other strategy.

If only the payoffs are taken as the independent variables and unconditional choice frequencies as dependent ones, a static mathematical model of the game would be represented by two functions:

$$S_1 = f_1(a_1, b_1, c_1, d_1, a_2, d_2, c_2, d_2).$$
$$S_2 = f_2(a_1, \ldots \ldots d_1, a_2, \ldots d_2).$$

Clearly, some restriction on the functions f_i are necessary to make a choice of such functions meaningful. We have seen in chapter 3 that the game-theoretic assumptions concerning utility scales, and the assumption that payoffs represent utilities, restrict the functions f_i to those that are invariant with respect to positive linear transformations of the payoffs (of each player independently). The simplest such functions are ratios of payoff differences in the form $(x_i - y_i)/(z_i - w_i)$, $i = 1, 2$, where $x_i, \ldots w_i$ are some permutations of a player's payoffs. Any function of such a ratio of differences is, evidently, also invariant under linear transformations.

If $x_i, \ldots w_i$ are all distinct, there are 12 such difference ratios, since each is determined by a choice of a pair for the numerator and can be of either sign. There are further ratios involving only 3 of the payoffs, but no fewer, since those involving only 2 must be either equal to 1 or to -1 or undefined, hence, trivial. Of these three-payoff ratios there are also 12, making 24 in all. However, as has been shown in chapter 4, it takes only 2 of them to generate all 24. Therefore, any function involving all 24 ratios can be expressed as a function involving only 2 of them. We shall return to this point in discussing the next experiment.

M. W. Steele and J. T. Tedeschi (1967) tested several difference-ratio models in an experiment using 42 game matrices, to be presently described. In addition, several other models were included that were not invariant under linear transformations. These were of the type x/y or $x/(y - z)$, or functions thereof.

The game matrices were constructed as follows. Designating the general numerically symmetric game matrix by 23.1, mean values were assigned to the payoffs as follows: $a = 100$; $b = 125$; $c = -50$; $d = -100$. Next, a possible range was assigned to each of the four

23.1
GENERAL 2X2 GAME MATRIX

payoffs: $0 \leqslant a \leqslant 205$; $0 \leqslant b \leqslant 245$; $-350 \leqslant c \leqslant 250$; $-1300 \leqslant d \leqslant$ 1100. The actual payoffs were considered to be normally distributed, with means as given above and with standard deviations approximately one-sixth of the corresponding ranges. The 42 matrices were constructed by independent random selection of each of the four payoffs from the corresponding populations. Through this process the following game species were obtained (cf. table 23.1).

TABLE 23.1   Games used in
Steele & Tedeschi's experiment.

Game #	Number of Variants
12 (Prisoner's Dilemma)	18*
66 (Chicken)	11
6 (No conflict Order D_2)	9
63 (No conflict Order D_0)	3
68 (Leader)	1

*In the text of Steele and Tedeschi's paper, the number of Prisoner's Dilemma games is given as 12. However, the authors define Prisoner's Dilemma as a game with b > a, d > c and, in addition, 2a > b + c. The latter condition was violated "in several cases" and so the resulting matrices were not counted as Prisoner's Dilemmas (in our taxonomy we do include them). In one of the matrices, a and b turned out to be equal. This game is borderline between #12 and #6. We have arbitrarily designated it as Game #6.

The precise number of games of each species is not important for the test of the model. However, as we shall see, the inclusion of game #66 has probably introduced a confounding factor.

Figure 23.1 shows the plot of B frequencies vs. the index given by

$$K = \log\left[(b - c)/(a - d)\right].$$

Taking the partial derivatives of K with respect to each of the four payoffs, we note that the model satisfies the monotonicity hypothesis (cf. p. 78). Therefore, the frequency of B choices should be a monotone increasing function of K. A glance at figure 23.1 suggests that this is the case. We note, however, that the increase of (B) with K is much clearer for positive values of K than for negatives ones.

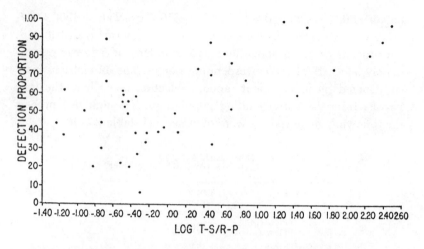

Fig. 23.1. Plot of relation between the index log (T-S)/(R-P) and defection proportion. Index on abscissa should be log (T-S)/(R-P) (after Steele and Tedeschi, 1967).

K is negative when $(b - c) < (a - d)$. In view of the inequalities $b > a$, $d > c$, this cannot happen in a Prisoner's Dilemma game. Therefore, the suggested model fits Prisoner's Dilemma games much better than other games. In fact, a positive monotone relation between K and (B) is not suggested when K is negative. Now, K can be negative in Chicken, because in that game $d < c$. The implication is that the monotonicity hypothesis may be violated in Chicken. Indeed, analysis of correlations between (B) and K in individual matrices reveals nonsignificant but *negative* correlation coefficients, suggesting that as d decreases (increases in magnitude when negative), (B) may tend to increase, at least in some variants. We may have here a corroboration of our conjecture (cf. p. 242) that in some range of d (punishment for double defection) in Chicken, defections may actually increase as the punishment gets more severe. Steele and Tedeschi state a similar conjecture.

Fifteen indices (models) in all were used by the authors. These fifteen indices had a .778 multiple correlation with (B). That is to say, the payoff structure of the game accounts for somewhat more than one half the total variance of strategy choices. From the total correlation matrix, the contributions of each of the indices has been calculated. Of the total variance *accounted* for, the following four have contributed 74 percent: log $[(a - c)/(a - d)]$ 21 percent; log

$(b-c)/(a-d)$ 20 percent; $\log (b/(a-d))$ 19 percent; R/T 14 percent.[1]

Note, however, that the "contributions" to the total correlation accounted for by the other indices is an artifact of linear analysis, because all of the remaining indices, except two or three whose contributions are negligible, are *functionally* related to the above mentioned. For instance, $b/(a-d)$ is clearly a function of $\log (b/(a-d))$. Thus, if the value of one is known, observing the value of the other adds no information. But one is not a *linear* function of the other; consequently, the correlation between the two is only .86 instead of 1.00. If we confine ourselves only to the indices invariant under linear transformations, then two of them (for instance, the first two mentioned above), contain all the information supplied by the payoffs. They account for about 25 percent of the total variance of choice frequencies in iterated symmetric games of several species.

We have already seen that the variance accounted for by the payoffs was reduced by the inclusion of Chicken, where the correlation between an index and (B) was of opposite sign. Consequently, there was an interaction between the effect of the index and the structure of the game. Including this interaction would have accounted for more of the variance. And, of course, individual differences among the players must be an important contribution to the total variance. This could be assessed if the players were tagged with a parameter.

J. S. Brew (1973) proposed a static model of Prisoner's Dilemma, in which a function of the payoffs is combined with a "personal" parameter, appropriately called the altruism parameter. The central idea of the model is that a player is concerned not only with his own payoffs but also with those of the co-player. His attitude toward the co-player, however, may range from "malevolence" to "indifference" to "benevolence." The malevolent player is interested in maximizing the difference between his own payoffs and the co-player's. Accordingly, he transforms the standard format of Prisoner's Dilemma (23.2) into a zerosum game (23.3). The "indifferent" player sees the pure Prisoner's Dilemma matrix. The "benevolent" player's utilities

---

[1] There is an apparent discrepancy in the text. On p. 201 (Steele and Tedeschi, op. cit) it is stated that the correlation between B and $\log (b-c)/(a-d)$ was .641, but on p. 203, the largest of the correlations is attributed to $\log (a-c)/(a-d)$ and is given as .52.

are the *sums* of his own and the co-player's utilities. Thus he sees the matrix as 23.4.

	C_2	D_2
C_1	R R	T S
D_1	S T	P P

23.2
PRISONER'S DILEMMA

0 0	$\frac{1}{2}(T-S)$ $\frac{1}{2}(S-T)$
$\frac{1}{2}(S-T)$ $\frac{1}{2}(T-S)$	0 0

23.3
PRISONER'S DILEMMA AS SEEN
BY A "MALEVOLENT" PLAYER

R R	$\frac{1}{2}(S+T)$ $\frac{1}{2}(S+T)$
$\frac{1}{2}(S+T)$ $\frac{1}{2}(S+T)$	P P

23.4
PRISONER'S DILEMMA AS SEEN
BY A "BENEVOLENT" PLAYER

	C_2	D_2
C_1	$(1+\beta)R$ $(1+\beta)R$	$\beta S+T$ $S+\beta T$
D_1	$S+\beta T$ $\beta S+T$	$(1+\beta)P$ $(1+\beta)P$

23.5
PRISONER'S DILEMMA AS SEEN
BY A PLAYER CHARACTERIZED BY β

0 0	T-S S-T
S-T T-S	0 0

23.6
PRISONER'S DILEMMA AS SEEN
BY A PLAYER WITH $\beta = -1$

2R 2R	T+S S+T
S+T T+S	2P 2P

23.7
PRISONER'S DILEMMA AS SEEN
BY A PLAYER WITH $\beta = +1$

In the transformed matrices, all payoffs (sums or differences of the original payoffs) have been multiplied by 1/2 for convenience.

Consider a player to be at some position in the "spectrum" between complete malevolence and complete benevolence. The player is characterized by a parameter β_i and sees the payoff matrix as a weighted average of matrices 23.3 and 23.4, the weights being $(1 - \beta_i)$ and $(1 + \beta_i)$, where β_i ranges from -1 to $+1$ (cf. 23.5). At one extreme ($\beta_i = -1$), the player is completely malevolent, since he sees the matrix as 23.6, where the payoffs have been multiplied by 2 and so represent the "difference" game. At the other extreme, $\beta_i = +1$, and the player sees the matrix as 23.7, a "sum" game. Note that the latter game is a no-conflict game, since $2R > T + S$ (a usual additional restriction in Prisoner's Dilemma), $2R > 2P$.

Having thus transformed the original matrix in accordance with his concern, the player now plays the game as if it were zerosum. That is, if the transformed game has a saddle point, he plays the pure maximin strategy, otherwise, the optimal mixed strategy.

From the generalized transformed matrix we can see that if the following inequalities are satisfied:

$$\beta_i > r_1' = (T - R)/(R - S),$$
$$\beta_i > r_2' = (P - S)/(T - P) \quad (i = 1,2),$$

then C is the dominating strategy and will be played exclusively. If both inequalities are reversed, D is the dominating strategy and will be played exclusively. If only one of the inequalities is satisfied, neither strategy dominates, and a mixed strategy will be resorted to. The mixture will depend on both difference ratios (which has been discussed in previous chapters as suitable indices of Prisoner's Dilemma) *and* the personal parameter β_i.

Assume now that β is distributed in the population in any way whatsoever. The probability that β is less than some specified value $\bar{\beta}$ is clearly an increasing function of $\bar{\beta}$. Therefore, the probability that the dominance of strategy D is "broken" for some player decreases as the smaller of the above two difference ratios increases. This suggests the ranking of numerically symmetric Prisoner's Dilemma games lexicographically, i.e., in the ascending order of Min $[(T - R)/(R - S), (P - S)/(T - P)]$, and in case of ties, in the ascending order of Max $[(T - R)/(R - S), (P - S)/(T - P)]$.

It is interesting to note that the indices r_1' and r_2' do not fully satisfy the monotonicity hypotheses.

We have, for example, both $\dfrac{\partial r_1'}{\partial S} > 0$ and $\dfrac{\partial r_1'}{\partial T} > 0$, which violates H_m (cf. p. 78). Nevertheless, the ranking of games in the descending order of expected C frequencies according to Brew's indices agrees very well with Rapoport and Chammah's data (cf. Brew, 1973, p. 357, table 7).

Brew compared his ranking of the seven variants of Prisoner's Dilemma used by Rapoport and Chammah (1965) with that based on their indices $r_1 = (R - P)/(T - S)$ and $r_2 = (R - S)/(T - S)$. Note that according to the hypothesis of monotonicity C must be monotonically related to r_1. However, C may be either increasing or decreasing with r_2. Accordingly, Rapoport and Chammah proposed two hypotheses, namely H_a: $\dfrac{\partial(c)}{\partial r_2} > 0$, and H_b: $\dfrac{\partial(c)}{\partial r_2} < 0$. Rankings of seven variants of Prisoner's Dilemma based on Brew's indices, on H_a, and on H_b are shown in table 23.2.

TABLE 23.2 Ranking of 7 variants of Prisoner's Dilemma by Brew's indices (r'_1, r'_2) and Rapoport-Chammah's indices derived from H_a and H_b. Comparison with ranking by observed C frequencies.

Var.	r'_1	r'_2	Observed rank	Brew's ranking	Rank by H_a	Rank by H_b
I	.05	.82	2	1=	1	3
II	.82	.05	1	1=	3	1
III	.82	.82	6	6	6	6
IV	.33	.33	3	3	2	2
V	.96	.96	7	7	7	7
XI	.33	.82	4	4=	4	5
XII	.82	.33	5	4=	5	4

Spearman's rank correlation
between theoretical and observed ranks   .982   .893   .964

An interesting by-product of Brew's further analysis is the inferred distribution of β in the population of players, which turns out to be bimodal, corroborating the conjecture we have made repeatedly that populations of players are bimodal with respect to several features related to game behavior.

Finally, we examine the general difference-ratio model (cf. p. 77) applied to all the seventy-eight games of the ordinal taxonomy played once. The data are taken from Frenkel's experiment (cf. chapter 7). We assume that the frequency of S choices in a 2×2 game is a linear function of

$$K = \frac{B(a-b) + C(a-c) + D(a-d)}{(a-b) + C'(a-c) + D'(a-d)},$$

where the coefficient of $(a-b)$ in the denominator has been set equal to 1 by the proper choice of units. Next, we estimate the parameters B, C, D, C', and D' by the least square method by fitting a regression line to the observed S frequencies plotted against K determined by the estimated values of the parameters and the payoffs a, b, c, and d of each game.

The product moment correlation coefficient between K and [S_1] turns out to be quite poor (.26). To be sure, near equality of the coefficients is not expected, because in our standard notation Row is generally underdog in asymmetric games. Still, even if the above values are accurate estimates of the correlation coefficients in the "parent" population, K accounts for only about one-fourth of the variance in Row's choices and a negligible fraction in Column's, in spite of the fact that five free parameters were used in determining each regression line. We are forced to conclude that it is probably futile to search for an index of the general 2 × 2 game, based on each player's consideration of his payoffs alone. This was already suggested by the significant effects attributed to competitive pressure (where each player compares his payoffs with those of the other) in Frenkel's experiment.

Nevertheless, the proposed index is not altogether worthless, for a plot of [S] against K enables us to identify the far-outlying games, those that violate strongly the hypothesized relation. We can then examine those games for some special features, thus generating psychological hypotheses concerning the pressures operating in them.

Frenkel pursued another tack, hinted at in chapter 14 (cf. p. 202). By grouping his ninety-six subjects into a few categories, each characterized by a specific decision rule, he was able to account for most of the variance in his experiment. Thus individual differences practically force themselves on the investigator's attention, even if he would like to "wash them out" in his experiment.

Nevertheless, the question is still not settled, in our opinion. The fact that each of Frenkel's subjects had to make over 200 choices might have forced the "across the board" decision rules. In an ideal experiment with single plays, independent populations should be tested on each game separately. We have already pointed out that the logistics of such an experiment are prohibitive. Still, the idea of discovering a "standard performance" for each game and for the variants within each species remains an attractive one. It seems worthwhile to try to work out an appropriate experimental technique.

24

Dynamic Behavioral Models

A dynamic model of a process typically leads to a determination of the time course of some variable of interest. In experiments on iterated games, time is conveniently measured by the ordinal number of a play ($t = 1, 2, \ldots$). Because individual choices are usually indeterminate, stochastic models seem to be the most suitable for iterated games. Typically, a stochastic model predicts the time course of a probability. However, since probabilities are not directly observable, they must be inferred, usually from observed frequencies in a population of players. For instance, a Markov chain model predicts the *probability* that a "system" will be in a given state at a given time, given that it was in some state at the previous moment of time. If the initial probability distribution of the states is assumed, the entire time course of probabilities can be derived. Observed fractions of a population of systems (i.e., players) in each of the states are then compared with the predicted probabilities.

In P. Suppes and R. C. Atkinson's monograph (1960), the Markov chain serves as a model of iterated 2×2 games, in particular, variants of all three games of complete opposition, #11, #45, and #75.[1] A special feature of Suppes and Atkinson's experiments is the probabilistic nature of the payoffs. When an outcome occurs, instead of

---

[1] Strictly speaking, the variant of game #45 was a limiting (degenerate) one, since two of Row's payoffs and two of Column's are equal. However, the essential feature of that game (one of the players but not the other has a dominating strategy) is preserved.

404

receiving a fixed payoff associated with that outcome, each player either receives or does not receive one unit of payoff with a probability associated with that outcome, while the other player does not receive or receives a unit of payoff with complementary probabilities. Thus the statistically expected payoffs to the two players sum to 1 in every outcome, and the game is constant-sum.

Were it not for the probabilistic nature of the payoffs, the results on games #11 and #45 would likely have been trivial, since in these two games at least one of the players has a dominating strategy and the pressures characteristic of games of partial opposition are absent. With probabilistic payoffs, the rational choice is not obvious; consequently, the results are not trivial. Nevertheless, because, formally speaking, games #11 and #45 have saddle points, game theory "predicts" 100 percent occurrences of the natural outcome (the saddle point) if the game is played by rational players. Since the observed frequencies of all four outcomes are far from 100 percent, the results can be interpreted as a refutation of the game-theoretic model (assuming that the utilities are monotonically related to the payoff entries.)

The game-theoretic predictions for game #75 (maximin strategy mixtures) are not corroborated either. It must be kept in mind, however, that the conditions assumed in the game-theoretic model are not quite fulfilled in Suppes and Atkinson's experiments, inasmuch as at the start of the experimental runs the players are virtually ignorant of the payoff structure. Only in the course of fairly long runs is it *conceivable* that they get some idea of the payoffs (which are statistical expectations) by estimating probabilities from frequencies of receiving the unit of payoff. Since we have no idea about how long it takes to get reasonable estimates of these probabilities, nor even whether it occurs to the players to try to achieve such estimates, we cannot consider these experiments to be a meaningful test of the game-theoretic model. (For this reason, an account of these experiments was not included in chapter 21.)

It appears, in fact, that the original purpose of the experiments was to test not the game-theoretic models but rather some stochastic learning models (the monograph is dedicated to W. K. Estes, who first developed these models), and that a comparison of stochastic learning-theory predictions with those of game theory was an afterthought. The novel feature of the learning experiments, as these seem to have been conceived, was the introduction of interactions between pairs of learning subjects, whereby one of them is right when the other is wrong. It is this opposition that formally identifies the learning situation with a game of complete opposition.

The three games used are shown in 24.1–24.3. The payoff entries represent the probabilities that the player in question receives the unit of payoff.

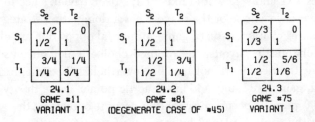

	S_2	T_2
S_1	1/2	0
	1/2	1
T_1	3/4	1/4
	1/4	3/4

24.1
GAME #11
VARIANT II

	S_2	T_2
S_1	1/2	0
	1/2	1
T_1	1/2	3/4
	1/2	1/4

24.2
GAME #81
(DEGENERATE CASE OF #45)

	S_2	T_2
S_1	2/3	0
	1/3	1
T_1	1/2	5/6
	1/2	1/6

24.3
GAME #75
VARIANT I

The first stochastic learning model tested was the single stimulus sampling model (cf. p. 87). The probabilities of reinforced responses in this case are the entries of the game matrices. Taking Row's payoffs to be those in the generalized 2×2 game (cf. p. 7), namely a_1, b_1, c_1, and d_1, Column's are correspondingly $a_2 = 1 - a_1$, $b_2 = 1 - c_1$, $c_2 = 1 - b_1$, $d_2 = 1 - d_1$. We drop the subscripts and refer to Row's payoffs as a, b, c, and d.

The single stimulus sampling model leads to a four-state Markov chain (cf. p. 85) where the four states are the four outcomes. For convenience of notation we label the four states 1, 2, 3, and 4 respectively. Row's and Column's learning parameters will be denoted by θ_R and θ_C respectively. Then the matrix of transition probabilities will be:

$$
\begin{array}{c|cccc}
 & 1 & 2 & 3 & 4 \\
\hline
1 & a(\theta_R - \theta_C) + 1 - \theta_R & a\,\theta_C & (1 - a)\theta_R & 0 \\
2 & c\,\theta_C & c(\theta_R - \theta_C) + 1 - \theta_R & 0 & (1 - c)\theta_R \\
3 & (1 - b)\theta_R & 0 & b(\theta_R - \theta_C) + 1 - \theta_R & b\,\theta_C \\
4 & 0 & (1 - d)\theta_R & d\,\theta_C & d(\theta_R - \theta_C) + 1 - \theta_R
\end{array}
\tag{24.1}
$$

From this matrix the asymptotic probabilities of the four states (that is, of the four outcomes) can be calculated. They are

$$u_j = \frac{\gamma_j \rho + \delta_j}{\gamma + \delta}, \quad j = 1,2,3,4. \tag{24.2}$$

Here $\rho = \theta_R / \theta_C$, and the remaining quantities are defined as follows:

$$
\begin{aligned}
\gamma_1 &= c(1-b)(1-d) + (1-c)(1-b)d \\
\gamma_2 &= a(1-b)(1-d) + (1-a)b(1-d) \\
\gamma_3 &= (1-a)(1-c)d + (1-a)c(1-d) \\
\gamma_4 &= (1-a)(1-c)b + a(1-c)(1-b) \\
\delta_1 &= cb(1-d) + c(1-b)d \\
\delta_2 &= ab(1-d) + a(1-b)d \\
\delta_3 &= (1-a)cd + a(1-c)d \\
\delta_4 &= (1-a)cb + a(1-c)b \\
\gamma &= \gamma_1 + \gamma_2 + \gamma_3 + \gamma_4 \\
\delta &= \delta_1 + \delta_2 + \delta_3 + \delta_4.
\end{aligned}
\tag{24.3}
$$

The magnitudes of the learning parameters, θ_R and θ_C can be estimated from the protocols. However, since the test of a stochastic model usually involves populations of subjects, there is recourse to a simplifying assumption, namely that every subject is characterized by the same learning parameter θ. If $\theta_R = \theta_C$, $\rho = 1$. The payoff parameters, a, b, c, and d being given, the model predicts the u_j without free parameters. Table 24.1 shows comparisons between observed values of u_j, those predicted by the single stimulus element stochastic learning model, and game theory.

It is quite clear that, whereas the stochastic learning model predicts the asymptotic frequencies quite well, game theory is far off the mark. As has been pointed out, the game-theoretic model is not refuted out of hand, because of the conditions of the experiment. We

TABLE 24.1 Comparison between observed S frequencies in 3 constant-sum games in Suppes-Atkinson's experiments and those predicted by game theory and by a stochastic learning model.

Game #	Obs.	(S_1) Predicted by learning model	Predicted by game theory	Obs.	(S_2) Predicted by learning model	Predicted by game theory
11	60.6	66.7	100	73.1	70.0	100
81	67.0	66.7	100	60.2	61.1	100
75	60.5	60.0	33.3	64.9	63.3	80

shall, therefore, return to it later. Here we shall pursue further tests of the stochastic model. The model predicts not only the asymptotic frequencies but also the transition probabilities of the four-state Markov chain given by the entries in (24.1). In it, the learning parameters θ_R and θ_C enter separately instead of only as a ratio. Therefore, even if we assume $\theta_R = \theta_C = \theta$, we must estimate θ. Maximum likelihood estimates of θ suggest a value close to 0.6. Using this value, we obtain the theoretical transition probability matrices of the three games by substituting into the general transition probability matrix. It will suffice to compare the theoretical matrix of transition probabilities with those observed in one game, since the agreement is immediately seen to be poor.

	1	2	3	4
1	.4	.3	.3	0
2	.6	.4	0	0
3	.45	0	.4	.15
4	0	.15	.45	.4

	1	2	3	4	
1	.43	.19	.30	.08	
2	.52	.19	.22	.07	
3	.47	.12	.31	.10	
4	.28	.16	.37	.19	(24.4)

Theoretical Markov chain
for Game #11 (on the basis
of estimated θ = .6).

Observed transition
frequencies in Game #11
(after Suppes and Atkinson
1960).

The discrepancies are considerable. Thus, although the single element stochastic model predicted the asymptotic choice frequencies quite well, it failed the test with regard to the more detailed structure of the process.

Among other models considered by Suppes and Atkinson was the so-called generalized conditioning model. Here also only one conditioning element is postulated. However, instead of being conditioned to the reinforced response with certainty, this element becomes conditioned to it with a certain probability. Now eight conditioning parameters are involved instead of two, namely:

c_{11}: the probability that the element is conditioned to S_1 when S_1 was chosen and reinforced;

c_{12}: the probability that the element is conditioned to S_1 when S_1 was chosen but not reinforced;

c_{21}: the probability that the element is conditioned to S_1 when T_1 was chosen and not reinforced;

c_{22}: the probability that the element is conditioned to S_1 when T_1 was chosen and reinforced.

The four conditioning parameters d_{ij} (i, j, = 1, 2) are similarly defined with reference to Column's choice (i.e., S_2).

The parameters c_{ij} and d_{ij} having been estimated from data, Suppes and Atkinson obtained the following comparison between the predicted transition probabilities and the observed transition frequencies. The observed transition frequencies are shown in parentheses in table 24.2.

TABLE 24.2 Markov chain transition frequencies predicted by the generalized conditioning model compared with observed transition frequencies in Suppes-Atkinsons's experiment. Observed frequencies in ( ).

| | Game #11 | | | | Game #81 | | | | Game #75 | | | |
	S_1S_2	S_1T_2	T_1S_2	T_1T_2	S_1S_2	S_1T_2	T_1S_2	T_1T_2	S_1S_2	S_1T_2	T_1S_2	T_1T_2
S_1S_2	42 (43)	19 (19)	30 (30)	09 (08)	38 (38)	27 (26)	23 (25)	12 (11)	38 (37)	22 (23)	29 (28)	11 (12)
S_1T_2	54 (52)	20 (19)	19 (22)	07 (07)	48 (50)	31 (31)	13 (11)	08 (08)	54 (54)	24 (25)	15 (15)	07 (06)
T_1S_2	47 (47)	11 (12)	32 (31)	10 (10)	34 (30)	19 (20)	27 (28)	20 (22)	35 (36)	17 (16)	28 (30)	20 (18)
T_1T_2	30 (28)	17 (16)	36 (37)	17 (19)	29 (32)	34 (36)	19 (15)	18 (17)	27 (28)	35 (35)	18 (17)	20 (20)

As is apparent, the agreement is excellent throughout. Comparison between observed and predicted asymptotic choice frequencies is shown in table 24.3.

TABLE 24.3 Predicted and observed choice frequencies over the last 200 plays in Games #11, #81, #75 in Suppes-Atkinson's experiment.

| | (S_1) | | (S_2) | |
Game #	Pred.	Obs.	Pred.	Obs.
11	67	61	70	73
81	67	67	61	60
75	60	61	63	65

Clearly, the generalized conditioning model fits the data better than the single stimulus model with certain conditioning of the reinforced choice since, in addition to predicting the asymptotic choice probabilities as accurately as does the single stimulus model, it predicts much more accurately the transition frequencies. The improvement is not surprising in view of the fact that the generalized conditioning model makes use of more parameters—four (setting $c_{ij} = d_{ij}$) instead of one ($\theta_R = \theta_C$). Another consequence adding credibility to this model is that the estimated values of c_{ij} are in accordance with the inequality $c_{11} > c_{21} > c_{12} > c_{22}$ in all three games. Recall that the second subscript refers to the choice reinforced, "1" referring to S_1 and "2" to T_1. Further, all c_{ij} are probabilities that the stimulus element becomes conditioned to S. It follows from the above inequality that the outcome (i.e., whether the choice of S was reinforced or not) has more effect upon the conditioning than the choice that was made. To put it in another way, the instrumental conditioning model is in this instance more relevant to the observed behavior than the classical conditioning model, a situation-specific answer to a standing question in learning theory.

Two games of partial conflict and one no-conflict game were used by Suppes and Atkinson for further tests of the stochastic learning models. These are shown in 24.4–24.6.

	A_2	B_2
A_1	1 / 3/4	1/4 / 1
B_1	5/8 / 1/2	5/8 / 1/4

24.4
GAME #82
VARIANT I

	S_2	T_2
S_1	1 / 3/8	0 / 1
T_1	3/8 / 5/8	5/8 / 0

24.5
GAME #73
VARIANT II

	A_2	B_2
A_1	4/5 / 4/5	0 / 0
B_1	0 / 0	1/2 / 1/2

24.6
GAME #83
VARIANT I

The first of these games is from the complete set, since Column's payoffs in T_1S_2 and T_1T_2 are equal. However, the game is quite close to game #15 in the ordinal taxonomy. It would be identical with that game if either c_2 were slightly increased or d_2 slightly decreased. Note that game #15 is of order D_2 and has a stable natural outcome. We should, therefore, expect very few departures from the natural outcome from players with full information. However, as in the case of the constant-sum games, the payoffs of the above nonconstant-sum games were probabilistic. As we have seen, under this condition the assumption of "rationality" does not hold even for constant-sum games with saddle point where both players have dominating strategies. The other game of partial conflict is game #73 of the ordinal taxonomy. The no-conflict game corresponds to either game #59 or game #60. It has no competitive pressure.

In Suppes and Atkinson's notation, each entry of the game matrices is a quadruple of probabilities corresponding to the events that both players guessed correctly, that only Row did, that only Column did, and that neither did. From these, the expected payoffs of the players in each outcome can be determined, and these are the entries in 24.4–24.6.

Assuming that the game-theoretic model predicts an equilibrium outcome in each game, we can compare it with the generalized conditioning model. The comparison in games #82 and #73 is shown in table 24.4. The comparison is shown in terms of the expected payoffs to each player, instead of strategy mixtures.

TABLE 24.4 Comparison between game-theoretic and learning theory models of Games #82, #73. Predicted expected payoffs and average payoffs observed in Suppes-Atkinson's experiment.

| | Game #82 | | Game #73 | |
	$g(R)$	$g(C)$	$g(R)$	$g(C)$
Predicted by game theory	.750	1.000	.500	.460
Predicted by learning theory	.687	.827	.499	.618
Observed	.708	.808	.517	.597

Again the stochastic learning model turns out to be by far the better predictor. The agreement between the observed transition frequencies and those predicted by the generalized conditioning model (cf. p. 86) are again very good (cf. Suppes and Atkinson, 1960, p. 125).

In game #83, both S_1S_2 and T_1T_2 are equilibria. The game is not Nash-solvable, since the equilibria are neither equivalent nor interchangeable (cf. p. 43). It is, however, solvable in the strict sense (cf. p. 45) and in Harsanyi's sense (cf. p. 46). The solution S_1S_2 is, of course, intuitively acceptable in this no-conflict game.

Comparison between the generalized conditioning model and Harsanyi's version of the game-theoretic solution is shown in table 24.5. The results on transition frequencies are analogous to previous ones.

The probabilistic payoffs used by Suppes and Atkinson were a carryover from the experimental techniques suggested by the stochastic learning models in the study of individual learning. The game-theoretic aspect of their experimental situation became appar-

TABLE 24.5   Comparison between game-theoretic and
learning theory models of Game #83.
Predicted expected payoffs and average
payoffs observed in Suppes-Atkinson's experiment.

	g(R)	g(C)
Predicted by game theory (Harsanyi's model)	.800	.800
Predicted by learning theory	.449	.449
Observed	.426	.426

ent when the "probability of being correct" was interpreted as the expected payoff associated with an outcome. It turns out that probabilistic payoffs considerably simplify the task of testing the models, because the "probability of guessing correctly" is incorporated into the probability that a stimulus element will be conditioned to the response just made. However, this single stimulus conditioning model, while it predicts accurately the asymptotic choice frequencies, fails when applied to the dynamics of the process, specifically to the transition probabilities of the Markov chain. The generalized conditioning model, which succeeds, amounts to assuming conditional probabilities of choices. It is identical to the four-state Markov chain model derived from the "propensities" (cf. p. 87).

In what follows, this model will again be applied to iterated Prisoner's Dilemma, where the payoffs are deterministic; that is, when the players have all available information. As it will turn out, the model fails in that context.

Rapoport and Chammah (1965) tested the one-step Markov chain as a dynamic model of Prisoner's Dilemma. As we have seen, this model is derived from the generalized conditioning model of stochastic learning theory (cf. p. 86). Assuming both players to be endowed with the same conditioning parameters, x, y, z, and w, the matrix of transition probabilities becomes:

	$S_1 S_2$	$S_1 T_2$	$T_1 S_2$	$T_1 T_2$	
$S_1 S_2$	x^2	$x(1 - x)$	$(1 - x)x$	$(1 - x)^2$	
$S_2 T_2$	yz	$z(1 - z)$	$(1 - y)z$	$(1 - y)(1 - z)$	(24.5)
$T_1 S_2$	zy	$z(1 - y)$	$y(1 - z)$	$(1 - y)(1 - z)$	
$T_1 T_2$	w^2	$w(1 - w)$	$(1 - w)w$	$(1 - w)^2$	

The asymptotic state (outcome) frequencies will be:

$$(CC) = \frac{aw^2 + 2wyz}{(1 - x^2)(a + 2w) + 2yz(1 + w - x) - w^2(2 - a - 2x)}$$

$$(DD) = \frac{b\tilde{x}^2 + 2\tilde{x}\tilde{y}\tilde{z}}{(1 - \tilde{w}^2)(b + 2\tilde{x}) + 2\tilde{y}\tilde{z}(1 + \tilde{x} - \tilde{w}) - \tilde{x}^2(2 - b - 2\tilde{w})}$$

$$(CD) = (DC) = \frac{1}{2}[1 - (CC) - (DD)],$$

(24.6)

where $a = 1 - y - z$, $b = 1 - \tilde{y} - \tilde{z} = -a$.

Suppose now we substitute the estimated values of x, y, z, and w averaged over all available protocols involving the seven variants (cf. p. 233) to calculate the asymptotic outcome frequencies and compare them with those actually observed. We shall find that in every case the observed asymptotic outcome frequencies for the symmetric outcomes C_1C_2 and D_1D_2 are larger than those predicted by the Markov chain, whereas the frequencies of the asymmetric outcomes C_1D_2 and D_1C_2 are smaller. Before we ascribe this discrepancy to the inadequacy of the model, we must remember that it may be due at least in part to a mathematical artifact. Namely, the averages of x, y, z, and w and those of the outcome frequencies were obtained by averaging these values over the subjects. Now as can be seen from (24.6), the asymptotic frequencies are not linear functions of the propensities. They are, in fact, quotients of two third degree polynomials. Therefore, we cannot expect that, even if in each individual case the values of the propensities when substituted into (24.6) correctly predict the outcome frequencies, the same will be true of the averaged values with respect to the averaged outcome frequencies. A numerical example will illustrate this point.

Consider two populations, one with x = .9, y = z = .4, w = .2; the other with x = .7, y = z = .2, w = .1. Averaging these values, we find for the combined populations x = .8, y = z = .3, w = .15. The outcome frequencies predicted for both populations and for the fictitious population with the average values of the propensities are shown in table 24.6 compared with the outcome frequencies averaged over the two populations. Note the discrepancies in the direction predicted.

Aside from this artifact, however (which can be avoided by proper estimation procedures), the one-step Markov chain fails as a model

TABLE 24.6   Comparison of outcome and choice frequencies predicted by the Markov chain models for a population with x=.5, y=z=.4, w=.2 (1); a population with x=.7, y=z=.2, w=.1 (2); a population with x=.8, y=z=.3, w=.15 (3); and the means of outcome & choice frequencies of populations 1 and 2 (4).

	(CC)	(DD)	2(CD)	(C)
(1)	34	33	33	50
(2)	05	75	20	15
(3)	19	54	27	33
(4)	11	57	32	27

of iterated Prisoner's Dilemma in two obvious ways that are manifested without recourse to statistical tests. First, the asymptotic values of the outcome frequencies are reached much later than they would be if the Markov chain were indeed the underlying process by any reasonable assumption of the values of the propensities. Second, no stationary Markov model can account for the characteristic reversal in the time courses of (C) and (CC) almost invariably observed in the time courses of massed protocols.

How good a model is depends on what one expects from it. If the expectations are "modest," models that meet them are readily found. In that case, the difficulty is, as a rule, not that of finding an adequate model but of deciding among several that are equally adequate. As one increases the demands on what the model should predict, one can subject the models to a selection process.

Another way of assessing models is by noting whether the parameters involved in them are "meaningful" in the context of the experiments. For instance, in the context of game experiments, the conditional choice frequencies have rather suggestive psychological meanings (cf. chapter 9). Thus, if the one-step Markov chain determined by these parameters were an adequate model of an iterated game, the natural next step would be to study the dependence of these parameters on independent variables of interest. Note that, if the Markov chain were an adequate model, this would imply that the conditional choice frequencies are constant in a given iterated game, unlike the cruder measures, such as the outcome frequencies or the individual choice frequencies, which usually are taken as the measures of performance.

We have already noted that in iterated games, especially in Prisoner's Dilemma, the choice frequencies are highly correlated over pairs. The high correlation is doubtless due to the interaction between the players. Thus the individual characteristics of the players are submerged. They may be masked even in asymmetric games, obscuring the characteristics of the unequal roles. If, on the other hand, a model reveals parameters that are "inherent" in the players, the interaction effects can be separated from those inherent characteristics.

In spite of the fact that the one-step Markov chain has proved to be inadequate as a model of iterated Prisoner's Dilemma, the parameters of that model are "more inherent" in the players than the choice frequencies. This is demonstrated by the lower correlations between the propensities compared with the correlations of their choices. The comparison is shown in table 24.7.

TABLE 24.7 Comparison of correlations between C-choices and x-propensities [Rapoport and Chammah (1965), p. 190].

	$\rho_{C_1 C_2}$	$\rho_{x_1 x_2}$
Men	.97	.79
Women	.87	.34

In searching for a model with "more deeply seated" psychological parameters, Rapoport and Chammah turned to the linear stochastic learning model, which, recall, is the limiting case of the multi-element model discussed in chapter 4.

Under the combining classes assumptions, the model leads to the following recursive equations.

Let $p(t)$ be the probability that Row will choose C on play t. Then,

$p(t+1) = \alpha_1 p(t) + (1 - \alpha_1) \lambda_1$, if the outcome of play t was $C_1 C_2$;
$p(t+1) = \alpha_2 p(t) + (1 - \alpha_2) \lambda_2$, if the outcome was $C_1 D_2$;
$p(t+1) = \alpha_3 p(t) + (1 - \alpha_3) \lambda_3$, if the outcome was $D_1 C_2$;
$p(t+1) = \alpha_4 p(t) + (1 - \alpha_4) \lambda_4$, if the outcome was $D_1 D_2$.

The respective equations for Column's choices are, of course, analogous.

Note that the probability of choosing C is affected on each play (provided the value of the corresponding α is not 1) regardless of what outcome occurs, since if the tendency to choose D is enhanced or inhibited, so is the tendency to choose C, the two being complementary probabilities.

The model contains sixteen parameters, eight for each player, so that the task of estimating them would be extremely laborious. Accordingly, Rapoport and Chammah resorted to some simplifying assumptions, suggested on common sense grounds. These assumptions relate to the λ's, which, recall, are equal to the asymptotic values of the corresponding choice probabilities.

The first simplifying assumption is that, if the outcome C_1C_2 occurred exclusively, the probability of choosing C would tend to 1 in the limit. That is to say, the longer cooperation between the two players persisted, the more their tendency to continue cooperating ("not to rock the boat") would be enhanced.

The second simplifying assumption is that, if the outcome C_1D_2 occurred exclusively, the probability that Row would continue to choose C would approach zero in the limit. That is to say, the longer a player's unilateral attempt to initiate cooperation is ignored (or exploited) by the co-player, the less likely it is that the effort will continue. Mutatis mutandis, the same assumption applies to Column when D_1C_2 occurs exclusively.

In accordance with these two assumptions, λ_1 is set equal to 1 and λ_2 equal to 0 for both players.

The next assumption is perhaps not as easily justified. If D_1C_2 were to persist exclusively, then the probability that Row chooses C will tend to zero in the limit. This is tantamount to assuming that the "martyr" invites further exploitation. We cannot be sure that this is predominantly the case. However, the assumption does little harm in practice, because protracted "martyr runs" in Prisoner's Dilemma are rare, which is a justification for setting $\lambda_2 = 0$. Thus, setting λ_3 equal to zero is to assume merely that repetitions of D_1C_2 will always enhance Row's tendency to keep choosing D as long as they occur and analogously for Column.

About λ_4 we are not in a position to make an intuitively compelling assumption. On the one hand, D_1D_2 is a "punishing" outcome for both players, which would suggest that its continued occurrence would inhibit further D choices. On the other hand, continued occurrence of D_1D_2 could destroy any hope in either player that it is possible to break out of the trap. Self-enhancing distrust would be reflected in setting $\lambda_4 = 0$, whereas the "punishment" suffered in

D_1D_2 would suggest setting $\lambda_4 = 1$. Therefore, the value of λ_4 was left undetermined, so that it became a "free" parameter. Thus, assuming equal values of the learning parameters in all players, the model was reduced to five free parameters, α_1, α_2, α_3, α_4, and λ_4.

To put this model to a rigorous test requires doing two things. First, the parameters would have to be estimated from some sample of the data. Given the values of the parameters so estimated, a large number of different statistics predicted by the model would have to be compared with the corresponding statistics observed in the data. Confidence in the model would be the more justified, the more statistics were accurately predicted. However, our purpose here is not to evaluate the adequacy of the stochastic learning model but merely to see what it suggests. Interesting suggestions are to be conjectures for generating hypotheses, which, if sufficiently interesting, would justify experiments specifically designed to test them more and more rigorously.

With this aim in mind, Rapoport and Chammah tested the stochastic learning model only very roughly. The parameters were not estimated from the statistics of the data but simply "fudged" to give reasonably fitting time courses by computer simulation. Next, the only comparisons made were between the simulated and the observed time courses and the variances of outcome frequencies and of choice frequencies in the seventy pairs who played the seven variants of Prisoner's Dilemma.

Comparisons between simulated and observed time courses are shown in figures 24.1–24.4. Judging by the naked eye, the fits are not too bad. Moreover, the characteristic initial decline in (C) and initial rise in (D_1D_2) are reproduced in the simulation but not the initial decline in (C_1C_2). The agreement between the observed variances and those produced by the simulated process are also fair (cf. table 24.8).

TABLE 24.8

	Var(C)	Var(C_1C_2)	Var(C_1D_2)	Var(D_1C_2)	Var(D_1D_2)
Observed	.091	.110	.006	.006	.080
Produced by simulation	.094	.134	.004	.004	.060

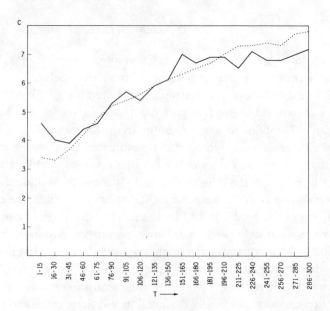

Fig. 24.1.   Comparison of observed time course of C (solid line) with that obtained from simulation (dotted line). Horizontal axis: number of plays. Vertical axis: C frequencies averaged over 140 subjects and seven variants. (Cf. Rapoport and Chammah [1965], p. 180.)

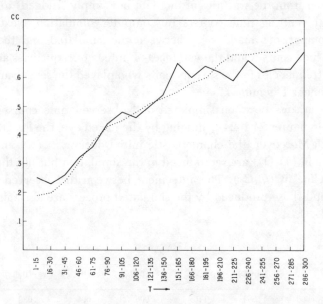

Fig. 24.2.   Comparison of observed time course of CC (solid line) with that obtained from simulation (dotted line). Horizontal axis: number of plays. Vertical axis: CC frequencies averaged over 140 subjects and seven variants. (Cf. Rapoport and Chammah [1965], p. 181.)

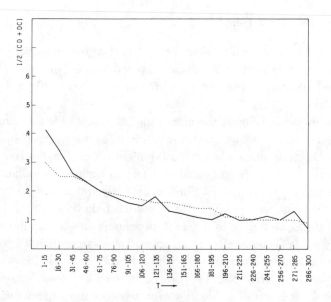

Fig. 24.3. Comparison of observed time course of ½ (CD + DC) (solid line) with
that obtained from simulation (dotted line). Horizontal axis: number of plays.
Vertical axis: ½ (CD + DC) frequencies averaged over 140 subjects and seven
variants. (Cf. Rapoport and Chammah [1965], p. 182.)

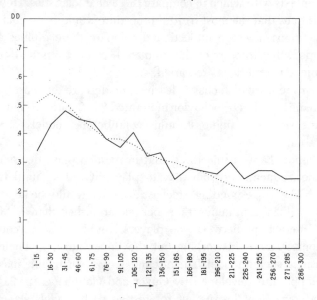

Fig. 24.4. Comparison of observed time course of DD (solid line) with that obtained from simulation (dotted line). Horizontal axis: number of plays. Vertical
axis: DD frequencies averaged over 140 subjects and seven variants. (Cf. Rapoport
and Chammah [1965], p. 183.)

Next, we examine the values of the "best fitting" parameters for conjectures they suggest about the supposed learning process in Prisoner's Dilemma. These are $\alpha_1 = .57$; $\alpha_2 = .40$; $\alpha_3 = .40$; $\alpha_4 = .74$; $\lambda_4 = .40$.

Recall that learning is the more rapid, the smaller is the value of α. Hence, we conjecture about the fictitious "average player" of Prisoner's Dilemma that he learns most quickly (i) to abandon cooperation when it is not reciprocated and (ii) to exploit the unilaterally cooperating co-player. Next, he learns fairly quickly to cooperate with the cooperating player. He learns most slowly either to break out of the D_1D_2 trap or to stay in it, depending on whether the probability of his C choice after D_1D_2 is smaller or larger than 0.4. These conjectures are meaningful only with reference to the fictitious average player. In principle, they can be derived also from individual protocols. It is questionable, however, whether the large amount of work involved in rigorous, statistically justified estimation would be effort well spent. Characterizing an individual with a set of parameters might be revealing and might suggest correlates of behavior in other contexts with which to compare these characteristics. However, it seems to us that the most fruitful procedure would be to characterize a fictitious "average subject" and compare these profiles as the population, the structure of the simulated "conflict situation," or the experimental conditions are varied.

It seems to us that stochastic learning models are the most promising dynamic models of behavior in iterated 2 × 2 games. They range from the simplest (single stimulus conditioning models) to arbitrarily complex ones.

In chapter 17 we conjectured that in iterated plays decisions are made not sequentially from play to play but rather "until further notice." The corresponding stochastic model would be a Markov process with a continuous time parameter rather than a Markov chain. Interactions between the players would introduce considerable complications in working out the time courses of choices on the basis of such a model. The attempt seems worthwhile inasmuch as the apparatus developed by Guyer and Gollub (cf. p. 94) provides a convenient instrument for testing such models experimentally. Models can be extended beyond the linear models (the last considered above) to learning models in which the subjects are assumed to modify their *propensities* rather than the probabilities of choices. Clearly, as the complexity of models increases, the number of parameters to be estimated increases rapidly. If such complex models are to be put to a rigorous test, the estimates of the parameters must be made from the data, which involves a prodigious amount of work to be carried out separately in each experiment. A cruder approach is to use computer simulation where parameters are "fudged" by trial and error to give the best fit. As the number of parameters to be so adjusted becomes large, it is always possible to obtain good fits to an arbitrary number of statistics. This reduces the models to ad hoc curve fitting, unsatisfactory from the point of view of the model builder who hopes to establish a theory with high predictive power. However, construction of a model with high predictive power is not the only legitimate goal of model building. Another is that of generating hypotheses based on interpretations of the "best fit" parameters. Here the "success" of the model is not the final goal but the point of departure of a theory. Once the parameters have been interpreted psychologically, the questions to be answered relate to the way these supposed "psychological constants" (constants in a given situation, that is) are affected by different variables. Assume, for instance, that by means of computer simulation we have obtained values of "higher order" learning parameters in a 2×2 game, such as the *rate of change* of the learning parameters assumed to be constant in linear stochastic learning models. One may expect that, while a learning parameter affecting the probability of response may not be constant, the parameter affecting the rate of change of the learning parameter may be. If so, the latter parameter would be a more fundamental characteristic of a subject or a pool of subjects than the former.

In order to get to these "deeper" parameters without paying an exorbitant price in time and labor, it may be justifiable to cut statistical corners. The simplification, of course, exacts a price of its own. One must abandon attempts to develop rigorously justified models in favor of suggestive and conceptually fruitful ones.

25

Concluding Remarks

Figure 25.1 shows the numbers of articles, books, memoranda, etc., published from 1952 to 1971, related to the subject of this book. There are three extensive bibliographies of the field (Guyer and Perkel, 1972; Shubik, Brewer, and Savage, 1972; Wrightsman, O'Connor, and Baker, 1972). There is, of course, a great deal of overlap in the bibliographies, but they differ in some respects.

The Guyer-Perkel bibliography contains only a few purely theoretical articles on game theory. Shubik, Brewer, and Savage include substantially more of these. The Wrightsman, O'Connor, Baker list contains a large number of items on social psychology, relevant only indirectly to experimental games as background or as sources of ideas that have stimulated gaming research. The Shubik-Brewer-Savage compilation contains many articles and books on simulation, business and war games, etc. This latter list is selective rather than exhaustive and covers only 551 items compared with about 900 in the Guyer-Perkel bibliography and about 1100 in Wrightsman, et al.

The Shubik-Brewer-Savage report is the most useful for an overview of the field. It classifies the items into several categories; for instance, mathematical sophistication (from "none" to "high"), purpose (theory, development, operational, teaching, etc.), qualitative assessment ("excellent" to "bad"), discipline (economics, social psychology, political-diplomatic-military), and even funding and classification (from "unclassified" to "top secret").

What interests us at the moment is the time course of the relative

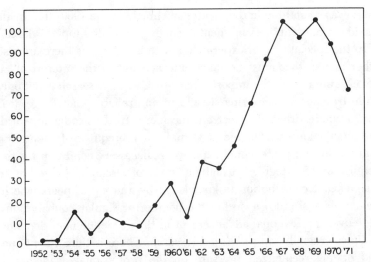

Fig. 25.1. Number of articles, books, memoranda, etc., published from 1952 to 1971, on various aspects of game experiments.

number of papers published since the early 1950s. It shows the effects of an "information explosion," mentioned by Shubik, et al. in their introduction. The "explosion" in the literature reviewed seems to have started in the early 1960s and to have reached a peak about 1967. After that, the curve levels off and possibly gives evidence of decline. It is impossible to say whether the decline is temporary, to be followed by further growth, or whether the peak was an "overshooting" to be followed by a somewhat lower plateau, or whether the phenomenon was a "fad" destined to peter out.

The fate of the field (the coupling of theoretical and experimental methods in the study of the structure of conflict) depends on a number of factors that contribute to or detract from its viability. Relentless natural selection operates not only on biological species, where it was first discovered and incorporated into the theory of evolution, but also in many other contexts; in the evolution of languages, of artifacts, and of ideas, for instance. Viability means a potential for reproduction, and what is written on any subject is certainly a "reproduction" of ideas, which, in any published item, serve as stimuli for other published items. The extent to which this "reproduction process" is reflected in the volume of publications depends partly on the fruitfulness of the ideas or, rather, on their *perceived* fruitfulness. And this depends, in turn, on the ideational climate. Evidently, there was something in the ideational climate in the 1960s that made the ideas inherent in experimental games and related topics "viable."

In the special area of experiments with 2 × 2 games there are also other factors that must be taken into account in the interest of an honest appraisal of the importance of this work. Research is not only an instrument for acquiring significant and reliable knowledge; it is also a wherewithal of career advancement. In the academic world, the acquisition of a degree is virtually a prerequisite for entering that world in a professional capacity. A necessary condition for the acquisition of a degree is usually a "piece of research," judged to be a significant contribution to knowledge by a group of peers who in their time were also awarded the degree for similar contributions. Moreover, professional advancement in the academic field depends, at times crucially, on *published* research. There is thus a continual and openly recognized pressure on the professional academic to "produce" research.

Now, the field of experimental games offers a lively opportunity to produce a publishable paper, especially in experimental psychology or experimental social psychology. All that is needed is a selection of some "interesting" independent variables that constitute either a characteristic of the subjects or of the conditions in which they are put. The subjects' game behavior constitutes easily recordable and easily quantifiable data. The work (aside from the design and the mechanics of experiments) consists of processing the data, that is, teasing out the features relevant to the hypotheses posed and applying more or less routine procedures of statistical evaluation that provide answers to questions posed. If the results are "positive" (i.e., statistically significant) and the answers are of sufficient interest to the academic community that comprises the particular discipline, the chances of publishing the resulting paper are limited only by the capacity of the journals receptive to the research undertaken. Moreover, this capacity depends, in part, on interest in the particular research and tends to be expanded as the volume of research grows. Thus a "positive feedback" that may account for the "explosion" sets in.

Needless to say, being ourselves engaged in experimental games, we do not believe that the above, somewhat cynical, explanation entirely accounts for the evident "success" of the field. We mention it only as a factor that must be recognized in order to avoid self-deception. So, having got this reservation off our chests, let us pose the substantive question. What has been learned or can be learned from research on experimental games, in particular the very simplest of these—the 2×2 games, that can be regarded as a "significant contribution to knowledge"?

Questions of this sort are inescapable in any society that supports certain activities through its institutions, since the questions relate to the values prevalent in the society which the supported activity presumably serves and thereby justifies support.

With few exceptions, all the work on experimental games was done in North America, and practically all the work on 2×2 games was done in colleges and universities. The above question, therefore, must be answered either in terms of values prevalent in North America, especially in its institutions of higher learning, or in terms of values which, although not presently dominant, ought to be dominant in the opinion of the person who answers the question.

The expansion of research of all kinds in the United States since World War II in terms of sheer quantity of facilities, support, personnel, and output has been unprecedented in history. Although expansion has been worldwide, of course, we suspect that the United States has contributed far more than its "normal" share. Reasons for this phenomenon are to be sought, we believe, in the prestige acquired by what is understood as "science" in consequence of power conferred on those who can utilize its applications. It has become somewhat trite to refer to the atomic bomb explosions at the close of World War II as the turning point in the popular estimation of "science." We believe, however, that there is much truth in that interpretation. In the popular mind, science is justified as the source of power. What is in the popular mind creates an ideational climate, thus an input into the political climate, and thence to policies and institutional practices.

This is one side of the picture. The obverse side is also present in the ideational climate, namely that power conferred by science is a danger to man. Again the atomic bomb is cited in almost every popular discussion of the contemporary human condition. What is lacking, it is often asserted, is man's ability to exercise control over himself as well as over the forces of nature, which he has learned from science. If physical science confers on man the power to control his physical environment, then there must be a way of making social science serve an analogous function, to confer upon man the power to control "himself," that is, his social environment. The parallel verbal construction—physical science is to physical environment as social science is to social environment—makes this projected expansion of the role of science reasonable and promising.

Now, physical science owes its prodigious success to its method in which the formidable power of mathematical deduction is coupled to observations of quantifiable events. It has appeared to many that what is needed to make the social sciences as prestigious and as fruitful as the physical is an extension to studies on man of the "hard" scientific method.

"Hard" science deals with observables. In fact, successful predictions of what will be observed are the only corroborations of the truth of genuinely scientific theories. The "observables" of the social environment are forms of human behavior. (This was pointed out by the behaviorists already at the beginning of this century in connection with what they said psychology ought to be concerned.) Therefore, quantifiable behavior ought to provide the empirical basis of "hard" social science.

The first science related to human behavior that started gathering hard quantifiable data from controlled experiments was psychology. At first these data were only remotely relevant to theories of behavior, the earliest psychological experiments having been concerned with the senses (psychophysics) and with rote learning (memorization of nonsense syllables, for example). As the experimental method spread to what is now called social psychology, attempts were made to simulate certain forms of social behavior in the laboratory or else to elicit answers to questions about how a subject would behave in a social situation. For instance, in a typical sociometric experiment, the subject is asked to name persons whom he "likes," "considers best friends," "would rather work with," etc. Data so obtained can be represented by a directed graph, whose salient properties reveal something about the structure of a social group. In personality assessment, subjects are frequently asked to fill out questionnaires about their attitudes or reactions to social situations. The answers are quantified on some kinds of scales designed especially for the purpose of personality assessment.

Two questions arise in connection with this methodology. One concerns the legitimacy of inferring behavior from verbal answers;

the other concerns the consistency or validity of the scales on which these answers are quantified. Game experiments obviate both of these questions. The subjects' choices in game experiments *are* behavior, not verbal descriptions of would-be behavior, and the quantification of these choices presents no problem of scaling. Frequencies, being dimensionless, are represented on an absolute scale, the "strongest" of all measurement scales, which provides the widest latitude of mathematical manipulations.[1] Next, the social context of which game experiments are supposed to be a representation is of the greatest interest in social psychology. It represents conflict in its peculiar human context, where choices among available alternatives based on "strategic calculations" are at least partial determinants of behavior.

Intense popular interest in conflicts of this sort is manifested in the tremendous popularity of parlor games that simulate real-world conflicts of interest ("Monopoly" and its innumerable variants) and in best sellers like Eric Berne's book, *Games People Play,* in which social situations and human relations are depicted as "games." These are not formal games of strategy, of course, but rather descriptions of "gamesmanship," a subject about which game theory has nothing to say. However, as pointed out, the ideational climate being strongly influenced by verbal parallels, "game theory" has become a household word, and we are frequently asked whether our experiments (which, we explain, are experiments in social psychology) have anything to do with "games people play" in contexts depicted in Berne's book.

In summary, the "success of the field" that encompasses all forms of game behavior can be attributed to the following factors.

1. Receptiveness to the idea that "social science" is sorely needed as a counterbalance to the awesome power of man over nature, which far outstrips man's ability to manage his social self.

2. The conviction that, to serve as a source of reliable knowledge, social science should become "hard," hence, rely on "objective" data, preferably gathered under controlled conditions; hence, that the experimental arm should become part of the social scientist's arsenal.

3. The recognized importance of conflict as a matrix of social events—in fact, as *the* component of the human condition that makes

---

[1] In this connection, see Luce (1959).

it imperative to "close the gap" between the physical and the social sciences.

These are the factors that create an ideational climate favorable to "research on conflict" and, perhaps, "research on conflict resolution." Besides these, there are factors in the specific ideational climate in the academic community (where most research is done) that single out game experiments as an attractive tool.

4. The laboratory is a time honored locale of "hard" research.

5. The game experiment captures the essentials of specifically human conflicts, where "rationality" is at least partly involved and where cross pressures of opposed and parallel interests operate. (This latter conception of human conflict is, of course, what makes the mixed-motive game appear to be the especially appropriate research tool and accounts for the wide popularity of the Prisoner's Dilemma game.)

6. Data on game experiments, especially on the simplest games, can be cheaply gathered in large quantities (making for statistical stability of the results) and can be readily quantified (providing answers, supported by statistical significance, to clearly formulated hypotheses).

Before we return to the question posed above, "What has been learned or can be learned from research on experimental games?" we must consider another source of interest in the field spurred onward by the idea that game theory may be the mathematical foundation of strategic science. As is well known, the foundations of game theory were laid by J. von Neumann, who first considered the logical structure of a game of strategy involving two players with diametrically opposed interests, each having available a finite set of strategies. As mentioned in chapter 3, von Neumann was able to prove that in every such game there is an optimal strategy available to each player, optimality being quite naturally defined in terms of maximizing payoffs under the constraints of the game (von Neumann, 1928). The idea that an "optimal" strategy can in principle be found in a conflict situation has a strong appeal to a decision maker who finds himself in such situations and who has faith in the power and relevance of science in the context of "problem solving." Again, the ideational climate prevailing in postwar years, especially in the United States, contributed to the receptivity on the part of policy makers and decision makers involved in competitive business or in diplo-military pursuits (or at least of their academically trained advisors) to the idea that game theory can be developed into a tool of rational decision in conflict situations—an applied science helpful for finding "optimal strategies." Research in game theory, it would seem, could be directed to supplement what has become known as operations research, which is concerned with finding optimal strategies in games against nature or one-person games.

Indeed, the interest in game theory amid the intellectual sectors of military circles is attested by the many conferences on the subject sponsored by military institutions, and by the support given to game-theoretical investigations by the research arms of those institutions; for instance, the Rand Corporation, the Office of Naval Research, et al. Also, tactical or logistic exercises depicted as formal games are now embodied in military education. Although, for the most part, these are only textbook exercises, tailored to be tractable (like the "word problems" in algebra textbooks), they are clearly intended to train students in rational, strategic thinking.

It is important to note that the games used as illustrations of military problems are, almost without exception, two-person zerosum games—and for very good reasons. First, these games depict players as "pure adversaries," as they are typically depicted in models of military confrontations. Second, two-person zerosum games are games wherein individually rational, optimal strategies can be clearly defined, hence, they can be "solved" in the sense of finding a strategy that can be prescribed to a rational participant in a conflict, where "rationality" in the contexts considered is compellingly defined as the pursuit of one's own interests.

In 1958, T. C. Schelling published a paper (later expanded into a book) in the *Journal of Conflict Resolution* entitled "The Strategy of Conflict: Prospects for Reorientation of Game Theory." There he pointed out that the situation depicted by the two-person zerosum game is only a very special case of human conflict, whereas, in most conflicts, the interests of the participants clash only partially. Partly their interests coincide; that is, outcomes exist that both (or all) players prefer to other outcomes. For instance, the global conflict between the two super powers in the post-World War II era was certainly generated by clashing interests. However, both super powers seemed to prefer the nonoccurrence of at least a nuclear war between them to an occurrence. Even in war, Schelling argued, adversaries are often forced into tacit cooperation, avoiding battle in certain circumstances, or refraining from the use of certain weapons in order to forestall retaliation, for example.

Such situations, if they can be depicted by formal models, are, of course, representable by *non*constant-sum games, and Schelling pointed out the importance of developing a theory of such games. We believe that Schelling's paper, and the book based on it published shortly afterward (Schelling, 1960), were an important stimulus to the development of the experimental approach to game behavior. (Some no-conflict games with problems of coordination in the absence of communication were used by Schelling as vivid examples.)

Although Schelling turned attention to the *cooperative* aspects of nonconstant-sum games, the development of the "theory" advanced by him took a different direction. One aspect of nonconstant-sum games that is totally absent in two-person zerosum games is communication, whether explicit, as in cooperative games, or tacit, as in noncooperative (especially, iterated) games. Clearly, communication in zerosum games serves no purpose. The interests of the players being diametrically opposed, communication cannot be used to establish cooperation and, with it, the achievement of outcomes preferred by both players.[2] In particular, in two-person zerosum games with saddle points, communication about intended moves or selected strategies can make no difference if the game is played by completely rational players, because the outcome of such games is theoretically known with certainty in advance. In games without saddle points, where mixed strategies are optimal, communication from one player to the other about his selected strategy *in any particular play* of the game can only hurt the communicator, for this knowledge enables the adversary to get a larger payoff than the maximin guaranteed by the optimal mixed strategy. False communication can be of value to the communicator if it is believed. However, in a zerosum game, there is no incentive to believe the communications of the adversary, if it is known that true communications from him can only hurt him.

The situation is radically different in a nonconstant-sum game.

---

[2] Bidding and bluffing in zerosum card games, although apparently acts of communication, are actually moves of the game itself, not communications *about* the game, which is what Schelling had primarily in mind.

Such games include situations where the transmittal of a true communication, together with credible evidence that it *is* true, can benefit the communicator and hurt the recipient. A clear example of this situation is the game of Chicken (game #66). In that game, if one player can somehow convince the other that he will choose T, the other, in choosing the strategy that maximizes his own payoff under the circumstances, inadvertently awards the largest payoff to the communicator. The communication, if believed, *preempts* the outcome with the largest payoff. Mutatis mutandis, it is frequently to the advantage of a player to make himself incommunicado. For instance, someone who cannot possibly receive a message need not fear that his child will be kidnapped and is, in fact, immune to all forms of blackmail—provided, of course, that the kidnappers or the blackmailers *know* that he cannot be reached.

It is these aspects of nonconstant-sum games that Schelling singled out for attention. Nevertheless, the *objectives* of game-theoretic (and related) investigations in the school of thought influenced by him remained the same as those of applied zerosum game theory: a search for optimal strategies in conflict situations. An example of this direction is Robert Jervis's book *The Logic of Images in International Relations* (1970), essentially a book of gamesmanship in the context of diplo-military confrontations. To be sure, Jervis derived no clear cut "optimal strategies" on the basis of a rigorously developed theory. But his analysis of the role of bluffs and counter bluffs, of deception and "sincerity," of "credibility" and scepticism, of prudence and boldness in risk-taking, illustrated by interesting historical examples, is far-reaching and intriguing. It gives the impression of being a handbook for negotiators in the world of bullying, subterfuge, and deception, where foreign policy "in pursuit of national interests" is conducted.

In answering the question posed, we shall consider it both with reference to behavioral science and with reference to the ideational input of game theory, or rather of various conceptions of game theory by people who would like to put it to "practical use."

The results of the numerous experiments with 2×2 games discussed in the summaries of preceding parts fall roughly into four categories:

1. *Results strongly expected on common sense grounds.* Examples are the monotonicity hypothesis, according to which increasing the

payoff in a cell increases the frequency of choices associated with that cell; various hypotheses concerning communication and information, where introducing or withholding communication or information produces changes in frequencies of choices in the expected direction; the effectiveness of the Tit-for-tat strategy in eliciting "cooperation" in iterated Prisoner's Dilemma.

2. *Negative results,* which become better understood in the light of structural aspects of the game in question, an aspect often neglected by investigators, who pose only "psychological" hypotheses. Such results are especially common in experiments involving a programed player. Starting with the hypothesis that "cooperation begets cooperation; competition, competition," experimenters have adopted a standard practice in games with Prisoner's Dilemma, where the effects of "strategies with varying degrees of cooperation" used by the stooge are compared with reference to the subject's responses. Most experiments of this sort failed to reveal significant differences between "highly cooperative" and "highly uncooperative" (noncontingent) programed strategies. The results are disappointing in failing to confirm an ethically attractive hypothesis. However, the hypothesis ignores the structure of the game, in which the 100 percent D (uncooperative) strategy is the only rational one against *any* noncontingent strategy. The usual distinction between individual and collective rationality does not enter this situation, because collective rationality is meaningless if the other is simply part of a stochastic environment unresponsive to tacit communication.

Other negative results abound in attempts to relate game behavior to a large variety of "personality types." (There are some notable exceptions.) Since strategies "maximizing one's own payoff" cannot be unambivalently defined in a noncooperative game, the tacit identification of the "cooperative" choice in nonconstant-sum games with "altruism," "liberalism," etc., and of the noncooperative one with "selfishness," "authoritarianism," etc., seems dubious.

The iterated 2 × 2 game can be regarded as a learning experience. considerably complicated, to be sure, by the interactions between the players. It may be that learning ability is "orthogonal" to many aspects of personality. The few positive results reported in this area may be due to just those personality factors that are positively correlated with the particular learning ability required to establish "cooperation" in the iterated noncooperative 2 × 2 game.

3. *Hypothesis-generating results*. In our opinion, these are the most valuable contributions from gaming experiments to behavioral science. New hypotheses are naturally generated by unforeseen or surprising results. Results are unforeseen if no hypotheses are formulated, because, in the absence of preconceptions, results "in either direction" seem equally likely. They are surprising if they dramatically disconfirm a formulated hypothesis. Both types of results can provide stepping stones to developing behavioral theory in the direction of greater relevance to "real life." The often posed question about what we can learn from gaming experiments about actual motivations or behavior of people in real life must be answered honestly: next to nothing. But the unforeseen or surprising results of gaming experiments do suggest new, sometimes searching *questions about* conflict behavior. These questions can be answered only by extensive observations beyond the format of simple laboratory games.

4. *Quantitative results*. In social-psychological experiments, hypotheses and results are most commonly presented in the form "the more of this, the more of that." Such findings are on the lowest level of quantification. Very often, as we have seen, results of this sort are only confirmations of common sense expectations. Quantitative refinements can provide far from obvious answers to more specific quantitatively-formulated questions. We have tried to derive such results when we examined the *rates* of increase of choice frequencies (conditional and unconditional) in relation to changes in the payoffs. Our findings were only vaguely suggestive (cf. chapters 15 and 16). In principle, they could be made more precise if experiments could be performed with very large numbers of subjects, for then the statistical stability of the results could be assured. To be sure, individual differences would be washed out and, because of the traditional orientation of psychology, the results might become uninteresting to the psychologist. In our opinion, however, the "composite human subject" is interesting as an object of study in its own right, especially because next to nothing is known about the quantitative aspects of "his" behavior in the game situation. Having suggested psychological interpretations of choice frequencies, especially, of the propensities (conditional frequencies), we could examine the behavior of this composite subject as a function of all the independent variables already in use (as well as many others that we could think of) in

great quantitative detail and so get a clear picture of his "psychology."

One might ask of what use would this composite psychology be, in view of the fact that no "real" individual can be considered to be endowed with it. The answer depends on the value ascribed to knowledge. In a pragmatically oriented society, knowledge is valued as an instrument of control, sometimes manipulative control that confers advantages on the possessor of knowledge, but also benevolent control, as in the design of welfare policies, in enlightened pedagogy, therapy, etc. Unfortunately, emphasis on the prediction-and-control aspect of knowledge, even in the context of best intentions, detracts from the other great gift bestowed by knowledge—understanding and insight uncoupled from pragmatic advantages. True, in pragmatically oriented societies, "pure science" is often generously supported and honored. For the most part, however, the support is based on tacit expectations that the knowledge generated by "pure science" will eventually find its way to "practical" applications. The defenders of "pure science" are never at a loss to find dramatic confirmations of such expectations.

Insight and understanding may not confer upon us powers of control, but they may change *us* by guiding our concerns in new directions. Every value system has self-justifying values. We believe that an expansion of intellectual and conceptual horizons ought to be a self-justifying value in a society that purports to be humane. To the extent that the "composite individual" in a conflict situation may be a new concept, and because his "psychology" is still largely a closed book at least in its details, and to the extent that even a 2 × 2 game offers a rich variety of simulated conflict situations easily amenable to experimental study, we believe that work in the indicated directions is justified.

This brings us to the relation of the work described in this book to the expectations that game theory coupled with behavioral studies or observations may provide the decision maker "in pursuit of interests" with knowledge of how to conduct conflicts advantageously. In our opinion, the expectations are not justified. They could at best be realized in the context of the two-person zerosum game, because in that context optimal strategies can be singled out, at least in principle. Actually, applications of the classical theory of the two-person zerosum game to real-life conflicts are severely limited, because the formal models of such situations are far too abstract and simplified to represent the real situation with any degree of fidelity. The theory of differential games may be a notable exception.

An example of a differential game is that played by an intercontinental ballistic missile against a pursuing antiballistic missile. The strategies available to the latter are pursuit strategies; those available to the former are evasion strategies. Payoffs can be clearly defined in terms of times of interception, or of distance from the target at which interception occurs, if it does. Here the game models can be assumed to be reasonable approximations of reality, because the "players" are automata with fixed repertoires of strategies, and the outcomes, although they may be perturbed, say, by weather conditions, are not likely to be altogether invalidated by totally unforeseen events. The mathematics of differential games is much more complicated than that of classical games. Still, because of the very nature of scientific research, where in the last analysis there are no "secrets," least of all in mathematical research, sophisticated applications of game theory can lead only to ever-growing sophistication of automated warfare without necessarily conferring an advantage on either "player," except temporarily. It is difficult to see who would benefit by such a development except the professionals who may derive satisfaction from flexing their mathematical and technological muscles.

As for nonconstant-sum games, with which, as we have seen, experimental work is primarily concerned, it should be clear that the concept of *individually* optimal strategies remains for the most part unclear in that context. In fact, the theory of the nonconstant-sum game has been perforce centered on the problem of conflict resolution rather than on the problem of finding individually optimal strategies. In the theory of the cooperative N-person game (with more than two players), conflict resolution is actually the focal point of investigation. (Perhaps we shall some day devote a book to that theory and to the experiments it has inspired.)

We hope that the interest in experiments on nonconstant-sum, two-person—and eventually N-person—games persists and spreads to the extent of providing a discernible input to the ideational climate. The frequent mention of the field, in conferences on a variety of social problems, even in articles in the popular press, etc., may be signs that our hopes will be realized. If so, the impact of the ideas on the world where strategic conflicts are planned and conducted, the world of competitive business, competitive politics, and of geopolitics, will be a destructive rather than a constructive one. For it will shake the conviction—prevalent in that world and strengthened by a faith in "science"—that rationality in conflict is simply an extension of rationality in classical decision making (that of the actor in a stochastic environment) and that, consequently, strategic sophistication confers an advantage on a participant in any conflict. If our expectation is too sanguine, we can at least hope that the impact on ordinary mortals of insights inherent in a generalized theory of conflict will shake their faith in the wisdom supposedly conferred on the designers of global policies by strategic expertise. The solution of the most important problems confronting humanity evades us the moment we so much as *pose* the question "How do *I* play the game rationally?" The only promising way is to pose the question "How do *we* play the game rationally?" The shift of focus from "I" to "we" has been urged by innumerable religious leaders, social reformers, patriots, and revolutionaries. Extensive experience with the simplest nonconstant-sum games puts the necessity of the shift from "I" to "we" into a concrete situation where consequences of actions are immediate, and which a child can readily grasp. This is what we mean when we say that an important but neglected aspect of knowledge is the change it can produce in us, internally, rather than the power it confers to control the external world.

Author Index

Italic numbers enclosed in brackets refer to pages in The 2 × 2 Game.

Adorno, T. W., Frenkel-Brunswick, E., Levinson, D. J., and Sanford, R. N. *The Authoritarian Personality*. New York: Harper & Bros., 1969. [*325*]

Atkinson, R. C. and Estes, W. K. "Stimulus Sampling Theory." In *Handbook of Mathematical Psychology*, vol. II, edited by R. D. Luce, R. R. Bush, and E. Galanter. New York: John Wiley & Sons, 1963, pp. 121–268. [*87*]

Baxter, G. W., Jr. "Personality and Attitudinal Characteristics and Cooperation in Two-person Games: A Review." In *Cooperation and Competition: Readings in Mixed-motive Games*, edited by L. S. Wrightsman, Jr., et al. Belmont, Cal.: Brooks/Cole Publishing Co., 1972. [*327*]

Baxter, G. W., Jr. "The Effects of Information about Race of Other Player in a Two-person Game." Unpublished Ph.D. dissertation, Peabody College, 1969. [*294–96*]

Bixenstine, V. E., Potash, H. M., and Wilson, K. V. "Effects of Level of Cooperative Choice by the Other Player on Choices in a Prisoner's Dilemma Game, I." *Journal of Abnormal and Social Psychology*, 66 (1963): 308–17. [*263*]

Braithwaite, R. B. *Theory of Games as a Tool for the Moral Philosopher*. Cambridge: Cambridge University Press, 1955. [*32, 60, 61, 62, 169, 229, 352*]

Brew, J. S. "An Altruism Parameter for Prisoner's Dilemma." *Journal of Conflict Resolution*, 17 (1973): 351–67. [*399–402*]

Bush, R. R. and Mosteller, F. *Stochastic Models for Learning*. New York: John Wiley & Sons, 1955. [*87*]

Chammah, A. M. "Sex Differences, Strategy, and Communication in Mixed-motive Games." Unpublished Ph.D. dissertation, University of Michigan, 1969. [*265*]

Cowan, G. "The Machiavellian: Manipulator or Failure in Self-presentation?" *Proceedings*, 77th Annual Convention, American Psychological Association, 4 (1969): 357–58. [*272*]

Crowne, D. P. "Family Orientation, Level of Aspirations, and Interpersonal Bargaining." *Journal of Personality and Social Psychology*, 3 (1966): 641–45. [*330–32*]

437

Crumbaugh, C. M. and Evans, G. W. "Presentation Format, Other-person Strategies, and Cooperative Behavior in the Prisoner's Dilemma." *Psychological Reports*, 20 (1967): 895–902. [265]

Deutsch, M. "Trust and Suspicion." *Journal of Conflict Resolution*, 2 (1958): 265–79. [291, 320–21]

———. "Trust, Trustworthiness, and the F-scale." *Journal of Abnormal and Social Psychology*, 61 (1960): 138–40. [325–26]

Edwards, J. and Gordon, R. "Performance of Female and Mixed Pairs in a Threat Game." University of Toronto, 1973 (unpublished). [317–20, 339]

Evans, G. "Effects of Unilateral Promise and Value of Rewards upon Cooperation and Trust." *Journal of Abnormal and Social Psychology*, 69 (1964): 587–90. [258]

Fox, J. "The Learning of Strategies in a Simple Two-person Zero-sum Game without Saddlepoint." *Behavioral Science*, 17 (1972): 300–308. [357–58]

Frenkel, O. "A Study of 78 Non-iterated Ordinal 2 × 2 Games." University of Toronto, 1973 (unpublished). [134, 135, 198–204, 211–28, 230, 240, 354, 402–3]

Gahagan, J. P., Long, H., and Horai, J. "Race of Experimenter and Reactions to Threat by Black Preadolescents." *Proceedings*, 77th Annual Convention, American Psychological Association, 4 (1969): 397–98. [264]

Gahagan, J. P. and Tedeschi, J. T. "Strategy and the Credibility of Promises in the Prisoner's Dilemma Game." *Journal of Conflict Resolution*, 12 (1968): 224–34. [264]

Gallo, P. S., Jr., Irwin, R., and Avery, G. "The Effects of Score Feedback and Strategy of the Other on Cooperative Behavior in a Maximizing Difference Game." *Psychonomic Science*, 5, 10 (1966): 401–2. [272]

Gordon, D. Unpublished doctoral dissertation, University of Michigan, 1972. [358, 364–94]

Guyer, M. and Gordon, D. "Effects of Parameter Changes in a Threat Game." University of Michigan, 1972 (unpublished). [245–56, 273–82, 319–20]

Guyer, M. and Hamburger, H. "A Note on 'A Taxonomy of 2 × 2 Games.'" *General Systems*, 13 (1968): 205–19. [31]

Guyer, M. and Perkel, B. *Experimental Games: A Bibliography (1945–71)*. Ann Arbor: University of Michigan, Mental Health Research Institute Communication #293, 1972. [422]

Guyer, M. and Rapoport, A. "Information Effects in Two Mixed-motive Games." *Behavioral Science*, 14 (1969): 467–82. [165, 300–305]

———. "2 × 2 Games Played Once." *Journal of Conflict Resolution*, 16 (1972): 409–31. [215–23, 228]

Hamburger, H. "Separable Games." *Behavioral Science*, 14 (1969): 121–32. [32]

Harford, T. C., Jr. and Hill, M. "Variations in Behavioral Strategies and Interpersonal Trust in a Two-person Game with Male Alcoholics." *Journal of Clinical Psychology,* 23 (1967): 33–35. [*270*]

Harford, T. C., Jr. and Solomon, L. " 'Reformed Sinner' and 'Lapsed Saint' Strategies in the Prisoner's Dilemma Game." *Journal of Conflict Resolution,* 11 (1967): 104–9. [*270*]

Harris, G. "An Experimental Study of a Threat Game." University of Toronto, 1973 (unpublished). [*203, 204*]

Harris, R. J. "A Geometric Classification System for 2 × 2 Interval-Symmetric Games." *Behavioral Science,* 14 (1969): 138–46.

———. "An Interval Scale Classification System for All 2 × 2 Games." *Behavioral Science,* 17 (1972): 371–83. [*32, 81, 83, 84*]

Harsanyi, J. C. "Rationality Postulates for Bargaining Solutions in Cooperative and Non-cooperative Games." *Management Science,* 9 (1962): 141–53. [*45–46, 68, 351, 411*]

Howard, N. "The Mathematics of Meta-games." *General Systems,* 11 (1966): 187–200. [*205*]

Kaufmann, H. "Similarity and Cooperation Received as Determinants of Cooperation Rendered." *Psychonomic Science,* 9 (1967): 73–74. [*272*]

Kaufmann, H. and Becker, G. M. "The Empirical Determination of Game-theoretical Strategies." *Journal of Experimental Psychology,* 61 (1961): 464–68. [*363*]

Kilgour, M. "On 2 × 2 Games and Braithwaite's Arbitration Scheme." In *Game Theory as a Theory of Conflict Resolution,* edited by A. Rapoport. Dordrecht: D. Reidel Publishing Co., 1974. [*61*]

Knapp, W. M. and Podell, J. E. "Mental Patients, Prisoners, and Students with Simulated Partners in a Mixed-motive Game." *Journal of Conflict Resolution,* 12 (1968): 235–41. [*263*]

Knox, R. E. and Douglas, R. "Low Payoffs and Marginal Comprehension. Two Possible Constraints upon Behavior in the Prisoner's Dilemma." In *Cooperation and Competition: Readings in Mixed-motive Games,* edited by L. S. Wrightsman, Jr. et al. Belmont, Cal.: Brooks/Cole Publishing Co., 1972. [*287–89*]

Lave, L. B. "Factors Affecting Cooperation in the Prisoner's Dilemma Game." *Behavioral Science,* 10 (1965): 26–38. [*264*]

Lieberman, B. "Experimental Studies of Conflict in Some Two-Person and Three-person Games." In *Mathematical Methods in Small Group Processes,* edited by J. H. Criswell et al. Stanford: Stanford University Press, 1962. [*355–57, 58*]

———. "Human Behavior in a Strictly Determined 3 × 3 Matrix Game." *Behavioral Science,* 5 (1960): 317–22. [*354 fn*]

Luce, R. D. "On the Possible Psychophysical Laws." *Psychological Reviews,* 66 (1959): 81–95. [*427*]

Luce, R. D. and Raiffa, H. *Games and Decisions.* New York: John Wiley & Sons, 1957. [*45*]

McClintock, C. G., Harrison, A., Strand, S., and Gallo, P. S. "Internationalism-Isolationism Strategy of the Other Player and Two-person Game Behavior." *Journal of Abnormal and Social Psychology*, 67 (1963): 631–36. [*270*]

McClintock, C. G. and McNeel, S. P. "Reward Level and Game Playing Behavior." *Journal of Conflict Resolution*, 10 (1966): 98–102. [*258*]

Malcolm, D. and Lieberman, B. "The Behavior of Responsive Individuals Playing a Two-person Zero-sum Game Requiring the Use of Mixed Strategies." *Psychonomic Science*, 2 (1965): 373–74. [*361–62*]

Marin, Gerardo. "Cooperation in the Prisoner's Dilemma and Personality Correlates: A Non-Existent Relationship." *Peace Research*, 5, 6 (1973): 29–32. [*327, 329*]

Morehouse, L. G. "One-Play, Two-Play, Five-Play, and Ten-Play Runs of Prisoner's Dilemma," *Journal of Conflict Resolution*, 10, 3 (1966): 363–66.

Nash, J. F. "Equilibrium Points in N-Person Games." *Proceedings of the National Academy of Sciences*, U.S.A., 36 (1950): 48–49. [*43, 411*]

———. "Two-person Cooperative Games." *Econometrica*, 21 (1953): 128–40. [*53, 55, 59, 68, 97, 364*]

Oskamp, S. "Effects of Programmed Strategies on Cooperation in the Prisoner's Dilemma and Other Mixed-motive Games." *Journal of Conflict Resolution*, 15 (1971): 225–59. [*261–63, 264, 341*]

———. "Effects of Programmed Initial Strategies in a Prisoner's Dilemma Game." *Psychonomic Science*, 19 (1970): 195–96.

Oskamp, S. and Kleinke, C. "Amount of Reward as a Variable in the Prisoner's Dilemma Game." *Journal of Personality and Social Psychology*, 16 (1970): 133–40. [*258–60, 265*]

Pancer, Mark. "Approval Motivation in the Prisoner's Dilemma Game." Unpublished bachelor's thesis, University of Toronto, 1973. [*231, 316*]

Radlow, R. "An Experimental Study of 'Cooperation' in the Prisoner's Dilemma Game." *Journal of Conflict Resolution*, 9 (1965): 221–27. [*258–59*]

Radlow, R. and Weidner, M. F. "A Two-person Game with Unenforced Commitments and Its Relation to 'Cooperative' and 'Noncooperative' Non-constant-sum Games." *Journal of Conflict Resolution*, 10 (1966): 497–505. [*305–8*]

Raiffa, H. "Arbitration Schemes for Generalized Two-person Games." In *Contributions to the Theory of Games, II, Annals of Mathematics Studies, 28*, edited by H. W. Kuhn and A. W. Tucker. Princeton, N.J.: Princeton University Press, 1953. [*58, 59, 352*]

Rapoport, Amnon and Mowshowitz, A. "Experimental Studies of Stochastic Models for the Prisoner's Dilemma." *Behavioral Science*, 11 (1966): 444–58. [*266–70*]

Rapoport, Anatol and Chammah, A. M. *Prisoner's Dilemma*. Ann Arbor:

University of Michigan Press, 1965. [*93, 153, 199, 212, 232–40, 266, 285–87, 311–17, 401, 412–20*]

Rapoport, Anatol and Chammah, A. M. "The Game of Chicken." *American Behavioral Scientist*, 10 (1966): 10–14; 23–28. [*241–42*]

Rapoport, Anatol, Chammah, A. M., and Guyer, M. Research Report, NIH-MH 04238–06, March, 1967. [*223–31*]

Rapoport, Anatol and Dale, P. S. "The 'End' and 'Start' Effects in Iterated Prisoner's Dilemma." *Journal of Conflict Resolution*, 10, 3 (1966): 363–66. [*316*]

Rapoport, Anatol and Guyer, M. "A Taxonomy of 2 × 2 Games." *General Systems*, 11 (1966): 203–14. [*19, 22, 23, 30, 34, 133, 180*]

Rapoport, Anatol, Guyer, M., and Gordon, D. "A Comparison of Performance of Danish and American Students in a 'Threat Game.'" *Behavioral Science*, 16 (1971): 456–66. [*317, 333–36*]

Rapoport, Anatol and Perner, J. "Testing Nash's Solution of the Cooperative Game." In *Game Theory as a Theory of Conflict Resolution*, edited by A. Rapoport. Dorcrecht: D. Reidel Publishing Co., 1974. [*134, 368, 387–91, 394*]

Schelling, T. C. *The Strategy of Conflict*. Cambridge, Mass.: Harvard University Press, 1960. [*429, 430*]

Scodel, A. "Induced Collaboration in Some Non-zerosum Games." *Journal of Conflict Resolution*, 6 (1962): 335–40. [*270, 272*]

Sermat, V. "Cooperative Behavior in a Mixed-motive Game." *Journal of Social Psychology*, 62 (1964): 217–39.

———. "The Effect of Initial Cooperative or Competitive Treatment upon a Subject's Response to Conditional Cooperation." *Behavioral Science*, 12 (1967): 301–13. [*264, 271–72*]

Shubik, M. "Some Experimental Non-zero-sum Games with Lack of Information about the Rules." *Management Science*, 8 (1962): 215–33. [*299–300, 344*]

Shubik, M., Brewer, G., and Savage, E. *The Literature of Gaming, Simulation, and Model-building: Index and Critical Abstracts*. Report R-620-ARPA. Santa Monica, Cal.: Rand, 1972. [*422*]

Steele, M. W. and Tedeschi, J. "Matrix Indices and Strategy Choices in Mixed-motive Games." *Journal of Conflict Resolution*, 11 (1967): 198–205. [*396–99*]

Suppes, P. and Atkinson, R. C. *Markov Learning Models for Multi-person Interactions*. Stanford: Stanford University Press, 1960. [*352, 404–12*]

Swensson, R. G. "Cooperation in the Prisoner's Dilemma Game: I. The Effects of Asymmetric Payoff Information and Explicit Communication." *Behavioral Science*, 12 (1967): 314–22. [*308–10*]

Swingle, P. G. "Exploitative Behavior in Non-zero-sum Games." *Journal of Personality and Social Psychology*, 16 (1970): 121–32. [*296–98*]

Swingle, P. G. and Coady, H. "Effects of the Partner's Abrupt Strategy

Change upon Subject's Responding in Prisoner's Dilemma." *Journal of Personality and Social Psychology,* 5 (1967): 357–63. [263]

Terhune, K. W. "Motives, Situation and Interpersonal Conflict within the Prisoner's Dilemma." *Journal of Personal and Social Psychology,* Monograph Supplement, 8 (1968), no. 3, part 2, 1–24. [231, 320–25]

———. "The Effects of Personality in Cooperation and Conflict." In *The Structure of Conflict,* edited by P. Swingle. New York: Academic Press, 1970. [128, 327–28]

Von Neumann, J. "Zur Theorie der Gesellschaftsspiele." *Mathematische Annalen,* 100 (1928): 295–320. [5, 428]

Wallace, D. and Rothaus, O. "Communication, Group Loyalty, and Trust in the Prisoner's Dilemma Game." *Journal of Conflict Resolution,* 13 (1969): 370–80. [292–93]

Wichman, H. "Effects of Isolation and Communication in a Two-person Game." *Journal of Personality and Social Psychology,* 16 (1970): 114–20. [305–6]

Wilson, R. "Testing the 'Reversal Effect' in the Game of Chicken." University of Toronto, 1973 (unpublished).

Wilson, W. "Cooperation and Cooperativeness of the Other Player." *Journal of Conflict Resolution,* 13 (1969): 110–17. [264]

Wilson, W. and Wong, J. "Intergroup Attitudes towards Cooperative vs. Competitive Opponents in a Modified Prisoner's Dilemma Game." *Perceptual and Motor Skills,* 27 (1968): 1059–66. [272]

Worchel, P. "Temptation and Threat in Non-zero-sum Games." *Journal of Conflict Resolution,* 13 (1969): 103–9. [197 fn, 237]

Wrightsman, L. S., Jr., O'Connor, J., and Baker, N. J., eds. *Cooperation and Competition: Readings in Mixed-motive Games.* Belmont, Cal.: Brooks/Cole Publishing Co., 1972. [422]

Wrightsman, L. S., Jr., Lucker, W., Bruininks, R., and O'Connor, J. "Effects of Extensiveness of Instructions upon Cooperation in a Prisoner's Dilemma Game." In *Cooperation and Competition: Readings in Mixed-motive Games,* edited by L. S. Wrightsman et al. Belmont, Cal.: Brooks/Cole Publishing Co., 1972. [289–90]

Game Index

The first (arabic) numeral(s) under each matrix is the number by which the particular game is labeled throughout the text. Roman numerals following indicate the variant of that game, correspondingly numbered throughout the text; e.g., 8-V stands for game #8, variant V (five).

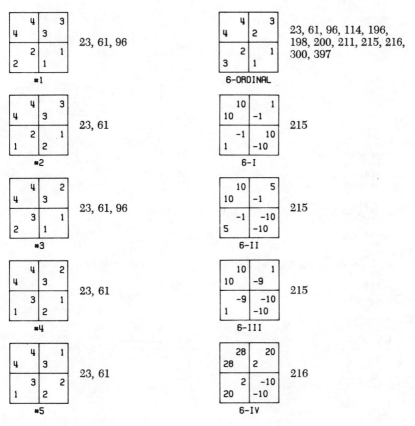

23, 61, 96   #1

23, 61   #2

23, 61, 96   #3

23, 61   #4

23, 61   #5

23, 61, 96, 114, 196, 198, 200, 211, 215, 216, 300, 397   6-ORDINAL

215   6-I

215   6-II

215   6-III

216   6-IV

443

28 / 28	20 / 12
12 / 20	-10 / -10

6-V   145, 146, 149, 216

28 / 28	20 / 19
19 / 20	-10 / -10

6-VI   216

3 / 3	2 / 4
4 / 2	1 / 1

*7   25

3 / 3	2 / 4
4 / 1	1 / 2

*8   25

3 / 3	1 / 4
4 / 1	2 / 2

*9   25, 96

3 / 2	2 / 4
4 / 1	1 / 3

*10   25

3 / 2	1 / 4
4 / 1	2 / 3

11-ORDINAL   30, 96, 353–54, 404

1 / -1	-10 / 10
10 / -10	-1 / 1

11-I   137

1/2 / 1/2	0 / 1
3/4 / 1/4	1/4 / 3/4

11-II   406, 407, 409

2 / 2	1 / 4
4 / 1	3 / 3

12-ORDINAL   28, 31, 45, 68, 96, 104, 133, 151, 153–55, 197–99, 203, 211, 224–25, 230–40, 257, 259, 293, 397

-1 / -1	-10 / 10
10 / -10	9 / 9

12-I   213, 224, 233, 285, 296

-9 / -9	-10 / 10
10 / -10	1 / 1

12-II   213, 225, 233, 285

-1 / -1	-10 / 10
10 / -10	1 / 1

12-III   152, 199, 203, 212–13, 224–25, 233, 236–39, 285

-1 / -1	-2 / 2
2 / -2	1 / 1

12-IV   212, 224, 233, 285

-1 / -1	-50 / 50
50 / -50	1 / 1

12-V   212, 224, 233, 236, 286

-1 / -1	-4 / 4
4 / -4	3 / 3

12-VI   237, 240

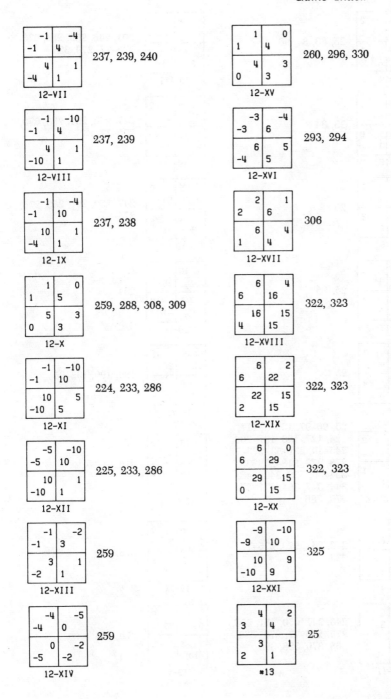

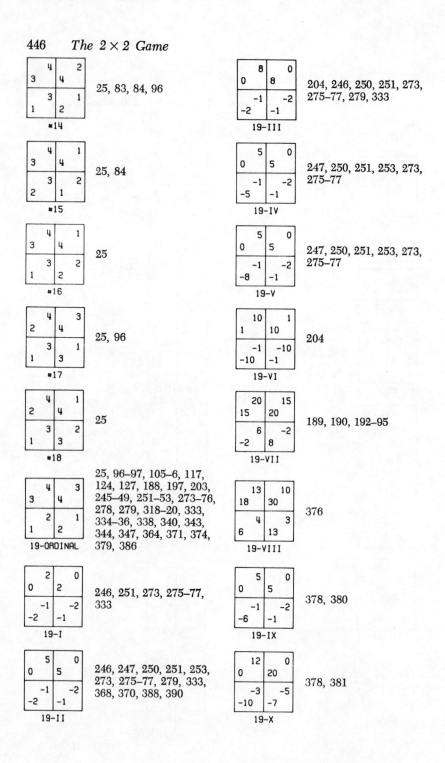

#14	4 2 / 3 4 / 3 1 / 1 2	25, 83, 84, 96
#15	4 1 / 3 4 / 3 2 / 2 1	25, 84
#16	4 1 / 3 4 / 3 2 / 1 2	25
#17	4 3 / 2 4 / 3 1 / 1 3	25, 96
#18	4 1 / 2 4 / 3 2 / 1 3	25
19-ORDINAL	4 3 / 3 4 / 2 1 / 1 2	25, 96–97, 105–6, 117, 124, 127, 188, 197, 203, 245–49, 251–53, 273–76, 278, 279, 318–20, 333, 334–36, 338, 340, 343, 344, 347, 364, 371, 374, 379, 386
19-I	2 0 / 0 2 / -1 -2 / -2 -1	246, 251, 273, 275–77, 333
19-II	5 0 / 0 5 / -1 -2 / -2 -1	246, 247, 250, 251, 253, 273, 275–77, 279, 333, 368, 370, 388, 390

19-III	8 0 / 0 8 / -1 -2 / -2 -1	204, 246, 250, 251, 273, 275–77, 279, 333
19-IV	5 0 / 0 5 / -1 -2 / -5 -1	247, 250, 251, 253, 273, 275–77
19-V	5 0 / 0 5 / -1 -2 / -8 -1	247, 250, 251, 253, 273, 275–77
19-VI	10 1 / 1 10 / -1 -10 / -10 -1	204
19-VII	20 15 / 15 20 / 6 -2 / -2 8	189, 190, 192–95
19-VIII	13 10 / 18 30 / 4 3 / 6 13	376
19-IX	5 0 / 0 5 / -1 -2 / -6 -1	378, 380
19-X	12 0 / 0 20 / -3 -5 / -10 -7	378, 381

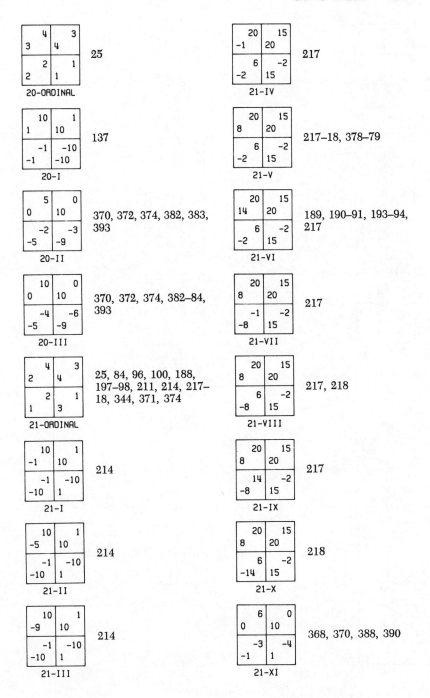

4	3
4	3
1	2
2	1

#22   24

4	1
4	2
2	3
3	1

#30   24, 61

4	3
4	3
1	2
1	2

#23   24

4	2
3	2
3	1
1	4

#31   26, 61

4	2
4	3
1	3
2	1

#24   24, 61

4	1
3	2
3	2
1	4

#32   26, 61

4	2
4	3
1	3
1	2

#25   24, 61

4	2
3	1
3	1
2	4

#33   26, 61

4	3
4	2
1	2
3	1

#26   24

4	1
3	1
3	2
2	4

#34   26, 61

4	1
4	2
2	3
3	1

#27   24, 61, 300

4	2
2	3
3	2
1	4

#35   26

4	1
4	3
2	3
2	1

#28   24, 61

4	1
2	3
3	2
1	4

36-ORDINAL   26, 168, 196, 198

4	1
4	3
2	3
1	2

#29   24, 61

10	-10
-1	1
1	-1
-10	10

36-I   137

```
    2 |  1
 2  | 4
    3 |  4
 1  | 3
  48-ORDINAL
```
28, 178–83, 186, 187, 198, 211, 215, 218, 219

```
   -1 | -10
-1  | 10
    1 | 10
-5  |  1
    48-I
```
214

```
   -1 | -10
-1  | 10
    1 | 10
-10 |  1
   48-II
```
214

```
   -1 | -10
-1  | 10
    1 | 10
-20 |  1
   48-III
```
214

```
   12 |  -4
12  | 25
   18 | 25
3   | 18
   48-IV
```
218

```
   12 |  -4
12  | 25
   18 | 25
-4  | 18
    48-V
```
218–19

```
   12 |  -4
12  | 25
   18 | 25
-10 | 18
   48-VI
```
218

```
   12 |  -4
6   | 25
   18 | 25
-4  |  9
   48-VII
```
219

```
   12 |  -4
6   | 25
   18 | 25
-4  | 18
  48-VIII
```
219

```
   12 |  -4
6   | 25
   18 | 25
-4  | 24
   48-IX
```
219

```
   12 |  -4
-3  | 25
   18 | 25
-4  | 18
    48-X
```
219

```
   4 |  3
3  | 4
   1 |  2
2  | 1
    #49
```
27

```
   4 |  3
3  | 4
   1 |  2
1  | 2
 50-ORDINAL
```
27, 254–56, 279–82, 340

```
   5 |  0
0  | 5
  -3 | -2
-5 | -1
    50-I
```
254, 255, 280, 281

```
   5 |  0
0  | 5
  -6 | -2
-5 | -1
   50-II
```
254, 255, 256, 280, 281

```
  10 |  1
1  | 10
 -10 | -1
-10 | -1
   50-III
```
281

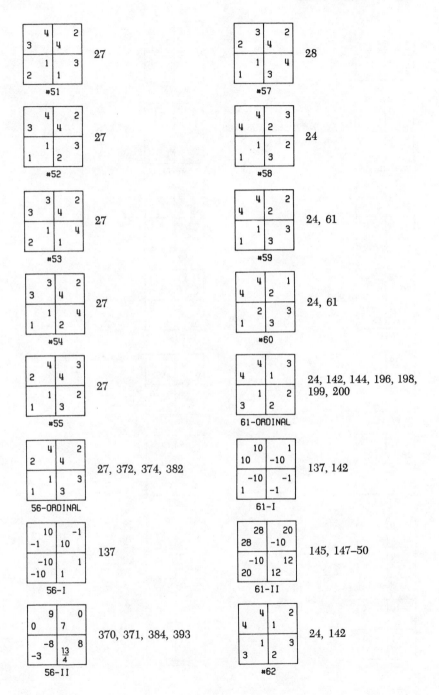

4 / 4	2 / 1
1 / 2	3 / 3

*63

24, 45, 46, 61, 142, 397

10 / 5	-3 / 0
0 / -3	5 / 10

64-VII

345

4 / 3	1 / 2
2 / 1	3 / 4

64-ORDINAL

27, 60–62, 168, 196, 198, 220, 227, 344, 371, 374

12 / 3	-12 / -4
-3 / -9	3 / 12

64-VIII

368, 370, 389, 391

19 / 5	-7 / 4
4 / -7	10 / 19

64-I

220

9 / 10	3 / -3
3/2 / 1	7 / 15

64-IX

376

19 / 10	-7 / 4
4 / -14	10 / 19

64-II

220, 389

13 / 1	-11 / -8
-9 / -10	7 / 4

64-X

376

19 / 10	-7 / 4
4 / -7	10 / 19

64-III

169–77, 220

20 / 0	0 / -13
-5 / -9	9 / 4

64-XI

376

19 / 10	-7 / 4
4 / -1	10 / 19

64-IV

220

4 / 2	1 / 3
2 / 1	3 / 4

*65

27

19 / 17	-7 / 4
4 / -7	10 / 19

64-V

220

3 / 3	4 / 2
2 / 4	1 / 1

66-ORDINAL

29, 32, 47, 49, 61–62, 80, 105, 133, 151, 197–99, 205, 211, 214, 227, 228, 231, 241–45, 262, 270–72, 340, 397

10 / 1	-10 / -1
-1 / -10	1 / 10

64-VI

137

1 / 1	10 / -1
-1 / 10	-2 / -2

66-I

141, 213

68-V

	12 \ 12	21 \ 15
	15 \ 21	−16 \ −16

221

69-VI

	−1 \ −1	1 \ 10
	10 \ 1	−10 \ −10

137

68-VI

	−1 \ −1	10 \ 1
	1 \ 10	−10 \ −10

137

#70

	4 \ 3	1 \ 2
	2 \ 4	3 \ 1

29, 44

69-ORDINAL

	2 \ 2	3 \ 4
	4 \ 3	1 \ 1

29, 61, 105, 159, 165–67, 197, 200, 222, 301, 303

#71

	3 \ 3	1 \ 2
	2 \ 4	4 \ 1

29, 44

69-I

	8 \ 8	22 \ 24
	24 \ 22	−5 \ −5

221

72-ORDINAL

	2 \ 3	1 \ 2
	3 \ 4	4 \ 1

29, 44, 60, 84, 178–80, 184–87, 198, 222, 223

69-II

	8 \ 8	14 \ 16
	16 \ 14	−5 \ −5

222

72-I

	5 \ 9	−10 \ 5
	9 \ 26	26 \ −10

141, 222

69-III

	8 \ 8	14 \ 24
	24 \ 14	−5 \ −5

160, 221, 222, 300

72-II

	5 \ 15	−10 \ 5
	9 \ 26	26 \ −10

222, 223

69-IV

	8 \ 8	14 \ 30
	30 \ 14	−5 \ −5

222

72-III

	5 \ 24	−10 \ 5
	9 \ 26	26 \ −10

222

69-V

	8 \ 8	9 \ 24
	24 \ 9	−5 \ −5

221

72-IV

	5 \ 15	−10 \ 5
	16 \ 26	26 \ −10

223

72-V

5	−10
15	5
24	26
26	−10

223

72-VI

−1	−10
1	−1
1	10
10	−10

137

73-ORDINAL

4	1
2	4
2	3
3	1

29, 44, 84

73-I

10	−10
−1	10
−1	1
1	−10

137, 141, 142

73-II

1	0
3/8	1
3/8	5/8
5/8	0

410, 411

∗74

4	1
2	3
2	3
4	1

29, 44

75-ORDINAL

3	1
2	4
2	4
3	1

30, 44, 353–54, 404

75-I

2/3	0
1/3	1
1/2	5/6
1/2	1/6

406, 407, 409

75-II

1	−10
−1	10
−1	10
1	−10

137

75-III

2	−6
−2	6
−1	5
1	−5

357, 358

∗76

3	1
2	3
2	4
4	1

29, 44, 84

∗77

2	1
2	4
3	4
3	1

29, 44

∗78

2	1
2	3
3	4
4	1

29, 44, 48

79-ORDINAL

2	2
2	1
1	1
2	1

31, 34

79-I

1	1
1	−1
−1	−1
1	−1

227, 258

79-II

150	150
150	0
0	0
150	0

227, 258

79-III

300 / 300	300 / 100
100 / 300	100 / 100

227, 258

79-IV

10 / 10	10 / -10
-10 / 10	-10 / -10

227

79-V

20 / 20	20 / -20
-20 / 20	-20 / -20

227, 258

80-ORDINAL

4 / 1	3 / 1
2 / 1	1 / 1

no reference

80-I (COLUMNS REVERSED)

3 / 3	4 / 3
0 / 3	1 / 3

296

81-ORDINAL

2 / 2	1 / 3
2 / 2	3 / 1

406, 407, 409

81-I

1/2 / 1/2	0 / 1
1/2 / 1/2	3/4 / 1/4

137, 406

82-ORDINAL

4 / 3	1 / 4
2 / 2	2 / 1

411

82-I

1 / 3/4	1/4 / 1
5/8 / 1/2	5/8 / 1/4

410, 411

83-ORDINAL

3 / 3	1 / 1
1 / 1	2 / 2

412

83-I

.8 / .8	0 / 0
0 / 0	.4 / .4

410, 411

84-ORDINAL

1 / 3	2 / 2
3 / 1	1 / 3

no reference

84-I

-3 / 3	1 / -1
9 / -9	-3 / 3

355, 361–62

85

2 / 2	1 / 1
1 / 1	2 / 2

47

Subject Index